Gigon/Guyer

GIGON
GUYER

Gigon/Guyer Architects

Works & Projects 2001–2011

Lars Müller Publishers

EXHIBITING

WORKING

REBUILDING

LIVING

All dimensions indicated are in meters.

The small, three-digit numbers used throughout refer to the project numbers in the Index of Works & Projects.

Acknowledgments

In connection with this publication and the exhibition at the ETH Zurich, we wish to extend our heartfelt thanks to the individuals, companies, foundations, and institutions for their generous support—so many that they are listed in the book's appendix.

We owe a debt of gratitude to the gta (the Institute for History and Theory of Architecture at the ETH Zurich) and in particular to Philippe Carrard for giving us the opportunity of showcasing our architectural designs in the main hall of the ETH Zurich from December 2011 to January 2012.

We are very pleased to publish this book with Lars Müller, who designed our very first book, *Werkstoff,* many years ago.

For the independent views of our work offered by Gerhard Mack, Arthur Rüegg, and Philip Ursprung, we are immensely grateful, as we are for the stimulating conversation with Martin Steinmann and Patrick Gmür.

Our profound thanks also go to the artists who have collaborated with us over the years—Adrian Schiess, Harald F. Müller, and Pierre André Ferrand. They have not only enriched our architectural designs, but have added substance to this book as well.

The photographic contributions to the Prime Tower by René Burri, Katalin Deér, Heinrich Helfenstein, Valentin Jeck, Walter Mair, Christian Scholz, Annelies Štrba, Erik Steinbrecher, Joël Tettamanti, and Thies Wachter provide a many-faceted view—both artistic and generic—of this building, the first of its kind in the city of Zurich. This invaluable input deserves our gratitude, as do the contributions of all the other photographers who have documented our buildings over the years.

This book in itself is an expression of our profound gratitude to all the clients who have given us the opportunity of building for them. Sincere thanks to all of you.

To the many engineers, landscape architects, specialists, and consultants who have helped us along the way—you have our deepest respect and gratitude.

We also wish to express our great appreciation of the many craftsmen we have had the privilege of spurring on, and who have taught us so much in turn. They are the ones who have transformed our ideas and designs into reality.

Finally, we also dedicate this book to our entire staff and all our collaborators—from trainees to architects. You have all contributed immensely to the success of our projects and, we hope, will continue to do so in future.

Exhibitions and books, like architecture, are the work of many.

Annette Gigon and Mike Guyer

Foreword

How can ideas and buildings be communicated, how can they be presented and represented? The exhibition at the ETH Zürich and the simultaneous publication of this book map out two directions. The first path is tried and tested: the publication provides a sequel to our 1999 book. The second is more experimental: an exhibition of limited duration uses linear time, namely the moving pictures of film projections to heighten the sense of space and compensate for the lack of depth in two-dimensional representation. Everyday movements in and around the buildings, which rarely feature in classic architectural photography, animate the buildings portrayed in this medium. Looking at the projects in this book also entails a temporal dimension. The projects are revealed, one after the other, in the form of photographs, drawings, and texts, to readers following their own rhythm. What is more, the book can still be read, re-read, and consulted long after the film projectors have been packed away.

In the book, built projects feature side by side with designs that exist only in the form of data and models. All that separates them is the thickness of the paper itself, so that diverse architectural designs stand side by side: the buildings are large and small, striking and modest, new and remodeled, everyday and exceptional, created for cities, green spaces, and urban agglomerations. They are loosely grouped together in the book: buildings for living, working, learning, exhibiting. A separate section deals with approaches to existing architecture, in the form of extensions, conversions, and remodeling.

With their widely varied functions, purposes, specifications, and budgets, the projects are neither condensed to form a city between the covers of this book, nor do they fuse into a stylistic canon of our architectural practice. Our projects are individual explorations, each one focusing on a specific site, its history, architectural heritage, and its future urban potential. They are concentrated modelings of the earth's crust, aimed at shaping an accessible other that shelters us, that gives us space and spatiality.

Annette Gigon and Mike Guyer

EXHIBITING

Subtle Shifts and Tentative Openings

Gerhard Mack

Kirchner Museum Davos

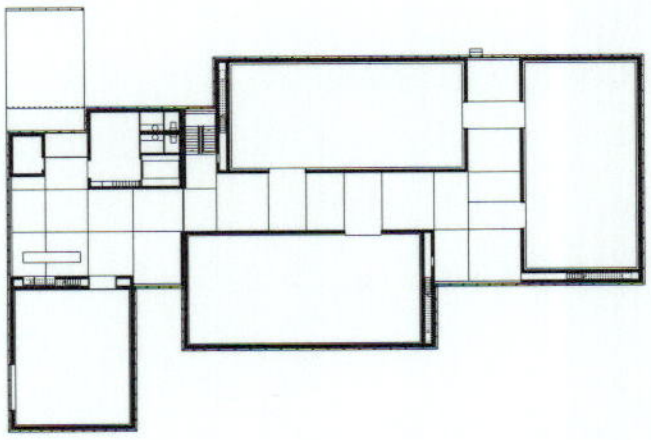

Floor plan

When the Kirchner Museum in Davos 00A opened its doors in September 1992, the architects Annette Gigon and Mike Guyer were catapulted overnight to the very top of their profession as contemporary museum designers. Dedicated to the leading German expressionist artist Ernst Ludwig Kirchner, who lived in this mountain community from 1917 until his death in 1938, the museum embodies the presence and elegance befitting a public building of this kind. However, it does not gain these qualities from the conventional pathos formulae of museum architecture, but from a simplicity diametrically opposed to all that shaped the new museums of the 1980s. The flat-roofed building, its four galleries topped with light spaces, is enveloped in an industrial-style glass skin with etched areas of glazing through which the insulation shimmers. Anyone looking at the building from above will see broken glass glinting on the rooftop instead of the usual gravel. In spite of obvious affinities with functional industrial buildings, the proportions in combination with the alternating transparency and opacity of the glazing indicate that there must surely be something different within. The museum echoes the famous flat-roofed architecture of Davos but primarily in order to create a crystalline form that triggers associations with the spiritual and intellectual world of modernism that emerged during Kirchner's own lifetime, when it was sometimes even symbolized by a crystal. Simplicity of form and clarity of material also feature inside the building as shown by the clear distinction between corridors and exhibition spaces: concrete for the former and wooden floors, white walls, and ceilings illuminated by cleverly channeled natural light in the latter.

The focus here is on the very aspects that were neglected in the most talked-about museum buildings of the 1980s, such as Hans Hollein's Museum Abteiberg in Mönchengladbach (1982) or James Stirling's Neue Staatsgalerie in Stuttgart (1984): the exhibition spaces themselves and the display of art and artifacts. One of the accepted requirements of architecture—already formulated in the early twentieth century by Alfred Lichtwark, the then director of the Hamburg Kunsthalle, in a scathing critique of Karl Moser's Kunsthaus Zürich in 1912—is that it should create spaces that provide the best possible conditions for the presentation of exhibits and the way visitors encounter art. This approach reflected not only the modernist tradition in Switzerland, as embodied by Hans Leuzinger's exemplary 1952 design for the Kunsthaus in Glarus, but also corresponded to the then prevailing attitudes.

In his 1986 lecture *Das Kunstmuseum, das ich mir erträume* (The Art Museum I Dream Of) at Kunstmuseum Basel, artist Rémy Zaugg defined the museum as a place for both "the artwork and the individual."[1] He went on to outline in minute detail the parameters that would govern such a building: placement, external appearance, the relationship between public and more private areas, floors, walls, ceilings, verticality and angularity, alignment, orientation, size and height of rooms, the position of doorways, the subtle integration of such details as smoke alarms and emergency exit signs as well as the illumination and hanging of the works themselves. This was based on the vision of an encounter between two independent and equal partners. Viewers are free to choose which works and rooms to visit, and in which order; they stand and look at the exhibits face to face. The exhibits, in turn, are free of all hierarchical order: historical structures and the linear sequence of rooms attendant upon them are swept aside in favor of loosely grouped galleries. In this respect, Zaugg speaks for his generation. Donald Judd, Georg Baselitz, and many others have expressed similar views. Franz Erhard Walther was even able to realize his ideas in his design for the Kunsthalle Ritter in Klagenfurt.

The museums by Gigon/Guyer place two aspects of Zaugg's museum concept at the very heart of their design approach: the rule of simplicity and the focus on almost clinically isolated conditions for the appreciation of art. Their architecture, at least as far as the interiors are concerned, stands firmly in the service of the presentation of art. They have developed an entire museum typology on the basis of this premise.

Kirchner Museum Davos, exhibition space

For instance, Zaugg calls for museums to be located in the middle of the city among the "butchers, bakers, and

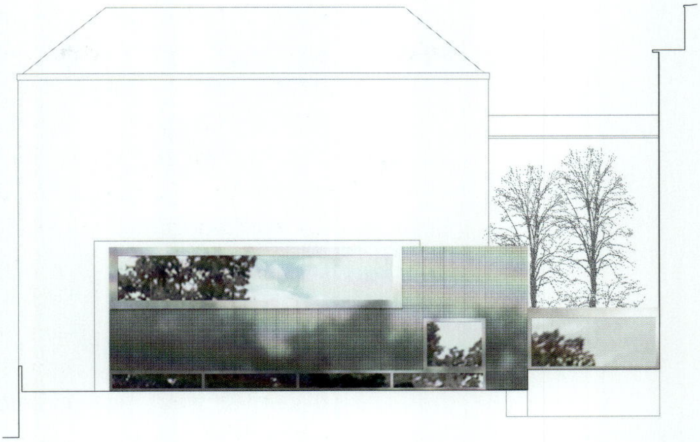

Extension of Kunstmuseum Basel, 2001 competition

Extension of Folkwang Museum, Essen, 2007 competition

candlestick makers."[2] so that they are an integral part of everyday life. Similarly, Gigon/Guyer have long made a concerted effort to ensure that their museum designs, as demonstrated by their external appearance, look perfectly natural and self-evident. Many of them are pavilions or at least suggest such lightweight structures. That applies equally to the Kirchner Museum and to their 2007 competition design for the extension of the Museum Folkwang in Essen 193. For the latter, they propose closing off the existing complex of buildings, aligned along both sides of an axis, with new structures and connecting them visually by means of a glass façade with metal latticework. Gigon/Guyer's 2008–09 competition design for a new Munch Museum and Stenersen Museum Collections on the Oslo Fjord (p. 130) proposes placing the massive building on a stilted platform so that it hovers above the water. And their competition-winning 2001 design for the extension of Kunstmuseum Basel 095, though never built, envisaged a pavilion clad in metal grids of varying thicknesses that would have had the appearance of a light garden architecture set within the previously publicly inaccessible courtyard between the museum and the Laurenzbau.

These proposals may well be indicative of the architects' preference for materials that channel light—especially glass, which is, of course, particularly suited to museums. Its transparency may also be seen as having a certain democratic

Extension of Kunstmuseum Winterthur

The Nelson-Atkins Museum of Art, Kansas City, MO, 1999 competition

New Museum of Contemporary Art, New York, NY, 2003 competition

appeal (not to mention the fascination it holds in modernism in general). Such considerations aside, Gigon/Guyer often use glass not only for its practical and functional qualities, but also as a gesture of understatement, as a means of creating a dialogue with the existing surroundings, and as a way of avoiding solipsistic positions. The glass panels for the 1995 extension of the Kunstmuseum in Winterthur 003 are normally used in industrial construction and, as such, they are a signal of pure understatement. Parking down below and art above: the solution owes much to the shoestring budget available at the time, but it also puts an entirely different focus on the art than does the neoclassicist building by Rittmeyer & Furrer. Art is an everyday commodity. While we need cars for mobility, art helps to train our perceptions and the way we see the world around us. It is a functional commodity rather than a cult object or an instrument of social distinction. The competition design submitted by Gigon/Guyer in 1999 for the Nelson-Atkins Museum of Art in Kansas City 050 featured lateral illumination, the intensity of which could be adjusted through glass panels with fine metallic weave inserts. The New Museum of Contemporary Art in New York, designed in 2003 as a landmark for an up-and-coming area of the city (p. 116), has a façade of mirroring and etched panes with diffuse runs in between that blur the two setbacks required by zoning law, so that, in a city

Museum Liner Appenzell

Extension of Städel Museum,
Frankfurt am Main, 2008 competition

dominated by skyscrapers, the building becomes an optical phenomenon that combines presence and dissolution. Their 2008 competition design for an extension to the Staedel Museum in Frankfurt 214 encloses the garden and features polished and variously folded chromium steel panels that alternate between mirroring the historic buildings and lending the new structure a presence of its own. The façade thus clearly marks out the new building, but also emphasizes its dialogue with the existing museum, which it complements.

The façades that Gigon/Guyer give their museum buildings are determined by a quest for the everyday even in those places where they set a landmark. The new entrance building of the Swiss Museum of Transport in Lucerne (p. 84) is a case in point: clad with industrial glass panels complemented by hundreds of wheels, aircraft and ship propellers, and rims that semiotically complement the exhibits within. The road transport hall on the same premises is entirely clad in an array of green, blue, and white traffic signs that grab our attention while at the same time striking a familiar chord. Even when the architects choose an unusual cladding, they remain true to the local vernacular. The Museum Liner 017 on the outskirts of Appenzell is undoubtedly a conspicuous landmark with its signature comb of diminishing sawtooth skylights. Yet at the same time, this industrial sawtooth roof is very much part of the local landscape, echoing the many small factories of the region's now defunct textile industry, just as the sheet metal cladding of its façade and roof echo Appenzell's traditional shingle-clad barns. Similarly, in spite of the textile quality of the cladding of beveled and perforated metal panels, the Kunst-Depot of Henze & Ketterer gallery in Wichtrach (p. 74) clearly references the vernacular of the barns with their pitched roofs and object-like hermeticism.

The fact that the entrance to this private building is as unassuming as the entrance to an industrial warehouse makes a great deal of sense. Those who focus primarily on the situation in which art is presented are likely to design the interface between the outer and inner worlds as casually as possible. Instead of creating a grand gesture to announce entrances, doorways, and foyers—as in such buildings as the Guggenheim Museum Bilbao or Tate Modern in London, to name just two very different examples—they are treated with utmost understatement. In terms of size, height, and layout, they fulfill a basic need rather than satisfying the desire for self-presentation and spectacle. These are places of arrival and service areas—not stages.

There is an evident duality inside these buildings. Wherever corridors connect up exhibition spaces, they either become secondary to them or are integrated into the overall scheme. The Kirchner Museum provides an excellent example of this. Raw concrete hallways access the much higher exhibition spaces which are flooded with light through glass roofing and skylights, allowing visitors to concentrate entirely on the exhibits themselves. In devoting painstaking care to the superb lighting created by a combination of artificial and natural light, as it changes with the seasons and the passing days, Gigon/Guyer have shown their consummate mastery of the white cube. In these rooms, it is possible to lose all sense of space and time. The everyday world is left behind, while ever-changing nature enters through the corridor windows. Only in their later designs, in which the galleries are directly interlinked, allowing a variety of routes through the building—as in Kunstmuseum Winterthur—do we find exhibition spaces opened up to the outside world by large windows that provide orientation.

Sammlung Oskar Reinhart, Winterthur

Anyone who makes understatement the hallmark of their authorship is positively predestined to enhance and bring out the very best in what already exists. In this respect, Gigon/Guyer have made a name for themselves as masters of detail. In 1997/1998, the rooms of the Oskar Reinhart Collection "Am Römerholz" 006 were analyzed and restored to their original state, from the parquet flooring to the re-instatement of blocked-up windows. The link between the residential villa and the later gallery building was sensitively remodeled. Three new exhibition rooms of varying proportions echo the existing galleries while at the same time signaling the transition between two discrete areas. The choice of materials and the overhead skylights lend the rooms a distinctive quality that makes them ideal for the small-scale temporary exhibitions that the museum occasionally stages to complement its permanent collection. Visitors find themselves in a tangible present nurtured by the history of the surroundings.

Remodeling of Kunstmuseum Basel, view from the large courtyard toward the cafe

Entrance hall with museum shop

New galleries around small courtyard

This keen awareness of historical architecture and attention to detail can also be observed in the restoration of Kunstmuseum Basel, which was completed in three phases between 2003 and 2007 (p. 330). When the former National Bank building was gifted to the museum, the art historical institute, its library, and the administrative offices were able to move into new premises. The former banking hall with its mahogany paneling, stucco ceiling, and skylight were restored and a library atmosphere was created using a mix of mass-produced fittings and custom-made furnishings partially designed in collaboration with Hannes Wettstein. The move freed up space in the museum for the presentation of art and allowed Gigon/Guyer to reinstate the building's former axial symmetry. The main courtyard is now framed by public areas, with the new cloakrooms on the left and, on the right, where the library aisle used to be, the seating, partially area of the cafe, which is now accessible and visible from the street thanks to two new wall apertures. Behind that, the rooms that formerly housed the library have been unified: the dark strip parquet flooring, the simple grid of neon tubes mounted directly on the ceiling, and the high doorways opening up to the joists all bring a certain cohesion to rooms that are otherwise of different sizes and with differently proportioned side windows. The result is a setting in which the classics of contemporary art can be displayed as intimately or as grandly as required. A new lighting system of neon tubes installed between the ceiling joists restores the sense of space in the entrance hall by turning the ceiling into a shimmering body of light that emphasizes its height. By moving the cloakroom and cafe, the ambulatory around the small courtyard has once again become an exhibition space, specifically for the presentation of contemporary sculpture. The Kunstmuseum itself has visibly regained its classical form, with a symmetry and clarity that bear eloquent witness to the understated approach taken by Gigon/Guyer.

Museum Folkwang, Essen, 2007 competition

The avoidance of dramatic gestures demands meticulous attention to the choice of materials and forms. If less is to be more, it has to be exquisite. Gigon/Guyer are known for their ability to innovatively recontextualize everyday materials and finishes. In doing so, they pursue a strategy of barely perceptible shifts. These range from the etched glazing of the Kirchner Museum to the programmatic glass panels and metal-clad sawtooth roof of the Winterthur museum extension to any number of more recent projects such as their 2007 design for the Museum Folkwang with its metal latticework, or the glass bricks proposed for the Landesmuseum für Kunst und Kulturgeschichte in Münster (2005) 164 and Kunsthaus Zürich (2008) (p. 124). A case in point is the Kunst-Depot in Wichtrach near Bern, completed in 2004. Henze & Ketterer Gallery, located in a country villa on the outskirts of town, needed an extension that would serve both as an art depot and a showroom. An adjacent plot, tapering sharply at a fork in the road, was available for development. While the ground floor has been fitted out as a storage area with a small presentation space, the upper floor is regularly used for exhibitions of contemporary art. The building has the air of a hybrid between the pastoral idyll of a traditional Bernese farmhouse and the apartment blocks that have mushroomed over the past thirty years. It seems both strange and familiar. It is familiar because it has the look of a classic, two-story gable-ended building that is exactly how we expect a house to be. But its floorplan and façade are somewhat disconcerting. In

Landesmuseum für Kunst und Kulturgeschichte, Münster, 2005 competition

Kunst-Depot, Henze & Ketterer Gallery, Wichtrach

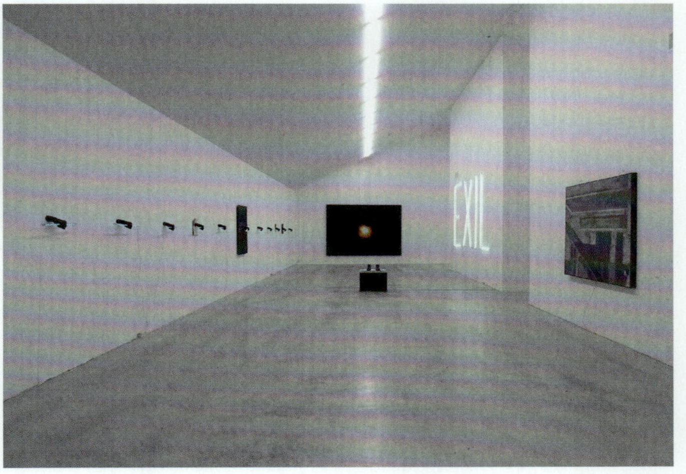

order to make the best possible use of the space, the architects built it on the basis of a trapezoid that is almost a parallelogram. The roof and walls are clad with Tetra panels normally used in warehouse construction and bound together to form a sculptural volume. This object-like quality is heightened by the way the panels have been installed: they envelope the structure like a gown with its inner lining placed directly onto the insulation and its outer layer not quite reaching the ground. At the rear of the building, this outer layer is slightly parted from the wall so that the gown opens a little, making the trapezoidal layout less obvious. This sense of ambiguity is further heightened by the slanting roof panels folded at angles, which echo the parallelogram of the floorplan and ironically reference the traditional architecture.

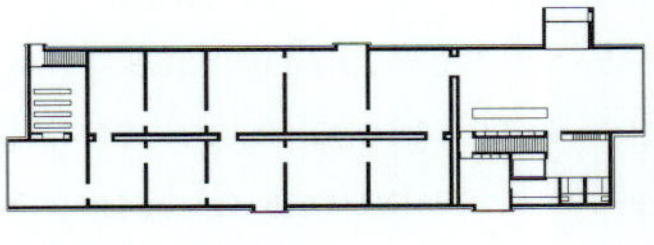

Museum Liner Appenzell, exhibition spaces

In the case of the Kunst-Depot, the small shifts between façade and interior space go hand in hand. The shell is an expression of the inner form. The sense of mild confusion continues inside the building, for instance on entering the upper floor and facing a wall without noticing at first sight that it is slightly off-kilter. This sculptural handling of space is a key element in many of Gigon/Guyer's projects. The rooms in the Museum Liner, for instance, are of steadily diminishing size. This is not immediately evident, though the movement of the body and the decreasing number of strides required to move from one doorway to the next, together with the discrepancy between the two large

Albers-Honegger Donation, Mouans-Sartoux

end rooms and the smaller galleries, all create a sense of intimacy while at the same time denoting the kind of constriction that is familiar to us from our own homes, in which the rooms are not vast halls. The pictures on the walls and the sculptures in the rooms suddenly seem supersized, or take on the personal air of things we have lived with for years. The very dimensions of the rooms themselves create a sense of intimacy, while the ceiling height prevents excessive proximity.

This is precisely the kind of spatial atmosphere that the artist Gottfried Honegger and his partner Sybil Albers sought for their collection of abstract art when they launched a competition in 1999. Their collection was housed in a small chateau in Mouans-Sartoux near Cannes (p. 62) and was to become the center of an educational institution where visitors could get to grips with art and hone their perception. In the tradition of the Bauhaus, Honegger believes in the power of art to change society. He feels that when children train their senses in an art studio, they are less susceptible to the temptations and frustrations of the consumer society, if only because they experience the joy of developing their creativity. The new building for the collection would facilitate these objectives and further the use of the chateau grounds where he had already installed an art studio for children. One room in the new museum was to be available for public events, while a bookshop would provide a service otherwise unavailable in the village.

In their design for the Espace de l'Art Concret, Gigon/Guyer engage in a dialogue with the existing chateau. They adopt the form of a tower and interpret it in a contemporary syntax in the spirit of modernism. Whereas the three towers of the chateau are round and are integrated into a closed triangle, the new tower is square. The yellowish green coloring echoes and abstracts the green of the foliage, so that the tower can be read as symbolizing a tree. Artificiality as a strategy for approaching nature, which is a fundamental premise of the client's concrete art, becomes a design principle here. The new tower faces a steep slope, and the entrance spans the drop like a drawbridge. The foyer, the service entrance, and the separate entrance to the assembly hall take the form of bays with extensive

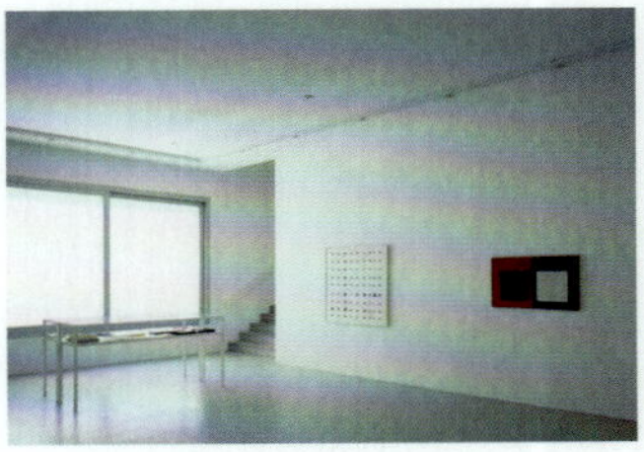

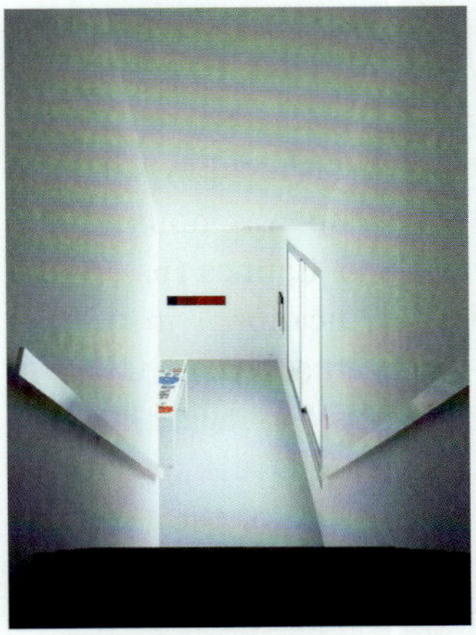

Albers-Honegger Donation, Mouans-Sartoux

glazed areas on three sides protruding from the square tower in an upward motion. This also forms the basic principle for the alignment of the rooms. They are grouped around the service core with its lift and two stairways and are juxtaposed at half-height. This draws the visitor gradually upwards from room to room, while the stairway forms a distinct transition. The individual half-stories are alternately open-plan or divided into small enclosed spaces with ceiling-height passageways between them. Concrete floors combined with white walls and ceilings ensure a low-key atmosphere, while the large windows introduce the outdoors, providing axial vantage points and visual orientation. The differing heights of the levels within the building give the visitor a palpable sense of rhythm, alternating between compact enclosure and spaciousness that lends a distinct presence to the works on display.

Gigon/Guyer have made a name for themselves as masters of elegant simplicity and now find that they are operating within an increasingly altered environment. Frank O. Gehry's Guggenheim Museum Bilbao of 1997 firmly established the boom in landmark buildings featuring sharply angular or biomorphic forms whose structural calculation requires highly sophisticated computer programs. Zaha Hadid was able to create her 2010 Constructivist-inspired designs for the MAXXI in Rome on a grand scale. The UNStudio of Ben van Berkel and Caroline Bos produced a conspicuously curvaceous museum for Mercedes-Benz in 2006. Architecture itself has become both an object and an event—something that towns can use to tout tourism. At the same time, art is changing. The ideal of the white cube no longer suits the needs of artistic strategies aimed at getting down and dirty by cultivating blurred boundaries and ambiguities in a frenzied bid to grasp a rapidly changing world. What's more, buildings over a certain size can no longer be designed as a simple combination of containers. Gigon/Guyer have responded to this changing situation with two basic principles: intensifying the relationship between their buildings and public space and designing museums like cities with streets, squares, and houses.

Munch Museum and Stenersen Museum Collections, Oslo, 2009 competition

This approach is perhaps most clearly articulated in their 2009 proposal for the Munch Museum in Oslo. The new building to house the art of Norway's most famous painter is intended as a complement to the existing opera house on the banks of the fjord and will be part of a cultural complex, forming a new and vibrant city district catering to a wide social spectrum. This can only be achieved with a mix of cultural, retail, business, and residential facilities that will attract people to the area even if they are not planning to visit the museum or the opera. In their competition design, Gigon/Guyer propose adding a new boulevard along the Paulsenkaia in the form of a long, curved promenade with alternating levels featuring apartments, restaurants, shops, bars, and galleries where people can drop in on their way to the opera or museum, or can simply sit and relax on the waterside steps. The museum itself appears as a grand villa in reddish brown concrete rising above the water, its five-sided structure dissolving at the edges into individual volumes. The entire building is set on a platform over the water, accessed by a long walkway redolent of an image by Munch himself. Visitors pass along this walkway as though on a procession route, leaving terra firma to enter the world of art. But those who come here simply to enjoy the spectacular views of the fjord and the city, or just to take a look at this new landmark building, are also more than welcome.

On the ground floor, a spacious, open foyer with entrances on all sides links the building and the platform as a cohesive entity. This is where the restaurant, shop, lecture hall, and conference rooms are situated. At the center, a stairway whose crystalline form echoes the five-cornered floorplan leads to the two upper levels housing the offices and depots that are not open to the public; the top floor is reserved for the museum. The stairway is framed by a generously proportioned and inviting ambulatory zone that juts out over the fjord at all five end points, with huge panorama windows looking out on the surrounding scenery like a live screening in cinemascope format. Six hall-like gallery rooms branch off this open space. With their rectangular or trapezoidal floorplans and slightly slanted end walls, they create the kind of dynamic that was

Swiss Museum of Transport, 1999 competition

also explored in the Wichtrach Kunst-Depot. The absence of fixed walls, the adjustable ceiling heights, and the artificial lighting combine to provide maximum flexibility. For all its hints of classic modernism, redolent of villas built on piloti, the irregular and almost immaterial forms lend the entire building an air of openness and movement. This is also reflected in the design of the exhibition rooms, which responds to the way the expectations and attitudes of both artists and visitors have changed since the 1980s. The design for Oslo clearly seeks to combine an appropriate platform for art with the need for entertainment and diversity.

The bigger the projects become, the more the museums echo the urban model. This typology is already present in the Kirchner Museum. The circulation zone is turned inside out, as it were, and expanded to form plaza and street, so that the rooms accessed from that zone become buildings. This notion of the museum as city came fully into its own with the remodeling and extension of the Swiss Museum of Transport in Lucerne. The museum consists of a conglomerate of buildings created at various times for such diverse exhibits as trains, planes, ships, cars, and even television technology. The clients require flexible and sturdy premises along the lines of industrial halls for their prime exhibits and temporary shows, and they want them to be easily adapted to meet different needs. This is no place for overly refined layouts and subtle lighting. The complex task required

Road Transport Hall, façade study

several planning phases, in the course of which a building for road traffic with a circle of ramps and, later, with a shell made of old car bodies, was rejected. Similarly, the idea of recycling elements of a pavilion from the Swiss Expo 02 in Yverdon-les-Bains to form the roof of the restaurant was jettisoned. In the end, between 2005 and 2009, the heterogeneous and almost faceless complex was reorganized. The architects concentrated on an overall concept that would provide a solid infrastructure for large visitor numbers and, most importantly, substantially improve the use of space. For this, they proposed two extension buildings, which, also after several planning phases, were actually realized: a new entrance building, which closes off the grounds, is oriented towards the lakeside park, while at the same time acting as a huge bracket linking the neighboring units of the Cinemax and the high-rise with the planetarium. This creates an inner circular route that allows visitors to pass through all the different exhibition areas. The foyer, in a greenish-yellow color scheme, with ticket desks, shop, and cloakroom, opens onto the courtyard and a new restaurant. The first upper level has black boxes, and the second has conference rooms of varying sizes with panorama windows overlooking the lake.

2002 Expo pavilion, Yverdon-les-Bains

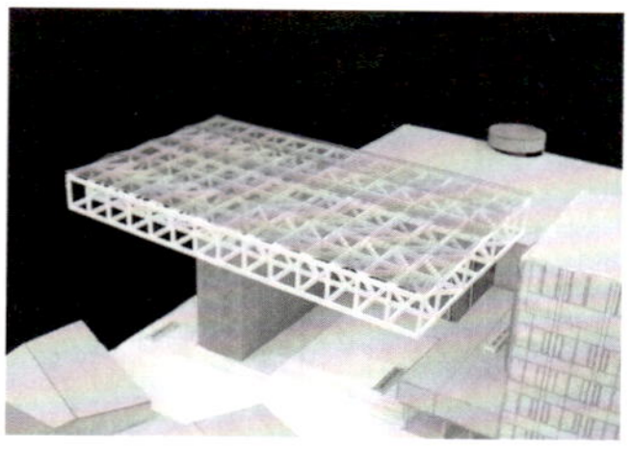

Swiss Museum of Transport, Lucerne, recycled steel structure of Expo pavilion as roof

As a counterpoint, a new building to showcase street traffic was placed at the rear end of the grounds, with a façade featuring 344 street signs (some used, some variations, some duplicates) indicating what is to be found in the multi-story space inside. Instead of the ramp proposed in an earlier design, Gigon/Guyer created an automated parking system, with a robot-operated lift, over the entire height of the rear wall of the building. The hall also provides enormous flexibility for exhibition designers. The alignment of the two new buildings creates additional space in the middle of the grounds for hospitality and catering facilities as well as open-air exhibitions and a children's play area. Like a city, the museum is built around a large plaza.

The design defines the Swiss Museum of Transport primarily as an urban planning module. This approach informs a number of projects by Gigon/Guyer in recent years. Their 2008 competition design for the extension of Kunsthaus Zürich, for instance, echoes the proportions and orientation of Karl Moser's building on the other side of the Heimplatz square, lending greater definition to an otherwise diffuse space. Subtly shifting the focus from the object itself to the overall situation is a strategy clearly demonstrated in two more recent designs. The new Cultural Center Les Arts in Gstaad (p. 144) has a concert hall at its center and spans two platforms of the railway station. Such a prestigious cultural facility calls for a distinctive landmark building, which must at the same time be compatible with the everyday comings and goings of a transport hub. The large structure, proposed by Gigon/Guyer in 2010, unites a number of heterogeneous functions and fragments them into smaller units. For instance, the roof is formulated as a variegated landscape of angles, slopes, and folds. Industrial and patrician elements are combined. In the exhibition areas, the folds form sawtooth skylights. Inside, this is contrasted by the impressive stairway that leads to the upper level, where the foyer, concert hall, and exhibition spaces are located, designed using the vocabulary of representative architecture. At the same time, the building as a whole lends definition to the Bahnhofsplatz.

Extension of Kunsthaus Zürich, 2008 competition

Cultural Center Les Arts, Gstaad, 2010 competition

A new museum district planned for Lausanne is also situated near the city's railway station. At its center is the Nouveau Musée cantonal des Beaux-Arts (MCBA, p. 150), whose construction has been delayed repeatedly for many years. Gigon/Guyer use the building in their 2011 competition design to articulate a sequence of pathways and plazas.

This time, in contrast to many of their other projects, they propose demolishing an existing historic building. The locomotive depot dating from 1911 will live on in the recycled bricks, in the silhouette rendered in the masonry of the façade, and above all in the simplicity of the elongated new building. With its two multi-story buildings at either end and its single-story central area for exhibition rooms, it is positioned so that it forms a passageway with the rear supporting wall of the grounds, providing access to the shops and galleries set into the remodeled wall arches at the northern boundary and leading to the two plazas at the entrance and the back of the MCBA. In a further construction phase, a separate building at the western end will house Musée de l'Elysée, while the plaza facing the entrance will be framed by the Museum for Design and Applied Arts (MUDAC). Mixed usage in another elongated building at the northern edge of the grounds, between the wall arches and the Musée de l'Elysée, reinvigorate a hitherto neglected urban area just behind the railway tracks.

Pronounced interest in the space in which the building is to stand was first expressed around the turn of the millennium in a unique, extremely distinctive project. In the 1980s, a number of archeological finds had indicated that the Battle of the Teutoburg Forest (or Varus Battle) took place in the year 9 AD near Bramsche-Kalkriese. Because this pivotal event in German history had been exploited by the Nazis for propaganda purposes, the state office for the protection of historic monuments (Landesdenkmalamt Osnabrück) wanted to free the location from that taint by creating a museum to mark the victory of the Germanic tribes over the Roman forces. One of their wishes was that such a museum would offer more than just a place to display the artifacts—many of them fairly unspectacular—that had been left among the dead bodies of the Roman soldiers and had lain in the ground for some two thousand years before being rediscovered. Therefore, part of the actual exhibition was to be the twenty-hectare field itself on which the Germanic warriors had prepared their ambush against the three Roman legions, complete with auxiliaries and camp followers. Furthermore, apart from the remains of an earthen rampart, no trace of the defenses remained

Historical photograph of traditional sod cutting

Archeological excavation: former rampart with layers of earth

Museum Kalkriese,
viewing platform

and the landscape has changed substantially over the centuries. The moorland on the northern side has been dried out and the terrain, leveled by centuries of agriculture in which the spreading of peat as a fertile topsoil, has raised the ground by one to one and a half meters, while the narrow corridor between the forest and the moor along which the Roman troops had to file in a procession stretching for an estimated six kilometers no longer exists. However, the conditions of the terrain are the key to understanding the outcome of the battle that caused the Romans to abandon their plans for expansion in Germany and withdraw permanently beyond the Rhine.

With their Archeological Museum and Park Kalkriese (p. 34) Gigon/Guyer first created the required museum building and then in 2009 added a visitors center echoing the brick architecture of the existing farmstead together with which it forms the entrance courtyard. The museum building takes the form of a simple steel framed structure whose brutalist cladding of rusted steel panels immediately signals that it is a foreign body set among the fields and woodlands. A structure elevated on stilts, with floor-to-ceiling windows that can be completely blacked out as required, provides a stark and unadorned environment ideal for flexible and versatile exhibition design. A tower rising above the entrance offers unrestricted views over the surrounding landscape and the scene of the battle. From

Wood-chip trails

here, visitors can survey the course of history from the vantage point of a military commander—a privilege that those who were involved in the events of two thousand years ago did not have. The landscape itself has been incorporated into the museum design with the formation of a line of steel poles that are clustered together in places where artifacts were found and spaced out where the defense ramparts are thought to have been.

However, it is the circulation through the museum that takes on a new and special significance in this particular design. This normally has the purpose of guiding visitors through a sequence of rooms in a way that combines both ease of orientation and variation, while drawing attention to the exhibits and keeping people interested. In contrast, the pathways and trails in Kalkriese actually place the emphasis on the physical perception of the space itself. Different materials are used to indicate possible historic positions and directions of movement that can no longer be precisely determined. The path trodden by the Roman soldiers is marked by an irregular alignment of steel panels; the freer movement of the Germanic warriors in the forest is suggested by scattered trails covered in wood chips. A relatively easily discernible route along which the Roman army marched is thus contrasted with a veritable spider web of short, interwoven woodland trails through which the Germanic warriors moved. Walking along these different

Steel-slab path

pathways, the visitor gets a tangible sense of just how exposed the Roman army was, and how swiftly and almost imperceptibly their opponents were able to dart out of the cover of the woods only to disappear among the trees again. Gigon/Guyer (together with landscape architects Schweingruber Zulauf) have adapted the grounds to reflect the presumed historic situation, by cutting down some existing trees and planting new ones. The fact that Integral Concept has contributed three pavilions dedicated to Seeing, Hearing and Questioning, while forging a link to modern warfare, reflects the educational requirements of the museum. Crucially, however, the fascination of this architecture lies largely in the fact that its purpose is not just to erect a building, but to articulate the psychology of a landscape, allowing visitors to experience the history of the place. Through this strategy, which is entirely in keeping with their reductionist approach and its subtle yet active implementation, Gigon/Guyer have tapped into a new dimension whose potential may well herald a turning point in classic museum design.

1 First published under the title *Das Kunstmuseum, das ich mir erträume oder der Ort des Werkes und des Menschen,* Cologne: Verlag der Buchhandlung Walther König, 1987. Reprinted in 1998 by Verlag für moderne Kunst, Nuremberg.
2 Ibid., p. 107.

Archeological Museum and Park Kalkriese, Osnabrück, Germany 038
1998–2002

For this project the site means more than just the location and its context; rather, it presents the actual theme of the intervention itself. It is an agricultural parcel approximately twenty hectares in size which, by virtue of the numerous archeological finds, is considered to be the long-sought location of the famous battle between the Germanic tribes and the Romans in the year 9 AD, referred to as the "Battle of Varus" or the "Battle of the Teutoburg Forest." Contrasting with classic archeological sites, where building remains form authentic illustrative material, here instead only thousands of scattered objects such as coins, sling bullets, and war masks were found when excavating this former battlefield. The sole exception is an earthen rampart, in a heavily flattened form, discovered in the layers of earth. Therefore, the chosen landscape design and architectural means are primarily abstract in nature rather than representative, and more symbolic than figurative. The overall perspective is focused on the battle in 9 AD, but of course unavoidably also on the present, which is manifest amidst all the interventions that have now been carried out with the purpose of archeological investigation and museological presentation of the past.

Consequently, the project encompasses just a few measures to spark the visitor's imagination of the events that took place in this landscape: trees cleared away and reforestation, a partial reconstruction of the former terrain, the visualization of the former rampart, three path systems on the grounds, as well as three pavilions and a museum. The undertaking was developed in close cooperation with the landscape architects Schweingruber Zulauf and designers from Integral, Lars Müller (pavilions), and Ruedi Baur (scenography).

The Landscape
Landscape design measures aimed at visualizing the original site (vegetation, course of the terrain, make-up of the ground) were simply realized with the means—meaning the plant types and cultivation methods—of contemporary agrarian and forest cultivation. The existing forest has been supplemented with trees to the south in order to trace its former edge. To the north, on the other hand, it was partially cleared to form open fields in order to recall the expanse of the former moors. The open field in the area of the earlier moor has been left untouched as an agricultural meadow.

A Reconstructed Landscape Excerpt
An exception to this general way of dealing with the extant agrarian land is formed by a "reconstruction" of the earlier landscape covering an area of nearly 1,600 square meters. Here the former, lower course of the terrain has been exposed and planted anew based on current knowledge of the historical vegetation. A dense grove of oak and beech trees is to be found on the "Germanic side," as well as the reconstructed earthen rampart with its palisades. On the Roman side there is sandy ground that changes into a moor pond. Sheet-piling retaining walls in steel serve to anchor the terrain and demarcate the lower,

Historical vegetation and topography in the 9th century AD (hypothetical)

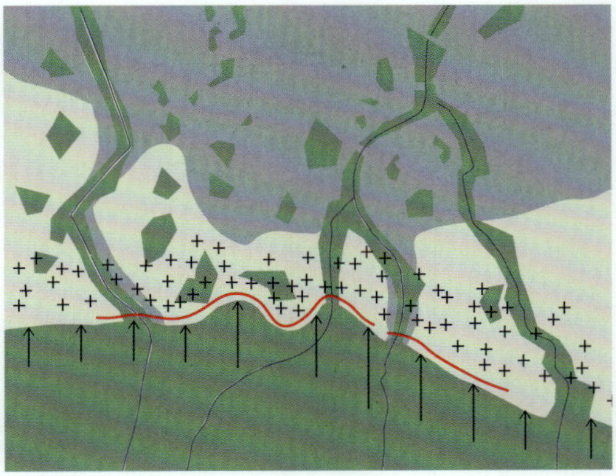

Vegetation and topography in the 9th century AD, battle positions, defenses (hypothetical)

Vegetation, aerial view, 1999

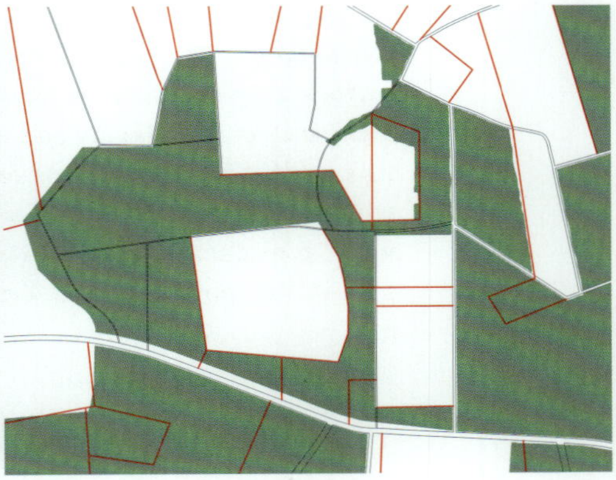

Vegetation with track system, 1999

Clearance and reforestation

Meadows and forest, 2002

reconstructed excerpt of the landscape in contrast to the contemporary topography and flora.

The Rampart
The location and assumed height of the former Germanic earthen rampart, including palisades built on top, has been marked by means of iron poles. Where archeological proof of the rampart's existence is at hand, the iron bars are placed closer together, and where it is not yet conclusive, they are placed farther apart.

The Path Systems
The probable course of the Roman Legion's route along the rampart, in difficult terrain between the slope and the moorland, is retraced by means of irregularly placed, large iron slabs. Individual slabs display historical Roman or contemporary written fragments. As the visitors proceed from one iron slab to the next they collect pieces of information from the ground, not unlike archeological work. Step by step, an image of the historical battle situation forms in their minds.

In contrast, narrow wood-chip paths are laid out across the ground to form a net-like pattern representing the positions of the Germanic warriors in the forest. This inconspicuous path system also symbolizes their freedom of movement through the forest, their various possibilities for attack and retreat, their camouflage, and their familiarity with the woods.

A further series of paths, contemporary in nature, is superimposed on the landscape interventions with their martialistic connotations. Its geometry is derived from the existing contemporary agricultural tracks. This network of paths allows visitors, besides being able to explore the positions of both the Romans and the Germanic warriors, to "change sides" and move around as in a landscaped park.

Archeological Museum and Park Kalkriese, Osnabrück, Germany

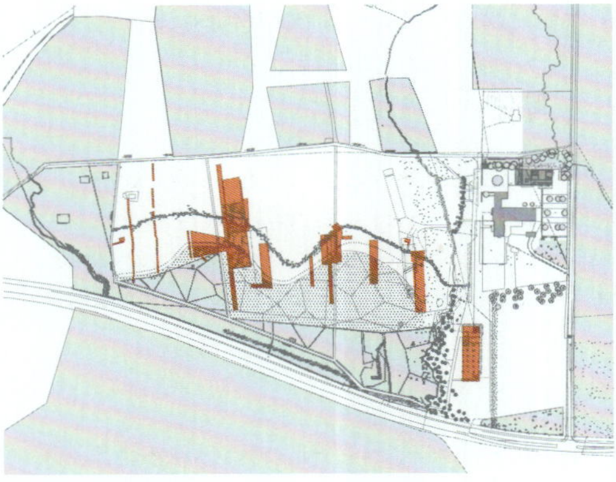

Archeological excavations up to the year 2000

Assumed rampart marked with iron poles

Landscape sunk to historical levels

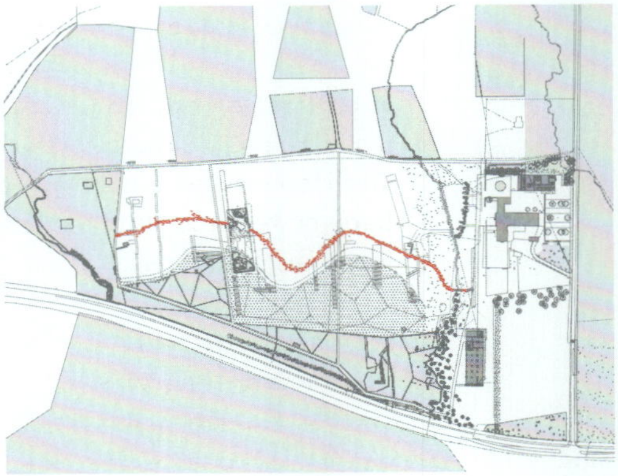

Roman positions symbolized by steel slabs

Positions of Germanic warriors symbolized by wood-chip trails

New and existing field tracks, gravel

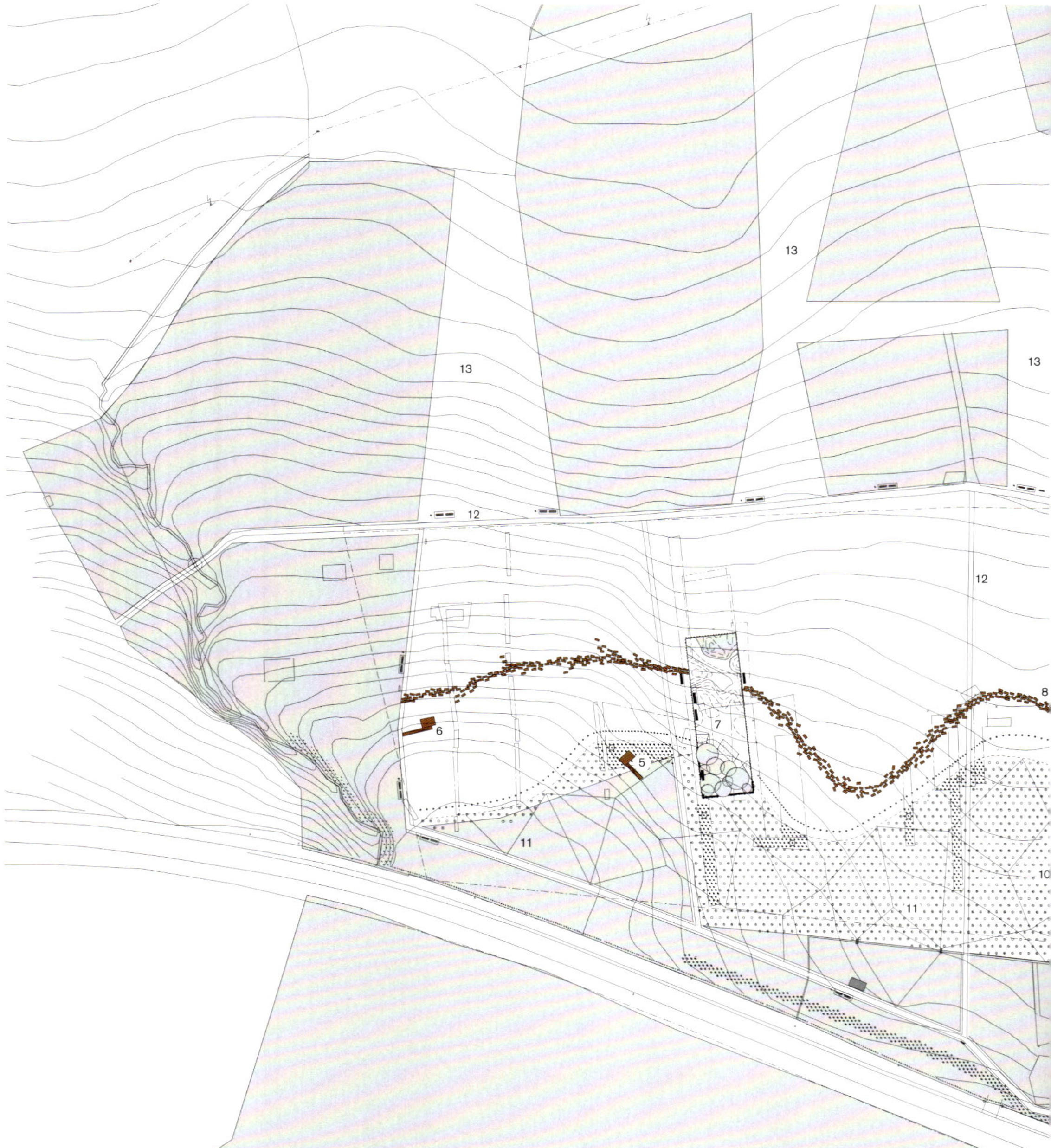
13
13
13
12
12
8
6
7
5
11
10
11

Archeological Museum and Park Kalkriese, Osnabrück, Germany

Situation plan

1 Niewedde farmstead
2 New Visitors Center
3 Museum
4 "SEEING" Pavilion
5 "HEARING" Pavilion
6 "QUESTIONING" Pavilion
7 Reconstructed landscape sections
8 Roman positions symbolized by steel slabs
9 Earthen rampart symbolized by iron poles
10 Reforestation
11 Germanic positions symbolized by wood-chip trails
12 Field tracks
13 Clearance

Earthen rampart indicated by iron poles

"Excavated landscape"

Entrance to "excavated landscape"

Steel-slab path

Wood-chip trails

The Pavilions

Three pavilions on the field serve as "perception instruments" to both broaden and question the impressions gained outdoors. The first pavilion, called "SEEING," projects the exterior world by means of a camera obscura upside down onto a glowing hemisphere. Akin to the function of the human eyeball, what one sees is pictured on this oversized glass "retina." The visitors can see how they see. Without electricity, this glass hemisphere brightens the darkened room in a mystical manner.

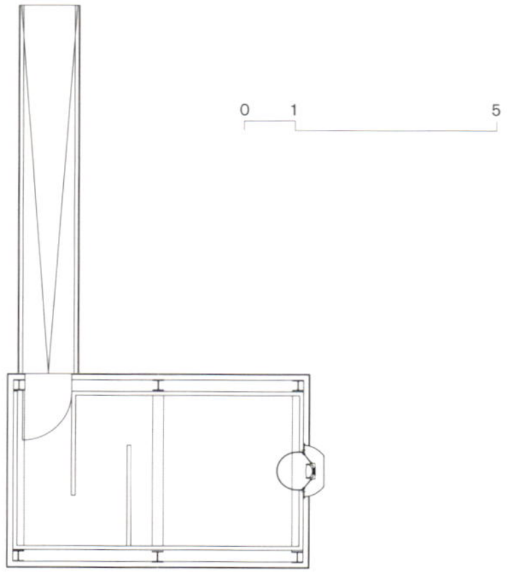

Floor plan

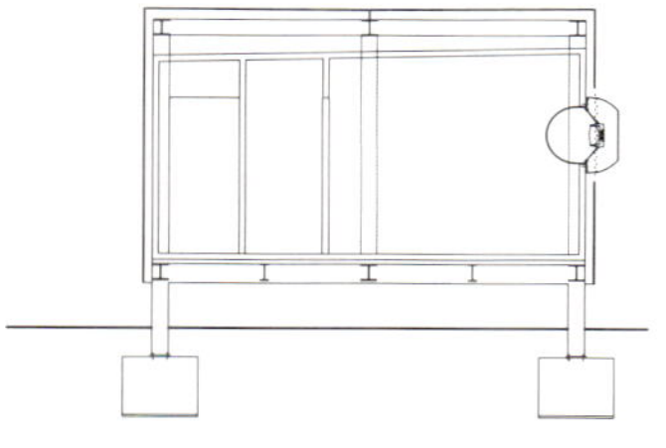

Section

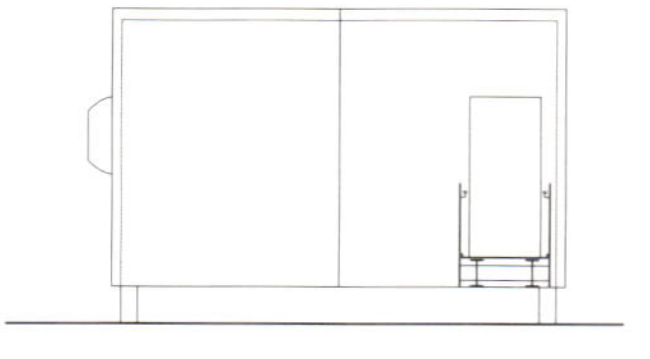

Elevation

"SEEING" pavilion

Camera obscura projection onto a glass hemisphere

The pavilion "HEARING" is equipped with a sizeable acoustical pipe that transmits the sounds of the outside world into a sound-insulated room. The pipe can be turned by hand and directed toward sources of sounds in order to listen carefully, to eavesdrop, and to intercept outside noises from within the insulated shelter: the chirping of birds, street noise, voices.

Archeological Museum and Park Kalkriese, Osnabrück, Germany
Pavilions

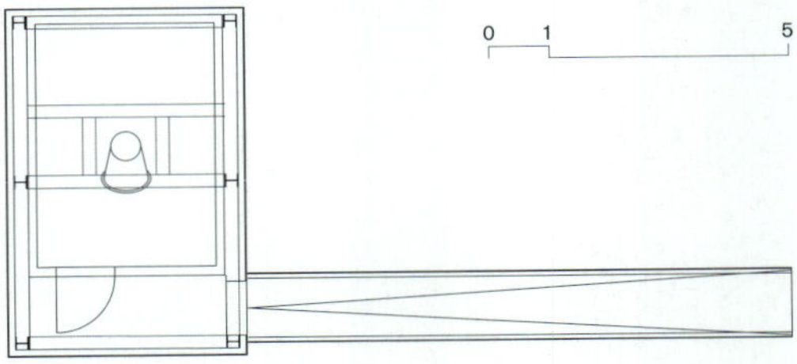

Floor plan

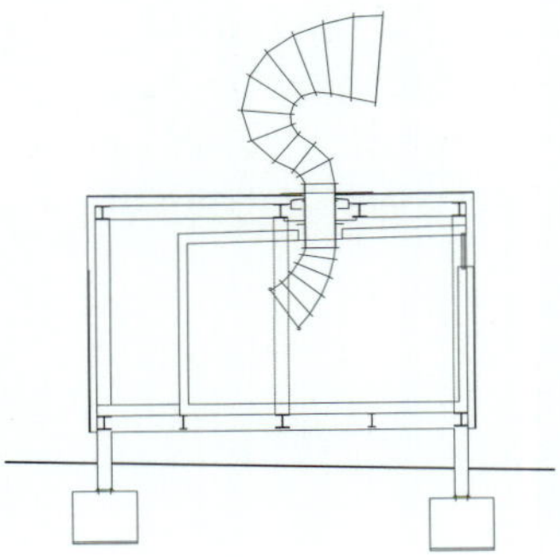

Longitudinal section

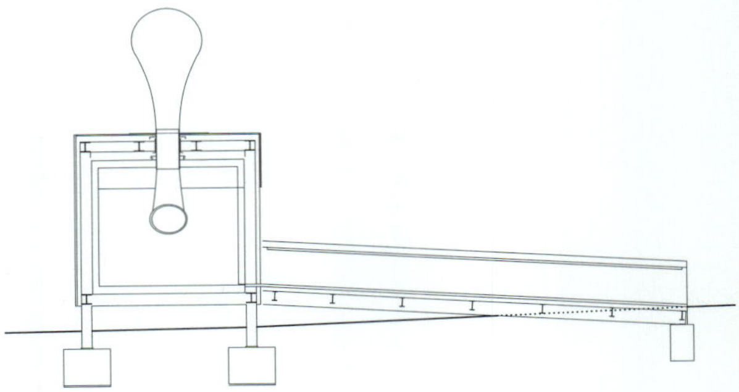

Cross section

In the last pavilion, called "QUESTIONING," a wall with slit-like openings stands opposite a wall with nine television monitors. A compilation of current news broadcasts makes it terrifyingly clear that still to this day, two thousand years later, conflicts continue to be fought out with aggression and violence.

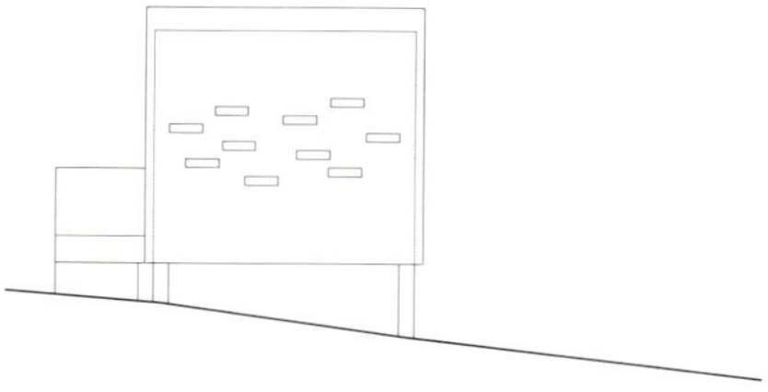

Elevation

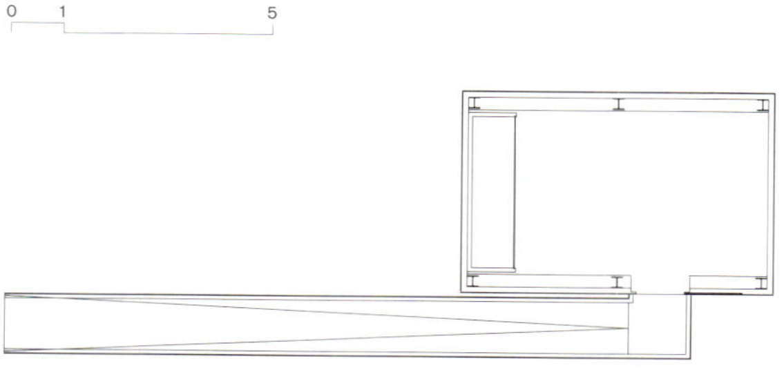

Floor plan

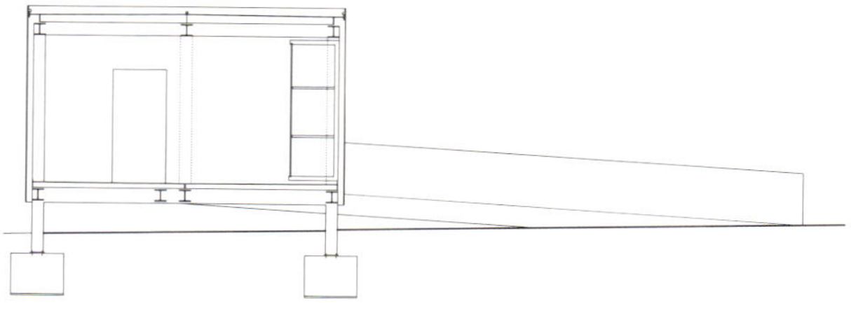

Section

Archeological Museum and Park Kalkriese, Osnabrück, Germany
Pavilions

The Museum

The museum consists of a single-story volume raised up from the ground, with a tower-like structure on top. A bird's eye view of the landscape and the one-time battlefield can be taken in from nearly forty meters high. The actual exhibition is to be found in the torso of the building, where the recovered artifacts are stored and displayed. A darkened, undivided room allows for the unfettered staging of the manifold aspects and themes of this battle: the culture of the Romans, that of the Germanic tribes, the course of the battle itself, the archeological research, and the perception of the battle throughout history. The abstraction of the interventions in the landscape is balanced out here by the instructive, descriptive material provided in the exhibition. Here and there, large windows partially brighten the space and provide open views back out onto the landscape and the one-time battlefield.

The Materials

Like the pavilions, the museum is a steel frame construction clad with large, rusting steel plates. Steel plates were also used in the interior of the museum: rolled steel sheets as wall and ceiling facing and non-rusting steel for the plates on the floor.

The intention was to make the interventions clearly visible by reducing the materials employed. The museum with its pavilions, the retaining wall of the sunken landscape, the slabs forming the path, and the visualization of the rampart with poles are all made of a common building material: steel.

Steel can be worked to varying degrees: untreated, rusting, oiled, painted, galvanized, slag-covered, to name only a few. As building material it possesses various characteristics and was used here in the form of weatherproof or non-rusting or common steel as befit the various tasks at hand. The large dimensions employed distinguish the material of steel as "contemporary" in nature. At the same time, it is precisely the rusting of the steel that makes the transitoriness of material states so manifest. It is worth adding that the majority of artifacts recovered in Kalkriese are metallic in nature.

The Farmstead

As a functional supplement to the museum and park, parts of the existing brick structures of Niewedde Farm have been converted for catering and administrative use. The visitors' restaurant as well as museum offices for administration, education, and the archeologists are located here. Before the curious eyes of visitors, the latter will very likely continue to excavate and conduct research into the battleground in the coming years, contributing new finds and insights, and thus continuing to write the history of the battle. To pursue the history of the site, seminars, events, and conferences cover themes such as conflict avoidance, conflict resolution, and research into peace.

Archeological Museum and Park Kalkriese, Osnabrück, Germany
Museum

GEBIERT AUS IHRER SICHT DI

Archeological Museum and Park Kalkriese, Osnabrück, Germany
Museum

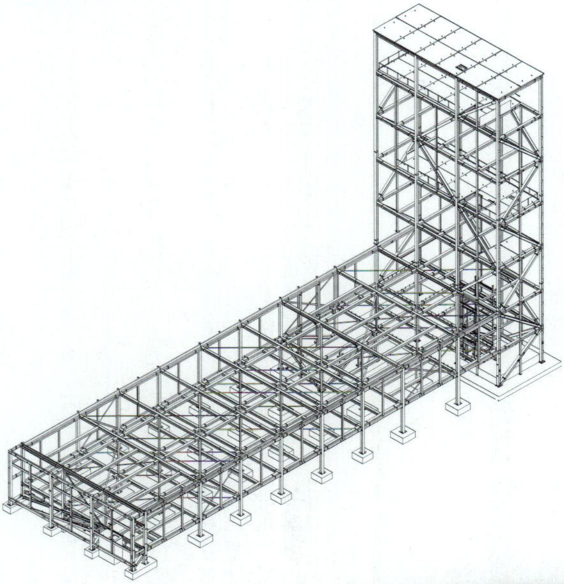

Steel structure

1 Entrance hall
2 Lecture rooms
3 Cloakroom
4 Exhibition anteroom
5 Exhibition
6 Education

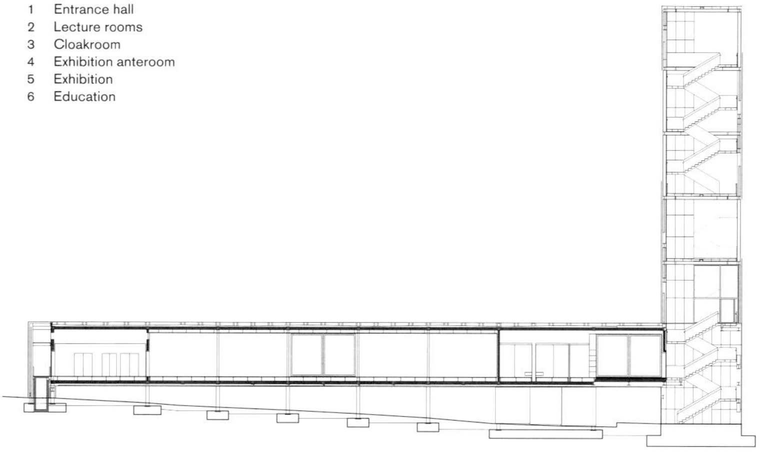

Section A–A

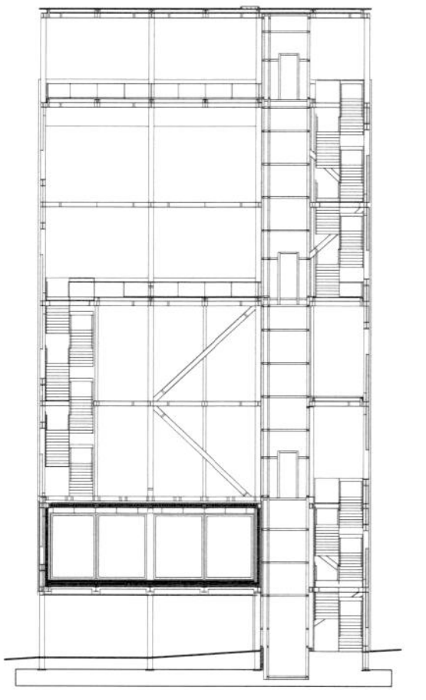

Section B–B

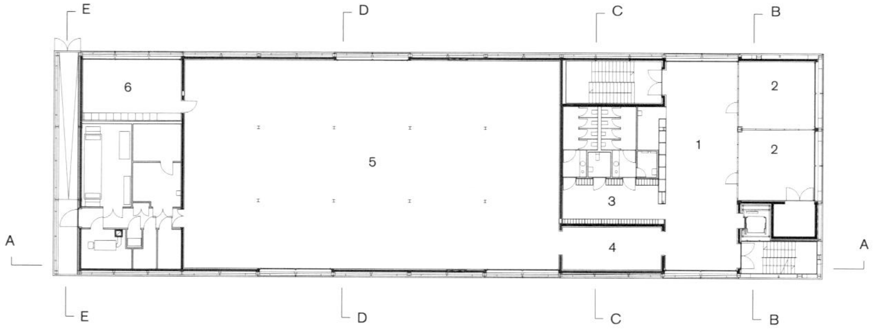

Exhibition floor

Section C–C

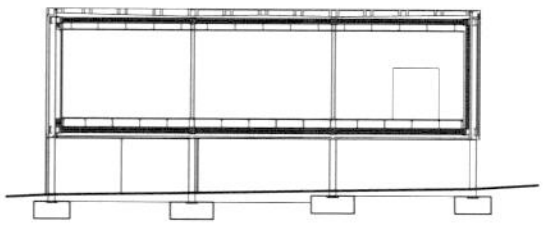

Section D–D

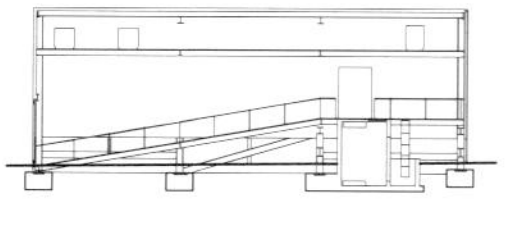

Section E–E

Archeological Museum and Park Kalkriese, Osnabrück, Germany
Museum

Museum entrance hall

Exhibition spaces, scenography by Integral Concept

Visitors Center, Museum Kalkriese, Osnabrück, Germany 177
2005–09

Added later, the visitors center now marks the entrance to the Archeological Museum Park. The ground floor houses the reception desk, museum shop, and a children's museum, while a multifunctional hall upstairs can be used as a large exhibition gallery or subdivided into smaller spaces by means of mobile partitions for use as meeting or conference facilities. Large windows on both sides offer views outdoors. The building is clad all around in facing bricks. The previous farmstead and the new building are united into a coherent ensemble by the material nature of their façades and together form an inviting courtyard.

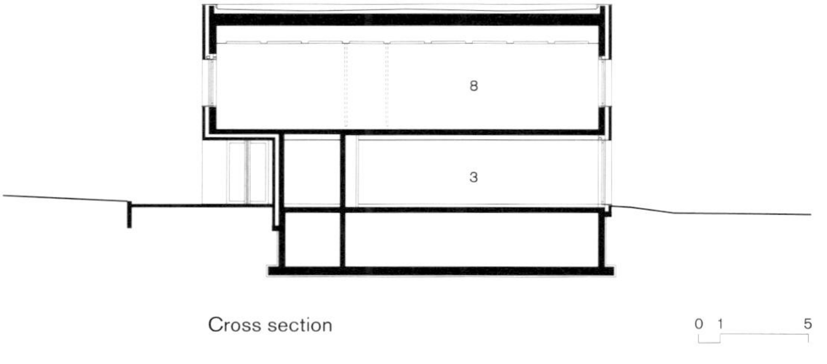

Cross section

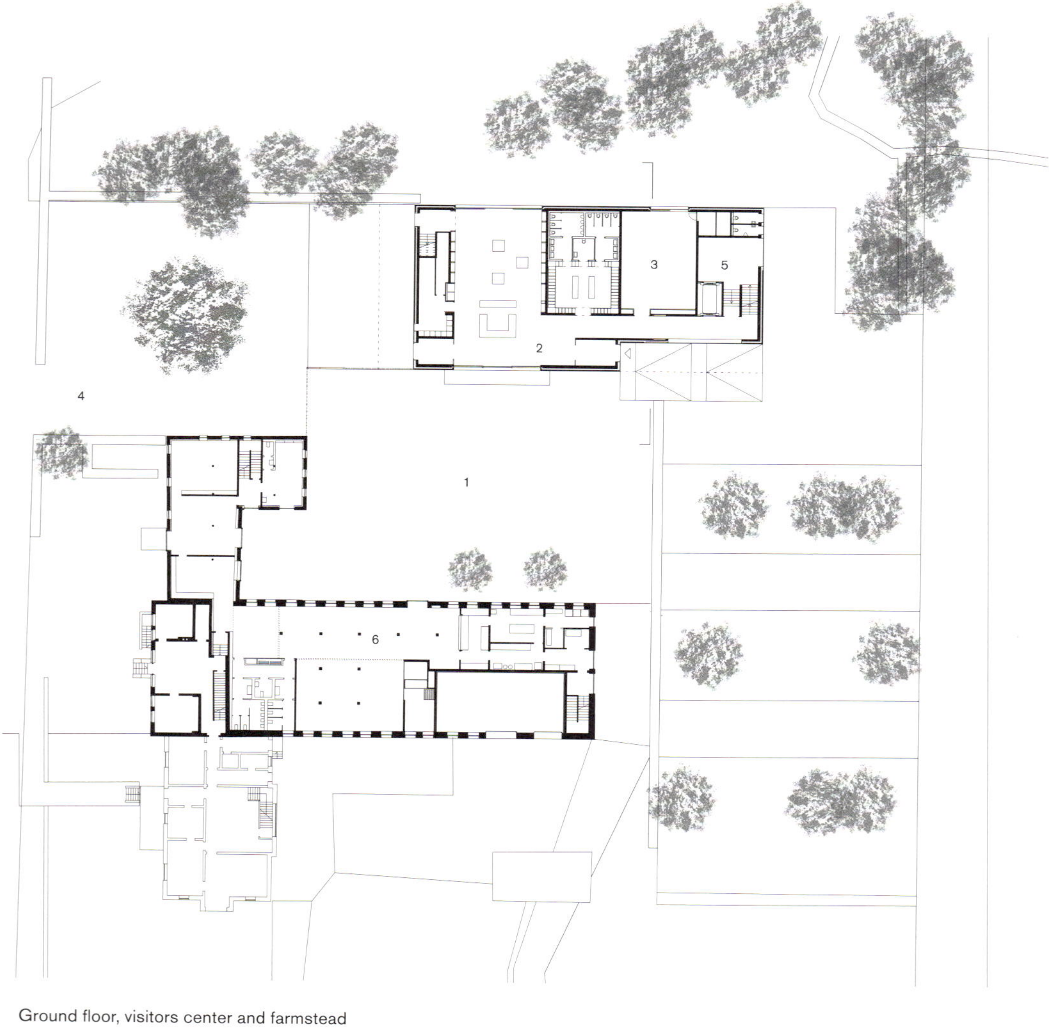

Ground floor, visitors center and farmstead

Visitors Center, Museum Kalkriese, Osnabrück, Germany

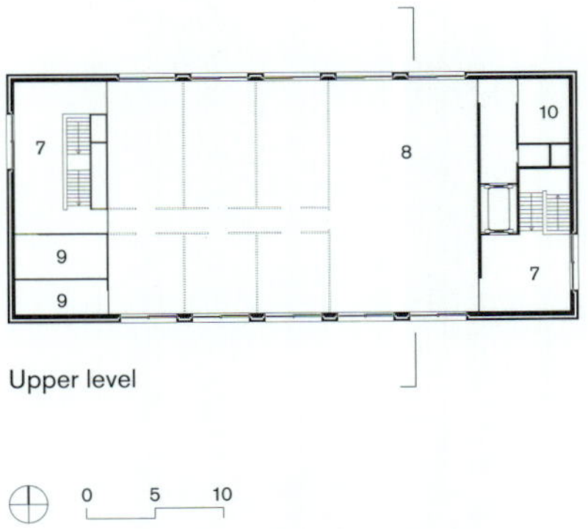

Upper level

1 Courtyard
2 Ticket desk/shop
3 Children's museum
4 Park entrance
5 Deliveries
6 Restaurant
7 Foyers
8 Exhibition space/potential conference area
9 Storage
10 Kitchen

Entrance area with museum shop

Hall on upper level

Albers-Honegger Donation 054 **and Préau des Enfants** 133
Espace de l'Art Concret, Mouans-Sartoux, France
1999/2001–03

1 Château of Mouans-Sartoux, Espace de l'Art Concret (EAC)
2 Albers-Honegger Donation
3 Préau des Enfants
4 Ateliers des Enfants

The new museum for the Espace de l'Art Concret (EAC) was built on the occasion of the donation of the Albers-Honegger Art Collection, parts of which had been displayed since the 1990s on a rotational basis in the castle of Mouans-Sartoux. The castle rooms will mainly be used for temporary exhibitions in the future. The new museum is the second freestanding annex on the castle grounds, following a children's painting studio called the Espace Art, Recherche, Imagination designed by architect Marc Barani. A third small building, the Préau des Enfants, was erected shortly after the museum. Both are set in a steeply sloping wooded area within the surrounding park.

The museum building's minimal, square-shaped ground plan and its tower-like structure with cantilevered elements made it possible to insert it into the wooded site with as little disruption to the existing trees as possible. Its position on a slope enables ground-level access at various building levels. A projecting section forms both the entrance to the museum and a bridge to the path outside. The access area for the public conference space and for deliveries also projects from the main volume of the building.

The museum entrance is elevated half a story above the first exhibition level. The galleries, connected by open stairs, are arranged at half-story level and form a spiral tour through the building. Two closed, sky-lit staircases serve as escape routes and also offer visitors a short path back to the entrance after finishing their tour. In addition to the lift, these staircases form an interior vertical connection between the conference space and the other rooms on the lower levels.

The arrangement of the galleries along the façades, the lateral lighting via the windows, and particularly the proportions of the spaces recall those of a large home rather than resembling a classic museum. Although the windows do not provide the even illumination often thought desirable in galleries, this solution meets the express wishes of the donors, who wanted natural light that would enable the works of art to engage in a vivid dialogue with the world outside and to be seen under a variety of lighting conditions. The windows are placed at differing heights in the galleries. Double-paned and resembling box-type windows, the outer pane of glass is affixed to the exterior of the façade to offer primary protection from wind and rain, while the inner pane, which can be opened, provides thermal insulation. Between the two windows, and thus shielded from the weather, fabric blinds afford protection from the sun. The blinds can be closed if desired, transforming the windows into sources of pure light, like glowing panels.

The building is constructed of poured concrete, which is painted a light yellow-green, in anticipation of the moss and algae that the nearby trees will eventually cause to cover it. Intriguingly, this color generates two diametrically opposed effects. On the one hand, it glows in contrast to the surroundings; on the other, it forms a harmonious background for the changing colors of the trees.

The donors' commitment to art education is expressed again in the nearby Préau des Enfants, an open concrete structure in the forest where the children's drawings and painting studies are exhibited.

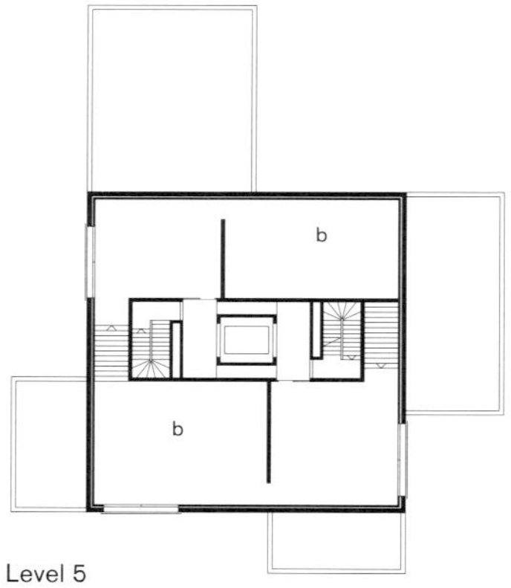

Level 5

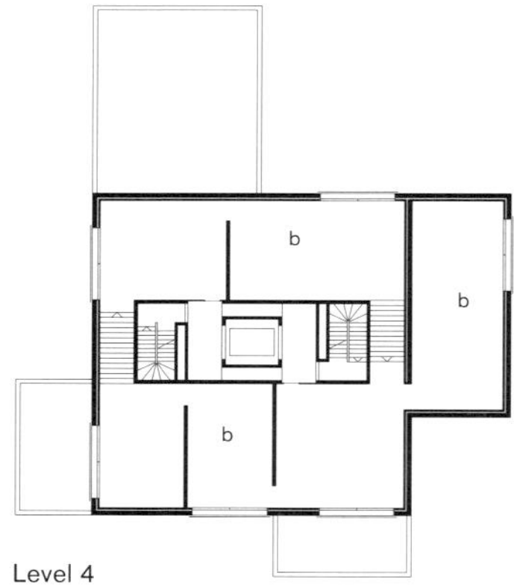

Level 4

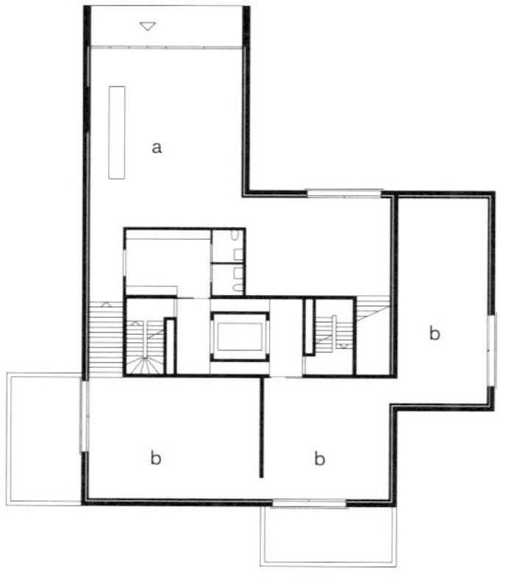

Level 3

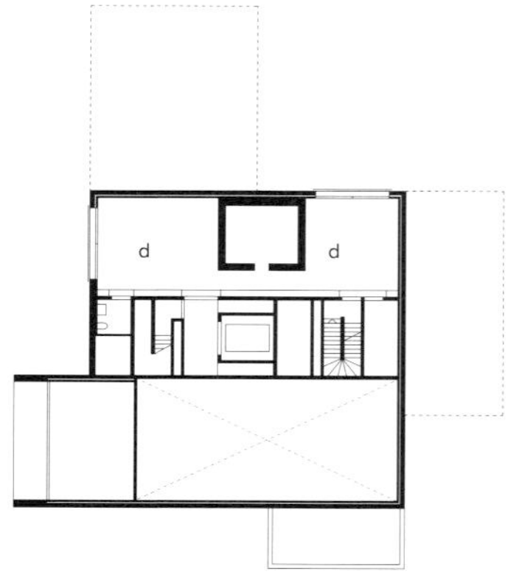

Level 2

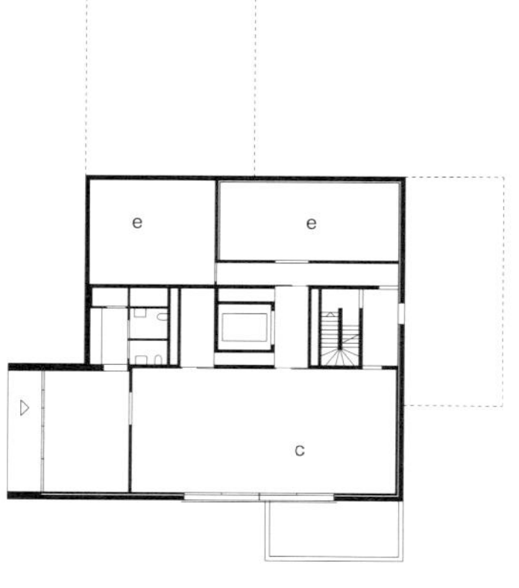

Level 1

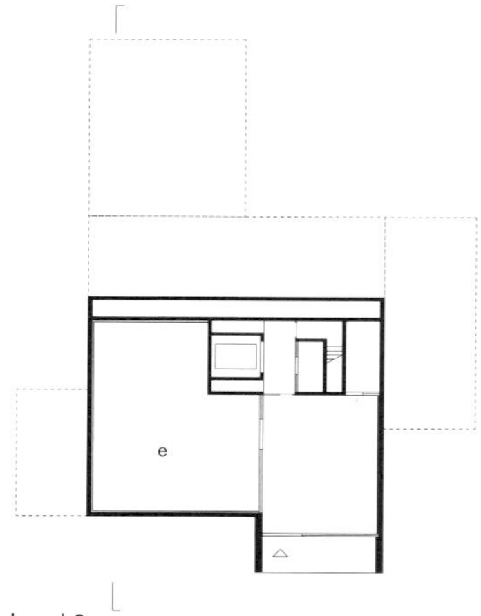

Level 0

Espace de l'Art Concret, Mouans-Sartoux, France
Albers-Honegger Donation

a Museum entrance
b Exhibition spaces
c Conference room
d Offices
e Storage

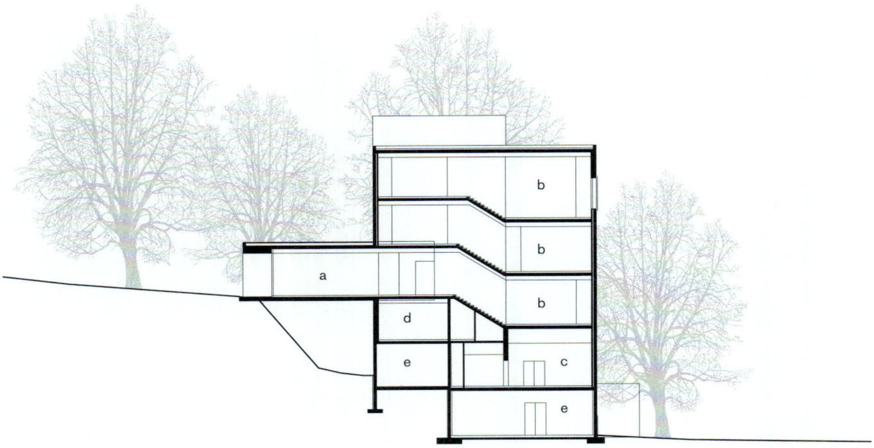

Section

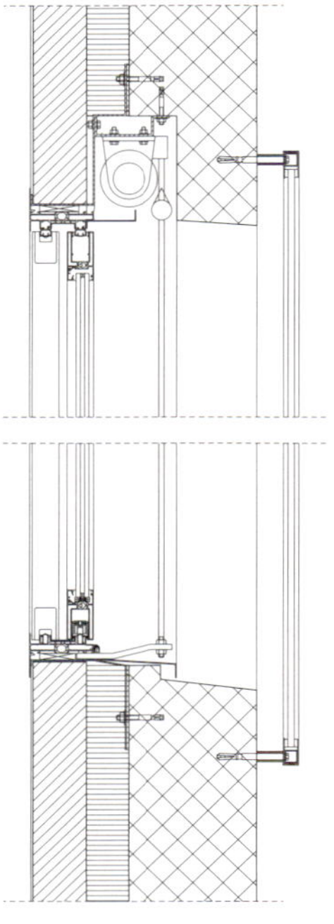

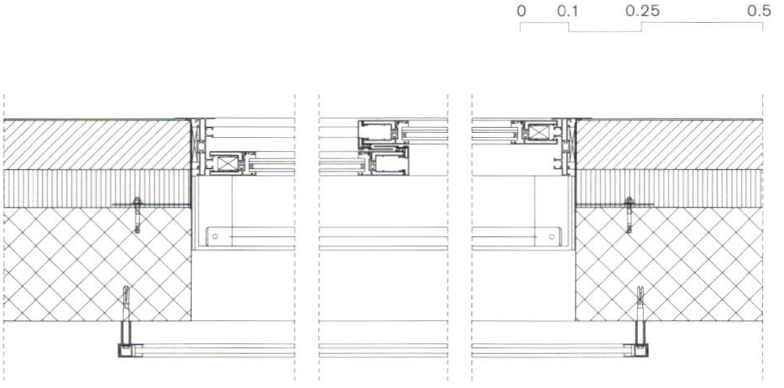

Construction detail

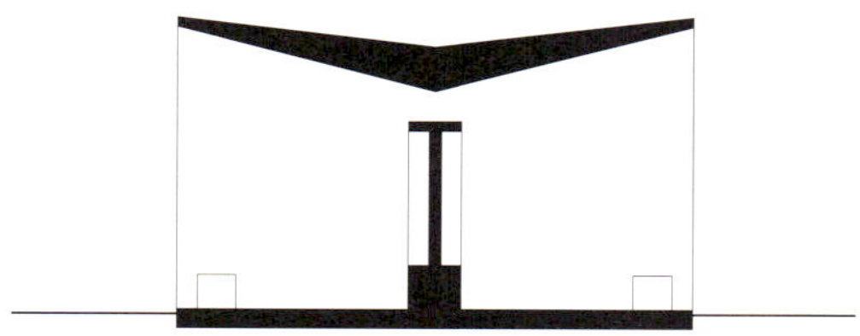

Section

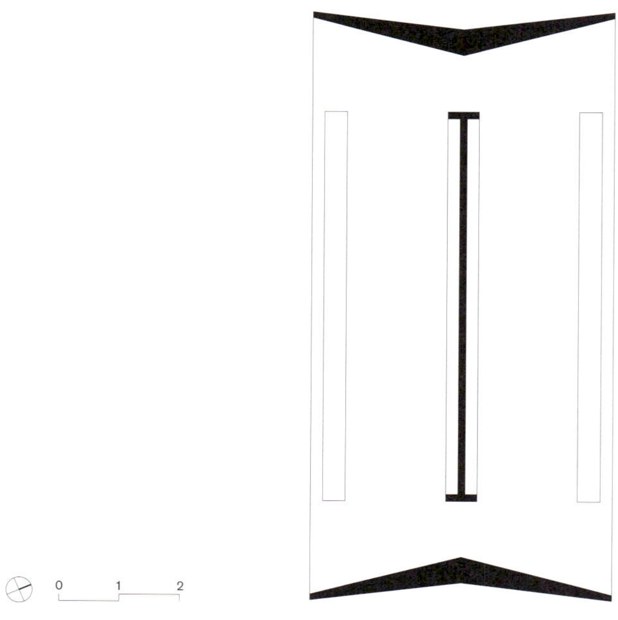

Floor plan

Espace de l'Art Concret, Mouans-Sartoux, France
Préau des Enfants

Kunst-Depot, Henze & Ketterer Gallery, Wichtrach, Switzerland 110
2002–04

The Kunst-Depot built for the Henze & Ketterer Gallery is designed to provide storage space for works of art while also functioning as a showroom: a showroom not only for clients who wish to look at a work that is not currently on display in the nearby gallery, but also a space that can be used for the presentation of contemporary art. The two floors above ground allow for all three types of use, although initially mainly the top floor will be used as gallery space.

The plan is not subdivided. It is structured only by the staircase with adjoining sanitary block and kitchen facilities, and also by a central load-bearing service wall. Two windows on the ground floor and two on the top floor allow daylight viewing of the works, as well as providing a view of the surroundings.

To minimize the risk of water damage to the artworks, only air is used for heating and humidity control. And to ensure a stable climate inside the Kunst-Depot, the insulation and mass of the brick-and-concrete load-bearing structure were maximized: even the roof is made of concrete.

Both the roof and façades are clad in "Tetra" metal sheeting, a material commonly used for warehouses. The distinctive look of the building comes from dividing the cladding into two perforated layers. The outer shell is like a curtain wall and functions as a sunscreen. The smooth metal roofing sheets are rectangular, but folded over the edge of the roof at a slant to echo on the façade the irregular, trapezoidal plan of the building.

The plan results from a wish to optimize the space both inside and outside the building within the limits of the bell-shaped plot. The building's shape responds to the local building code, which calls for a pitched roof and eaves for new buildings located in the historic center of the village to match the imposing style of the traditional surrounding farmhouses.

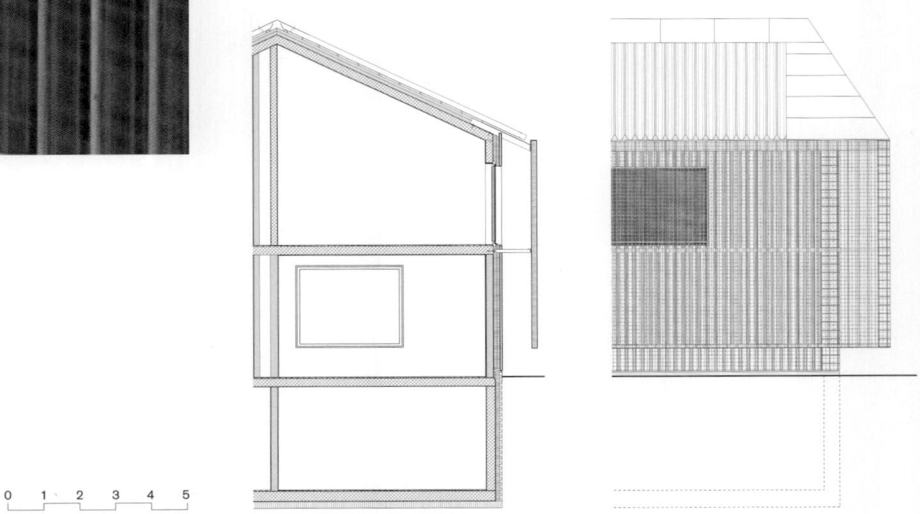

Construction detail

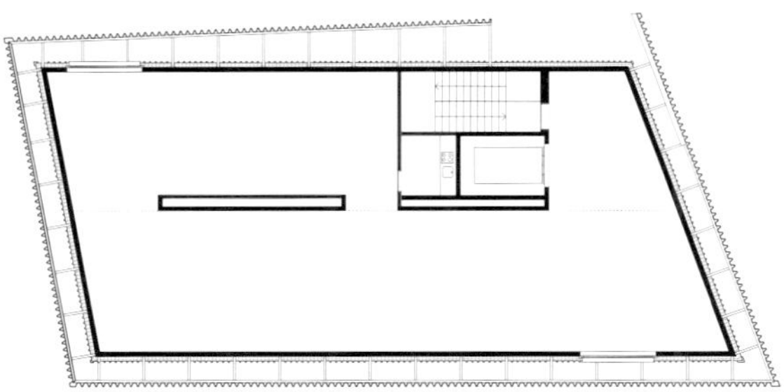

Upper floor

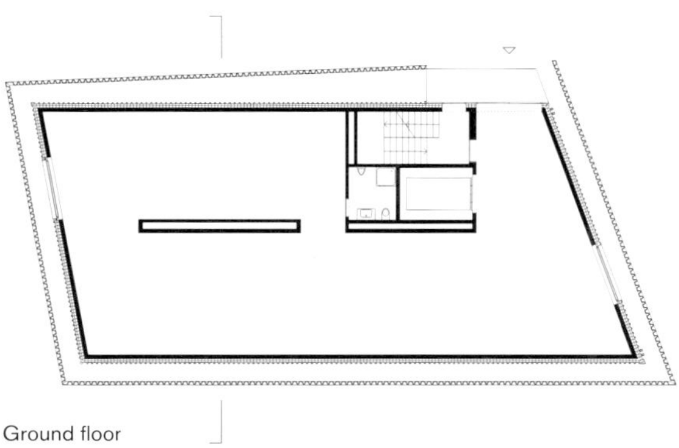

Ground floor

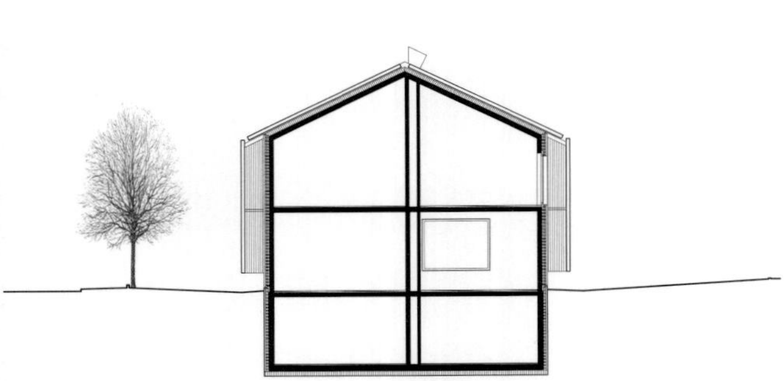

Cross section

piccard

Swiss Museum of Transport, Lucerne, Switzerland
Entrance Building and Road Transport Hall 166
1999/2005–09

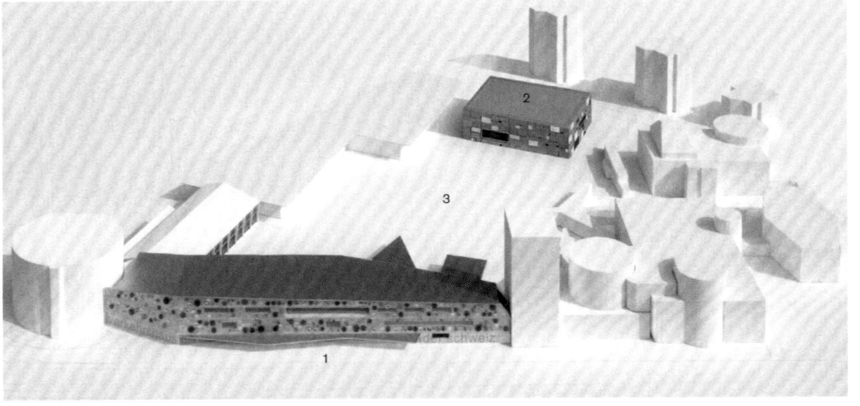

1 Entrance building
2 Road Transport Hall
3 Arena

The current project is based on the 1999 competition. At that time the brief represented an urban design vision for the gradual renovation of the museum complex with its various buildings exhibiting the different modes of transport, as well as a new building for the Road Transport Hall. During the first construction phase (2005–09) a new Entrance Building (FutureCom) was built in addition to the replacement of the Road Transport Hall. This urban design strategy enabled the creation of a central open courtyard (Arena), which in the new scheme will remain undeveloped, creating a setting for temporary, themed exhibitions as well as space for young visitors to run around and play.

The new Entrance Building forms a bridge-like link between the existing buildings on Lidostrasse (the Filmtheater, the Rail Transport Hall, and the high-rise with adjacent planetarium). The ticket office, shop area, and two restaurants are located on the ground floor—one restaurant offers table service and opens toward the lake, the other is conceived as a self-service restaurant that stretches out with fingers into the Arena. The exhibition areas for communication media, the new entrance to the Planetarium, and also the building services area are found on the first floor. The second floor accommodates the conference area, with a conference hall that seats 500 guests, a generous foyer, and three smaller meeting rooms. A large opening in the ceiling of the entrance hall affords views through the entire building—into the exhibition level and all the way up to the conference level.

The glass façades that provide protection from the elements also form more or less transparent "display cases" for all kinds of wheels, propellers, wheel rims, turbines, cogs, steering wheels, etc. These mechanical parts are densely hung on grids in front of the thermal insulation, shining and glinting through the blue-green glass panes of the façade. Seen at an angle, they submerge again behind the glass. Like a trophy display, the *omnium-gatherum* of recycled and dusted-off used metal together with pieces from the museum's collection pays homage to the wheel as a basic element of mechanical movement.

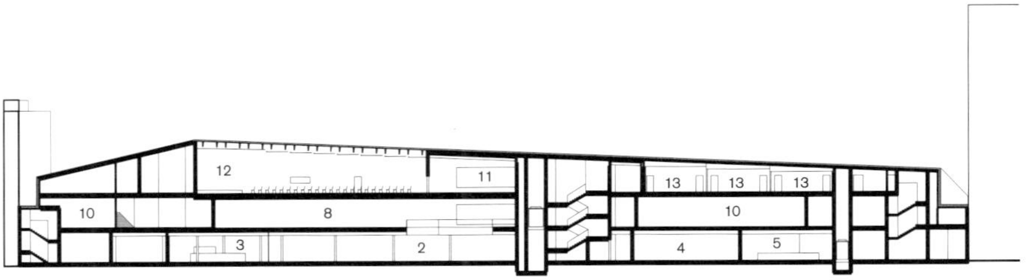

Section

1 Main entrance
2 Entrance hall
3 Shop
4 Restaurant
5 Kitchen
6 Filmtheater
7 Exhibition hall
8 Exhibition
9 Void
10 Building services
11 Foyer
12 Conference room
13 Meeting room

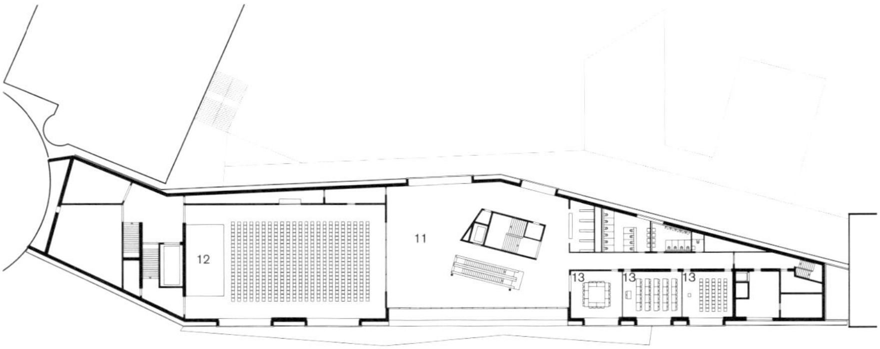

2nd floor

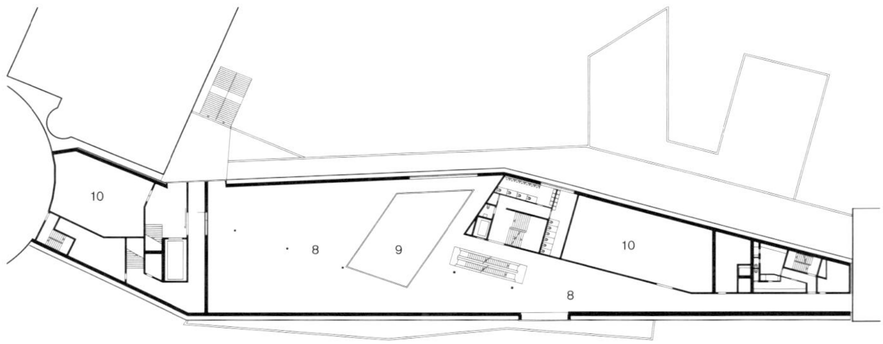

1st floor

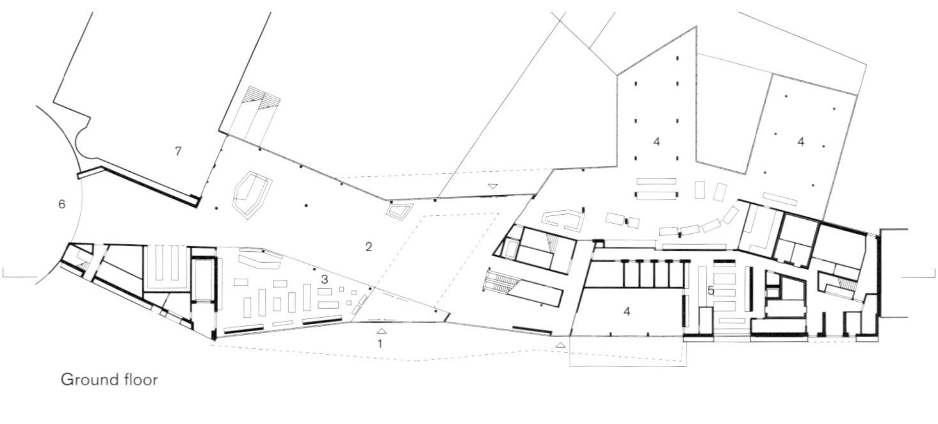

Ground floor

Conference level, foyer

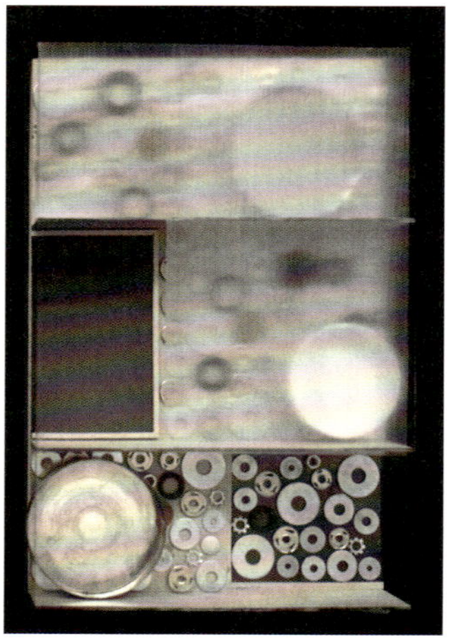

Design model

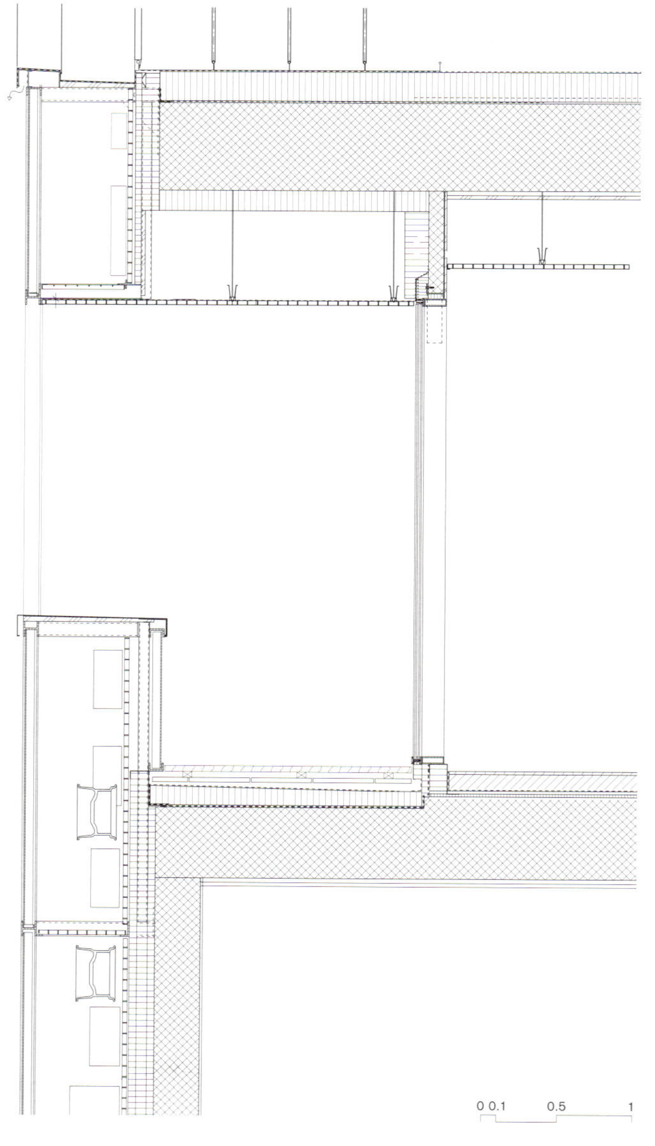

Section detail of façade

Conference level

Lausanne Moudon
Fribourg Bern
Payerne-Vignette
Grenchen
Arch
Büren a.A.
SORTIE
Fribourg
Romont
Z.I. La Maillarde
Basel/Bâle
La Chaux-de-Fonds Porrentruy
Industries
Münsingen
EuroAirport
Rubigen
Münsingen
Belp
Les Mosses
Aigle
Martigny
Z.I. Aigle
Service autos
Gipf-Oberfrick 650 m
Kirchberg
Alchenflüh
Langnau i.E.
Burgdorf
Zürich Basel
Solothurn
Langenthal
Solothurn
Industrie Neuhof
Epiquerez
Boudry
1000 m
Basel Liestal
Solothurn
Härkingen
Gäu/Gäupark
Fribourg
Bulle-nord
Z.i. Les Combes
Chez-le-Bart
Collonge-Bellerive
750 m
Fribourg
Rüegsauschachen
Lüterswil-Gächliwil
Divonne
Crassier
Eysins
Genève
Lausanne
Z.I. Ouest
Vallée-de-Joux
Cossonay Penthalaz
Lausanne
Penthaz
Eclépens
Daillens
Cossonay Orbe
Sullens
Boussens
Genève
Rolle
Genève
Lausanne
Gimel
Aubonne
Murten
Bern
Liestal
Egerkingen
Olten
CNG
Grauholz
2000 m
Bern
Lausanne
Aigle
Rheinfelden
Kaiserau
Genève
Gd-Saconnex
Lausanne
Ferney
Fret-Cargo
Champagne
800 m
Gd-Saconnex
Ferney
Palexpo Arena
Choindez 650 m
Genève-
Aéroport
900 m
Martigny
St-Maurice
Monthey
Luzern
Ost
Fully
Flughafen
Zürich
MIGROS
Le pays-Fraîcheur

Uhwiesen
Dachsen
Rheinfall
Wil Zentrum
Rickenbach
Wattwil
Zürich
Bern
St.Gallen
Tuggen
1000 m
Schaffhausen
Industriegebiet Wil
Deutschland
Rheinfelden
Basel
Kaiseraugst
Glattfelden
Basel
Zürich
Baden-West
1000 m
Flughafen
Flughofstrasse
Meilen
1000 m
Albula
Alp Grüm
Wallisellen
Oerlikon
Schwamendingen
Oberwil-Lieli
Zürich
Matzingen
Wängi
St.Gallen
Schaan
Vaduz
St.Gallen Neudorf
Heiden
60
St. Gallen
Wattwil
Uznach
Aarau
Sins
Gotthard
Luzern
Bünzen
1000 m
Rotkreuz
Hünenberg
Stans
Ennetmoos
Länderpark
Heiden
Rehetobel
St.Margrethen
Kreuzlingen
Rorschach
San Bernardino
Raststätte
Thusis
Cazis
Albula
Polizei
90 m
Landquart
Chur
UNIQUE
berufsfeuerwehr zurich airport
26

The concept for the new Road Transport Hall differs from the first design during the 1999 competition. Originally conceived as a three-story building with concrete shear walls, a load-bearing, glazed façade construction, and bridge-like ramps on the exterior, the new building is to have two stories, be more economical, and in particular offer greater flexibility. It is an exhibition building that in its rudimentary simplicity and as "dark-gray black box" is reminiscent of those buildings country-wide that are designed for the storage and housing of cars, i.e. multi-level parking garages and automobile repair shops. An automated parking system is employed here; a shelf-like structure operated by a mechanical lift displays the collection of cars densely positioned one above the other and out of reach. At the touch of a button, visitors can move one of the cars forward to look at it close up. The open areas on the first two levels provide space for running temporary theme-based exhibitions. A workshop shows the visitors how the vehicles are maintained and repaired.

The façade cladding of the mainly closed building volume is composed of sheet metal in differing formats and colors. Instead of standard façade sheeting, however, or metal from car bodies (as envisaged during the preliminary project), sheet-metal traffic signs have been recycled here: highway signs, guidance and information signs, warning signs, marker signs, and place-name signs. The signboard walls, which spatially delimit the Road Transport Hall, indirectly refer to the great freedom of mobility afforded by private transport, which is directed and regulated with the help of such boards. Furthermore, they also refer to numerous locations near and far that might be the home towns and cities of the visitors, who arrive via diverse traffic routes and using different modes of transport in order to discover more about the subject here. On the rear façade, toward the neighboring buildings, the signs are reverse-mounted, which means that the printed side faces the building while the untreated, metal side faces outward. Thus, the neighbors see these boards just as road users would see the signs meant for the oncoming traffic—from the back.

Swiss Museum of Transport, Lucerne, Switzerland
Road Transport Hall

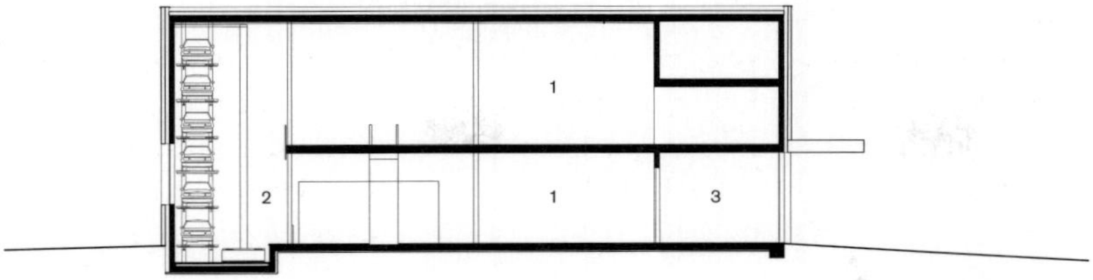

Section

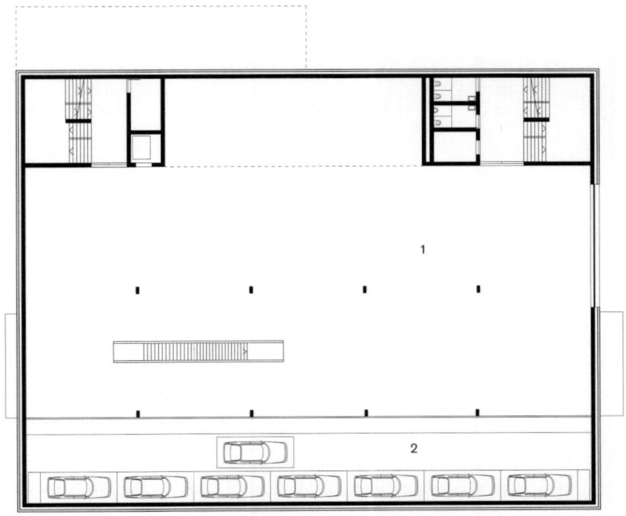

1st floor

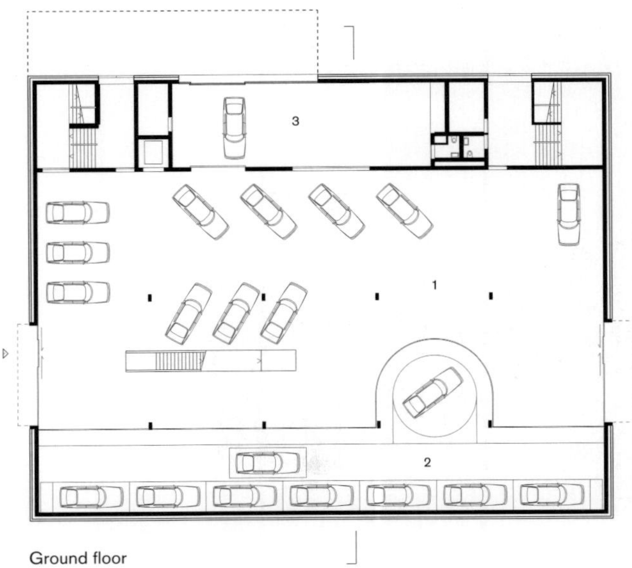

Ground floor

1 Exhibition
2 High-rise rack, parking robot
3 Exhibition workshop

0 1 5 10

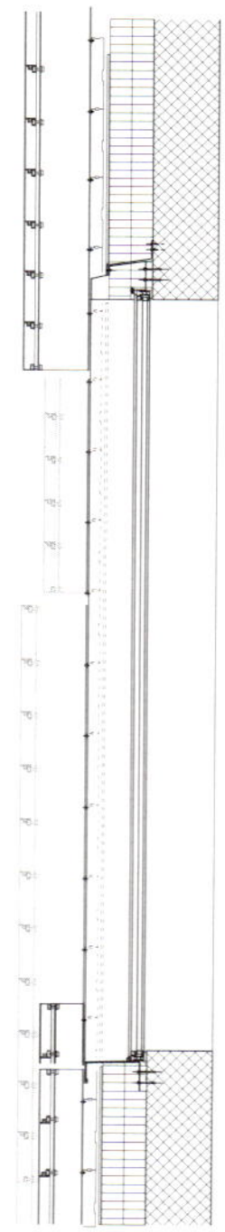

0 0.5 1

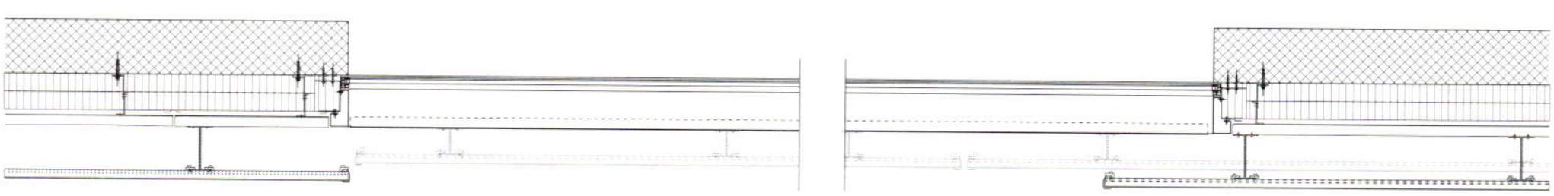

Construction detail

Bellinzona
E25
Lausanne
Genève
Lyon
E23
9
Lausanne 42 km
Orbe 12 km
Altstätten
Kriessern
St.Gallen
St.Margrethen
Geno
Milan
Dom
Brig
Genève-Centre
Jonction
Les Vernets
Meersburg
E25
1
250 km
St.Gallen 169 km
Zürich
Bern
Vacances
Sion
E35
2
Gotthard 125 km
Interlaken 112 km
Zug 64 km
Luzern 39 km
E35
2
San Gottardo
Lugano
Bellinzona Sud

Viamala

Bulle
Centre d'entretien Police
E27
12
Bern
Liestal
Egerkingen
Olten
CNG
9
Bex-Centre
TRANSIT
22
Wangen a.A.
3,5t
2,5m
Holzbrücke
Deitingen
Walliswil b.W.
Wangenried
Bosco / Gurin
TI
Breganzona
TI
Z.I. Orgamol Nord
Evionnaz
Yverdon
Prilly
1000
SWISSAIR

National Park Center, Zernez, Switzerland 112

2002 (Competition)

1 Visitors center, new build
2 Palace, administration
3 Former service building, seminar rooms

In Zernez, at the border between upper and lower Engadin, a visitor and administration center was opened in 1968 for the Swiss National Park, which was founded in 1914 and is the oldest of its kind in the Alps. Several decades later, the decision was made to adapt the center to contemporary needs, leading to a competition for reorganizing and expanding the functions that had, up to then, been housed in the historic Planta-Wildenberg Castle and other buildings. The new concept envisions a coherent architectural and landscaping plan for the entire area reaching from the old village road to the new bypass, without however competing with the village's existing landmarks.

While the administration of the national park is accommodated in the castle and an auditorium in the neighboring service building, the information center is given its own new building. This structure deliberately does not borrow its typology from the castle, but rather expresses the new use with an independent appearance. The elongated, mostly single-story structure with its folded roof and body-like openings more readily recalls a "natural" and "landscape" form than a building.

The layout and positioning of the building volume allow it to be entered from all sides – from the castle courtyard, from the canton road and from the old main street of the village via a newly created square. On the inside, a network of pathways connects the three entrances, simultaneously structuring the public areas, the non-public areas, and the areas subject to entry fees. Visitors move through the exhibition on a "circuit tour" punctuated by opportunities to look out onto the landscape, the mountains, the village, and the sky. The exhibition rooms are designed as continuous areas, which can also be flexibly divided into smaller room units. Alternating zones of dark and light are illuminated from the side and above.

The load-bearing structure for the roof and walls is made of concrete, which on the interior is partially left untreated and in other areas plastered, painted, or faced in wood. The exterior façades and roofs are clad in local scree. Together with the gravel areas outdoors, these take up a dialogue with the built environment and the natural landscape of the nearby national park.

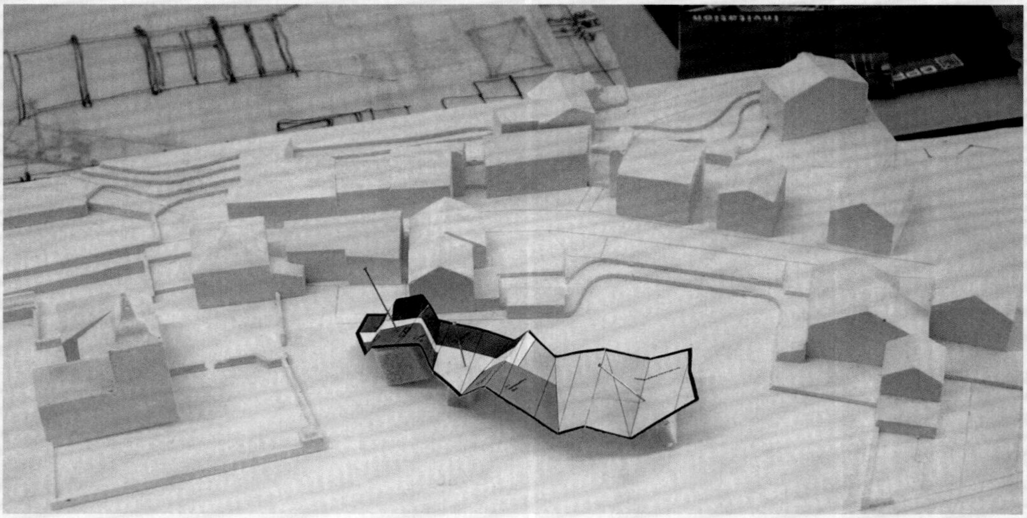

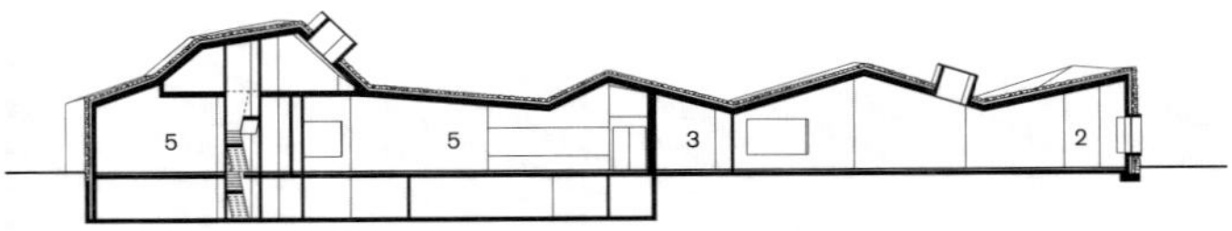

Section A–A

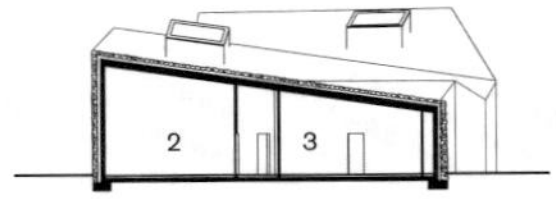

Section C–C

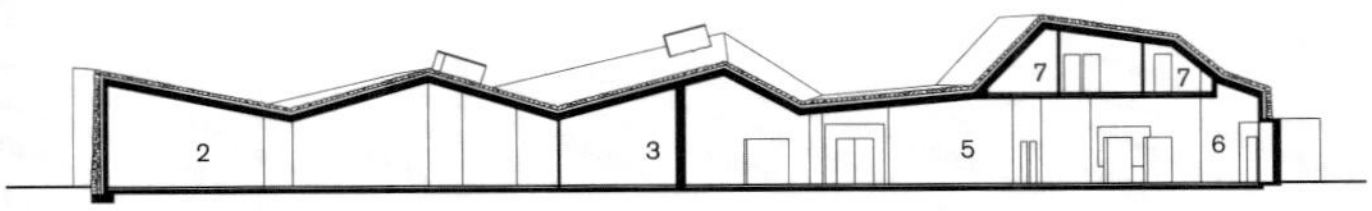

Section B–B

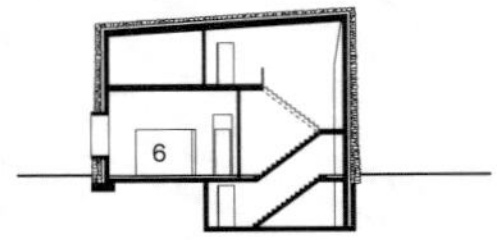

Section D–D

1 Hall
2 Exhibition
3 Lecture hall
4 Tourist office
5 Sales area
6 Cloakroom
7 Office
8 Library
9 Archive
10 Seminar room

Ground floor

West elevation

South elevation

View from Kantonsstrasse

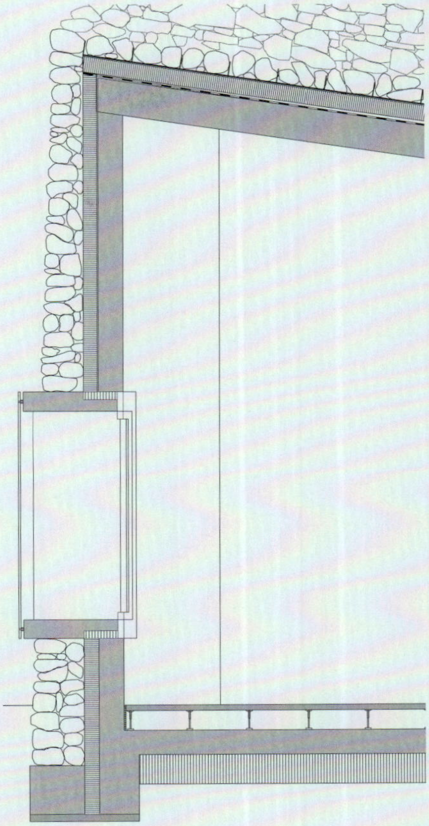

Construction detail

Scree fields in the National Park

Road construction, retaining walls

Extension of Rietberg Museum, Zurich, Switzerland 107
2002 (Competition)

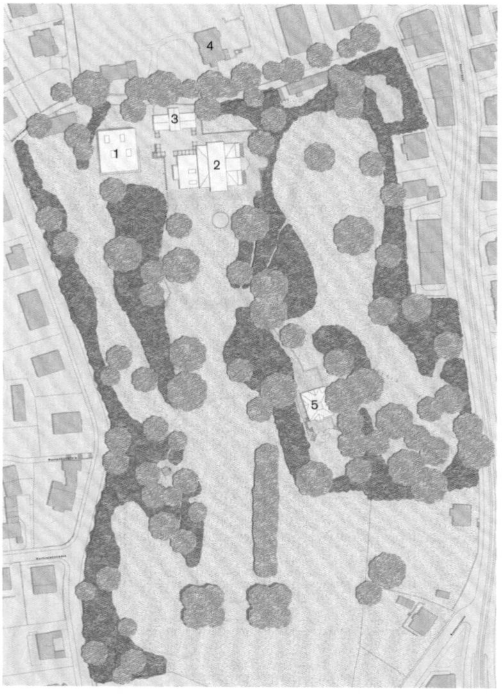

1 Museum extension, new entrance building
2 Villa Wesendonck
3 Service building
4 Villa Schönberg
5 Villa Rieter

In 1952 the Rietberg Museum for non-European art moved into Villa Wesendonck, situated in Rieterpark, one of Zurich's most beautiful parks. The villa, built in 1857 by Leonhard Zeugheer, is famed as one of the key examples of late Neoclassical architecture in Zurich. The new extension project was driven by the museum's growing need for more space even after the museum expanded in 1978 to incorporate the adjacent Villa Schönberg (Alfred Friedrich Bluntschli, 1888), which in the meantime has been restored by Arthur Rüegg and Silvio Schmed.

The design is based on a three-story cube, which rises up from a subterranean rhizome-like connecting building. An ensemble is generated by introducing the extension building alongside the two existing structures—Villa Wesendonck and its former services building—creating a new and adequate presence for the museum institution. The extension welcomes visitors from the street side, while receding into the background when viewed from the park. The appearance of the historical park is thus scarcely altered.

On the ground floor the new building houses the ticket desk and museum shop, along with a multimedia room, which is conceived as a flexible spatial enclosure with sliding dividing walls. The new permanent exhibition is located on the two upper floors. Generously proportioned stairways and an underground hallway connecting the two buildings provide access to the area for temporary exhibitions. This is designed as a flexible space for varied exhibition options and is artificially lit. In the new rooms for the permanent collection by contrast, natural light enters from above through skylights on the third level and on both floors through side windows that also offer vistas of the surroundings. The ceiling construction spans the entire space, allowing flexible uses of these rooms as well.

Above ground, the extension is clad with prefabricated concrete/glass-brick elements. Supplementing the windows, they also function as a source of diffuse natural light. The exterior of the building displays a subtle iridescent sheen, created by mixing quartz sand into the concrete and sand-blasting the cladding panels.

The design envisages just one simple change to Villa Wesendonck: a new stairway leads from the underground level directly into the villa's existing staircase.

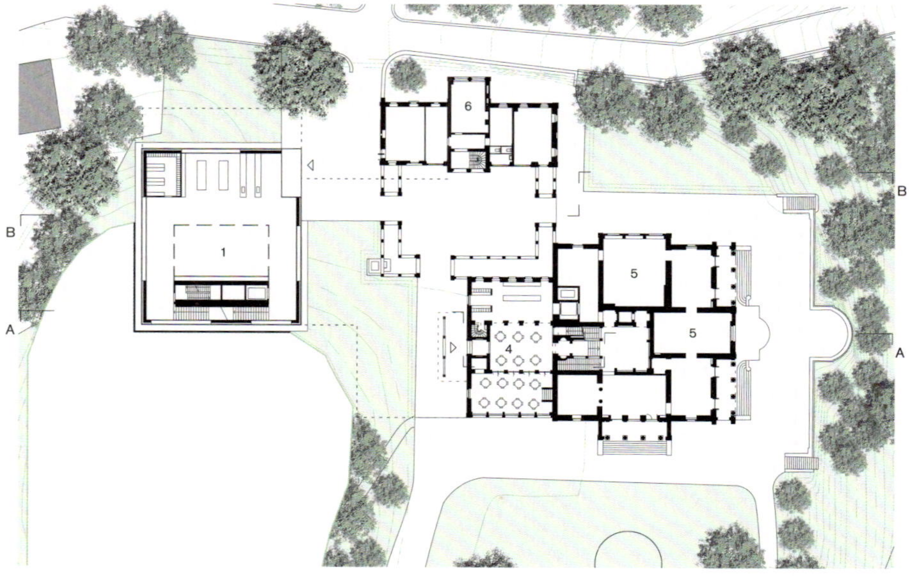

Ground floor

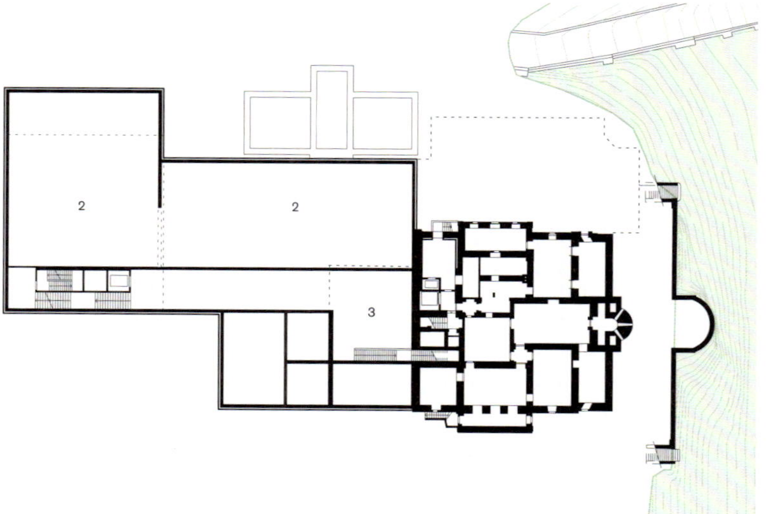

Lower floor

1 Entrance area
2 Temporary exhibition
3 Hall
4 Cafe
5 Permanent exhibition
6 Administration/education

Extension of Rietberg Museum, Zurich, Switzerland

South elevation

North elevation

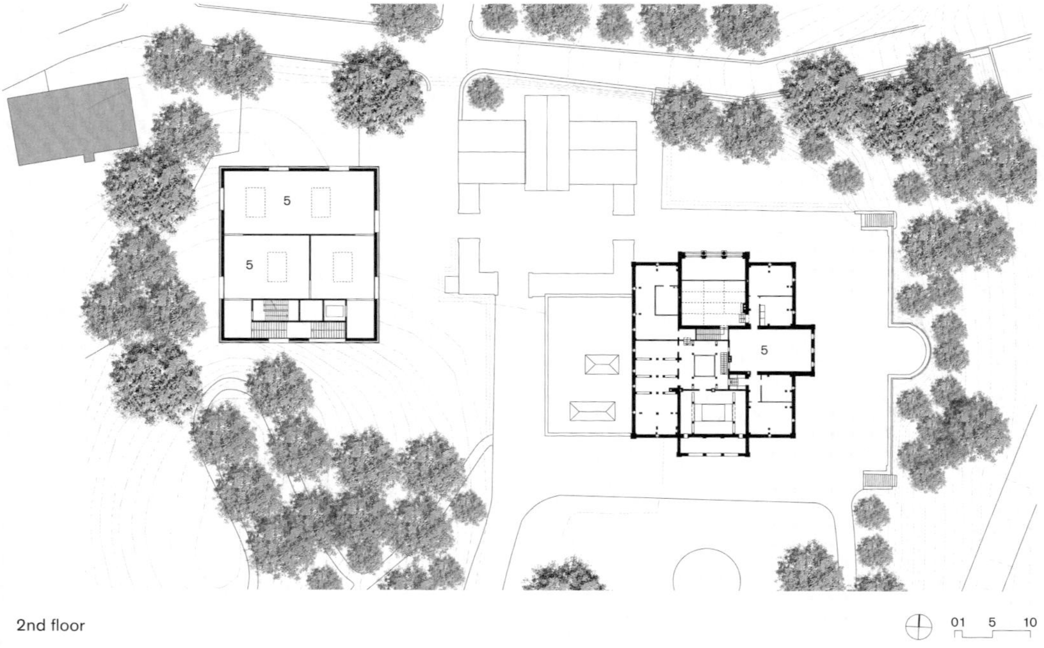

2nd floor

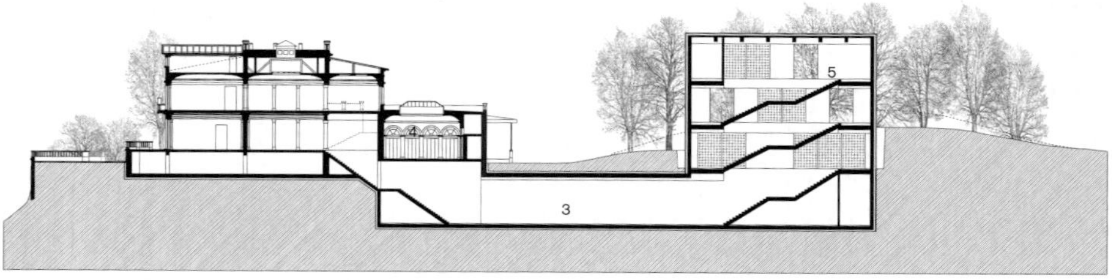

Section A–A

Section B–B

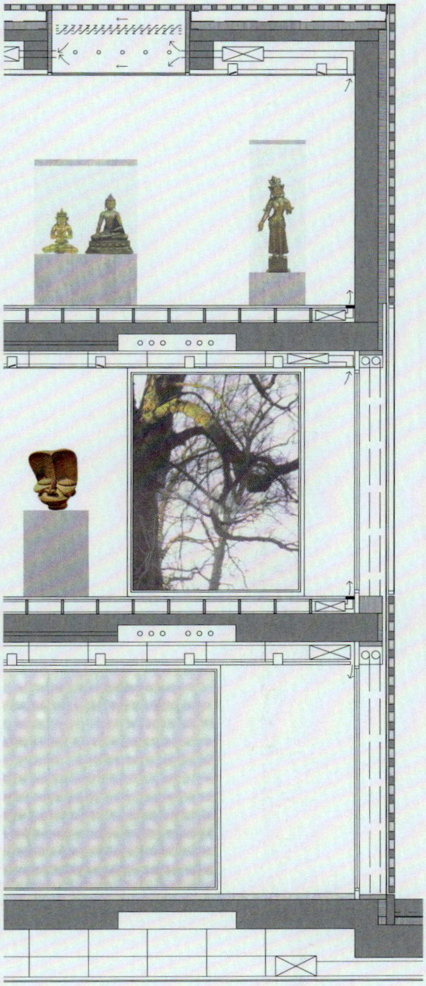

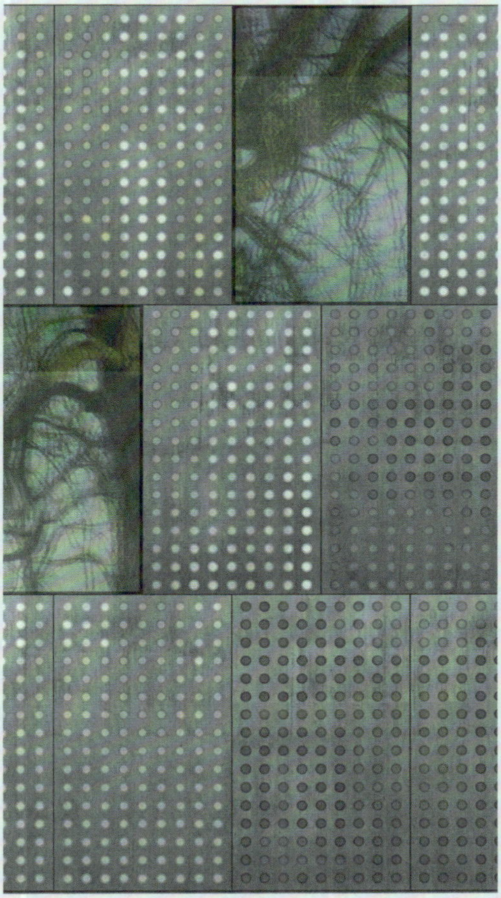

Construction detail

0 0.5 1

NEW MUSEUM
BARI HOTEL

New Museum of Contemporary Art, New York, NY, USA 122
2003 (Competition)

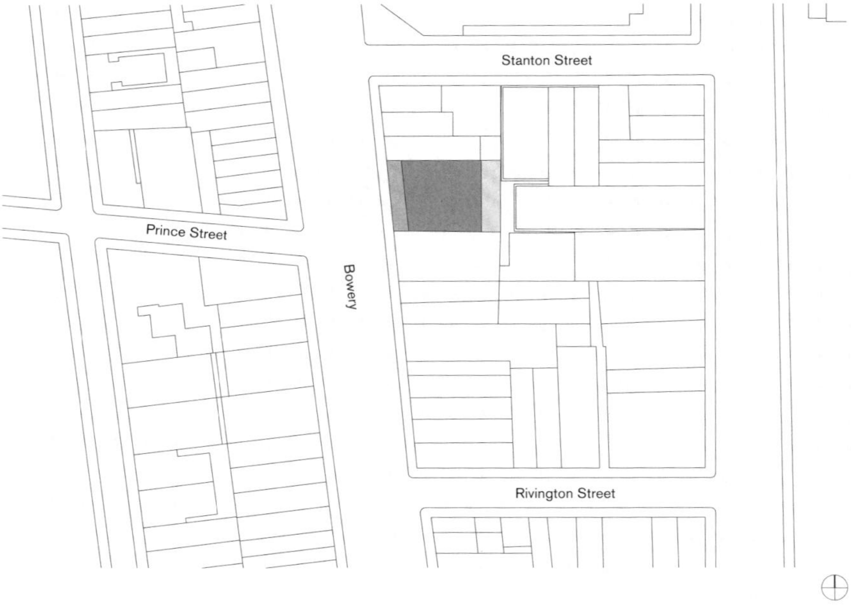

The New Museum of Contemporary Art was planned for insertion into a gap in the building row on the east side of the Bowery in the Manhattan district of Soho. The concept for the architecture of the museum is once more to place itself at the service of the art. In the competition brief, the client formulated the requirements for the building as follows: "The building should be so great that you can't miss it on the outside, and so great that you don't notice it on the inside."

The various functional areas of the museum are stacked in a 48-meter tower that is far higher than the neighboring buildings, while the base consists of a generously proportioned multi-story lobby that connects the interior with the exterior. The cloakroom, cash desks, museum shop, and vertical access facilities structure the space as orthogonal, mostly glazed cubes, with a special exhibition hall to the rear. The cafe is situated at the gallery level above the lobby, facing the street, and offset above it is a media lounge and the administration level.

The actual exhibition galleries are on the upper five floors, whose height ranges from 5.5 to 6.7 meters. The eccentric position of the main stairway and elevator shaft produces varying room depths, thus providing for a diverse circuit on each level. Due to a setback, a typical feature dictated by New York's building code, a terrace is created on level 7 that functions as resting place and lookout point on the way through the exhibition.

The exhibition galleries of the New Museum are basically conceived as "containers" for art. They are designed as clear-cut, mostly rectangular spaces evincing a carefully composed interplay of proportions, materials, and lighting. High side windows of etched glass bathe the galleries in even, diffuse daylight. The floors are made of poured concrete.

The façades reflect the various demands met by the building: the special features of the site, its construction, and the urban context. Various types of glass surface generate fascinating, diffusely flowing transitions between clear, reflective, and etched glass in which the surroundings appear as a mirror image, only to disappear again. The materials used are characteristic for New York, but are deployed here in an unconventional manner. The building's exterior makes the museum functions within legible, yet simultaneously obscures them; by both working and playing with the light it reveals itself to be a built "instrument of perception."

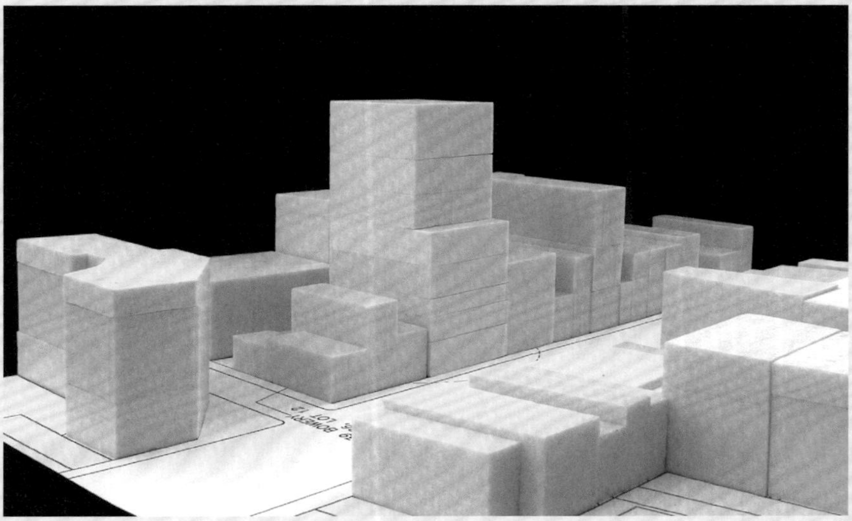

1 Theater
2 Backstage
3 Deliveries
4 Foyer
5 Tickets
6 Museum shop
7 Cloakroom
8 Exhibition
9 Cafe
10 Office
11 Void
12 Media area
13 Education
14 Reception
15 Conference room
16 Library
17 Building services

0 1 10

New Museum of Contemporary Art, New York, NY, USA

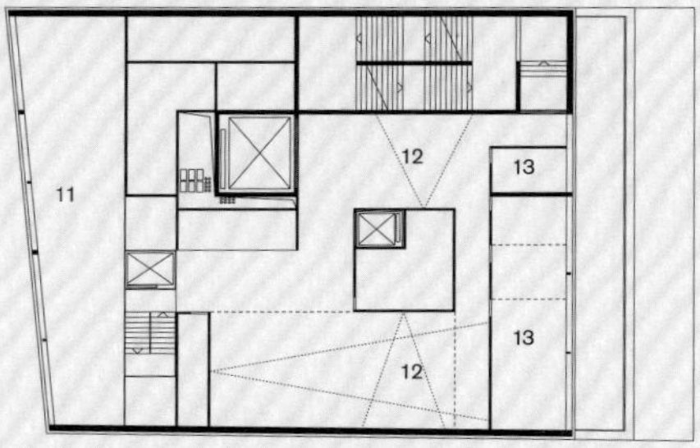

3rd floor

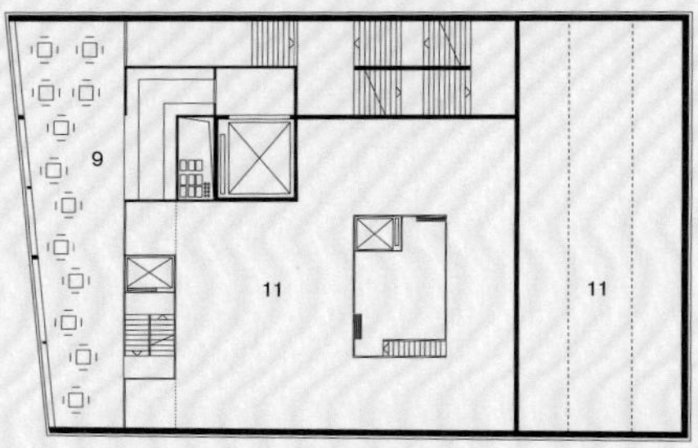

2nd floor

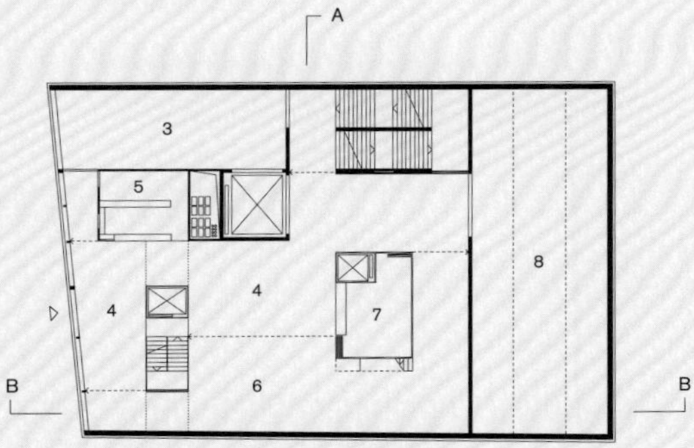

Ground floor

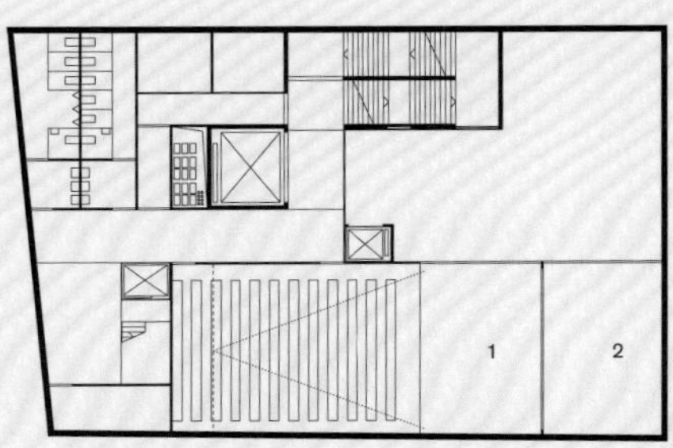

First basement level

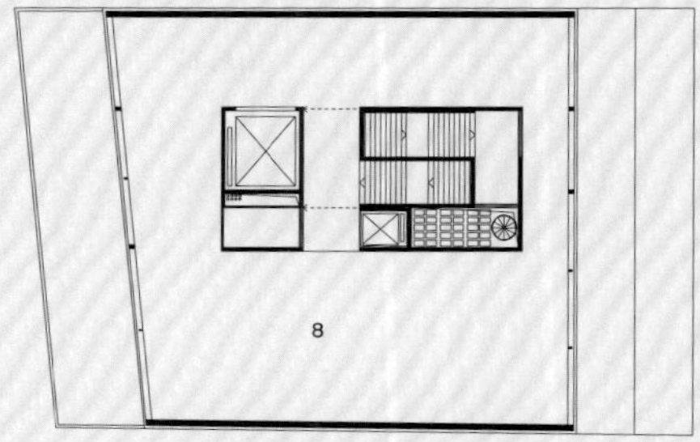

9th floor

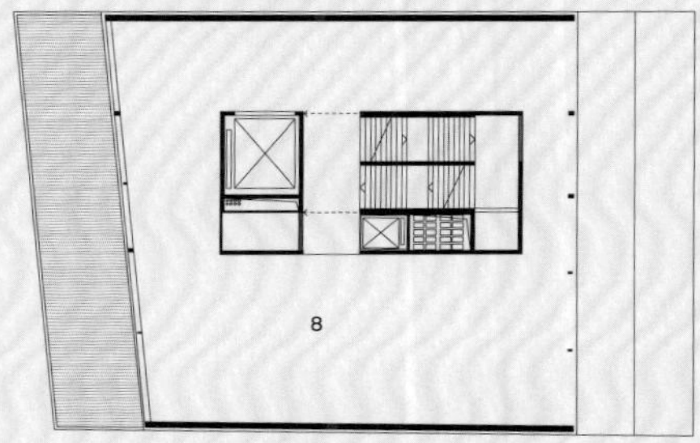

7th floor

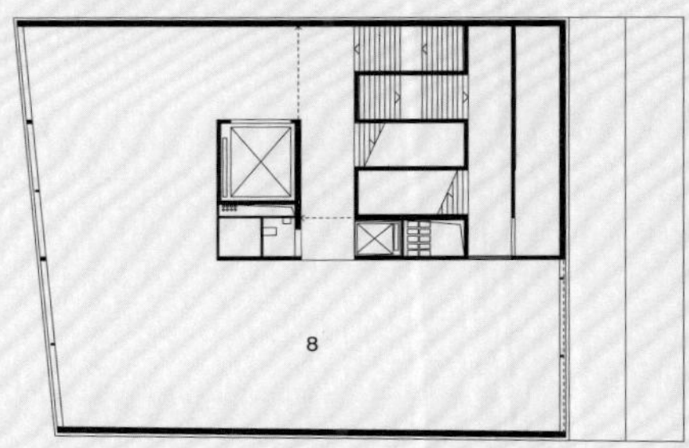

5th floor

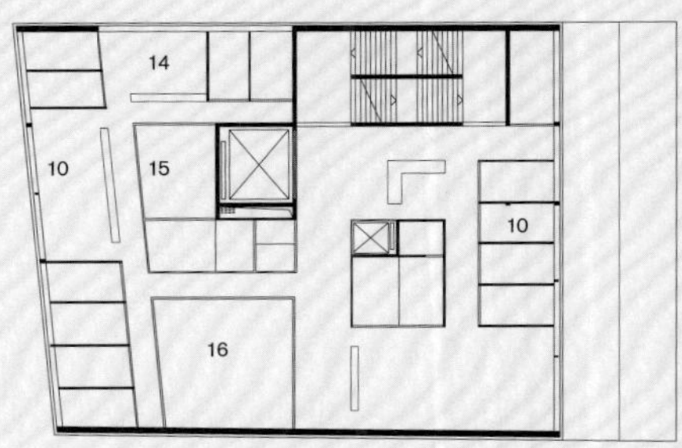

4th floor

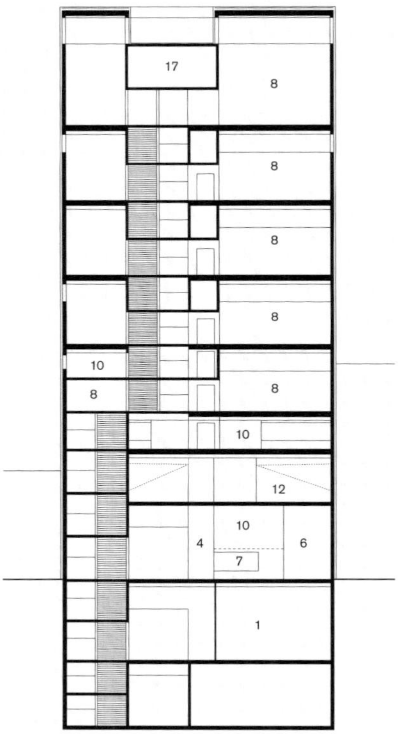

Section A–A

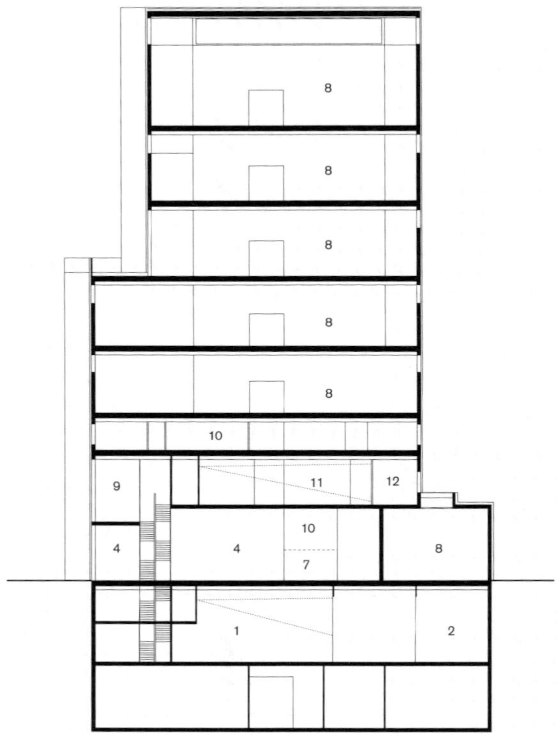

Section B–B

0 1 10

NEW MUSEUM
BARI RESTAURANT EQUIPMENT DEPOT
PIZZA OVENS, MIXERS, RANGES, FRYERS, REFRIGERATORS, FREEZERS, ICE MACHINES & BAKERY EQUIP.

Extension of Kunsthaus Zürich, Switzerland 225

2008 (Competition)

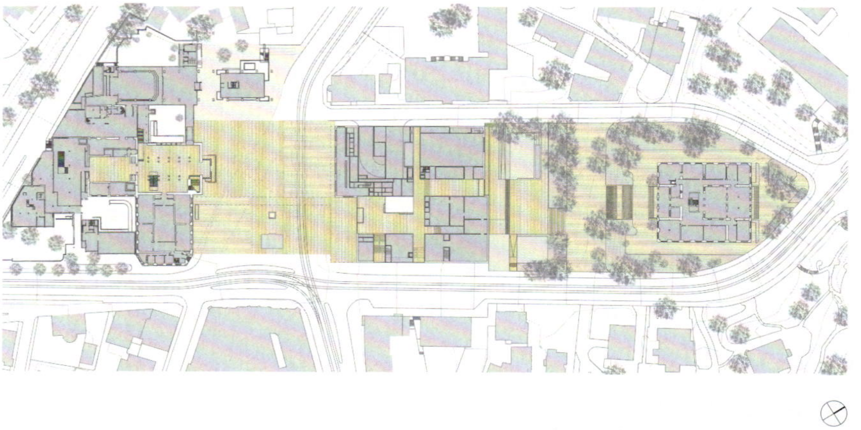

The competition design for the extension to Kunsthaus Zürich envisages, in a sense, a mirroring of the existing building. The new extension constitutes a companion piece to the older building, both spatially and in terms of its utilization. Taking this premise as the point of departure, Heimplatz square is transformed by means of continuous paving into an urban "stone carpet" linking the two museum buildings across the street that separates them. The new building opens up to Heimplatz with a projecting volume and a cutout portion facing the square, as a generous, welcoming gesture.

Like the institutional architecture along Rämistrasse, the new museum building boasts a substantial footprint, yet it also references the small scale of the buildings immediately adjacent to it through the configuration of the roof structures.

Inside the extension, a system of "squares and pathways" leads visitors to the open-access facilities and through to the garden at the back, as well as into the exhibition spaces. These "passageway spaces" form generously proportioned, light-filled circulation areas that provide orientation and offer vistas to the exterior, while also displaying artworks. They offer information, set the mood, and give visitors an opportunity to linger and relax.

In contrast, the main exhibition spaces are restrained, concentrated, rectangular rooms with light-diffusing glass ceilings. A range of different light solutions allows carefully controlled levels of daylight to enter the exhibition spaces, creating a lively atmosphere with natural light. To achieve this, daylight is focused into the building laterally through skylight superstructures set atop the building. Conversely, this has the striking effect of making the building glow with its own luminosity when the interior is brightly lit during evening events and residual light filters through to the exterior. The height of these skylight structures varies as a function of the depth of the exhibition spaces and the number of glazed faces on each skylight unit. This rule generates a roof landscape with an engaging relief effect.

The load-bearing structure is primarily in concrete, with steel deployed in the skylight areas. The façade is conceived as a translucent and "light-bearing" wall. It is composed of windows and concrete elements with glass bricks in a range of sizes. Some are more transparent or translucent, others less so, to reflect the distinct requirements of the particular parts of the building. Rear-ventilated elements made up of large-format etched glass bricks protect the lateral glazing in the roof-light units and their louvers. Where the glass bricks are set in front of the insulated load-bearing walls, they form "peepholes" affording occasional blurred glimpses of the wall construction. Glass as a construction material thus appears in a wide range of different manifestations: as matt or reflecting glass, as panes, "bricks," or solar elements; it may appear pixelated, "pointillist," or as a smooth expanse of glazing. Glass gives the building its characteristic appearance and conveys a sense that this is a museum building, an architectural genre whose primary function lies in harnessing light to enable the visual perception of artworks.

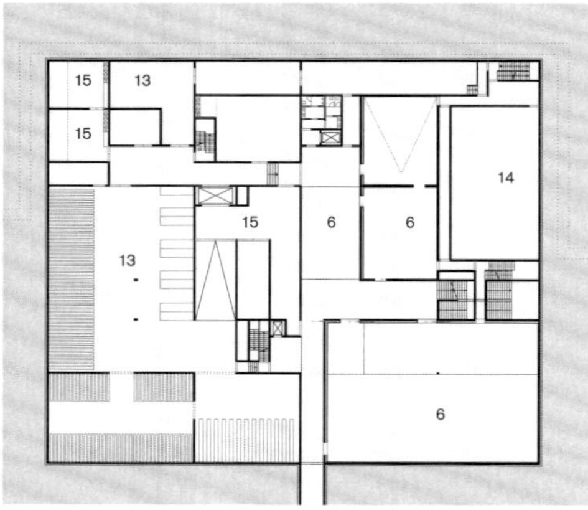

Second basement level

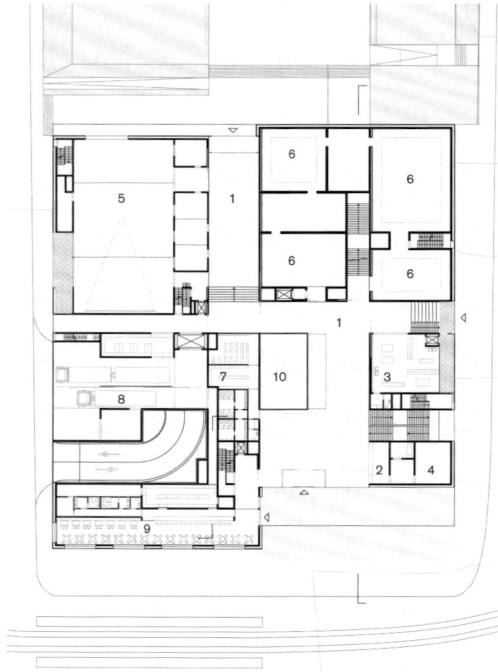

Ground floor

1 Foyer
2 Ticket desk
3 Museum shop
4 Office
5 Event hall
6 Exhibition/Gallery/Collection
7 Cloakroom
8 Deliveries
9 Cafe/Bar
10 Clear space
11 Group room
12 Education
13 Depot
14 Building services
15 Ancillary room

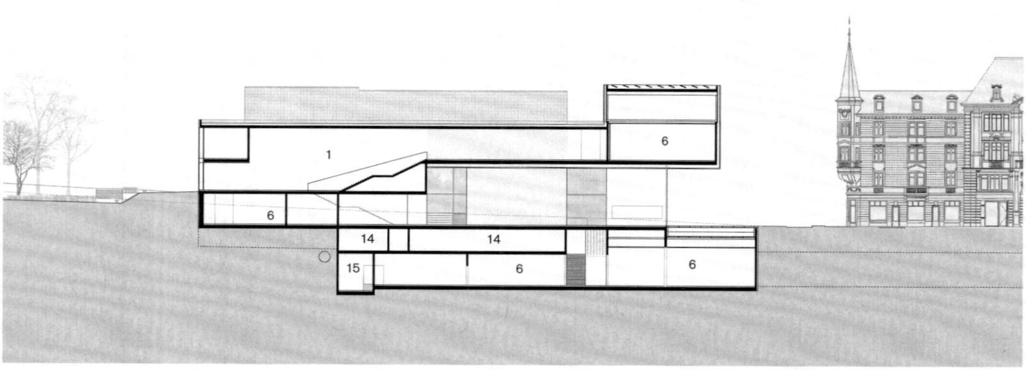

Section

1st floor

2nd floor

Central hall

Munch Museum and Stenersen Museum Collections, Oslo, Norway 232

2008–09 (Competition)

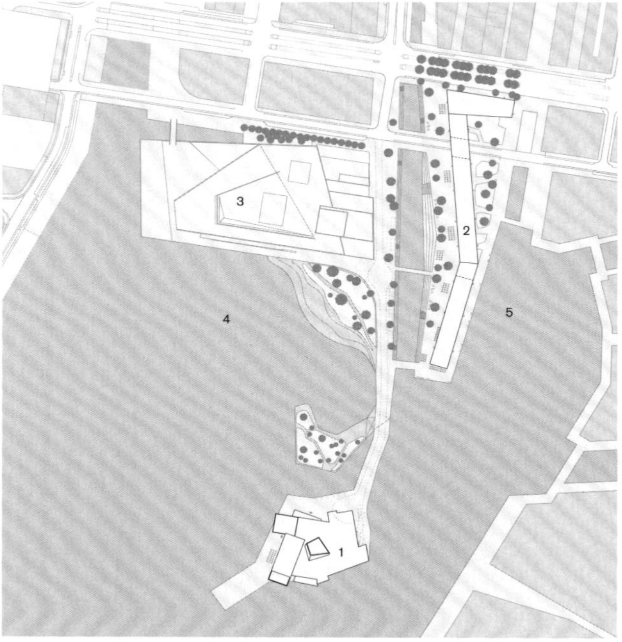

1 Munch/Stenersen Museum
2 Paulsenkaia development
3 New Opera
4 Bjørvika
5 Bispevika

The construction of a new Munch/Stenersen Museum in Oslo is part of the urban development plan for the former Paulsenkaia harbor site, which is to be given a boost by the appeal of the museum and the nearby Opera. On the reclaimed land of the harbor area adjacent to the new opera, a boulevard is envisioned, lined with buildings housing shops, cafes, and restaurants on the ground floor with offices and apartments above. Some harbor areas will be renaturalized, and steps to sit on along the banks of the Akersleva River are an invitation to linger by the water's edge. A wide, slightly sloping causeway will lead from the Opera up to the museum and reach further out over the water as a pier.

The Munch/Stenersen Museum is to rise like a "floating peninsula" between the Bjørvika and Bispevika fjords, hovering on piles above the water. Visitors enter the museum through a spacious foyer with adjoining restaurant, museum shop, and conference rooms and then continue on through a security passage, which is of central importance to the museum after the theft of the famous painting *The Scream.* An imposing staircase lit by a skylight above winds up to the exhibition level.

The six large exhibition halls can be accessed separately via a generous connecting space that not only provides an open area for introductions to guided tours and educational presentations, but also serves as an informal zone where guests can relax and enjoy views of the sea and the city in all directions through large picture windows.

The variously sized exhibition halls by contrast are places for quiet, concentrated art viewing. They offer the desired flexibility—able to be subdivided into smaller units or their ceiling height adapted as needed—as well as the explicitly requested illumination with artificial light.

The museum is set on concrete piles driven into the sea bed, which are visible and become part of the museum design due to the raised position of the platform several meters above sea level. The building hence fulfills the desired functions as a "beacon," while also alluding to the structural form of an oil platform or a majestic villa atop pilotis. Brownish-red concrete is used throughout as construction material, from the concrete piles to the central hall on the exhibition level.

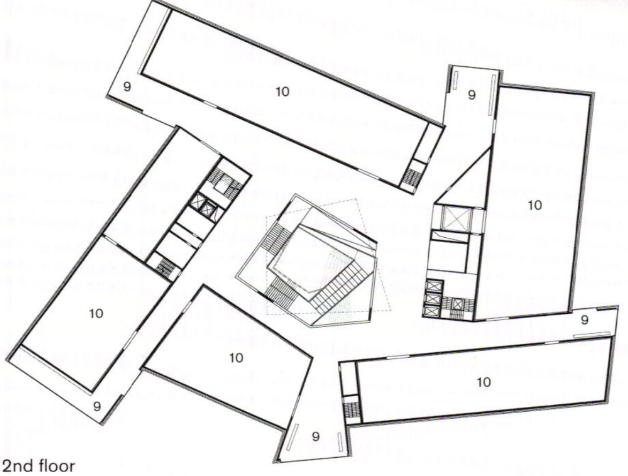

2nd floor

Ground floor

1 Foyer
2 Tickets/Information
3 Museum shop
4 Cloakroom
5 Restaurant
6 Auditorium
7 Conference room
8 Sponsors' area
9 Lounge/view
10 Exhibition
11 Offices
12 Ancillary room
13 Parking
14 Deliveries
15 Building services
16 Security passage

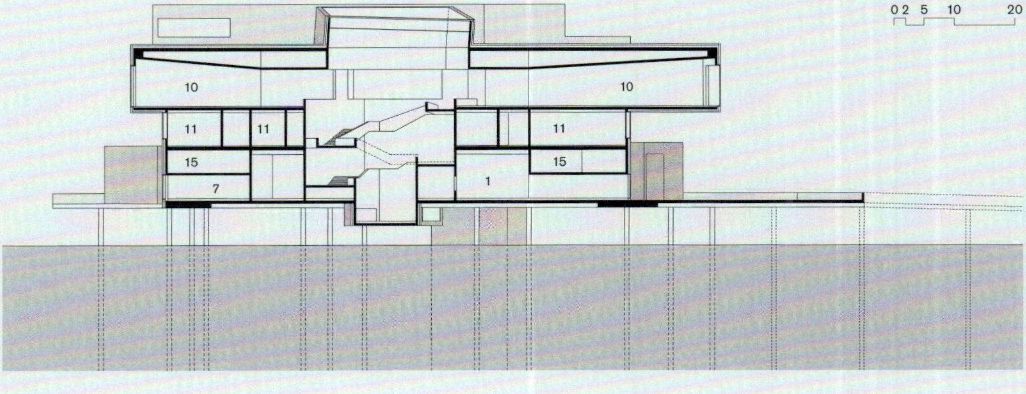

Section

Theater

ambiente
st. alban

Extension of Kunstmuseum Basel, Switzerland 245

2009 (Competition)

1 Extension
2 Kunstmuseum

Thanks to the donation of a property across from the existing Kunstmuseum, an opportunity arose for a further significant extension to the main building. The dimensions of the competition project respond to the proportions of the historic building by Paul Bonatz and Rudolf Christ, as well as to the scale of the neighboring buildings along Dufourstrasse. With its skylight superstructures and nuanced sculptural relief, the building volume also enters into a dialogue with the smaller-scale historical architecture of the St. Alban district. The structure of the façade and the materials selected facilitate integration of the voluminous extension into the urban fabric, without however foregoing the aspiration of making the new museum building a key player in the cityscape.

Direct access from Dufourstrasse is available for special events. However, the principal link to and access from the existing art museum is underground. In the historic building a cascading stair leads down to the wide connecting hallway, where already visitors can enjoy artwork on view. All the levels in the extension are linked via a broad two-flight stairway. The foyer and the delivery area for artworks are set on the ground floor. The collection is housed in rooms on the first floor and the lower level, while the second story accommodates temporary exhibitions.

The arrangement of the floor plan is based on rectangular exhibition rooms. The complex spaces set between them—including the foyer and the linking hallway—offer circulation routes as well as setting the tone and providing areas for art education activities. They punctuate the tour with vistas to the outdoors and also give visitors a chance to pause between rooms. On each floor there are several circuits through the exhibition rooms, which are sequenced by the interposed circulation spaces.

The exhibition rooms on the second floor enjoy natural light from above via a light-diffusing glass ceiling. The skylight superstructure above this captures the daylight through a glass roof equipped with etched panels and shade-roviding photovoltaic units arranged in a grid. On the first floor the rooms that house the collection are illuminated via a lateral skylight. The foyer faces onto the surroundings with large windows.

The building is constructed of concrete and steel components. The load-bearing concept is based on a cross-wall structure with the interaction of walls and ceilings. The surfaces in the intermediate zones and stairways, as well as the façades, are executed in beige limestone concrete. The façades are composed of different cast concrete "framing elements," set one above another, some flush with the surface and some recessed.

West elevation

North elevation

0 1 5 10

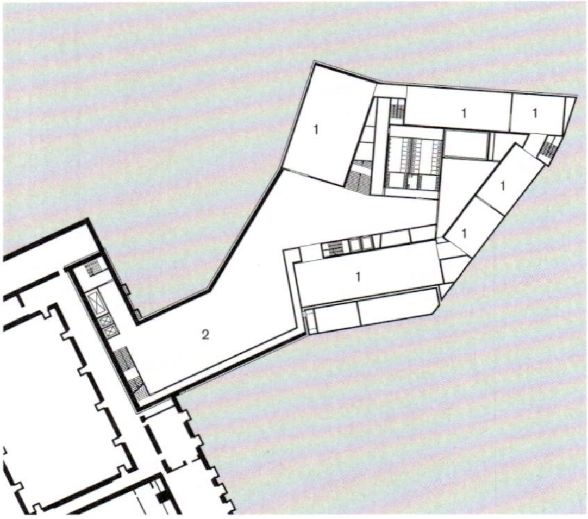

1 Collection
2 Connecting space
3 Ancillary room
4 Depot
5 Foyer
6 Extension of foyer
7 Deliveries
8 Art handling
9 Temporary exhibition
10 Offices
11 Library
12 Bistro

First basement level

0 1 5 10

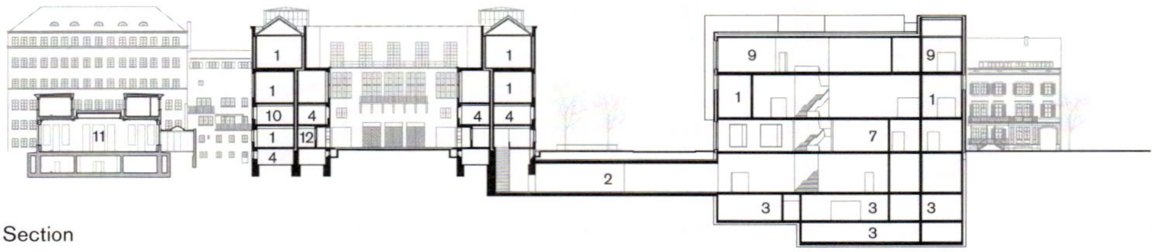

Section

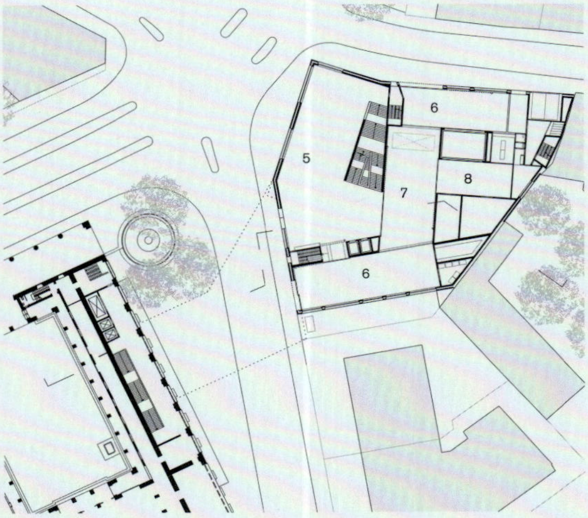

Ground floor

Façade elevation

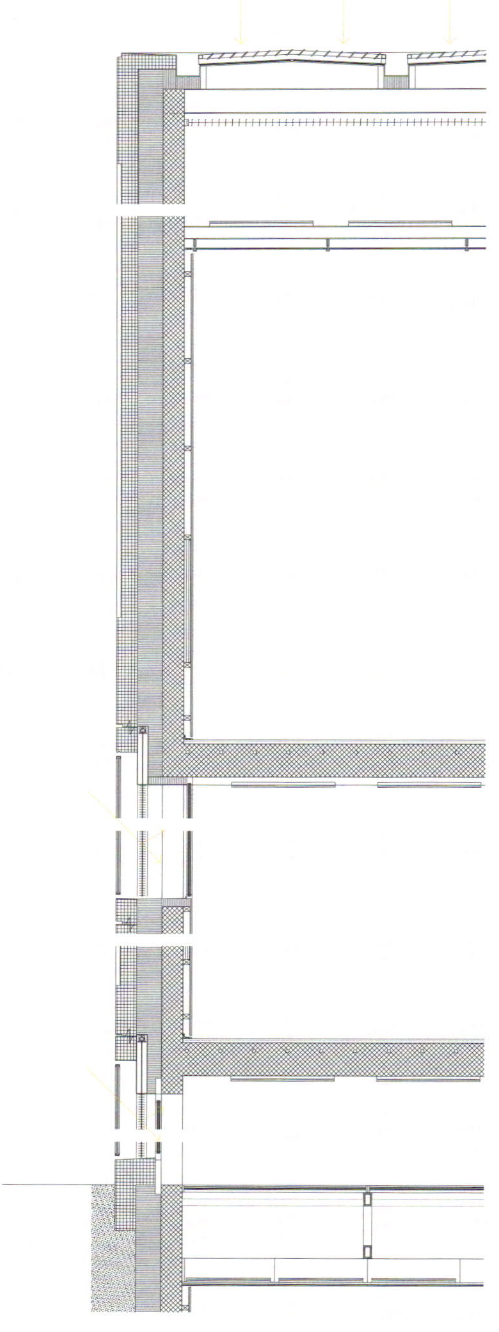

Construction detail

Extension of Kunstmuseum Basel, Switzerland

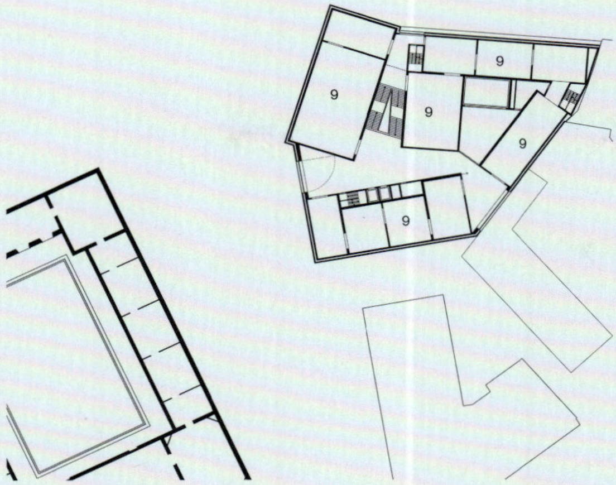

2nd floor

1st floor

Cultural Center Les Arts, Gstaad, Switzerland 250
2010 (Competition)

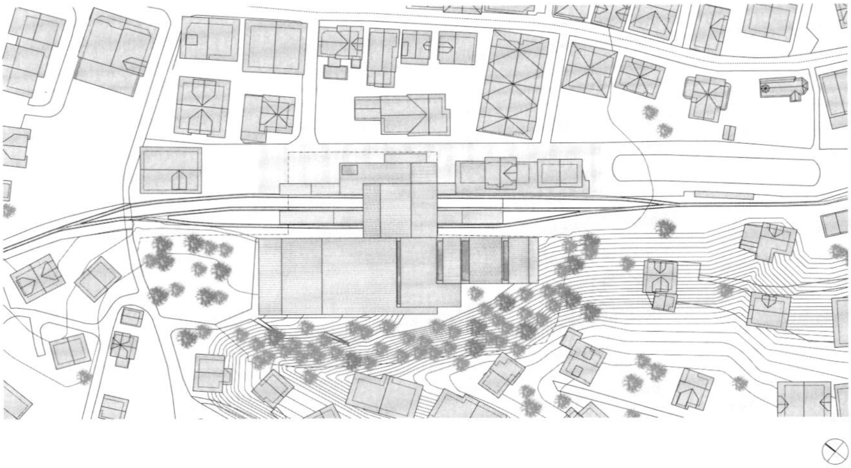

Gstaad has hosted the "Menuhin Festival" and "Sommets Musicaux" for decades. Reflecting the great international prestige of these festivals, future musical events are to be held in a new cultural center with a spacious concert hall, centrally located next to the station. This center will also house exhibition spaces and a restaurant.

The architectural and urban planning concept underpinning the design is inspired by the notion of a building that is imbued with a sense of the celebratory, yet at the same time is part of everyday life. The center's architecture features cosmopolitan touches, while remaining rooted in the local context and regional traditions. The large building on a sloping site responds to the square in front of the train station and the adjacent smaller built structures by means of a moderately proportioned wing that extends over the tracks in an open, welcoming gesture.

The roof, incorporating a variety of angles and different shapes, structures the building rhythmically and strikes a balance between expressive and traditional roof pitches. Above the exhibition space and the foyer, skylights are created by folds and bends in the roof. These convolutions settle into a more tranquil configuration over the concert hall and project outward to provide cover over the platforms and the smaller entrance volume on Bahnhofsplatz. Here, a wide stairway by the entrance provides access to the restaurant on the upper floor, which offers a view over the square. From this area the generously proportioned foyer leads into the concert hall and the exhibition spaces. Mineral materials were selected for the surfaces of the foyer and the museum area in the eastern part of the building. The rooms here have varied proportions and receive natural light via high shed roof elements or side windows. A circular path through the building leads down from the upper floor and back up again.

The design for the concert hall is based on a cuboid form. The finely modeled contours of its wooden paneling create a dense mesh of reflecting surfaces, producing rich, well-balanced acoustics. The visual impression in the concert hall is of a bright, warm, wooden space. Metallic particles—gold brass, nickel silver, and copper—shimmer in the pores of the wood, for the concert hall is interpreted as a massive spatial "instrument": a space that captures and reflects sounds and therefore "shines forth" in the materiality of wooden and metal musical instruments.

Two independent structures are utilized in the concert hall to ensure acoustic decoupling. The load-bearing structure is executed with concrete and steel girders, essential for the large spans and the varying configurations of the roof above the center's various spaces. The shell of the building, which is composed of copper sheets, functions as cladding for the roofs and façades, while at the same time forming a Faraday cage to protect against electromagnetic interference from the nearby railway. In addition, the copper's brown hue echoes the color palette of the traditional wooden buildings and integrates the contemporary structure into Gstaad's townscape.

Exhibition

Elevation to railway station

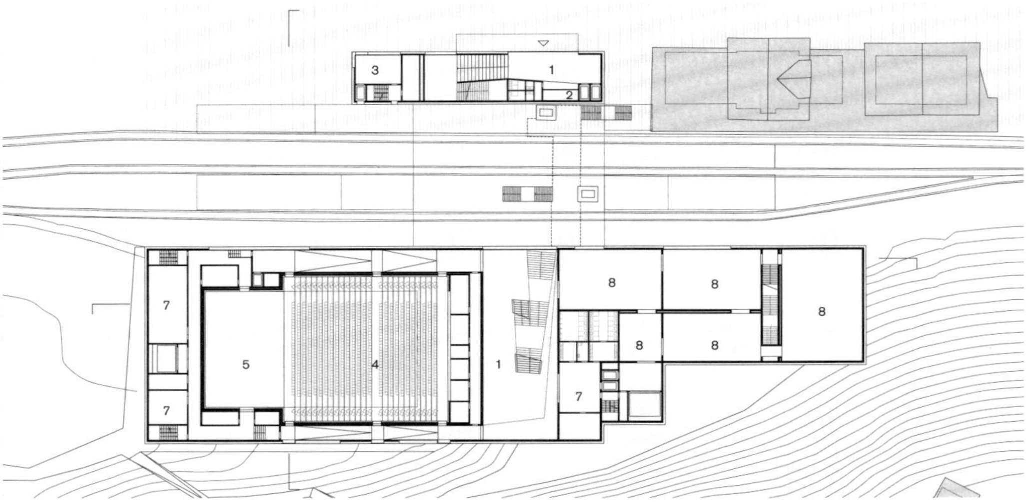

Ground floor

1	Foyer	9	Balcony
2	Tickets	10	Restaurant
3	Shop	11	Offices
4	Concert hall	12	Visitors' cloakroom
5	Stage	13	Artists' dressing rooms
6	Building services	14	Void
7	Depot	15	Parking
8	Exhibition		

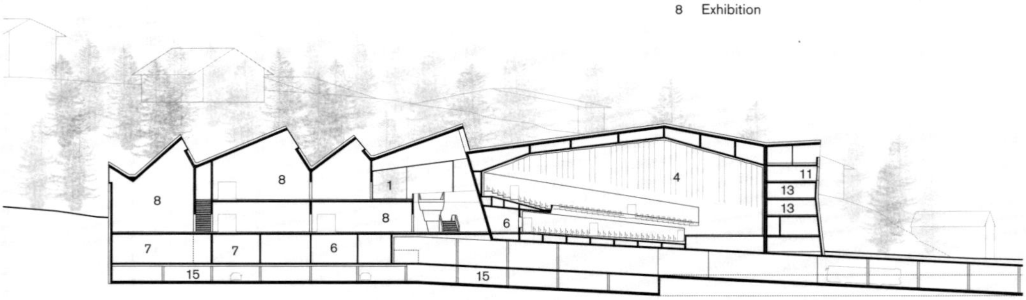

Longitudinal section

Cultural Center Les Arts, Gstaad, Switzerland

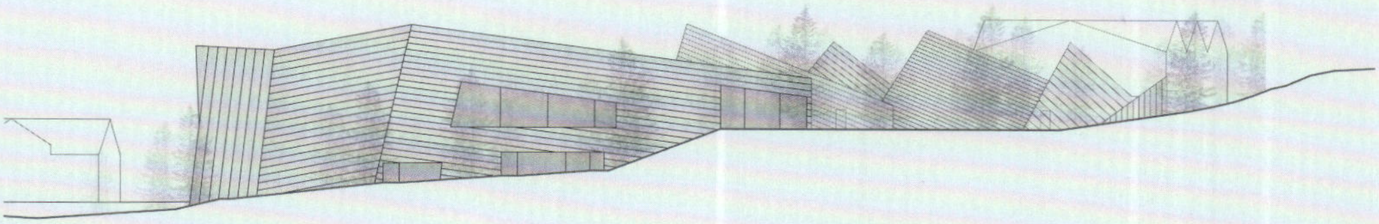

Elevation to forest

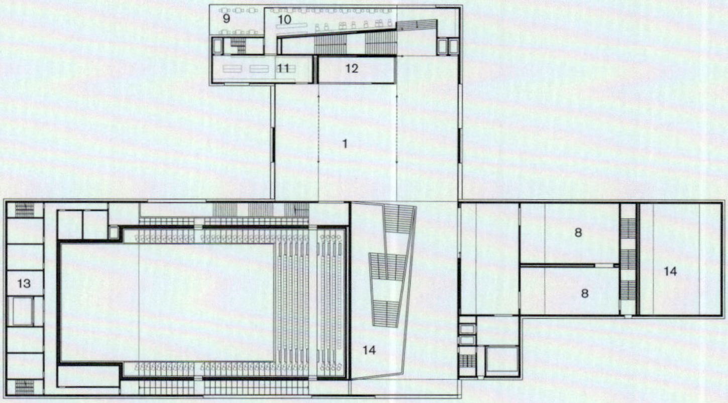

1st floor

Concert hall

Foyer

MCBA
CAFE

Nouveau Musée cantonal des Beaux-Arts MCBA, Lausanne, Switzerland 271

2010–11 (Competition)

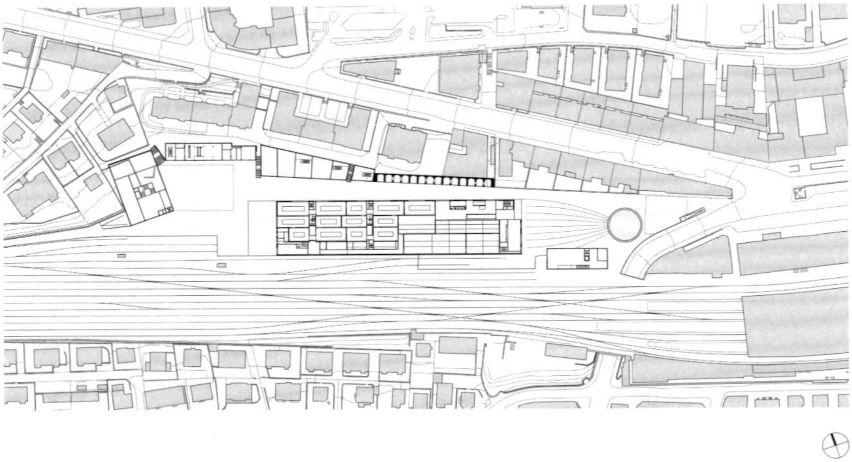

The competition concept goes against the competition organizers' plan to convert the existing locomotive depot into a museum, and instead proposes a new museum building. Neither the spatial dimensions of the depot, the heterogeneous structure of its architecture, nor its position offer real scope for the far-reaching transformation needed to create a public museum building with all its complex requirements. In contrast, the new museum confidently expresses its function both inside and outside the building, just as the locomotive depot itself once did on this site.

Other traces nonetheless evoke the history and ambience of this locus—the railroad tracks, the turntable, and the northern retaining wall with various rooms embedded in its structure. Last but not least, there are the finely detailed silhouettes of glazed and re-used bricks set into the new walls: these trace out the former positions of the walls and doors, as well as the general contours of the building that used to stand here, and ornament the new building.

The new, precise positioning of the museum creates two generously proportioned squares, providing space for two additional museum buildings in subsequent phases of development. The new building leaves a wide, bright passage through to the western part of the plot. Lined with small shops and galleries in the historic wall niches, this passage links the two squares. The definitive urban framework for the district will be completed in the future, with the northern border of the site developed as a raised garden terrace with pavilions, while the two smaller museums (mudac, Elysée), one in the eastern and one in the western part of the site, will mark the museum district's starting and ending points.

At two strategic points the primarily single-story volume rises up to form multi-story façades; fronting the square in the east, to clearly mark the building and the new district within the urban context, and on the side toward the rail tracks. The eastern part of the structure houses the areas dedicated to public functions (cafe, auditorium, museum education, and library), which the museum will share with other institutions that will join the "pôle muséal et culturel" in the future. The western part comprises the museum's workspaces and administrative areas, which are not open to the public.

The main focus is on offering visitors the best possible spatial ambience in which to encounter the artworks. All the exhibition areas on the ground level are configured to allow natural light to enter from above and to offer easily accessible, barrier-free visits. The main entrance to the museum is in the north-eastern corner of the building, looking toward the square and the passage, and is flanked by the bookshop and the cafe. After circling through the permanent or temporary exhibition, the route leads back into the main foyer, which also opens onto the "Espace projets," used for special exhibitions.

The elongated main body of the building offers space to deploy photovoltaic arrays across large expanses of the roof to generate electricity and supply the energy needed for the building services. A slender ribbed prefabricated support structure and in-situ recycling of demolition material to construct the load-bearing elements and the façade help to reduce the building's gray energy consumption. Old bricks from the walls of the former locomotive shed are used in conjunction with new bricks as the construction material for the external shell.

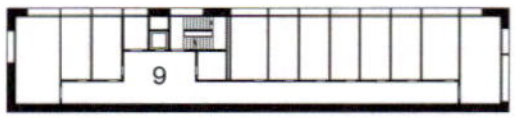

3th floor

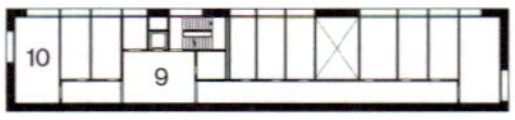

2nd floor

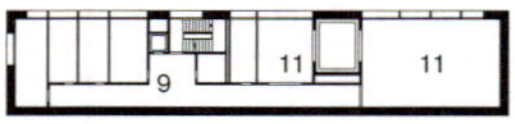

1st floor

1st 2nd 3th 4th floor

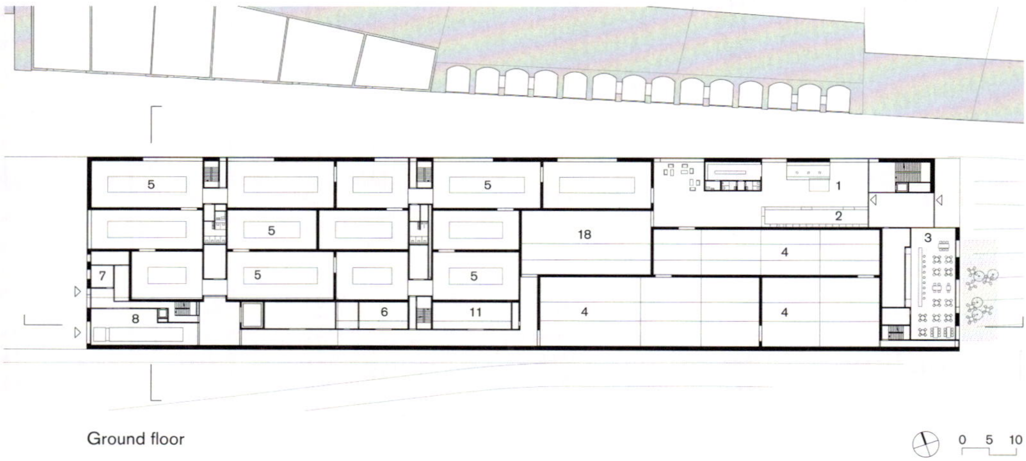

Ground floor

1 Foyer
2 Museum shop
3 Cafe/Restaurant
4 Temporary exhibition
5 Exhibition
6 Restoration
7 Personnel
8 Deliveries
9 Office
10 Conference room
11 Studio
12 Auditorium
13 Education
14 Library
15 Archive
16 Depot
17 Ancillary room
18 “Espace projets”

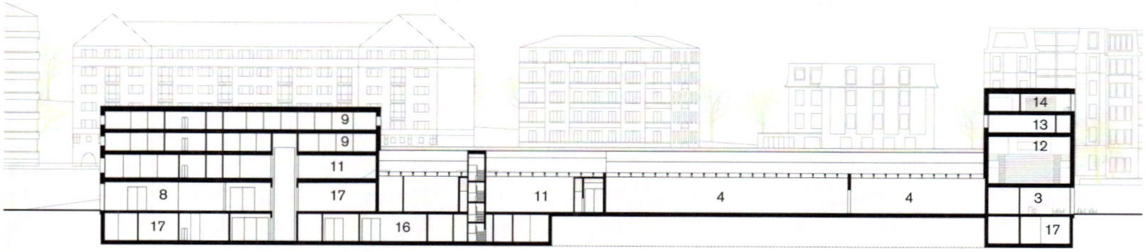

Longitudinal section

North elevation

South elevation

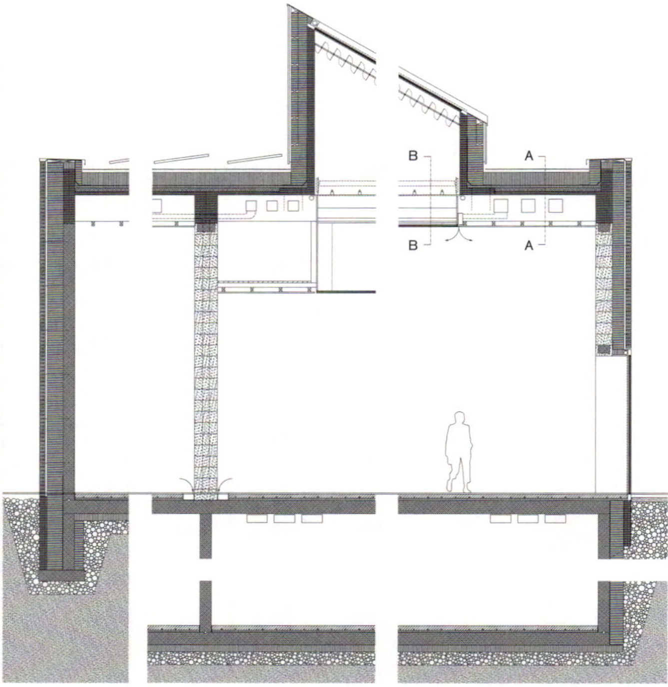

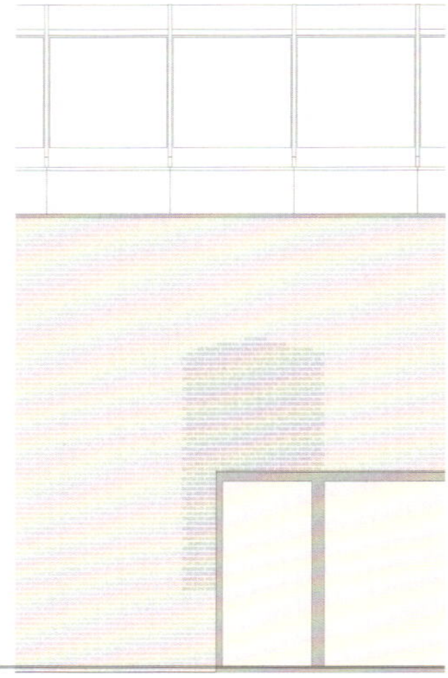

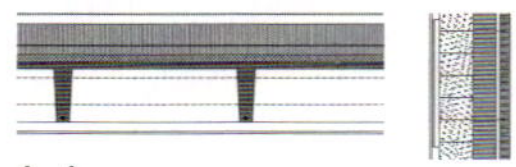

A–A

B–B

Construction detail

0 0.5 1

Nouveau Musée cantonal des Beaux-Arts MCBA, Lausanne, Switzerland

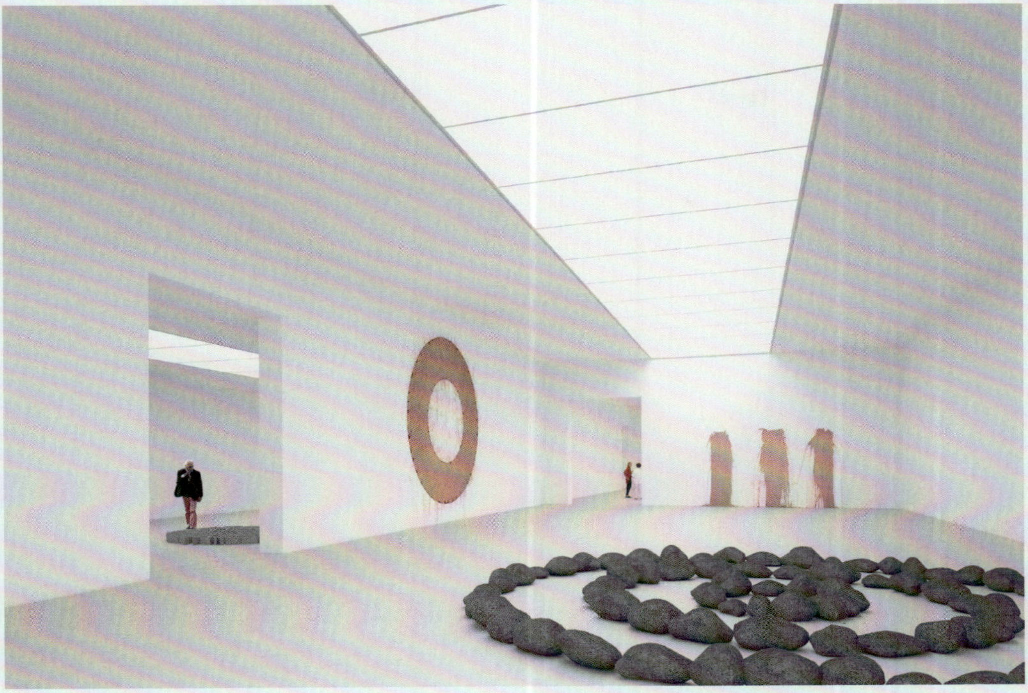

WORKING

Valentin Jeck

Annelies Štrba

Katalin Deér

Halle

Erik Steinbrecher

BEST
GPS
KUONI
BEST

Christian Scholz

Joël Tettamanti

Heinrich Helfenstein

HELLO
Stadt und Land mitenand

René Burri

Thies Wachter

COLT
INTERNET & TELECOM
GPS

Walter Mair

BRITNEY SPEARS
life sexy
Garten

Imaging a City: Gigon/Guyer in Zurich

Philip Ursprung

Zurich-West with Prime Tower

Gigon/Guyer's high-rise office building at the Maag-Areal in Zurich (p. 208) looks both natural and at ease in its surroundings. Even before the opening in 2011—while construction work was still under way—it already created the impression of belonging there, of being in exactly the right place. What is it that gives it such certainty? Why is no one up in arms against it? How is it that this building—this clearcut, green glass sculpture—imbues the whole area, even the gloomy infrastructure of Hardbrücke Station, with its unexpected beauty and presence?

One of the reasons for its success is that it refuses to comply with the conventional typology of high-rise office buildings. It is not conceived in the usual way as a purely vertical structure; it also has a horizontal sweep. It's dancing to its own tune. It's not joining in the hymn to heroic growth that resounds, louder than ever these days, from the chorus of metropolitan skyscrapers all over the world. On the contrary, this building is about differentiation, contradiction, complexity. Rather than simply stacking floor upon identical floor until they had fulfilled the remit, the architects have created an irregular, polygonal footprint and have allowed the building to expand outwards as it rises upwards. As a result it gives the impression that it couldn't go just on growing taller and taller by dint of additional floors. Yet it doesn't strictly appear self-contained, in the sense of a finely balanced, immutable painterly composition. For it is not linear, as such; it is like a crystal that could grow in different directions, a law unto itself—semi-controlled, semi-chaotic, semi-organic, semi-artificial.

Of course this high-rise office building is also utterly urban. The green glazing, the chrome finishes, and the polished stone surfaces do not seek to conceal the capital investment. The abruptly cut-off top is as blunt and punchy as you might expect from a landmark building in a new urban development at a high-density road and rail junction. It neither prettifies the clients' intention to make a handsome profit from this onetime industrial site at the edge of the city, nor does it try to hide the competitive thrust and cool calculations of its tenants from the financial services industry. The somewhat contrived name—Prime Tower—is typical of this. (Still, the clients did refrain from having the name emblazoned across the top of the building and, happily, the restaurant on the top floor is open to the public.) The lobby deliberately evokes the cool atmosphere of American corporate architecture in the international style. But the tower itself—and here we see how well Gigon/Guyer were able to sustain their own architectural autonomy—does not seek to glorify Capitalism, to transform it into an image of the sublime. It's not a celebration of growth and size—Koolhaas's "bigness"—as supposed forces of nature. It's not trying to naturalize Capitalism or to give it a voice as part of a city "skyline." In accepting this commission, Gigon/Guyer have not allowed themselves to be used but rather have taken the opportunity to reflect on the question of high-rise buildings and the city. Of course their design is a flexible response to the clients' requirements, but it is in no sense servile. There is nothing here of the "sense of historical sadness and negativity" that Jeff Wall diagnosed in the late architecture of Ludwig Mies van der Rohe and that moved him to declare, "Mies' response to the historical catastrophe of the 1920–50 period is to renounce the implicit utopian critique of the city contained within modernism, and to relinquish the city to its caesars: the speculators, bureaucrats, and real-estate developers. His gesture of withdrawal is deliberate and his architecture, in its perfected emptiness, expresses his submission to the modern forms of power which have apparently vanquished all opposition and rule over a chaotic, estranged mass."[1]

Ludwig Mies van der Rohe looking south from 860 Lake Shore Drive, Chicago

The Performance of Images

For passers-by the tower is a sculptural form that looks very different depending on where they are. From the trains arriving at the station, the wide side comes into view first, from a car crossing the Hardbrücke, the narrow side is first to appear. But neither close to nor from a distance does the tower allow itself to be reduced to a simple, basic form. Seen from the edge of the bus stop, the tower stands out sharply, shooting up into the sky. But seen from the hillsides around the edges of the city, it blends into the

Prime Tower with open windows

cityscape and even merges into its surroundings in certain lighting conditions. What we see and what we know are not the same. The tower is constantly presenting new faces to the world. It's not an abstract sign; it's a concrete image.

This notion of an image draws us into the contemplation of the work of Gigon/Guyer in a wider context. Ever since the 1980s art theory has used terms such as *iconic turn* and *visual turn* to define the greater interest in the visual aspect of art.[2] In a nutshell, *iconic turn* refers to the perception of phenomena primarily as images, rather than being read as texts, as had been the case in many areas since the earlier *linguistic turn*. While the term *iconic turn* sparked a fruitful debate in the art world that has been ongoing since the eighties, it has had little impact on architectural discourse. The notion of the image—like many related concepts, such as surface, illusion, theatricality, and effect—is (and always has been) derided by most architects. No doubt this has to do with the fact that they tend to equate "image" with "picture." in the sense of a two-dimensional, framed object. Thus, it is probably fair to say that "image" triggers the underlying fear that any reference to an external phenomenon could endanger the autonomy of architecture. Moreover, the term "iconic architecture" is not helpful, because it reduces the complexity of architecture to analogies with visual art. By contrast, the term "image" has the potential to sharpen our understanding of present-day architecture.

A definition of "image" that is still useful today was provided by the French philosopher Henri Bergson in his book *Matter and Memory,* first published in French in 1896. As he puts it, "Matter, in our view, is an aggregate of 'images.' And by 'image' we mean a certain existence which is more than that which the idealist calls a *representation,* but less than that which the realist calls a *thing*—an existence placed halfway between the 'thing' and the 'representation.'"[3] Thus Bergson does not reduce the notion of the image to a flat, picture-object. Instead, he formulates a concept according to which an image is not static but constantly in motion and engaged in a process of interaction. And he writes, "Here I am in the presence of images, in the vaguest sense of the word, images perceived when my senses are opened to them, unperceived when they are closed.

All these images act and react upon one another in all their elementary parts according to constant laws which I call laws of nature."[4]

Jean-Paul Sartre, who in some ways takes up where Bergson left off, goes even further when he defines the image as an "act."[5] Kevin Lynch, in his book *The Image of the City,* also regards the image as a dynamic phenomenon, and from this coins the term "imageability": "The concept of imageability does not necessarily connote something fixed, limited, precise, unified, or regularly ordered, although it may sometimes have these qualities. Nor does it mean apparent at a glance, obvious, patent, or plain. The total environment to be patterned is highly complex, while the obvious image is soon boring and can point to only a few features of the living world."[6]

If we postulate the image as a dynamically active—not merely passively replicating—actor, then it is easier to compare the work of architects (with very different agendas) such as Sauerbruch Hutton, Herzog & de Meuron, Peter Zumthor, Rem Koolhaas, Caruso St John, Toyo Ito, Iñaki Ábalos, Josep Lluís Mateo, Eduardo Souto de Moura, Christian Kerez and, of course, Gigon/Guyer. In the case of Gigon/Guyer the notion of an "image" positively demands consideration. On one hand, their work has always been about images. On the other hand, it has also been shaped by regular collaborations with visual artists such as Adrian Schiess and Harald F. Müller.

Human Dimensions

The first project that Annette Gigon and Mike Guyer took on in their newly formed architectural practice was the Kirchner Museum in Davos 00A. When it opened in 1992, the Kirchner Museum made the young architects' name overnight and is today regarded as a modern archetype of museum architecture in Switzerland. Like their high-rise building in Zurich, this design was already stunningly unconventional. Whereas windows have traditionally been taboo in museums because they distract attention from the exhibits, Gigon/Guyer introduced five panoramic windows or glass walls into their design, and placed them so prominently that they affect the visitors' perceptions

Kirchner Museum Davos, hall

Extension of Kunstmuseum Winterthur, exhibition space

wherever they are in the museum. It is impossible for visitors not to compare the paintings by Ernst Ludwig Kirchner with the sight of the real landscape outside the museum, which stays with them in their mind's eye as they progress through the exhibition rooms. In addition to this, whenever they like, they can glance out of the windows and see where they are in the Here and Now of their actual surroundings. The architects took a similar approach to their extension for Kunstmuseum Winterthur in 1995 003. Visitors to the new exhibition rooms find themselves faced with three very large windows, looking out onto the old trees and industrialists' villas that establish the new wing's spatial and historical context. Once again, the visitors' awareness of the views framed by the windows connects with their perception of the works on display, for here the White Cube framing the exhibition is, in turn, framed by its own surroundings.

In subsequent projects by Gigon/Guyer—specifically the residential buildings they have created since the 1990s—there has again been a particular focus on windows. One might explain the use of large-scale windows by pointing out that in the building trade double glazing is now available in much larger sizes than in the past and that this meets the expectations of today's clients who want abundant daylight and first-rate insulation. However, in the case of Gigon/Guyer the windows are never merely "solutions" to particular needs. They are also a "theme." which goes beyond immediate necessity in the sense that it is also about the production of images—both real and imagined.

One question that arose in connection with the work of Gigon/Guyer in recent years was whether they could make the leap from small and medium-sized architectural formats to those with much larger, urban dimensions. Their high-rise building at the Maag-Areal is proof that they are in fact able to integrate human dimensions into an urban design. Once again the key lies in the windows. The grid width of 1.35 meters, which is the basis of the building's structure, also defines the dimensions of the windows. Every second window, or in certain areas every third, is a manually operated, parallel-opening window, which adjusts the air-flow in the offices so that the people working

Detached House, Zurich

Montage of window elements in the Prime Tower

Prime Tower, 17th floor, tenant fit-out

John Hancock Tower, Boston, 1976, by Henry N. Cobb and I.M. Pei

inside have the feeling of making contact with the outside world, except in high winds or torrential rain, of course. The supporting concrete columns of the building's skeleton pass through open interior spaces, so that anyone can see them and touch them. And the corridors are organized in such a way that you can almost always see outside and don't have the feeling of scurrying through some labyrinth.

Passers-by, for their part, register the building as a structure that is occupied and in use, partly because they can clearly see the size of the windows. In contrast to the effect created by fully reflective façades, the people outside don't feel exposed and potentially under scrutiny, because they can in turn see what is going on inside the office-building. Some high-rises stress the power and exclusivity of those inside the building by means of mirror-glass façades that prevent anyone from even glancing inside. Fredric Jameson has compared this with the wearing of "reflector sunglasses which make it impossible for your interlocutor to see your own eyes and thereby achieve a certain aggressivity toward and power over the Other."[7] Not so Gigon/Guyer's buildings: the architects make a show of the inside as well as the outside. The façade does not appear abstract and homogenous, like that of the renowned John Hancock Tower in Boston (1976) by Henry N. Cobb and I. M. Pei. If anything it looks almost anthropomorphous, that's to say, like an accumulation of modules that relate to human scale. Gigon/Guyer use glass as a membrane that both separates and divides, but not as a vehicle for what was lauded for decades as "transparency." The very organization of the windows in their buildings demonstrates that the ideology of transparency is an anachronism. Instead they create striking architectural images for such diverse activities as working, living, or looking at art. These can even take on an emblematic air, as in the case of their Signal Box in Zurich (1999) 018, where the windows, like the eyes of a watchful spirit, gaze out over the tracks and the trains.

People do not feel overwhelmed by the size of the high-rise office building because they can relate to it. This in turn recalls the theoretical categories of the "sublime" and the "beautiful," as defined in eighteenth-century aesthetics. While the sublime is in every sense overpowering,

Signal Box, Zurich

CCTV Headquarters, Beijing, 2010, by OMA

Diagonal Industrial Building, Maag-Areal

overwhelming, and potentially threatening—but at a safe distance and hence a source of aesthetic pleasure—beauty relates to phenomena that the viewer can take in, comprehend, and locate. In terms of architecture today, a monumental structure such as OMA's China Central Television Headquarters in Beijing could be described as sublime, while Gigon/Guyer's high-rise building could rightly be described as beautiful.

Discontinuity

The anthropomorphic qualities of architecture, which help humans to orient themselves in relation to it, comprise not only spatiality but also temporality. So how do Gigon/Guyer respond to the history of a site? One of the reasons that they won the competition for the Maag-Areal design in 2004 was their skilled articulation of the entire area. Seen from a distance, the building is a notable landmark. From close up, however, it is clearly a component in an urban ensemble where old and new actively interconnect. The past—long-gone manufacturing industry—has not been entirely obliterated, but is made visible in the form of road-layouts and the Diagonal office building (p. 236), now a historic monument. The architects also fended off the danger of homogenization by ensuring that each of the associated buildings in the Maag-Areal has its own spatial system. The façade of the Cubus office building (p. 232) looks like a solid wall perforated with windows, in contrast to the crystalline finish of the high-rise. Meanwhile the Platform office building (p. 240), next to the railroad tracks, looks almost like a recumbent high-rise building. This is accentuated by the very spacious atrium—unique in Switzerland—which draws the outside world into the interior of the building.

In the same way that Gigon/Guyer deliberately resist spatial homogeneity and create differences, they also find ways to interrupt temporal homogeneity. They regard not only space but also history as a discontinuous phenomenon. Their buildings make a virtue of their own innate contradictions and in an urban context—a setting that is riddled with contradictions—precisely this quality sees them becoming important nodal points. The high-rise

Platform Office Building, atrium

building and its associated buildings do not fetishize the history of the place—they make no conservationist gestures preserving remnants of the past, as in the neighboring Schiffbau and Puls 5—nor do they expunge that same history. They simply respect the infrastructure left over from the industrial age, the brick buildings, chimney stacks, and factory bays. And they respect the evidence of Switzerland's economic boom during the 1960s and early 1970s and its idolization of mobility in the form of city highways and concrete flyovers. This dialogue with the city also includes two more extensive projects by Gigon/Guyer. On one hand the high-rise building communicates with their office building C10 at Lagerstrasse (p. 280), which—together with buildings by Max Dudler and David Chipperfield—will transform the site formerly occupied by the railroad and the post office into a new urban center and redefine the area's identity with what they themselves describe as a new "urban yard." On the other hand, the high-rise building also connects with the Löwenbräu site (p. 288), which is no more than a stone's throw away. Here the debate between old and new is even more explicit than at the Maag-Areal and the Europaallee. The old brewery building is marked out by its typical late-nineteenth-century brick façade. The reds and yellows that say "old factory" are taken up by the coloration and texture of the extension. The façade of one of the corner buildings is clad in gleaming, dark red, fired ceramic panels as if to commemorate the part of the building that had to be demolished to make way for the new. And the residential tower literally rises out of the ruins of the industrial age, respectfully extending over the older buildings and at the same time communicating across the rooftops with the high-rise building at the Maag-Areal. With its high-quality finish, the extension to the Löwenbräu exhibition spaces stands in distinct contrast to the brick façade of the old brewery. There is no attempt here to conceal the interventions by which the old has been transformed. At the same time, the architects also demonstrate very clearly that, with the art business being such an important economic factor in Zurich, they have developed a special formal language to reflect its presence.

Building site, Office Building C10, Lagerstrasse, Zurich

Building site, Löwenbräu-Areal, Zurich

It is a stroke of good fortune for the city that in recent years Gigon/Guyer have created a whole series of buildings in Zurich. During this time, rather than propagating a single, identifiable style, they have evolved mechanisms that allow their architecture to articulate the contradictions between old and new, large and small, private and public. And other architectural practices have been able to benefit from this without feeling the need to imitate their designs. The contradictions and discontinuities that are intrinsic to city life are not silenced by iconic landmarks but rather mediated by virtue of a multiplicity of operations which, as we have seen, are closely related to the concept of the "image." Gigon/Guyer's buildings are constantly producing, absorbing, and transforming images. They are open to what once was and what is yet to come. They are the outcome of a sequence of commissions and remits but they never play down their independence as architectural entities. They call to mind the advice once given to his readers by the American artist Robert Smithson: always to be aware of one's own role and never to relinquish responsibility. Or, as he himself said, "The artist should be an actor who refuses to act."[8]

1 Jeff Wall, "Dan Grahams Kammerspiel." in Jeff Wall, *Szenarien im Bildraum der Wirklichkeit. Essays und Interviews,* Dresden: Verlag der Kunst, 1997, pp. 89–187, here pp. 147–148a.
2 See David Freedberg, *The Power of Images: Studies in the History and Theory of Response,* Chicago: University of Chicago Press, 1989; Georges Didi-Huberman, *Devant l'image: Question posée aux fins d'une histoire de l'art,* Paris: Éditions de Minuit, 1990; Norman Bryson (ed.), *Visual Culture: Images and Interpretation,* Hanover, N.H.: University Press of New England/Wesleyan University Press, 1994; W. J. T. Mitchell, *Iconology: Image, Text, Ideology,* Chicago: University of Chicago Press, 1986; W. J. T. Mitchell, *Picture Theory: Essays on Verbal and Visual Representation,* Chicago: University of Chicago Press, 1994; Gottfried Boehm (ed.), *Was ist ein Bild?,* Munich: Wilhelm Fink Verlag, 1995; Christa Maar and Hubert Burda (eds.), *Iconic Turn, Die neue Macht der Bilder,* Cologne: DuMont Verlag, 2004.
3 Henri Bergson, *Matter and Memory,* trans. by Nancy Margaret Paul and W. Scott Palmer, New York: Urzone Inc., 1988, p. 9 (Introduction).
4 Ibid., p. 17.
5 Jean-Paul Sartre, *The Imaginary: A Phenomenological Psychology of the Imagination,* trans. by Jonathan Webber, Abingdon: Routledge, 2010, p. 4.
6 Kevin Lynch, *The Image of the City,* Cambridge, MA: The Technology Press and Harvard University Press, 1960, p. 10.
7 Fredric Jameson, *Postmodernism, or the Cultural Logic of Late Capitalism,* Durham, N.C.: Duke University Press, 1991, p. 42.
8 Robert Smithson, "A Refutation of Historical Humanism" (Manuscript, 1966–67), in idem., *The Collected Writings,* Berkeley: University of California Press, 1996, pp. 336–337, here p. 336.

KUONI

Prime Tower Office High-rise with Annex Buildings Cubus and Diagonal, Maag-Areal, Zurich, Switzerland 152
2004–11

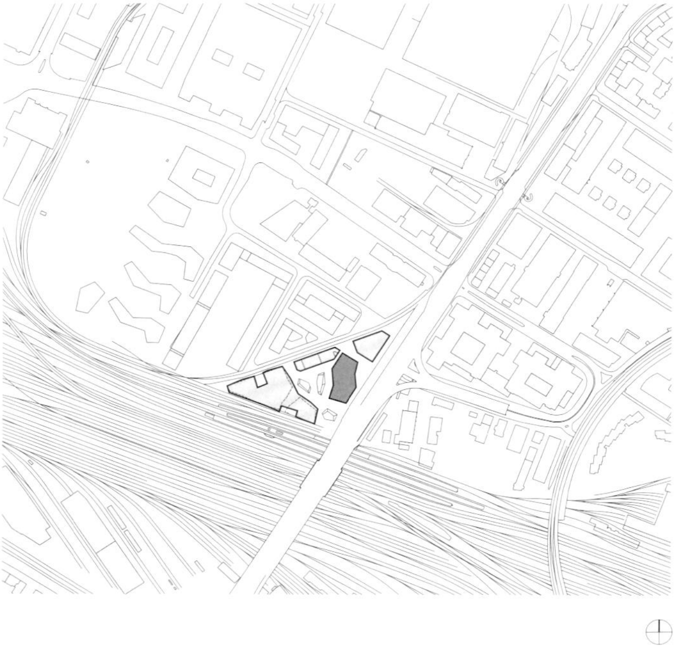

The location of the Prime Tower and its two annexes, the Cubus and Diagonal buildings, is part of a formerly almost inaccessible industrial site that is gradually being converted into a business and residential district with associated services. Situated in the immediate vicinity of Hardbrücke railway station and 126 meters in height, the high-rise is the tallest in Switzerland for the time being. It is not only a distinctive feature of the neighborhood, but also a landmark for the up-and-coming district of Zurich West.

The concept underpinning the Prime Tower is of a building that might be said to assume many guises, although its fundamental structure and the means deployed are relatively straightforward. The design aimed to find a floor plan arrangement that would maximize the number of well-lit workplaces, while also seeking to create a striking architectural form evoking differing impressions depending on the position from which it is viewed. The outcome of these efforts is a building on an irregular octagonal ground plan that confounds conventional expectations by broadening toward the top.

In terms of urban planning, the building's significance is twofold in relation to its impact when seen from nearby or from a distance. From afar, it appears as an abstract, elegant volume formed from greenish glass that changes depending on whether it is seen from the side (from the north or south) or head-on (from the east or west). The planes of the façade, oriented in various directions, reflect the light and the surroundings in different ways, articulating and subdividing the volume into what might be called gigantic "pixel surfaces." The impression the building makes when seen close-up also changes with the spectator's standpoint. These close-up views reveal that the projecting portions of the tower exert an integrating effect on the surrounding buildings.

At Geroldstrasse, an inviting outdoor area between the high-rise and the new neighboring Cubus office building leads to the entrance of the Prime Tower and toward the planned Lichtstrasse. In the southwest, a plaza is created in conjunction with the existing listed Diagonal building and the new Platform office building beside the railway.

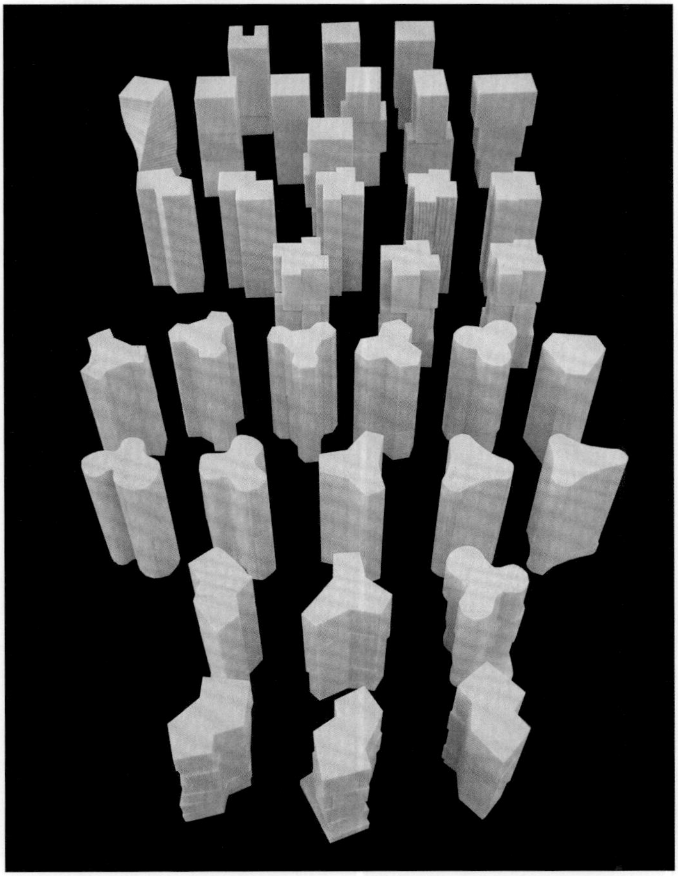

Volumetric studies, 2004 competition

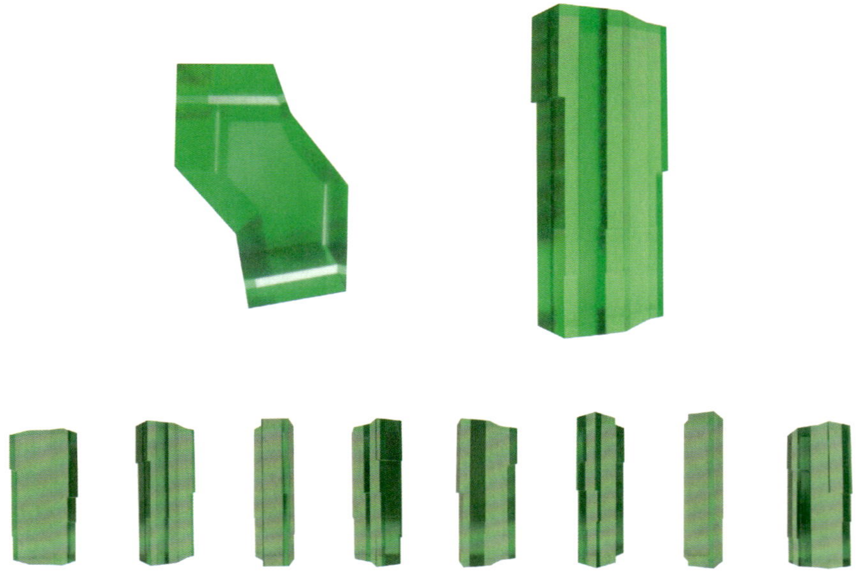

Design model

The ground floor of the Prime Tower houses retail spaces and a coffee bar for use by both office employees and passers-by. Special features on the top floor include a public restaurant, bistro with a bar, and a lounge, while a private conference area is available on the floor below.

The cores and emergency stairs are arranged so that up to four tenants can occupy offices on the same floor or, conversely, one business can occupy several floors with internal atriums and staircases. The projecting portions of the building create additional office space on the higher and therefore more sought-after floors, as well as providing greater variety when using the space for different types of offices.

The load-bearing skeleton structure of the tower is made of concrete with reinforcing cores. The variously sized cantilevered projections are supported by slanting the supporting columns over two or three stories. The façade is constructed from insulated triple glazing with a greenish tint. To enhance workspace conditions, and to meet fire regulations, which require smoke ventilation, alternating windows can be opened parallel to the building. The prefabricated windows are frameless on the exterior. They grant the polygonal building the multifaceted appearance of a greenish crystal.

welti-furrer

Prime Tower Office High-rise with Annex Buildings Cubus and Diagonal, Maag-Areal, Zurich, Switzerland

Ground floor

1 Prime Tower
2 Platform
3 Diagonal
4 Cubus

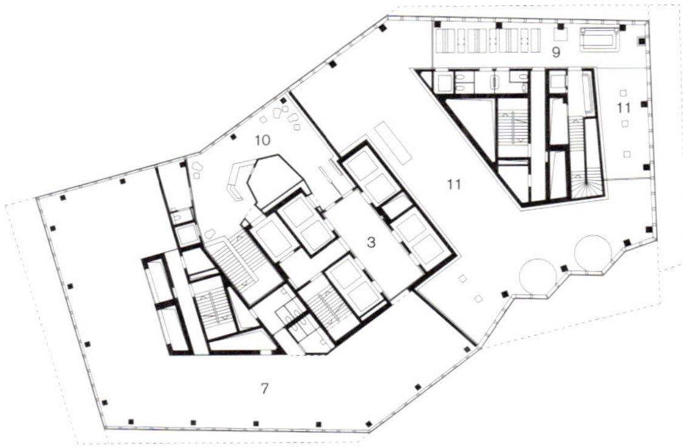

1st floor

1 Entrance hall
2 Security control
3 Elevator lobby
4 Underground parking access
5 VIP room
6 Facility management
7 Bank branch
8 Entrance to restaurant
9 Cafe
10 Reception for restaurant
11 Void

0 2 5 10

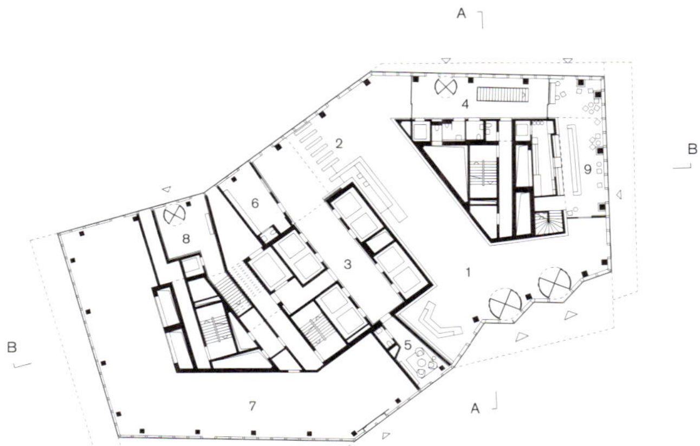

Ground floor

PRIMETOWER

12 Offices
13 Ancillary zone

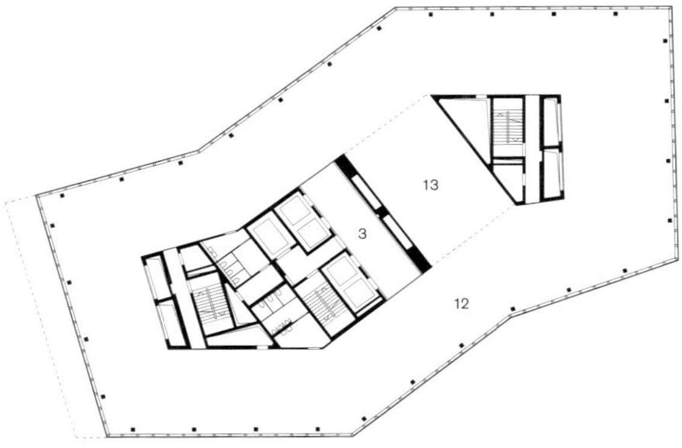

24th floor

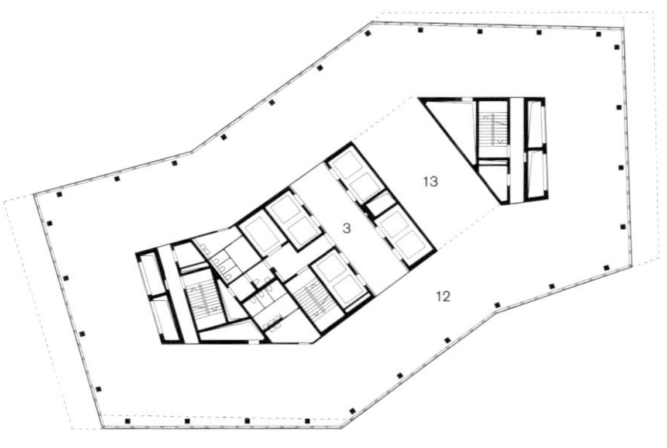

10th floor

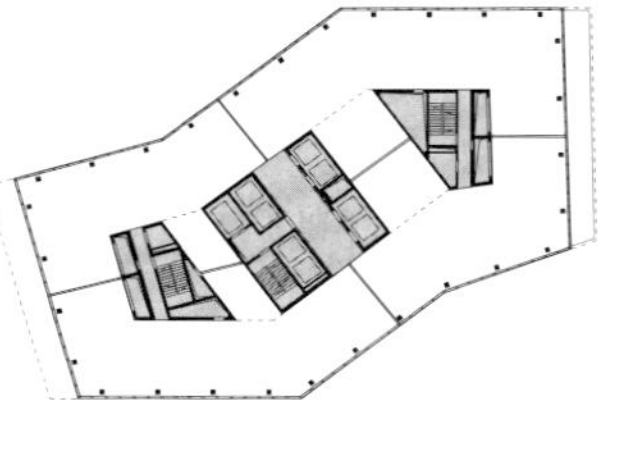

Individual offices

Combined offices

Open-plan offices

Division into four rental units

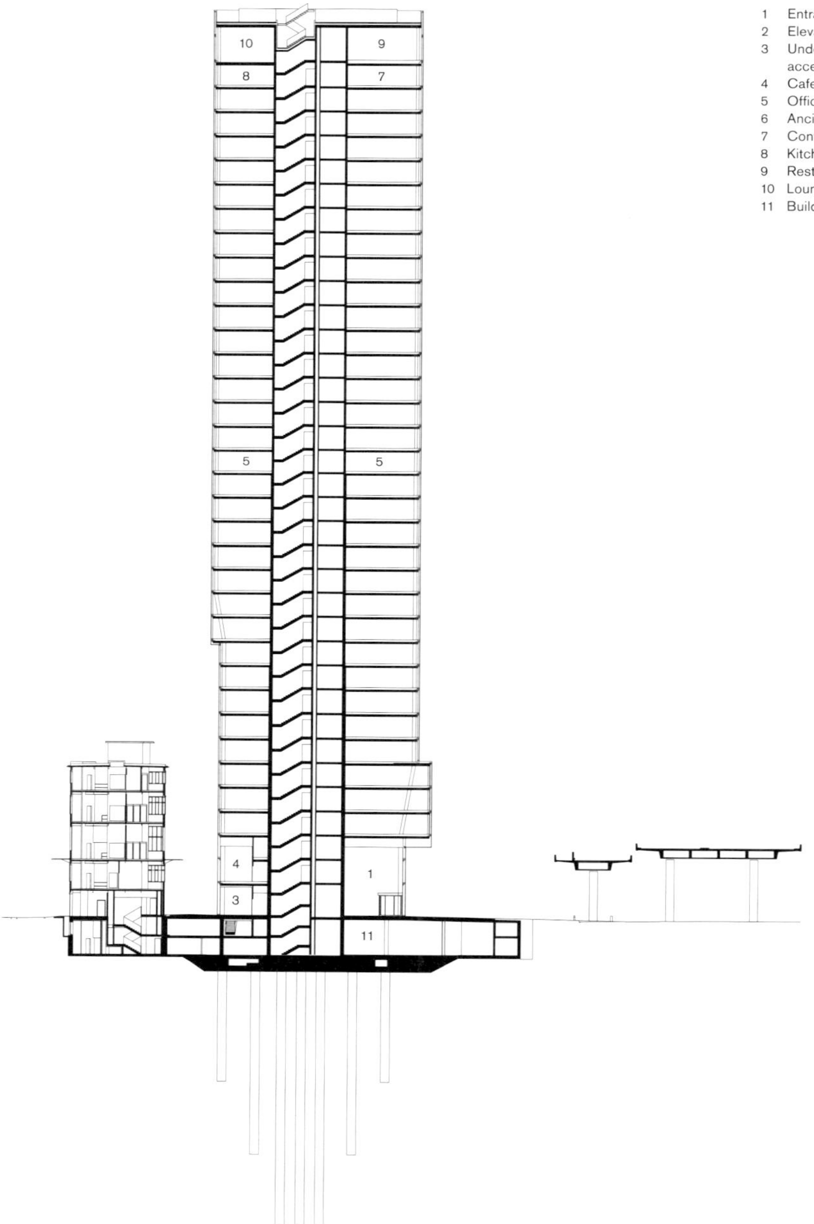

1 Entrance hall
2 Elevator lobby
3 Underground parking access
4 Cafe
5 Offices
6 Ancillary zone
7 Conference zone
8 Kitchen
9 Restaurant
10 Lounge
11 Building services

Section A–A

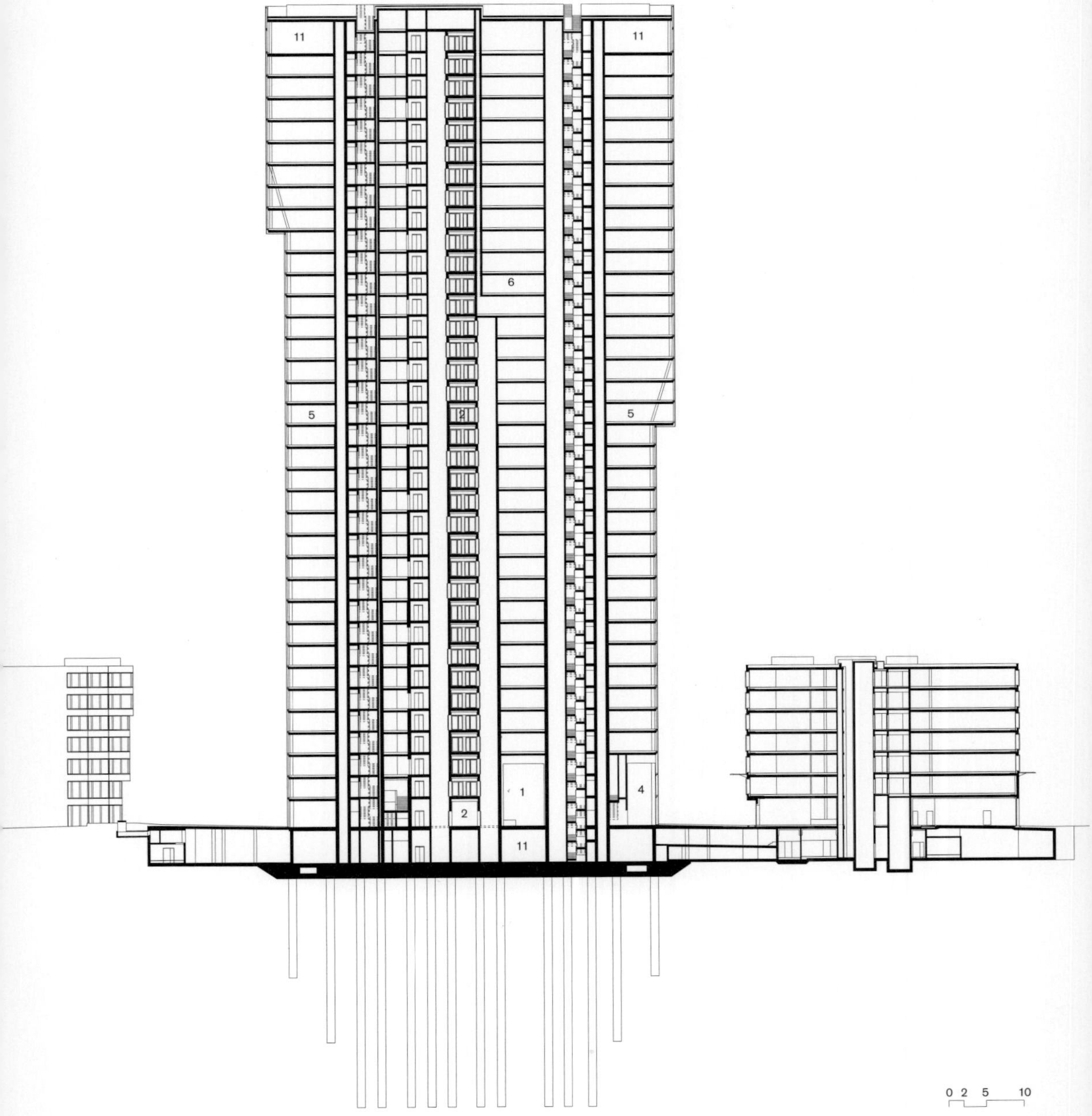

Section B–B

Prime Tower Office High-rise, Maag-Areal, Zurich, Switzerland

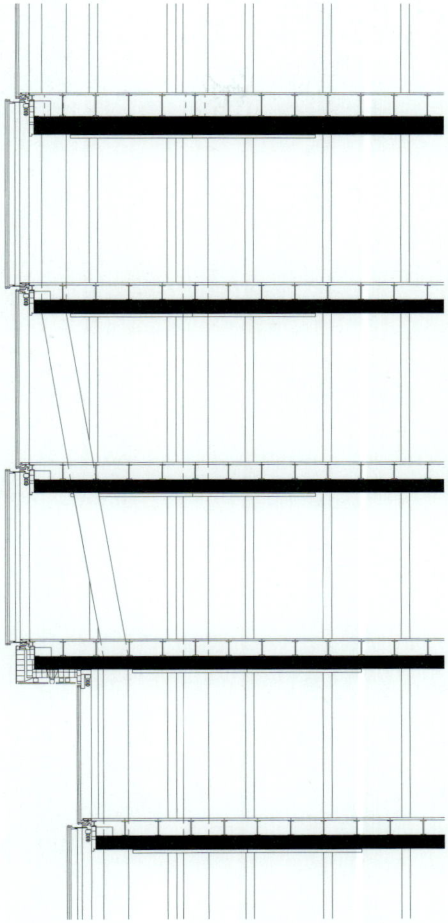

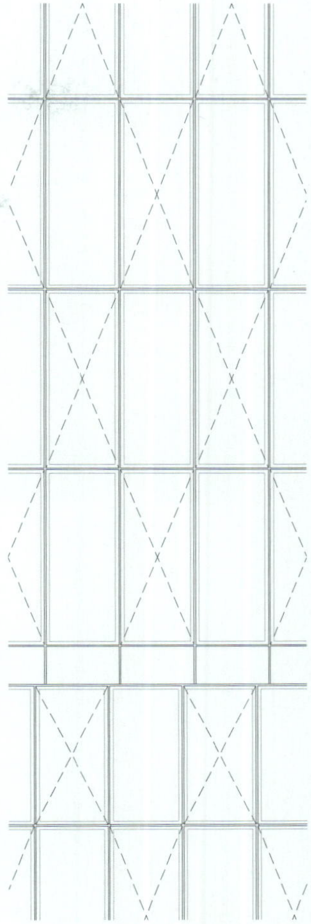

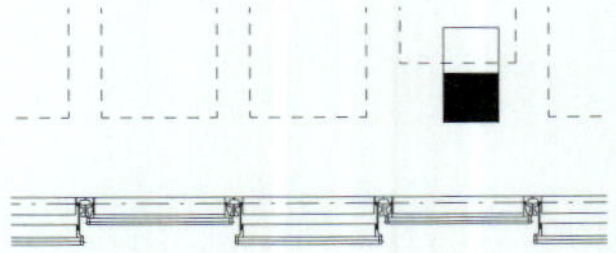

Construction detail

0 1 2

Tenant Fit-out for Homburger, Prime Tower, Zurich, Switzerland 155
2007/2010–11

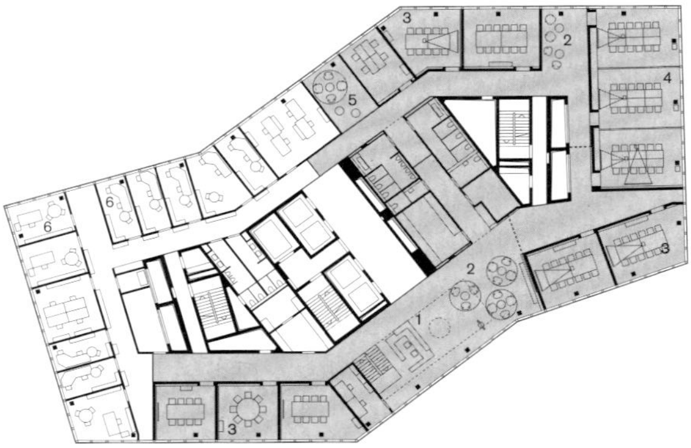

1 Reception
2 Waiting area/lounge
3 Customer meeting area
4 Conference area
5 Smoking lounge
6 Individual office
7 Internal meeting room
8 Staff kitchen
9 Archive

0 2 5 10

31st floor

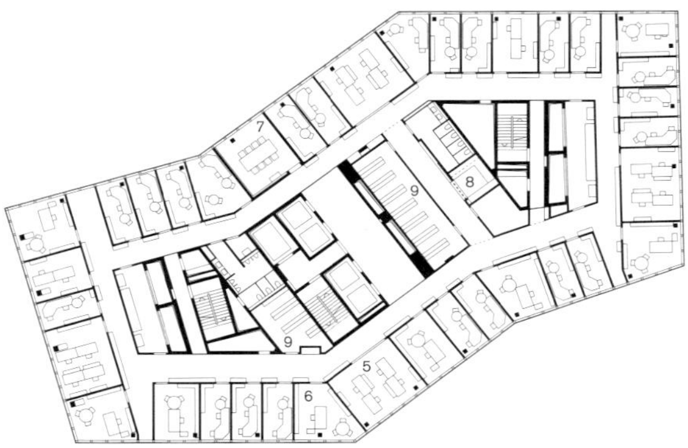

29th floor

The offices of the law firm Homburger extend from the 25th to the 32nd story of the tower. The reception area on the 31st floor has a double-height hall affording a sweeping view over the city. A number of rooms of various dimensions for meetings with clients and a large room offering the option of flexible partitioning are located adjacent to the reception. Dark parquet flooring in the circulation areas, carpeted floors in the meeting rooms, white walls and ceilings, reflective metal cladding, coordinated furnishings, and nuanced lighting combine to create a fitting ambience that also showcases different artworks. In the entrance-level spaces, a large-format light object by Olafur Eliasson and several wall paintings by Sol LeWitt can be found.

The layout of the internal work areas is defined by individual offices and access zones, which often have windows offering views over the city. The circulation areas on the various floors are lent distinct identities thanks to further art installations by Hans Danuser, Beat Zoderer, Katharina Grosse, Lang/Baumann, and Christian Kathriner which are all integrated into the overall design.

Tenant Fit-out for Clouds Restaurant, Prime Tower, Zurich, Switzerland 247
2010–11

1 Reception
2 Restaurant
3 Bar/Bistro
4 Lounge
5 Patio event space
6 Preparation kitchen
7 Elevator lobby
8 Reception/lounge
9 Large room
10 Meeting room
11 Kitchen
12 Office

0 2 5 10

35th floor

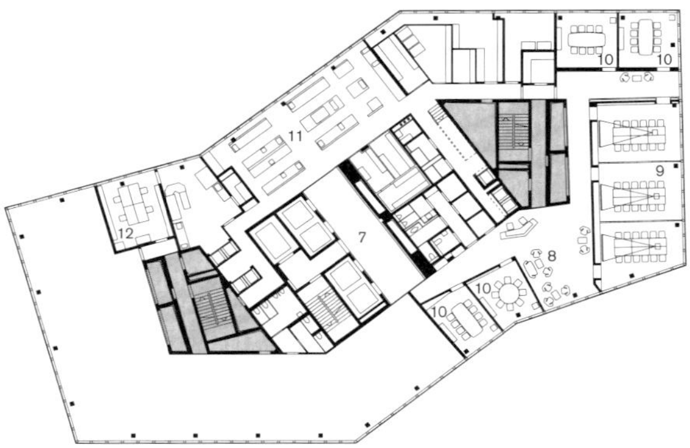

34th floor

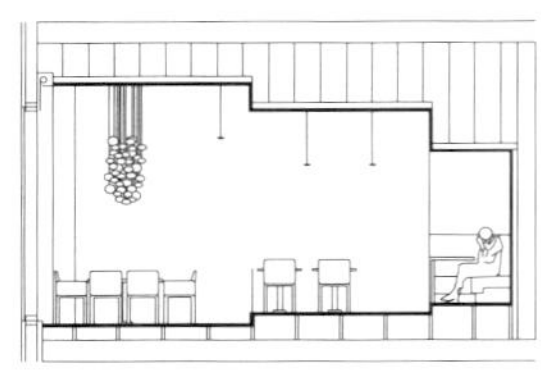

Section

0 1 5

119 meters above the ground, a literally "high-level" restaurant awaits guests, complemented by a bistro with bar, a lounge, and rooms for special events. On the floor below, conference rooms are available for rental. The various areas each have distinct atmospheres conjured by fine fabrics, parquet floors, wood-paneled walls, decorative plasterwork, metal facing, and various types of leather, textiles, glass, and mirrors. Gradations in the floor and ceiling of the restaurant and bistro open them up to the outside, making the panorama an even more impressive experience.

In the restaurant the mood is set by the light-colored translucent mesh ceiling, a motif carried over into the fabric blinds on the façade, along with a recessed seating niche. The ambience in the bistro is distinguished by warm copper-hued tones and a wood-paneled back wall, while the most striking features in the lounge are the brass bar with its meandering curves and a ceiling painting by Adrian Schiess.

Cubus Office Building, Maag-Areal, Zurich, Switzerland 152

2004–11

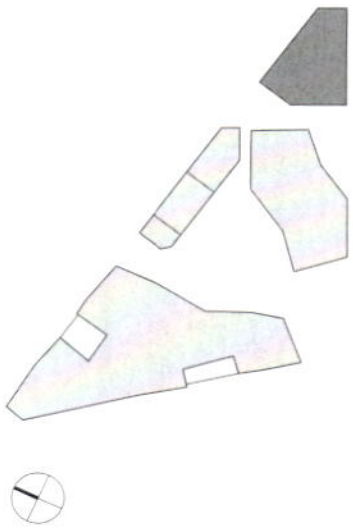

1 Shop
2 Deliveries
3 Garage entrance
4 Offices

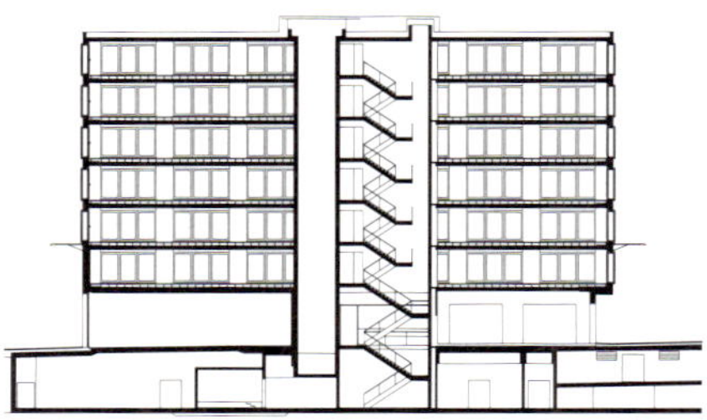

Section

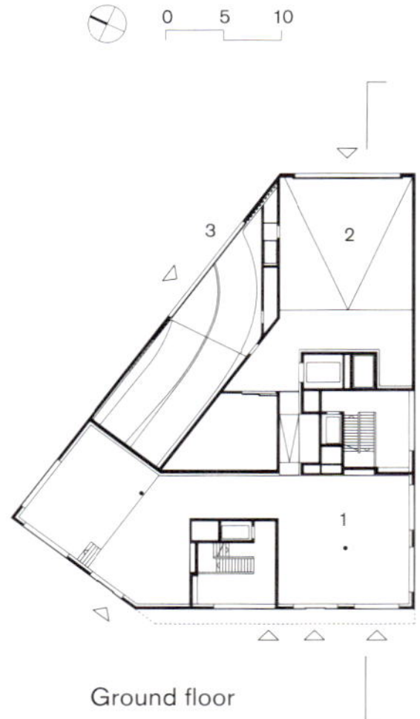

Ground floor

6th floor

The Cubus annex building, a seven-story structure with a pentagonal ground plan, houses offices on the upper floors and at ground level retail outlets, access to the parking garage, and deliveries for the entire complex. Of note here is that, due to the excellent public transport connections to this site, relatively few parking spaces are required. The load-bearing structure is executed in white-pigmented exposed concrete. Externally fixed glazing panels give the façade its character and help to reduce noise from the elevated road nearby.

Refurbishment of Former Diagonal Industrial Building, 152
Maag-Areal, Zurich, Switzerland, 2004–11

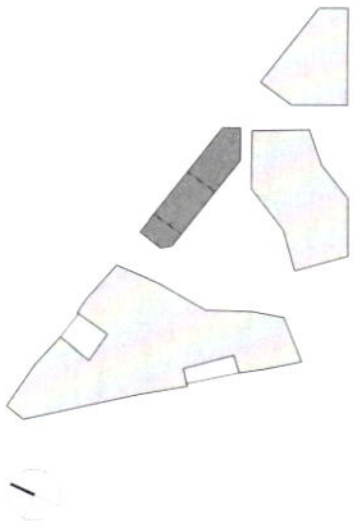

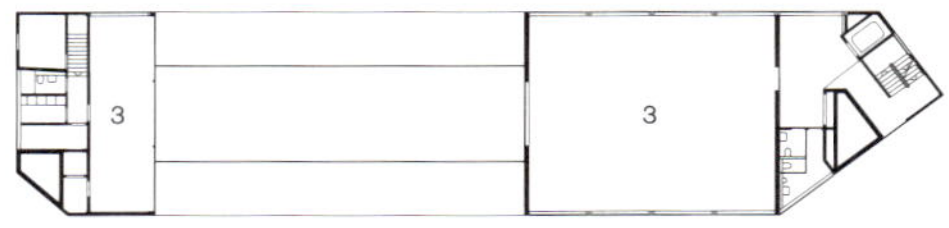

4th floor

1 Restaurant
2 Exhibition
3 Offices

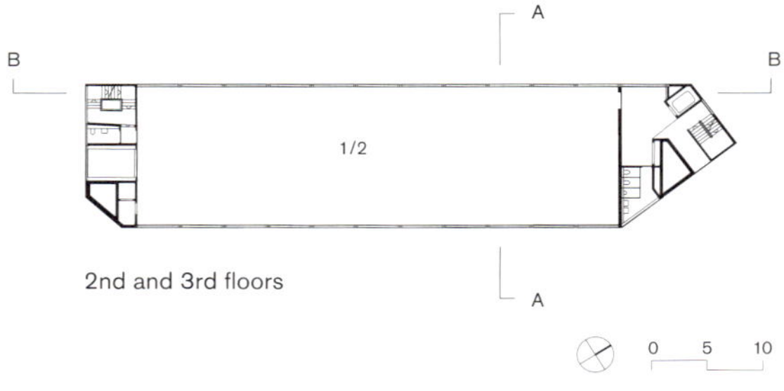

2nd and 3rd floors

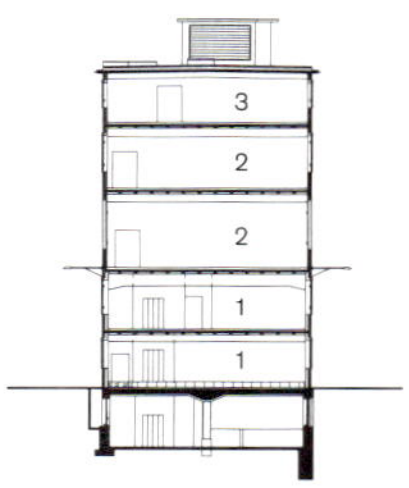

Section A–A

Section B–B

The Diagonal building, the former MAAG cogwheel factory, has been preserved as a fascinating architectural testament to the site's industrial past. The load-bearing structure and the façades have been carefully revitalized. The surviving slender glazing bars were restored and are complemented by insulating glazing on the interior. The Diagonal building contains a restaurant on the ground floor and gallery spaces on the upper floors.

1
pperswil
2
J
54

Platform Office Building, Maag-Areal, Zurich, Switzerland 197
2007–11

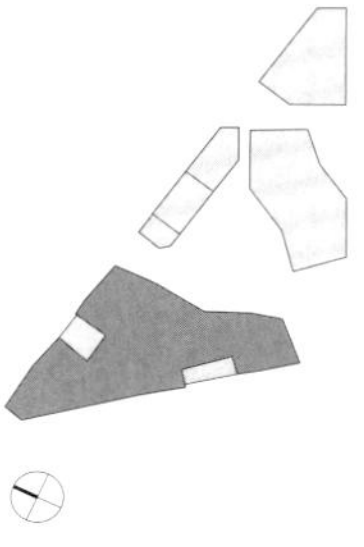

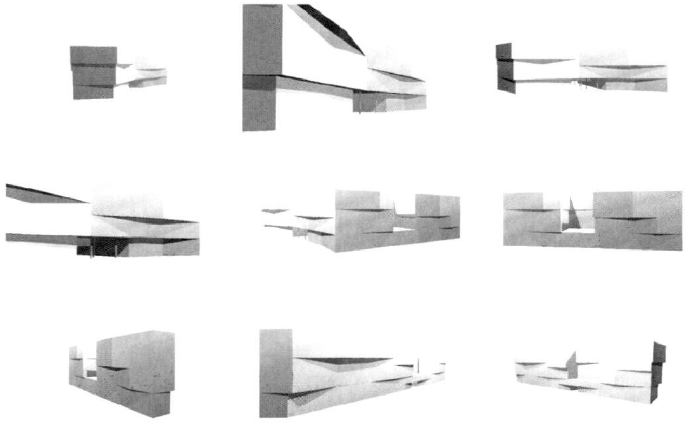

Model studies

In the immediate vicinity of Hardbrücke railway station, the seven-story office building called Platform completes the ensemble comprising the high-rise Prime Tower and its annexes Cubus and Diagonal. The building's volume, with various angles, reacts to the urban situation, providing a coherent link between the station and the new central square. A two-story-high passage through the building connects the square with the public pedestrian and bicycle path along the side of the tracks as well as with the new pedestrian underpass to Hardbrücke Station. In addition, the passage acts as a generous covered area outside the entrance foyer.

With its pronounced horizontal and layered design, the building contrasts with the Prime Tower nearby, effectively forming its reclining counterpart. As in the tower, the stories increase their floor area as the building rises, made possible by various projections. The volume of the building is also subdivided by courtyards that cut into the west and south sides and ensure well-lit office spaces within, as well as by the angular projections in the façade.

The central, prestigious entrance foyer forms an additional internal open area. A tall atrium flooded with natural light links the entrance level with the office floors above. Its function as a hub that lends the building its identity is additionally underlined by the open staircases and adjoining seating areas on the office floors. Dark glass balustrades mirror the space and the light in multifaceted reflections, creating a kaleidoscope effect.

Next to the entrance foyer on the ground floor are a restaurant, a cafeteria, and an auditorium. A wide, inviting staircase leads from the entrance level to the customer lobby on the first floor, from which the various conference rooms can be accessed. The levels above provide office space for around 1,000 staff. Although the building has been conceived as a corporate headquarters, the positioning of core facility areas permits a variety of office typologies if required in the future, including the division of each floor into a maximum of four separate rental units. Wall and ceiling paintings by Nic Hess, wallpaper and drapes by Lachmayer/Nobis and a textile sculpture by Ernesto Neto complete the interior.

To be able to meet changing spatial needs or different uses without radical structural alterations, the building has been designed as a load-bearing skeleton structure with reinforced cores.

The glazed façade is articulated by horizontally layered bands of parapets and windows. The double windows hold sunblinds in between and help reduce noise from outside. The inner windows can be opened for ventilation purposes toward the interim space of the double-skin façade. The slightly reflective outer glazing shell and parapets accentuate the building's folded structure.

4th floor

1st floor

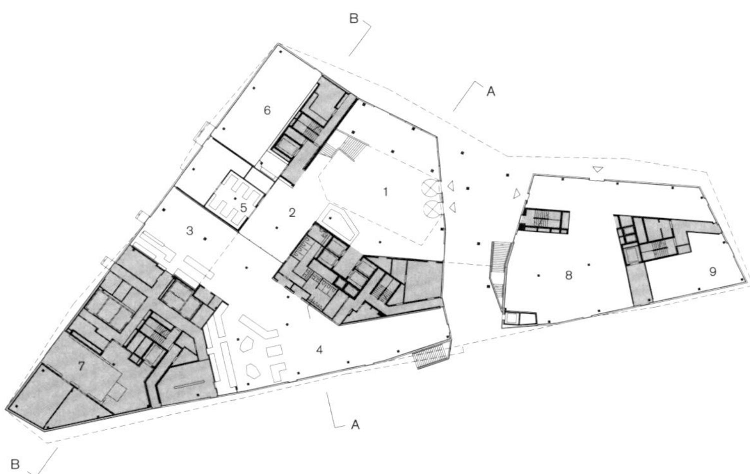

Ground floor

1 Entrance hall
2 Foyer
3 Cafeteria
4 Restaurant
5 Mail room
6 Auditorium
7 Deliveries
8 External gastronomy
9 Services
10 Customer lobby
11 Void
12 Customer meeting room
13 Office zone
14 Lounge
15 Internal meeting room
16 Think Tanks

0 5 10 20

ERNST & YOUNG

Platform Office Building, Maag-Areal, Zurich, Switzerland

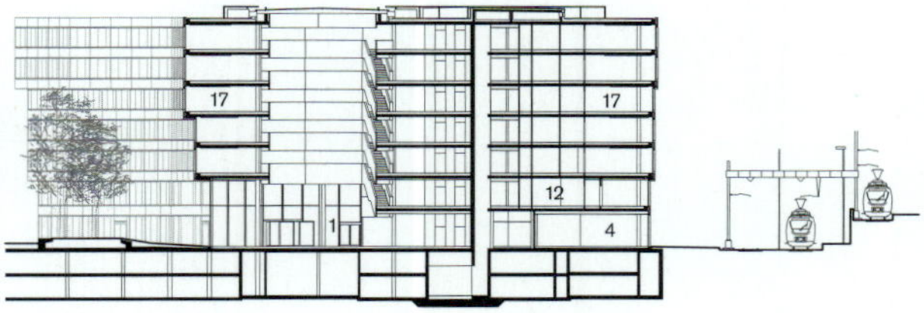

Section A–A

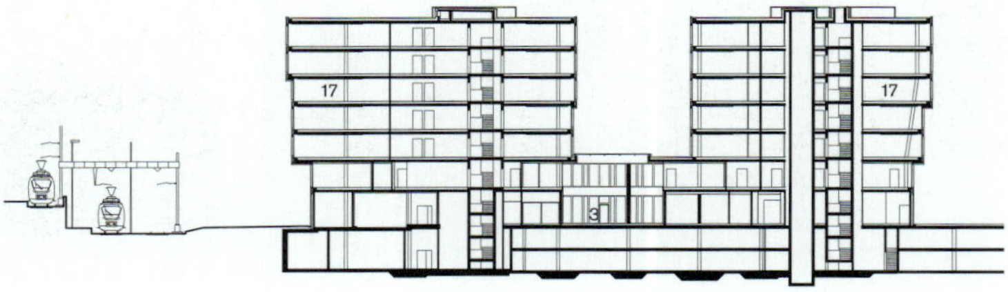

Section B–B

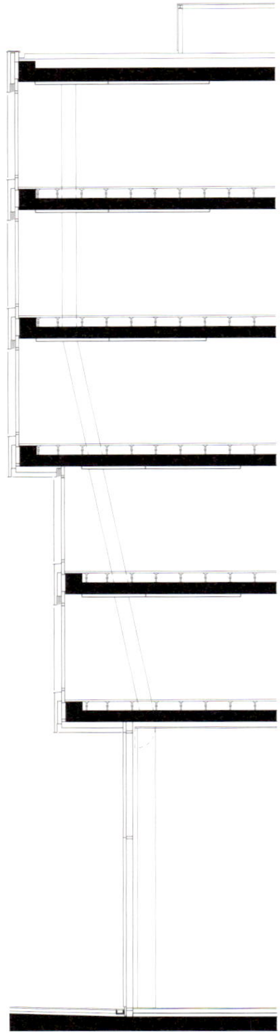

Construction detail

0 1 2

ZKB

Extension of Hardbrücke Railway Station, Zurich, Switzerland 270

2010 (Competition)

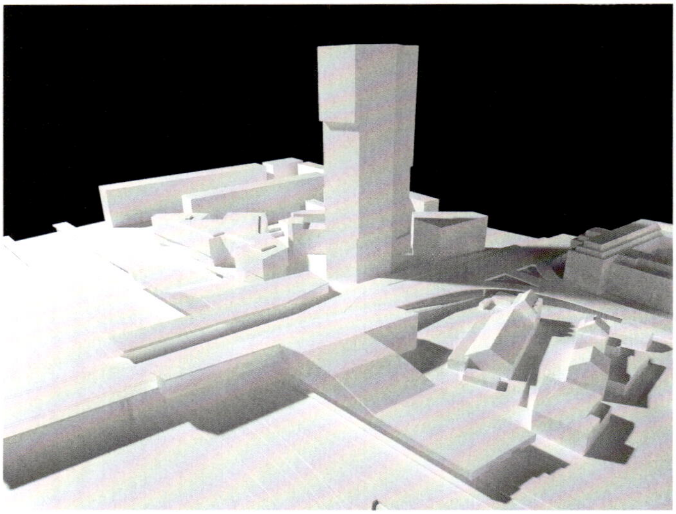

Hardbrücke station is to be upgraded to keep pace with urban development in the Zurich West area and to accommodate growing passenger numbers. The station acts as a central hub between the tracks, Hardbrücke bridge, and Hardstrasse, which runs below the bridge and ends in a square in front of the new station.

Passengers will enter the new station building from this ground-level square, Bahnhofsplatz, using escalators, stairways, or elevators to reach the bridge level, where in the future trams will share the bus stops. Two new concourses connected to the bridge lead down to the commuter train platforms. An intermediate level, forming a gallery in the high entrance hall, allows passengers to change to other lines and traverse the site without crossing the Hardbrücke traffic lanes.

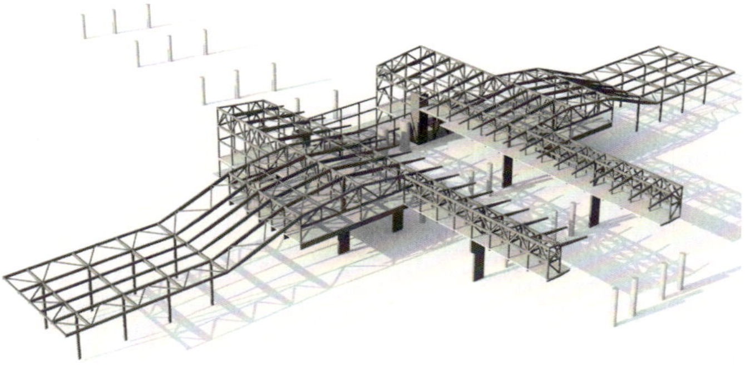

Main load-bearing structure

The narrow underground connecting tract currently in use will be taken out of operation and used exclusively for technical infrastructure. In conjunction with the existing passenger tunnel to the west, a generously proportioned new passenger tunnel in the eastern part of the site will help to further ease pedestrian traffic, particularly on the middle platform.

Roofs with multiple folds provide shelter for the platforms, sweeping up to Hardbrücke bridge in the east and west, then widening along the length of the bridge above the bus/tram stops and the entrance building. The latter establishes a link under the bridge between the two sides of the site. A nuanced building emerges, providing a spatial frame for the branching streams of passengers while confidently asserting its status as an autonomous structure.

In the platform area, the configuration of the structural system is coordinated with the structural axes of the bridge, offering optimum flexibility for future alterations to the track and platform layout. The load-bearing constructions of the concourses and roofs are entirely independent of the existing bridge structure.

Entrance hall, city level

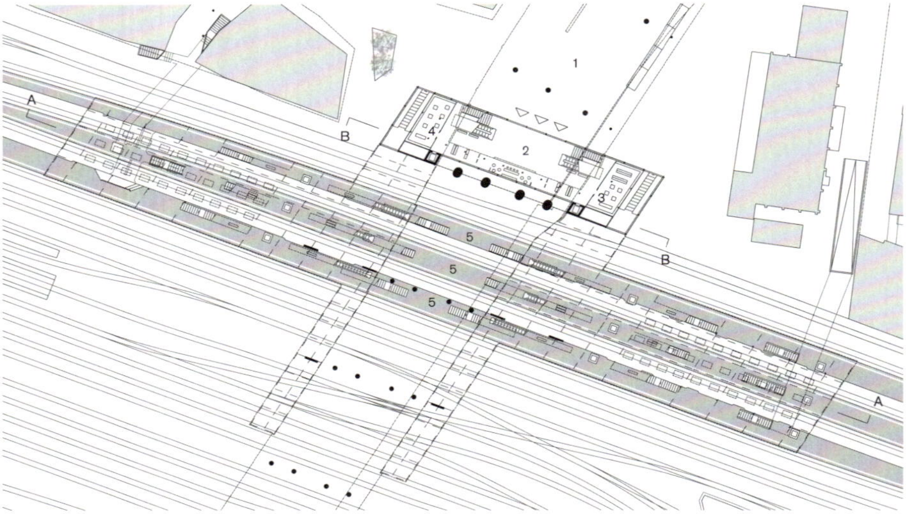

Floor plan, city level

1 Station forecourt
2 Entrance hall
3 Shops
4 Bar
5 Perrons
6 Distribution level, new concourse
7 Bus/tram stops

0 5 10 20

Railway station concourse, Hardbrücke level

Extension of Hardbrücke Railway Station, Zurich, Switzerland

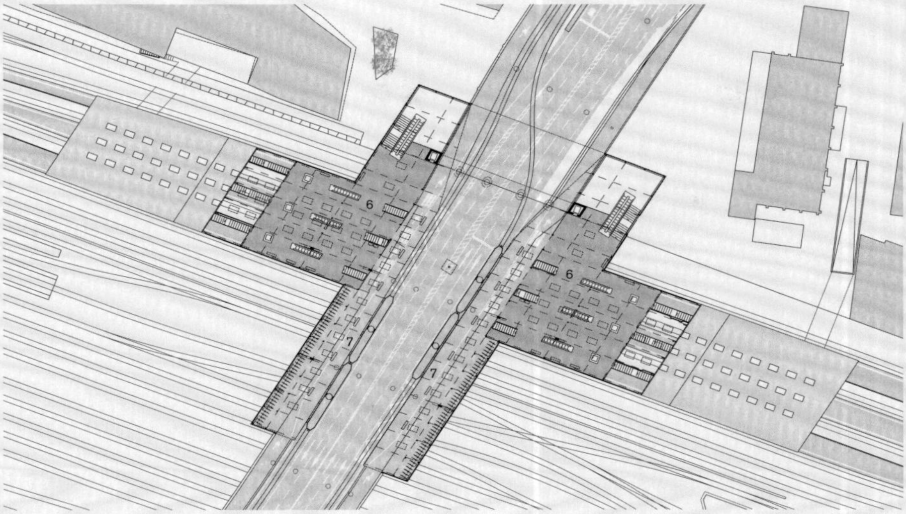

Floor plan, Hardbrücke level

South elevation

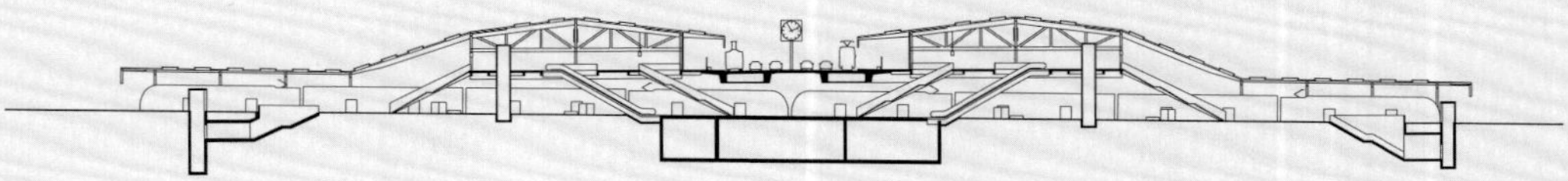

Section A–A

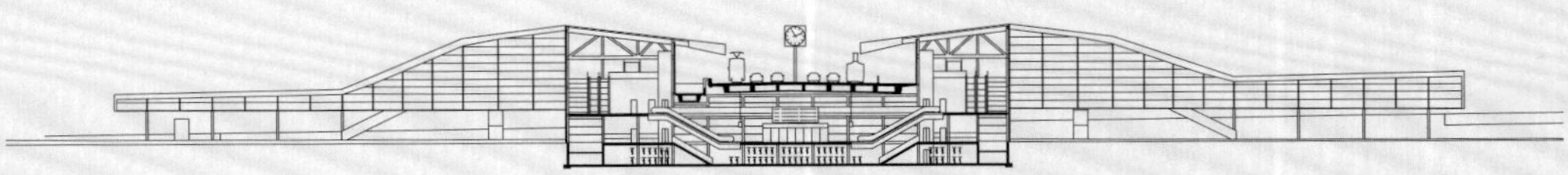

Section B–B

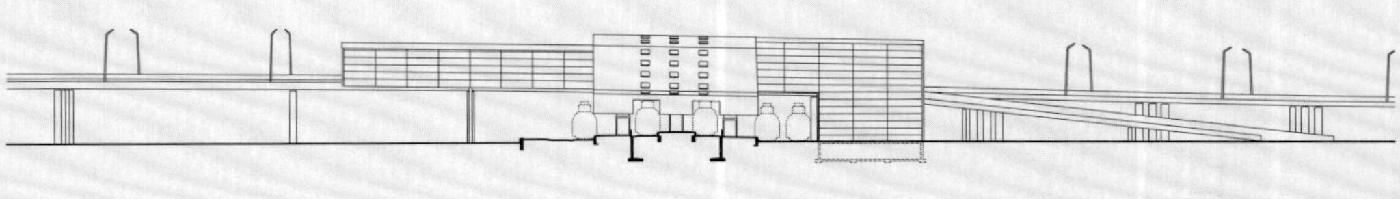

East elevation

Extension of Workshop School Buildings Appisberg, Männedorf, Switzerland 037

1998–2002

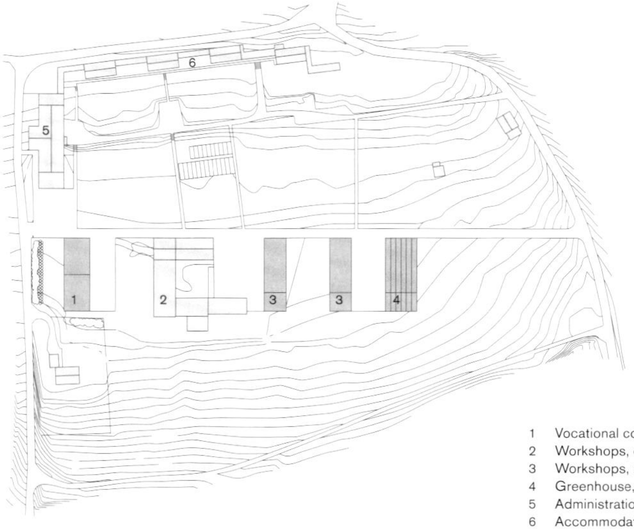

1 Vocational consultation, new build
2 Workshops, existing
3 Workshops, new build
4 Greenhouse, shelter, new build
5 Administration/canteen, existing
6 Accommodation, existing

The new extension of the Appisberg workshop school complex comprises a row of individual volumes along an internal access road opposite the existing 1930s buildings. The principle for the alignment of the new structures was defined by the position of the existing buildings. In keeping with the original layout by the Mertens brothers landscape architects, the center of the complex remains undeveloped as a large planted area that merges in the east with the open landscape.

The alignment of the building volumes parallel to the sight axes toward the lake and the mountains serves to accentuate these views rather than obscure them. The proportions of the new additions echo the scale of the historic buildings. Both tension and rhythm are generated by the way the spatial organization of the new volumes relates to the existing structures. Subtle differences in the dimensions and form of the individual volumes enrich this interplay.

With the exception of the greenhouse, all buildings are constructed mainly of in-situ concrete. The floor and ceiling slabs are supported by the load-bearing exterior walls and reinforcing service cores. The robust materials used for the exterior walls and windows respond to the high demands placed on them by the workshop and training functions. The greenhouse with its contrasting material properties signals the border of the site and the transition to the open landscape.

Two color tones are dominant in the complex. The orange of the historic buildings contrasts with the various green hues of the surroundings: in summer, the lush green of the meadows, the yellow-green of the fields, and the pale green of the distant hills, and all year round the dark green of the nearby forest. The opposite approach is taken by the new buildings, whose yellow-green shade echoes the tonality of their environment. Vibrant color intensity is achieved through several coats of transparent matt glaze, through which the materiality of the concrete still remains visible.

Aerial view, c. 1930
"Occupational Therapy Center for Tuberculosis"

Ground floor and upper floor
Vocational consultation

Ground floor and upper floor
Workshops

1 Wood workshop
2 Consultation room
3 Entrance hall
4 Metal and textiles workshop
5 Electronics workshop
6 Offices
7 Metal workshop
8 Recycling workshop
9 CNC workshop

Cross section
Vocational consultation

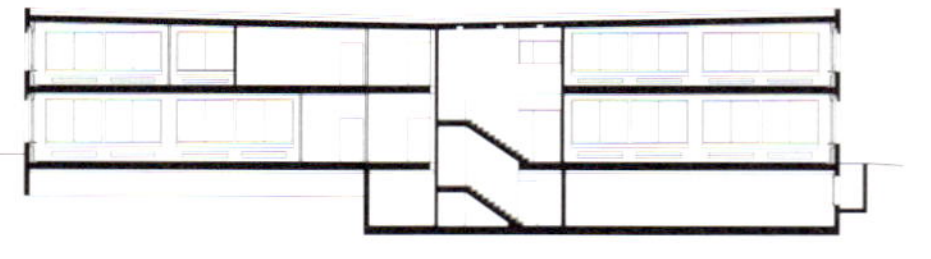

Longitudinal section

Würth Administration Building with Educational and Training Center, Rorschach, Switzerland 237
2009–13

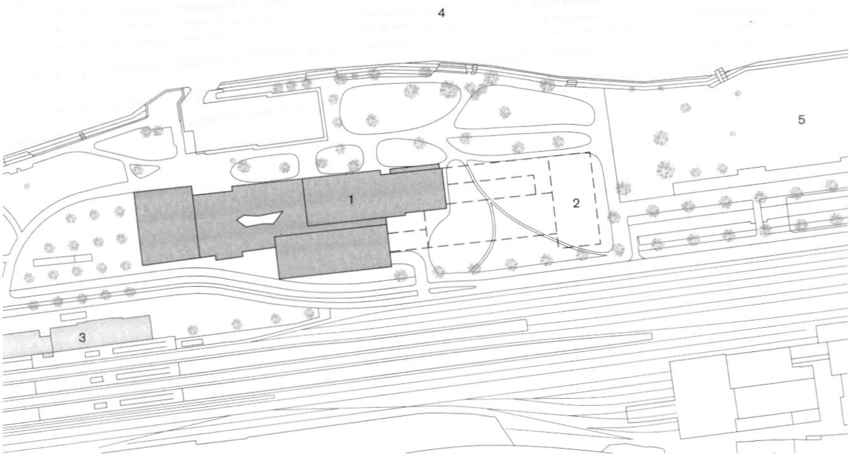

1 New build, Phase 1
2 New build, Phase 2
3 Railway station
4 Lake Constance
5 Bathing area

A greenish crystalline building responds to the unusual location of the site, set between the edge of Lake Constance and Churerstrasse. Walkers and passers-by experience a glass structure that oscillates between transparency and shiny reflective surfaces that multiply the natural beauty of the setting. The architecture affords views out to the surroundings, glimpses into the building, and sightlines through it to the park and lake.

The interior offers staff and visitors generously proportioned sequences of rooms—workspaces, communication areas, and leisure zones—as well as providing space for product presentations and art exhibitions. The structure responds to the train station building with lower volumes and reacts to the expanses of the park and lake with a higher segment. There are plans to add an extension on the eastern side in a future phase of construction. Toward the street, the volumes give shape to a range of external spaces through precisely defined projections and setbacks: in the middle is the entrance area, to the east the vehicle access and workshop zone, and to the west Bahnhofsplatz, the station square, which is expanded toward the lake. Maple trees set in a perpendicular configuration characterize this space, and also continue as rows along Churerstrasse.

Approaching from the station, a broad canopy signals the main entrance. The various user groups—visitors, people attending courses, and company staff—enter the building through a large lobby and are guided from this point to the different parts of the building. On the ground floor and first floor, the public functions—training and conference rooms, as well as the restaurant—are grouped around a foyer with an open courtyard in the center and are linked by a sweeping stairway. Both the conference area and the separate exhibition spaces can be accessed directly from the exterior, allowing the option of using these areas independently from the rest of the building. The exhibition area guides visitors from the entrance to two different-sized exhibition rooms, which are located on the first floor of the southern part of the building and are naturally lit from above. The structure of the shed skylight over the exhibition spaces simultaneously supports the enormous projecting canopy over the entrance. Office space extends over four stories in the highest part of the building, which is not open to the general public. Informal meeting areas with balconies facing the lake, transparent or closed-off meeting rooms, and individual offices alternate here with open-plan office areas.

A double glass envelope encases the building. The inner layer is made up of triple glazing and metal-clad thermal insulation. The external, back-ventilated layer is composed of offset greenish glass panes equipped with a fine mesh insert with a metallic luster. This creates a rhythmically articulated glass curtain that provides protection against wind from the lake and noise from the street and also against excessive heat and cold. The predominance of glass in the building materials is continued on the roof in the form of CIS photovoltaic panels.

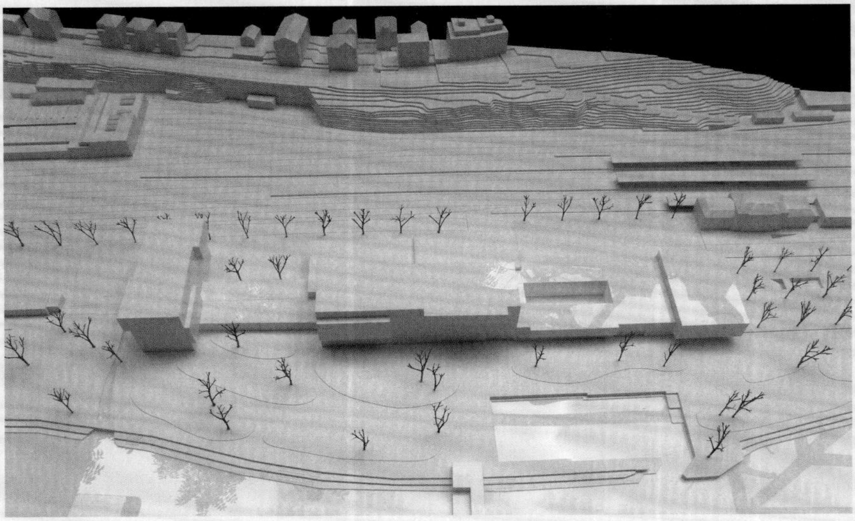

Competition model, Phases 1 and 2

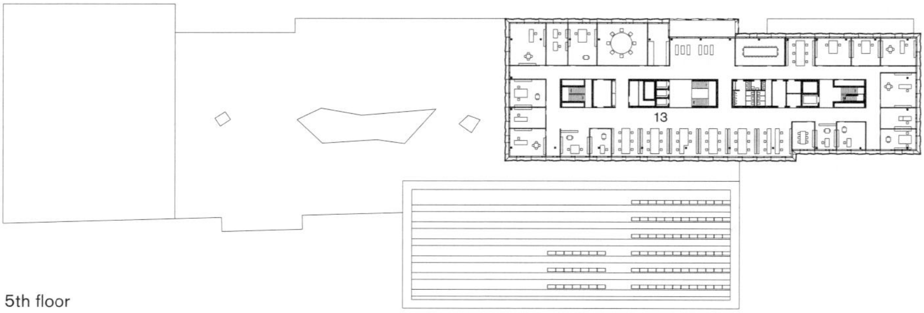

5th floor

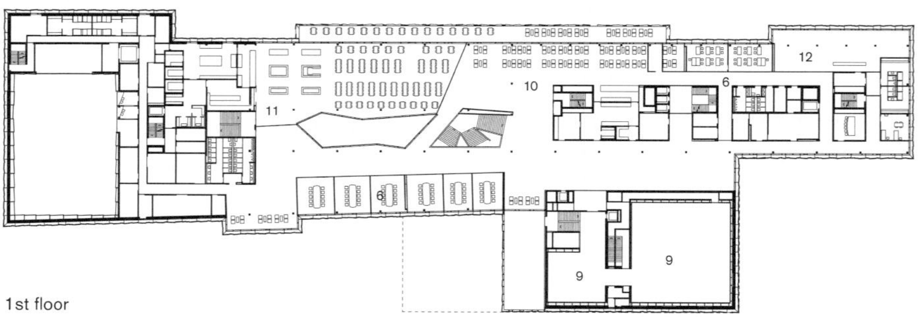

1st floor

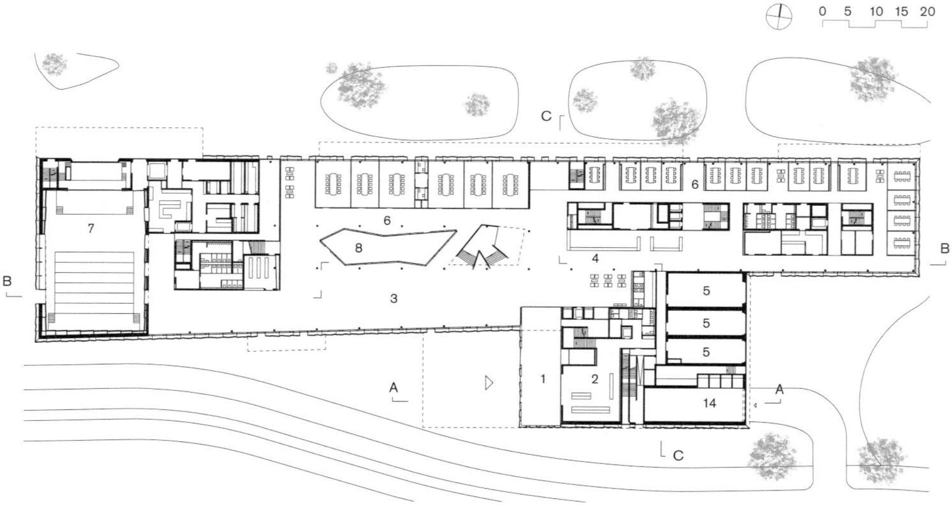

Ground floor

Würth Administration Building with Educational and Training Center, Rorschach, Switzerland

1 Entrance
2 Exhibition foyer
3 Lobby
4 Reception
5 Demonstration workshops
6 Conference/training
7 Congress room
8 Courtyard
9 Exhibition
10 Cafeteria
11 Restaurant
12 Fitness
13 Offices
14 Underground parking

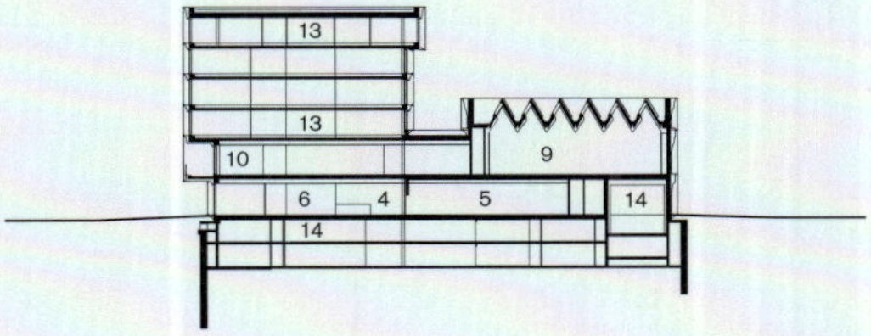

Section C–C

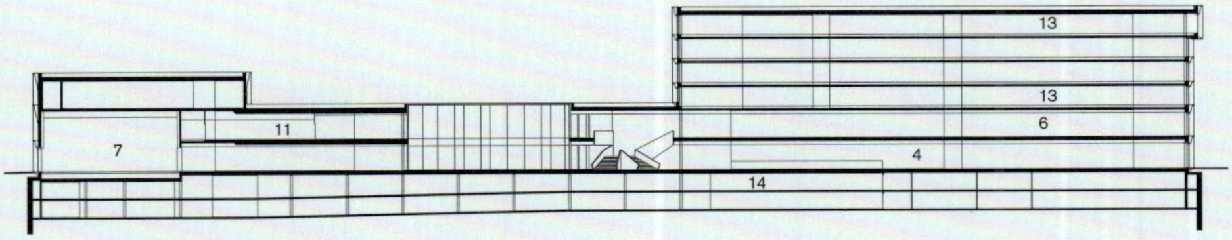

Section B–B

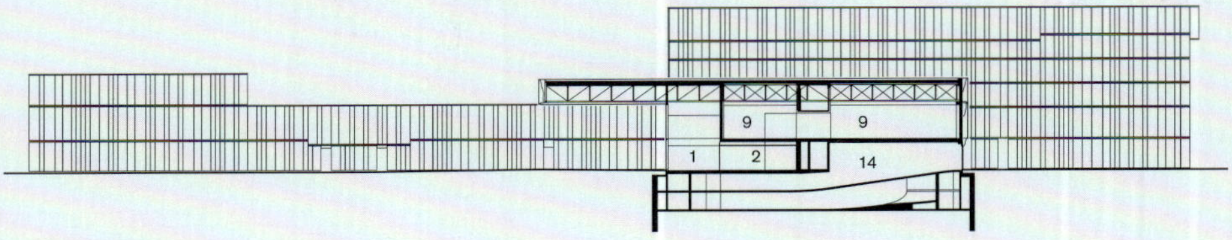

Section A–A

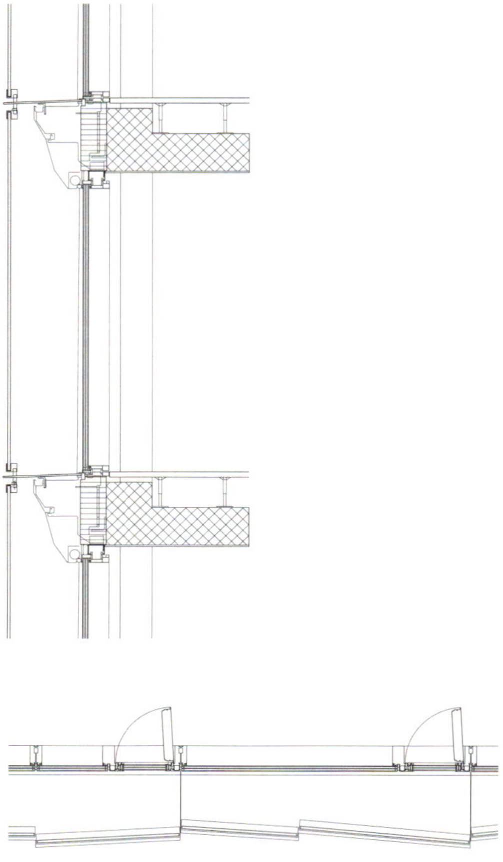

Construction detail

0 0.5 1 2

Mock-up façade

Rosau Office Building, Zurich, Switzerland, 2008–15 156
Refurbishment of Villa Rosau, Zurich, Switzerland, 2009–15 239

The new L-shaped office building opposite the Tonhalle on the corner of Gotthardstrasse and Claridenstrasse is integrated into the perimeter block structure along Claridenstrasse, while Villa Rosau and its surrounding gardens remain true to their historical conception. The green area forms a twin garden with the park of the Hotel Baur au Lac on the opposite side of the Schanzengraben canal. The newbuild marks the westerly end of the two gardens, whose beautiful trees border the public square Bürkliplatz.

The parks of Villa Rosau and Hotel Baur au Lac on Lake Zurich are important witnesses to the history of the city's development. The gardens flow around the villa and the new building, merging the perimeter block development with the solitary villa in the park to form a coherent ensemble. This convergence of architectural and organic garden design is a central theme, which assists the organization of the green space into different zones.

New Rosau Office Building
The new building offers the future long-term tenant, a banking firm, a prestigious place of business. Customers are received in an entrance hall situated in the part of the building facing the lake, from where they are accompanied to a lounge on the fourth floor, where several consultation rooms are at their disposal. An open staircase leads to the customer area on the third floor, with larger consultation rooms and conference rooms with vistas across the lake. Adjacent to the

entrance hall on the ground floor is the bank's seminar area, with an auditorium that seats 120 guests. At the corner of Gotthardstrasse and Claridenstrasse, a bakery with outdoor seating is planned, while two apartments are housed in the top two levels of the building section facing the Schanzengraben canal.

The structure is a skeleton frame with recessed columns and centrally located reinforcing concrete circulation cores. Vertical and horizontal profiles of architectural bronze arranged in varying rhythms articulate the façade. They take up, on a larger scale and with greater geometric regularity, the existing ornamental wrought-iron fences surrounding the gardens.

Refurbishment of Villa Rosau

In the course of the project for the new office building, Villa Rosau will be fundamentally refurbished. The historical villa was constructed by the architect Ferdinand Stadler in 1844/45. Research in the archives and surveys on site yielded information on the villa's historical condition and urban setting that provided the basis for the façade renovation and the basic fit-out. The building will continue to be used as the domicile of the "Club Baur au Lac" and comprises bar and restaurant spaces on the ground floor, clubrooms on the second floor, and meeting rooms on the top floor.

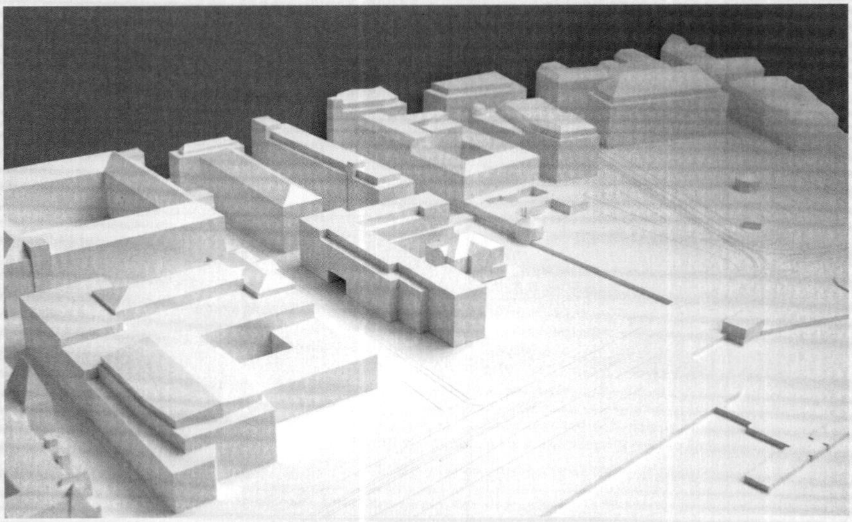

Façade detail

View from Gotthardstrasse

Rosau Office Building, Zurich, Switzerland

Ground floor

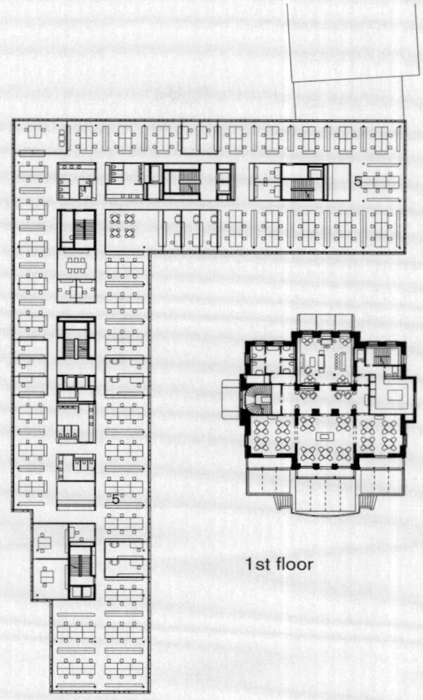

1st and 2nd floors

1st floor

1 Reception
2 Foyer
3 Auditorium
4 Seminar
5 Offices
6 Bakery
7 Customer area
8 Apartment
9 Management

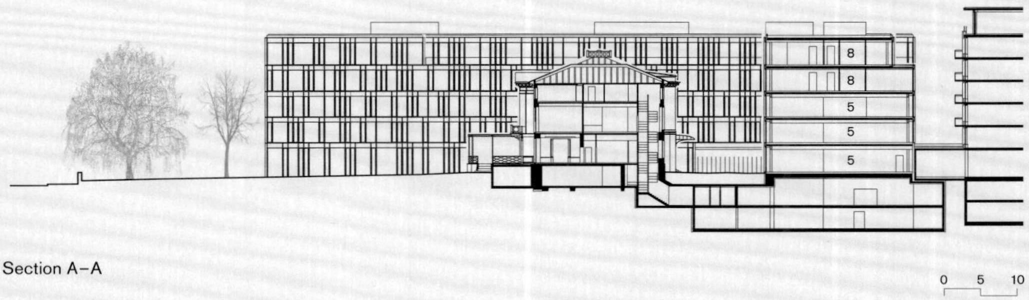

Section A–A

2nd floor

3rd floor

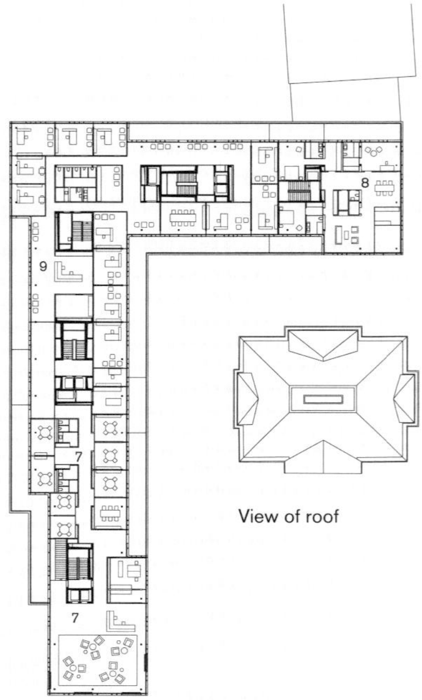

View of roof

Top floor

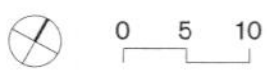

Refurbishment of Villa Rosau

1 Reception
2 Entrance hall
3 Bar
4 Restaurant
5 Terrace
6 Checkroom
7 Offices
8 Kitchen
9 Club recreation area/Bar
10 Club restaurant

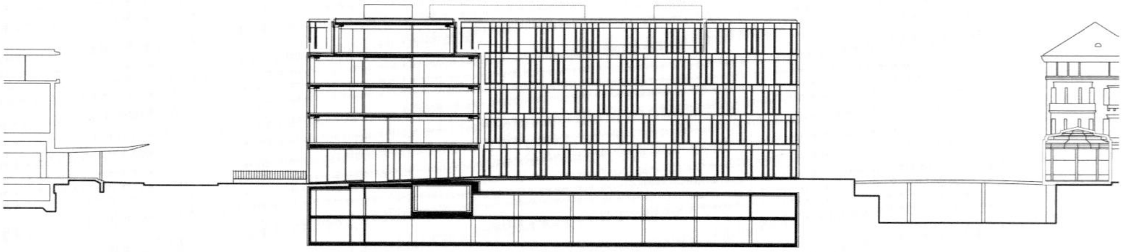

Section B–B

Refurbishment of Villa Rosau, Zurich, Switzerland

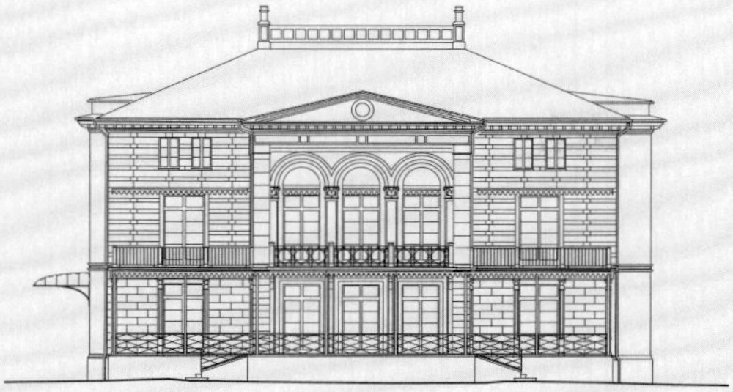

South façade

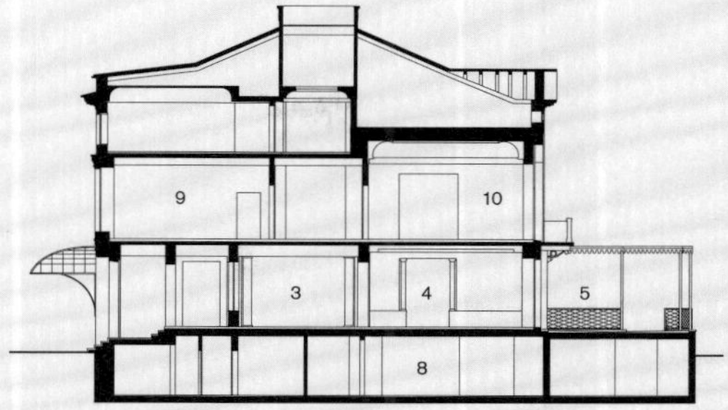

Section

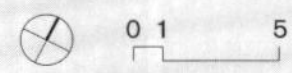

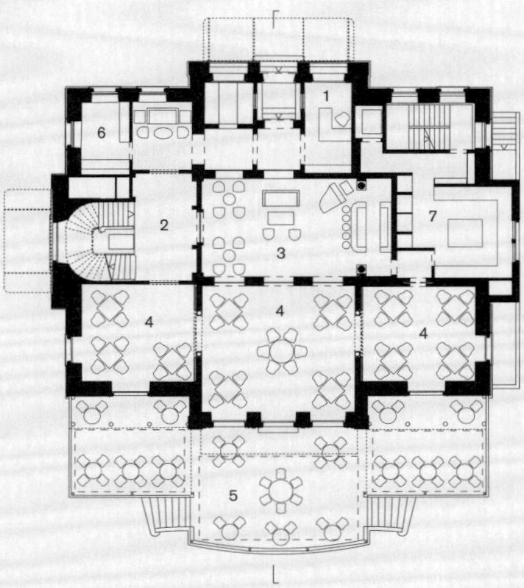

Ground floor

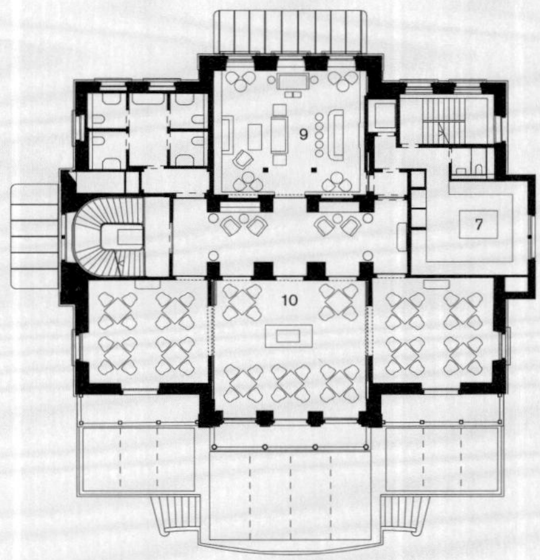

1st floor

Villa Rosau in its original form, c. 1850

South façade, 1909

CAFE Sí
CAFE
Sí

CAFE Si
UBS
BOSS
BOSS
CAFE
Si
BOSS

C10 Office Building, Europaallee 21, Zurich, Switzerland 206
2006–12

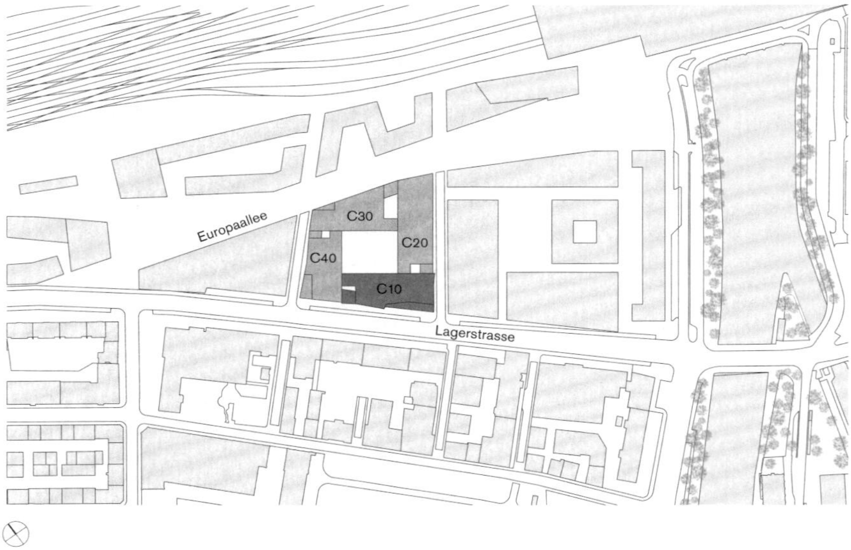

In the immediate vicinity of Zurich's Main Station, the formerly almost inaccessible infrastructure areas used by the Swiss Post and Swiss Railways are undergoing a decisive transformation. They are becoming part of the urban fabric, with public streets, squares, and courtyards. Four buildings are now arranged to form a perimeter block development between the new Europaallee and Lagerstrasse, surrounding a rectangular public courtyard easily accessible from all four sides.

A special characteristic of this complex is that the buildings were designed by different architects and therefore each has a distinct appearance and interior. Two were conceived by Max Dudler Architects (C30, C40), one by David Chipperfield Architects (C20), and the fourth by Gigon/Guyer Architects (C10). What is interesting from a volumetric and urban planning standpoint is the way the four buildings relate to the neighboring structures. Three bridges reach from one volume to the next and therefore allow circuits and connections on all the upper levels, while at the same time creating engaging entry passages.

Building C10 possesses a multifaceted volume that reacts to the various urban planning requirements, building regulations, and functional specifications and derives from them an unexpected articulation. Located on Lagerstrasse, it is set back from the building line on the first two levels, forming a covered entrance area as well as a welcoming gesture. Recesses and projections on the upper levels modulate the volume, forming the attic story and bridge connections, as well as enlarging the office space.

A cafe, a shop, and a generous entrance hall are located on the ground floor. This lobby can be accessed from the street as well as from the courtyard. It provides the main entrance to the office and conference rooms on the seven upper floors. A further access option is offered by a passageway encircling the courtyard on the first floor, which connects the four buildings.

Wide-spanning concrete floors, a few columns, as well as the staircase and elevator cores constitute the load-bearing structure of the building. Concrete was used in refined forms—as terrazzo and cast stone—for the flooring on the ground floor and in the staircases.

The double-layered building skin consists of an inner metal and glass façade with a varied rhythm of glass pane sizes and an outer, ventilated single glazing layer featuring a fine fabric with a metallic sheen. The outer panes provide wind protection for the sunshades and noise protection from the street and also afford privacy to those inside while not blocking their view out the windows. The outer glass panes are arranged at varying angles, generating additional slits for ventilation and, depending on the lighting conditions, a subtle play of different reflections. This lends the impression of a curtain-wall façade—in the truest sense of the word.

Mock-up façade

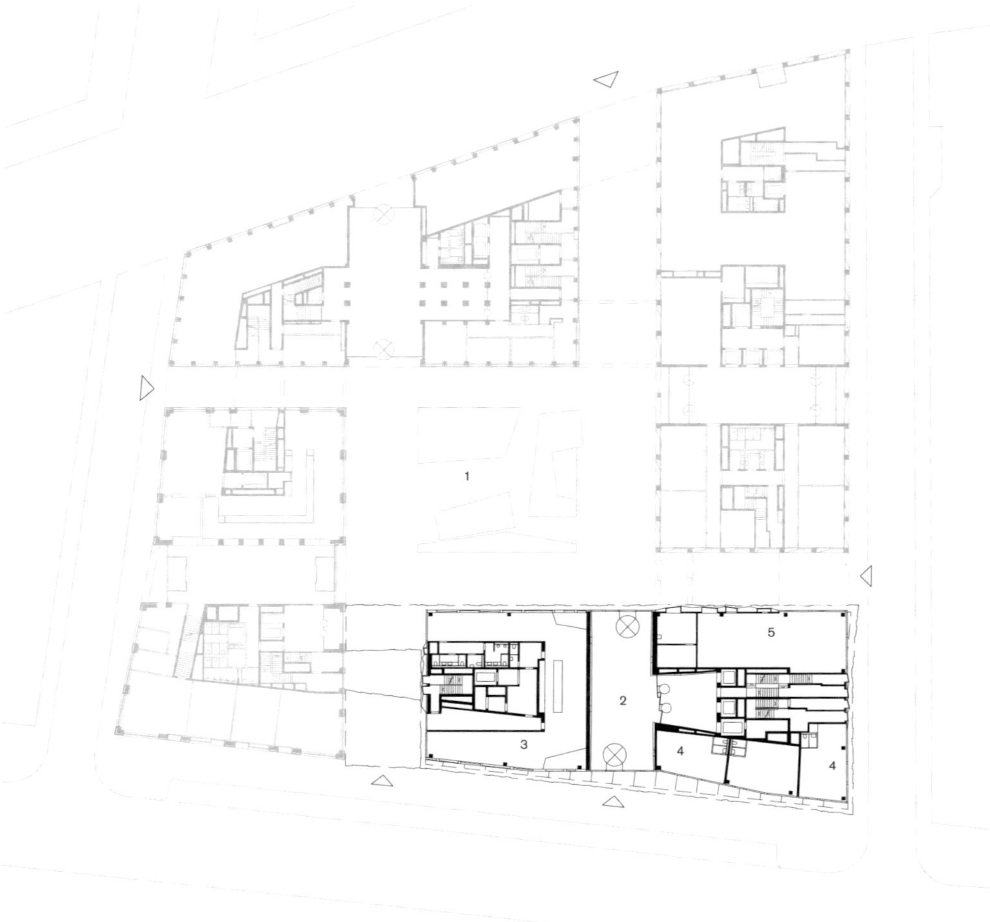

Ground floor

1 Public courtyard
2 Foyer
3 Cafe
4 Shop
5 Bicycle storage

0 5 10 25

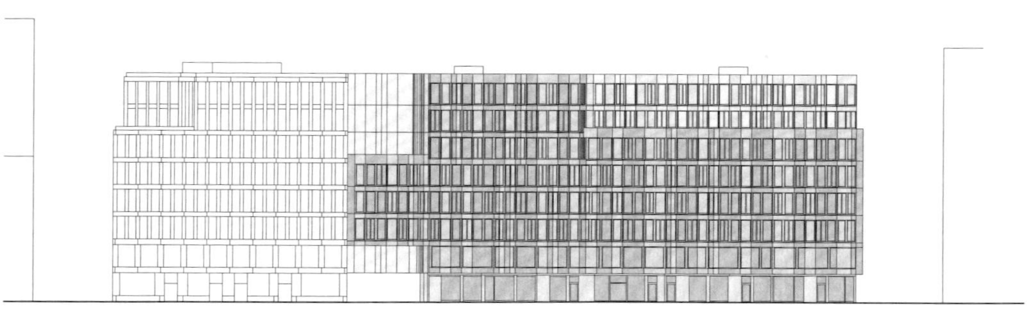

Elevation

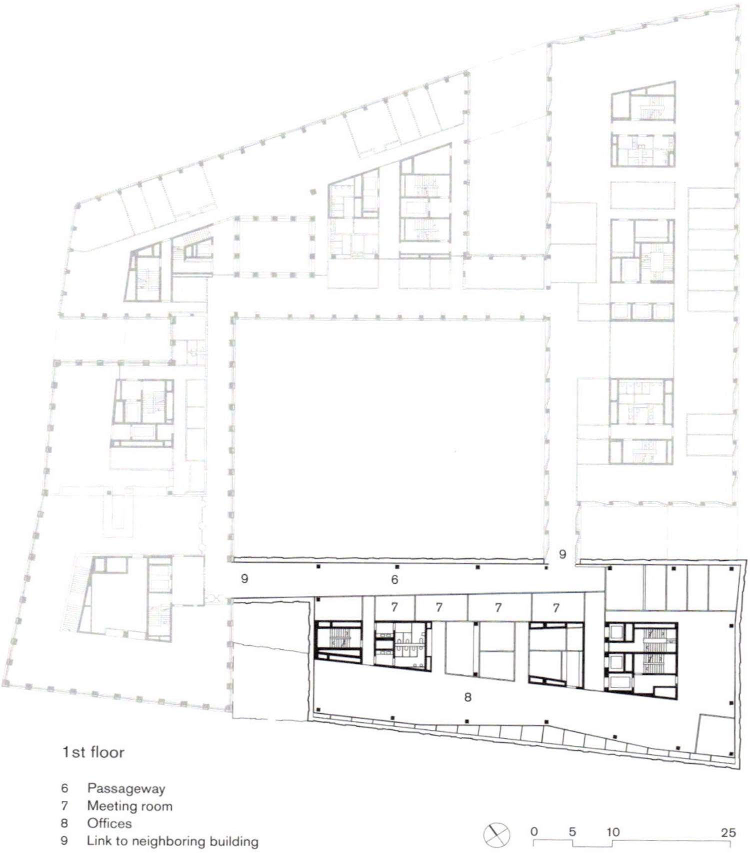

1st floor

6 Passageway
7 Meeting room
8 Offices
9 Link to neighboring building

Cafe

Foyer

Visualizations

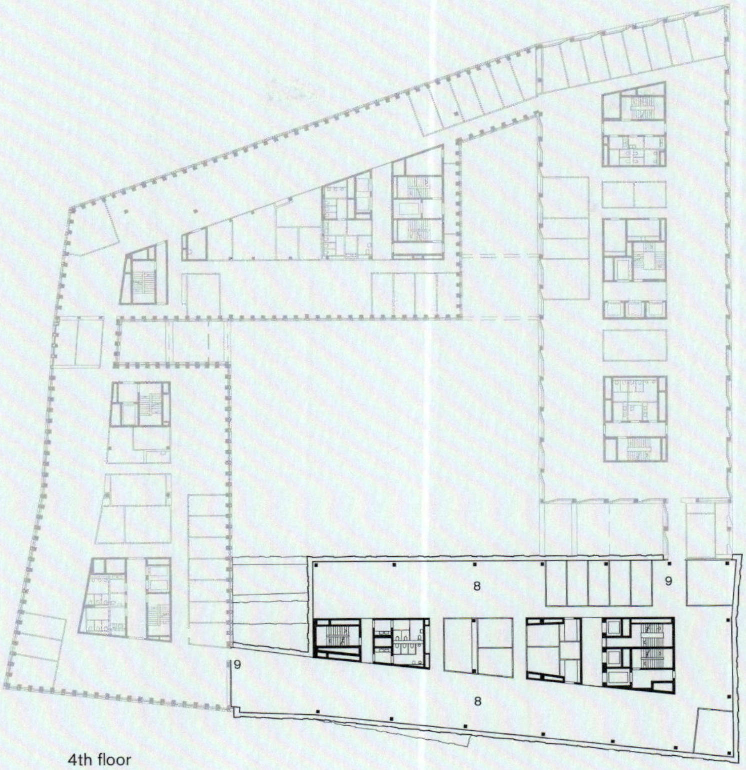

4th floor

Elevator area

1st floor passageway

LÖWENBRAU

Löwenbräu-Areal
Arts Center, Residential Tower, and Office Building, Zurich, Switzerland 118
2003–12

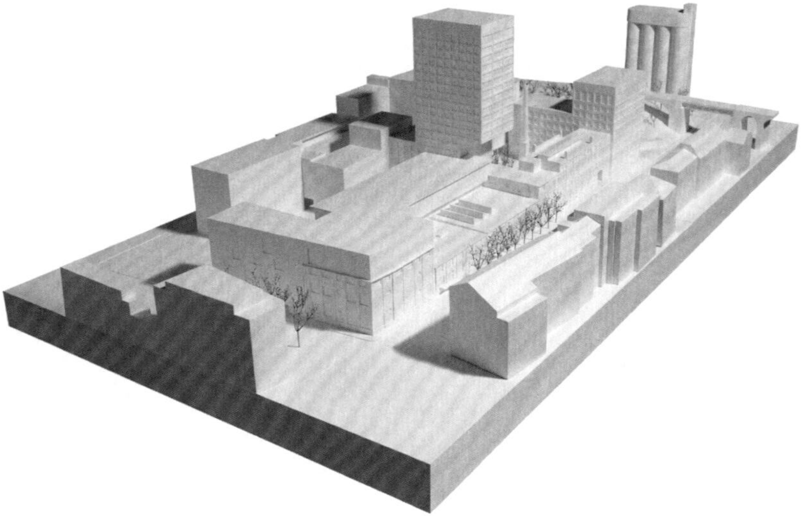

The history of the Löwenbräu complex, a former brewery, is one of frequent remodeling, adding on, and replacing parts of the existing buildings, whereby the change of use from a brewery to an art exhibition and gallery complex in the 1990s marked the crucial turning point. The new project is based on this most recent, successful conversion, while enhancing the variety of uses for this complex with new residential, office, and exhibition spaces. The preservation of the original historical building is an important step toward maintaining the identity of the former industrial district, rendering an important chapter in the city's history visible.

The concept for urban development here focuses on three structural changes in the form of new buildings within the existing complex: the *New West Building,* to offer additional space for the arts, the *New East Office Building,* and the *Central High-Rise Residential Building.* Together with the steel tower and the Swiss Mill silos, the high-rise residential building redefines the site's silhouette and—to a certain extent—even that of the city.

By adding buildings to the existing complex, a new urban ensemble can evolve—with the *Central High-Rise Residential Building* forming the focal point. The elongated, older structures with the former main brewery building on Limmatstrasse are framed by the addition of a further level on top of the Arts Center in the west and by the taller *New East Office Building* at the opposite end near the railway viaduct.

In future, the new Löwenbräu complex will be seen not just from the street and from a distance, but also from its two courtyards. The former *Brewer's Yard*—a listed historical site—provides access to the surrounding buildings as well as being a traffic-free outside space for relaxation. The new entrance to the art institutions is located in the open *Art Courtyard,* which also includes parking spaces for visitors and a delivery entrance.

Together with the entrance area to the art section and the additional story at this end of the complex, the *New West Building* projects at right angles and adjoins the former workshops on the courtyard side. It includes art exhibition rooms, guest accommodations, and offices. The exhibition spaces and a multi-function room can be partitioned as required. They are lit by side windows and are accessed directly from the entrance area to the art section. This entrance area has been conceived as a new, generously proportioned foyer with a staircase and elevators. The staircase is directly accessible from the lobby, which can be entered from Limmatstrasse or the courtyard.

The *Central High-Rise Residential Building,* with its large projection to the south, houses 37 apartments, one to four on each floor, which all face in several directions, affording views of the city, the lake, and the Limmat valley. The main volume of the high-rise is cantilevered out over a narrower base set in the *Brewer's Yard.* The 21 apartments in the base face southward onto the quiet courtyard. Service facilities are housed on the ground floor, in addition to a passageway between the two courtyards and the lobbies.

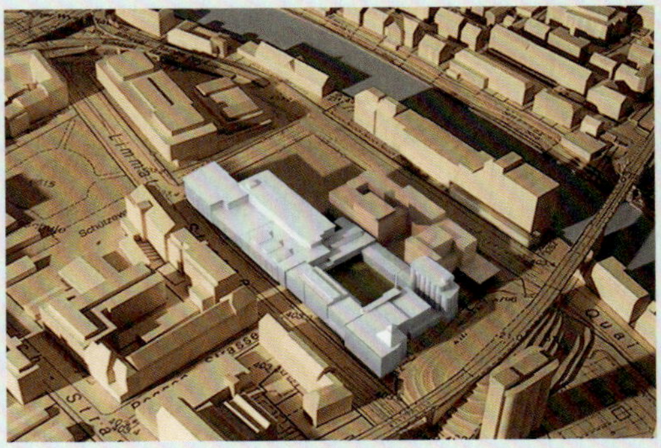

Existing buildings

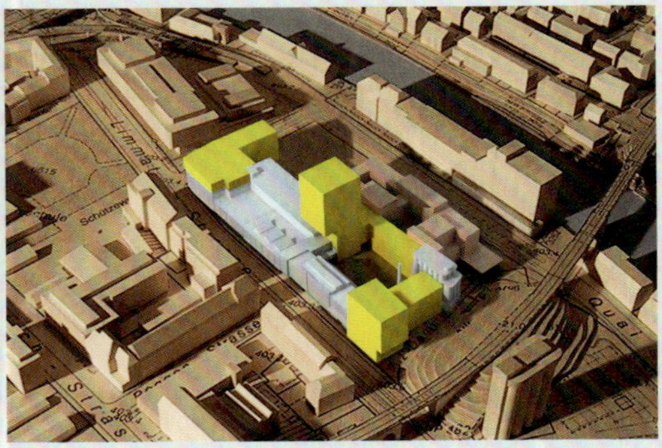

Project

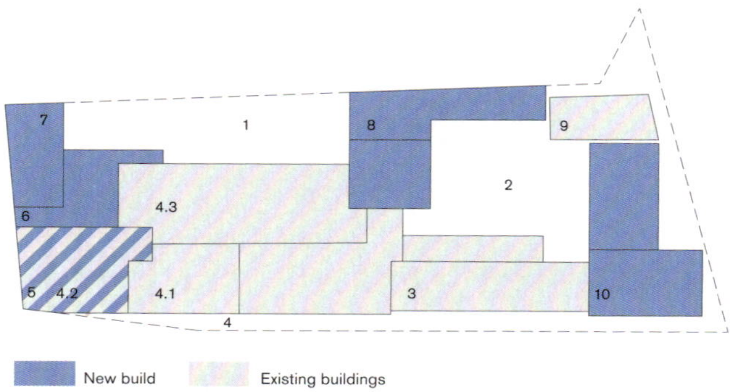

1 Art Courtyard
2 Brewer's Yard
3 Brewery, main building
4 Existing buildings
4.1 Keg room
4.2 Old workshops
4.3 Bottling plant
5 Arts Center added stories
6 Arts Center access area
7 Arts Center new build, west
8 Apartment high-rise, center
9 Silo
10 Office new build, east

The *New East Office Building* is also an angled structure with a higher section on Limmatstrasse and a lower segment between Dammweg and the *Brewer's Yard.* On the ground floor, the entrance lobby to the offices is located under the projection, whereas the gallery and retail spaces are accessed via the courtyard. The varied widths of the rooms on the upper office floors enable them to be adapted to suit a range of different office constellations. The façades of the *Central High-Rise Residential Building* and the *New East Office Building* are clad in molded ceramic elements with black and red glazed finishes that refer to the colored brickwork of the existing buildings. Double aluminum windows with additional ventilation slits comprise an external pane of plain glass and an inner pane of insulation glass with blinds in between. "Seasonal rooms" with specially designed windows that can be opened upwards provide a loggia-like outdoor space on sunny days.

The tower rises up above the row of various old and new buildings along Limmatstrasse as a dark, shimmering volume. The walls form grid patterns whose ceramic surfaces stand out from or merge with the window areas depending on the light, presenting a changing face to the city.

The red *New East Office Building* picks up on the fundamental character of the old buildings not only with regard to the materials used, but also in its coloration. The wavy structure, the gleaming materials, and the alignment of the windows, however, anchor the building firmly in the present.

The *New West Building* has been designed as a homogeneous, white concrete structure, insulated on the inside. The art spaces are equipped with box windows. While the new and old sections of this building are interwoven closely here in terms of their volumes and use, the material finish chosen for the addition sets it apart from the existing structure. A new ensemble is created that enables the expansive dimensions of the new volume to be clearly read and signals the presence of the arts within the complex.

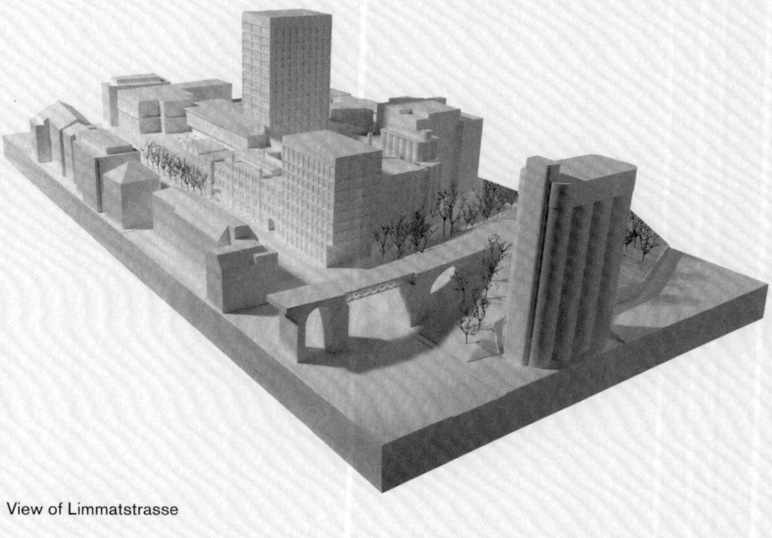

View of Limmatstrasse

2nd floor

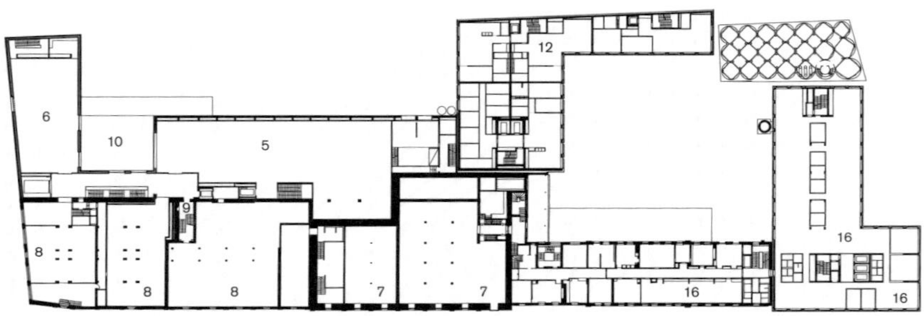

1st floor

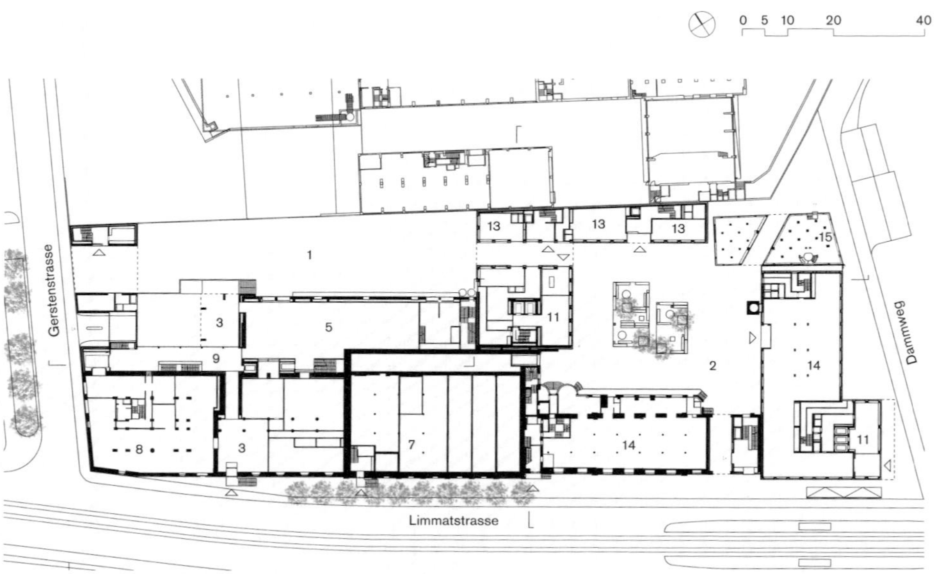

Ground floor

Löwenbräu-Areal—Arts Center, Residential Tower, and Office Building, Zurich, Switzerland

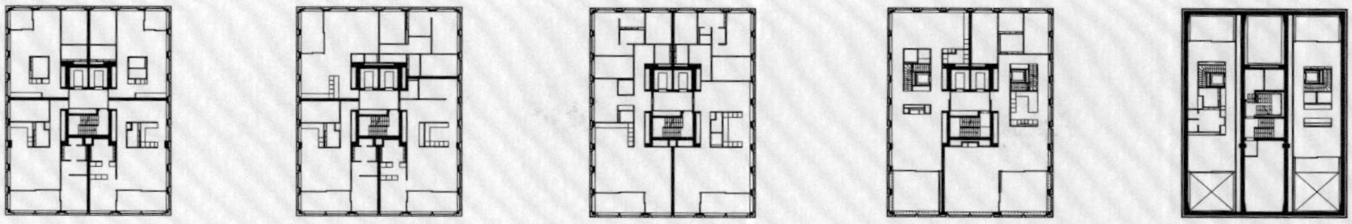

4 apartments
8th/11th

3 apartments
9th/12th/14th/15th/17th

2 apartments
10th/13th/16th/18th

Duplex
19th

Duplex
20th

Upper floors of apartment high-rise

1 Art courtyard
2 Brewery courtyard
3 Entrance area, art
4 Kunsthalle Zürich
5 Migros Museum
6 Artuma Holding
7 Daros Collection
8 Gallery
9 Access area, art
10 Terrace
11 Lobby
12 Accommodation
13 Commercial
14 Shop
15 Cafe
16 Offices
17 Silo

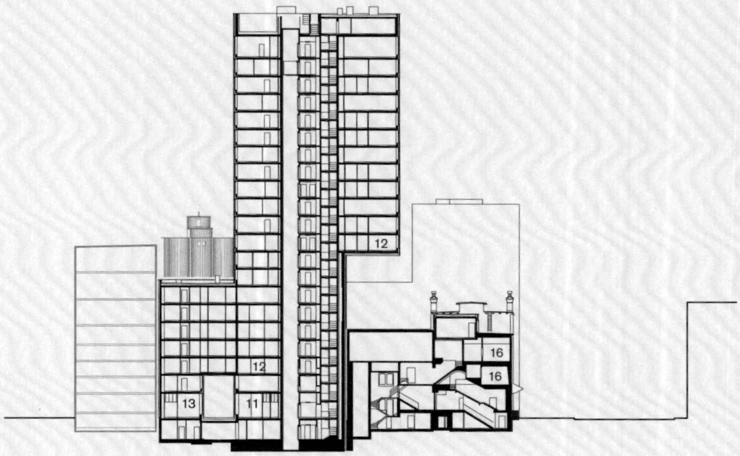

Cross section

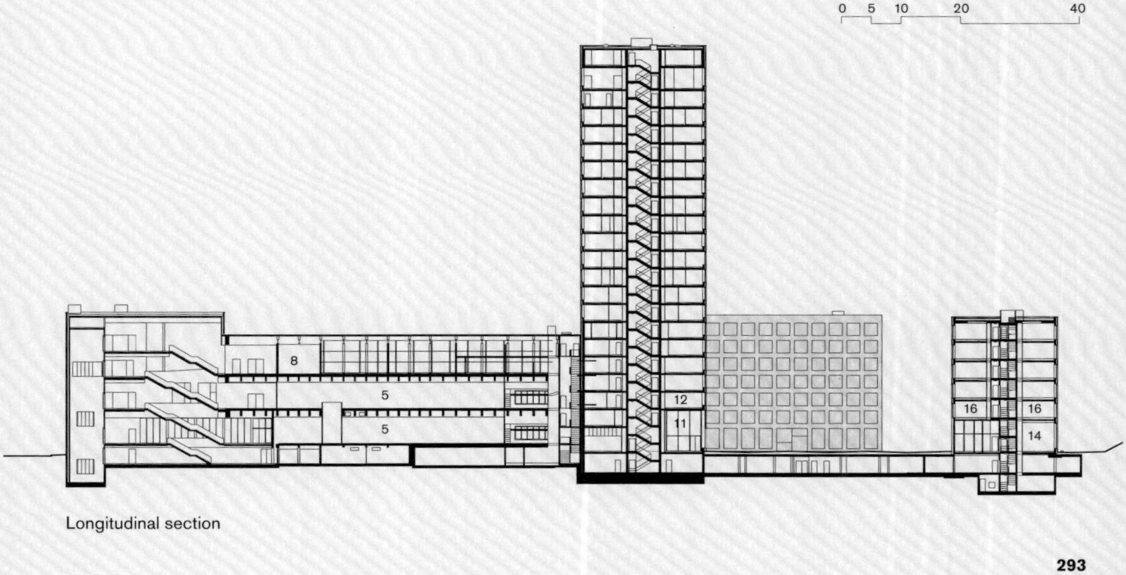

Longitudinal section

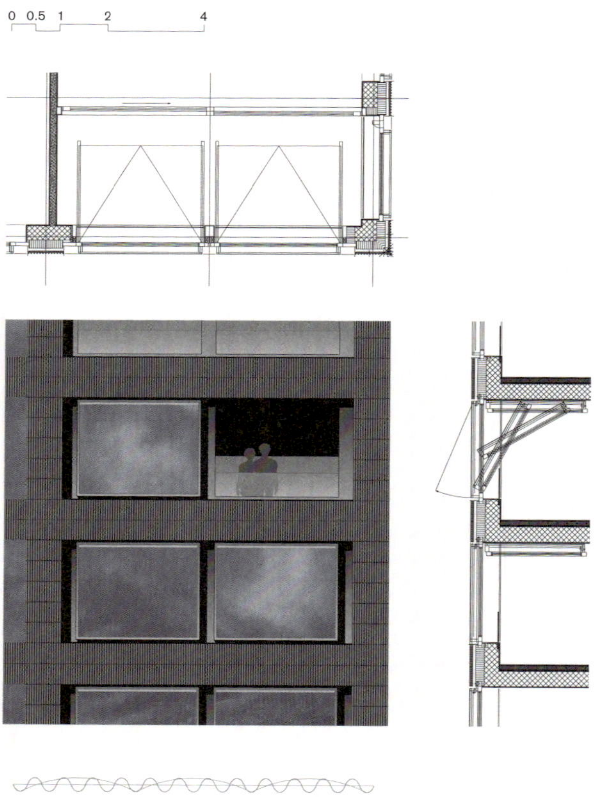

Façade of apartment high-rise, construction detail

Ceramic elements,
rear-ventilated façade cladding

Mock-up façade

Penthouse

Tower

Courtyard

Penthouse

Building site, 2011

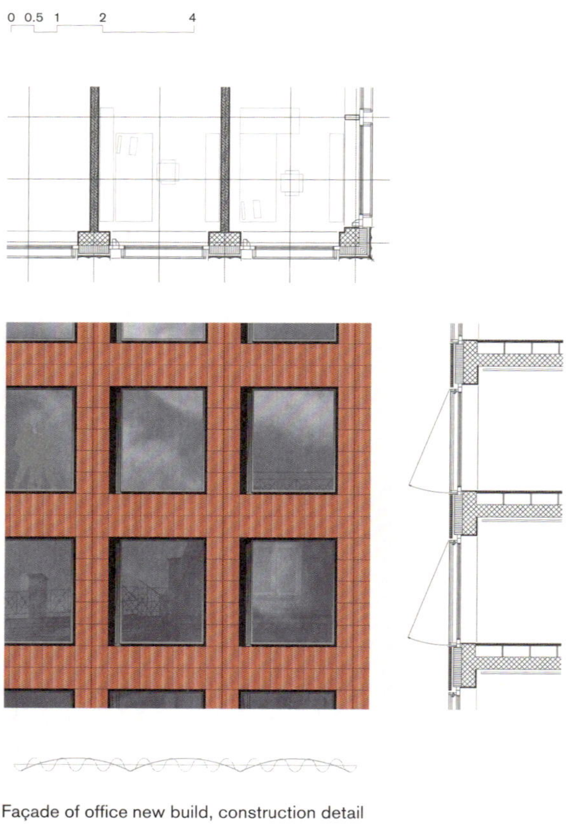

Façade of office new build, construction detail

Ceramic elements,
rear-ventilated façade cladding

Mock-up façade

"Blue Room," brewery, main building

Offices, new build, east

View from viaduct, Limmatstrasse

Merging of old and new

Exhibition space

Entrance to Arts Center on Limmatstrasse

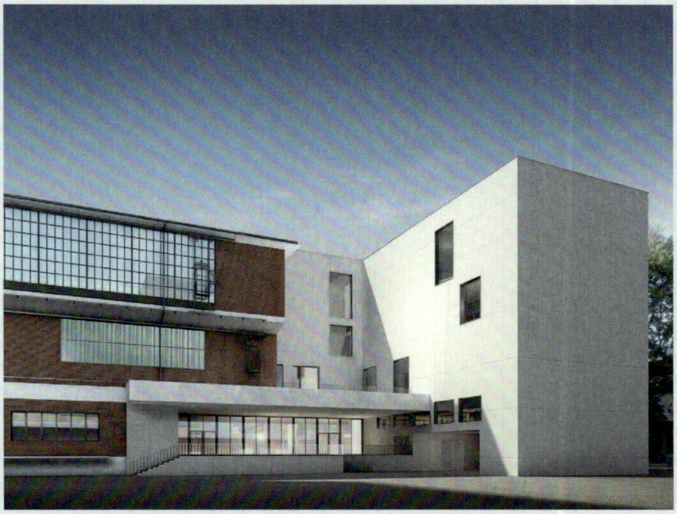

Courtyard entrance for deliveries

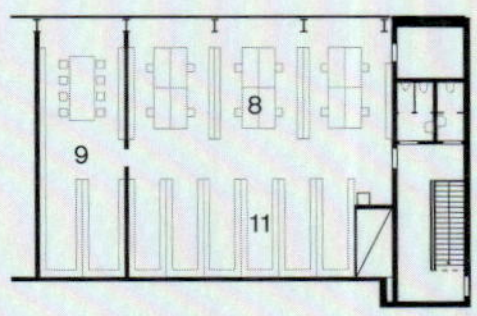

4th floor

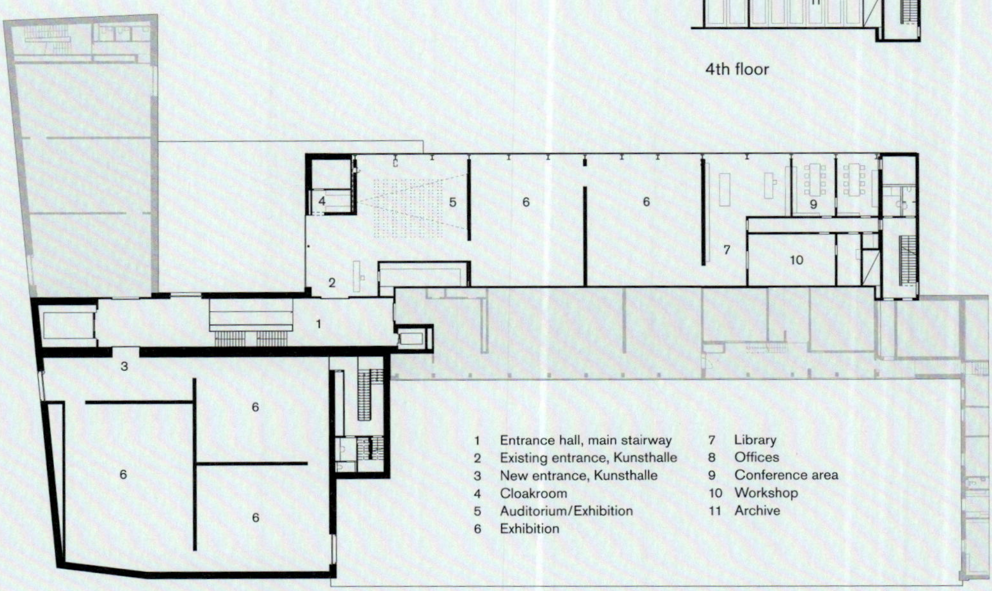

1 Entrance hall, main stairway
2 Existing entrance, Kunsthalle
3 New entrance, Kunsthalle
4 Cloakroom
5 Auditorium/Exhibition
6 Exhibition
7 Library
8 Offices
9 Conference area
10 Workshop
11 Archive

Kunsthalle, 3rd floor

REBUILDING

Forte, piano

On Some Conversions by Gigon/Guyer

Arthur Rüegg

Kirchner Museum Davos

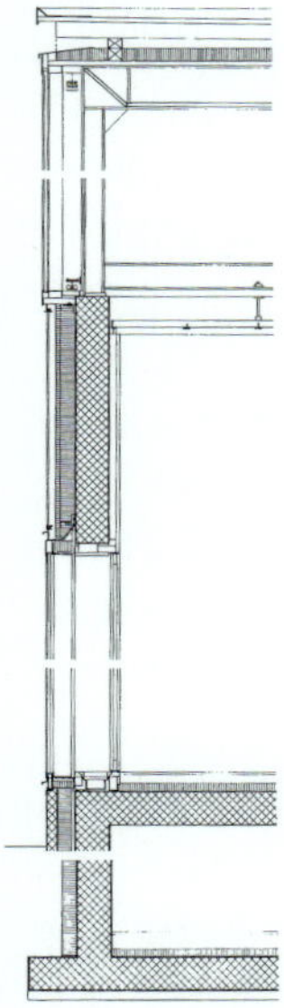

Section

Annette Gigon and Mike Guyer presented their first major exhibition in 1993, featuring just two completed buildings along with a smattering of material samples and a handful of projects, only one of which would ever be realized. That may not sound like very much. Yet with their Kirchner Museum 00A and their Restaurant Vinikus 00B—set barely three hundred meters apart on the lakeside promenade of the Swiss resort of Davos—they confidently outlined the parameters of a field that they would go on to plough with great success.

The museum and the restaurant represent two extremes —and not just in terms of function. On the one hand, there is the "white glass crystal, sparkling in a hard frame"[1] of the new museum building, its "hard, crystalline structure with regularly shaped planes shining in the Alpine light, shimmering and reflecting like sharply cut ice-cubes."[2] On the other hand, there is the restaurant: the conversion and extension of a complex of commercial buildings that had developed organically over the years along the watercourse of the Schiabach—a massive masonry-built structure with an irregular floor plan, perfectly molded into its surroundings. The existing single-story restaurant building had to be extended along the line dictated by the mountain stream in order to create a new space of adequate height. On one hand, this situation seemed to provide an excellent opportunity for architectural idealism, but it also placed enormous restraints on creativity, compounded by the imperative of exploiting maximum permitted lot coverage. Designing a new museum is the dream of every talented architect, but it does not necessarily follow that the task of converting commercial premises is little more than a compulsory exercise for pragmatically-minded specialists with legal and technical expertise.

The exhibition at the Architekturgalerie Luzern 00E and the beautiful catalogue that was published to accompany it are an eloquent manifesto against such hierarchal notions of architectural design. This is not because, as Johannes Gachnang wryly observed, "people are more interested these days in fine dining than fine art."[3] It is because Gigon/Guyer undertook both these projects with the same open-minded approach. Their express aim, as they have stated in relation to their most ambitious project so far—the Prime Tower in Zurich (p. 208)—is "for a building to emerge in this specific place whose height and shape, construction and materialization form a cohesive architecture that ... radiates."[4] This cohesion between the overall concept and the smallest detail can also be found in their two early buildings in Davos—both of which "radiate."

Kirchner Museum Davos, exhibition space

The Kirchner Museum is not an arbitrarily artistic product of creativity. In spite of being reduced to an abstract basic form, its crystalline exhibition spaces pay homage to the classical skylight galleries of the nineteenth century, incorporating all the elements of that era, including their distinctive materiality. The use of glass for the outer skin may suggest the dream of an Alpine architecture, or perhaps the smoothly polished stone cladding of nineteenth century urban buildings. Yet Gigon/Guyer's historical achievement lies in their ability to incorporate the then all-pervasive reality of layered façades and render it visible through the sense of depth created by the use of glass. In other words, they took the traditions of the vernacular and channeled them into the design process.

The themes for the renovation were derived primarily from the existing buildings, but their solutions were similar to those that would apply to a new building. For instance, when they were confronted with the need to create a façade that would fit in with the neighboring masonry, they chose a massive structure of high-insulation stonework. That meant exploring what was, at the time, a new alternative to the conventional façade system of substrate, insulation layer, and weatherproof finish, in order to achieve an unprecedented degree of thermal resistance. In this case, the interior of the restaurant itself is clad in large fiberboard panels, whose visually rhythmic seams recall the paneled walls of traditional Swiss inns. In the space between the inner wooden paneling and the exterior brickwork, there is room for the technical infrastructure—housing the services that are part of the genetic code, as it were, of such a project.

Restaurant Vinikus, elevation

Dining room

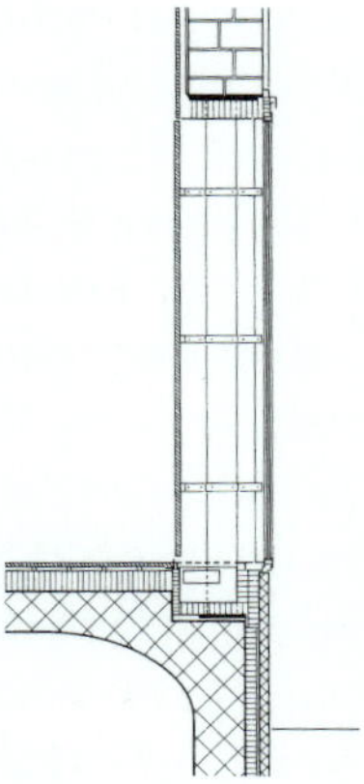

Section

While traditional themes enrich the modern architecture, the historic context of this conversion project is attenuated by contemporary structures and forms. Clearly, in their efforts to formulate an architectural character in extremely reduced form, the architects oscillate constantly between the two poles of abstraction (in the sense of modern art) and figuration (in the sense of traditional architecture). The procedure is subversive: what seems at first glance to be an excitingly abstract new building does have a strangely familiar look, while the unassuming conversion suddenly takes on an unexpected contemporaneity and presence. A glass front stretches the entire length of the façade on the ground floor of the Vinikus restaurant. Given the sheer mass of the masonry, it should not be there at all. A close-meshed steel frame bears the load. It is subtly integrated into the glasswork structure so that the side opening onto the Promenadenstrasse appears to be suspended in thin air. On driving into Davos, this slight visual distraction draws the gaze towards the obviously new structure and its huge, though delicate, lettering that spells out the name VINIKUS. The letters, half way up the building, are spread right across the full length of the glazed façade in a visual echo of the contemporary and exquisite character of the restaurant itself. The very fact that this has been created by leaving out parts of the finish—so that the letters shimmer through the thin coating in the form of raw rendering—merely reinforces the subversive sophistication of the architectural strategy.[5]

Basso continuo

Subsequent projects by the architects have demonstrated that this "phenomenological" approach—based only on the observation of the artifact—works equally well in dealing with the modification of historical buildings. The fundamental ideals, methods, and concepts of historic preservation,

Extension of Kunstmuseum Basel, 2001 competition, exhibition space

as outlined repeatedly by ETH Professor Georg Mörsch, indicate a certain trepidation with regard to an overly cavalier attitude towards historical architecture in which no monument appears to be safe from "purification, improvement and reconstruction."[6] If the historic substance is not to become a mere fossil, frozen in time, the pros and cons of remodeling have to be weighed up. This can sometimes involve so much red tape that architects become unwitting opponents.

In June 2001, Gigon/Guyer won the design competition for the coveted project of restructuring and extending the Kunstmuseum Basel (p. 330), which had arisen thanks to a gift of the former National Bank building, known as the Laurenzbau. Their design was based on the premise of retaining as much as possible of the existing architecture while avoiding any kind of visual competition with it. The core element of the design proposal was a pavilion-style extension occupying the open space between the former banking hall of the Laurenzbau and the adjacent, private garden of the Zum Raben building.[7] The subtly formulated extension, illuminated by box-mold windows with etched glazing, was to comprise six large rooms, with basement workshops and storage areas intended to relieve the pressure on the old buildings. However, before the project moved ahead, the plan to add this extension was scrapped, which meant that the architects had to focus entirely on modifying the 1936 Kunstmuseum designed by Paul Bonatz and Rudolf Christ and the Laurenzbau, built some ten years earlier to a design by Suter & Burckhardt.

If the conversion of these two superb buildings can be described as masterful, then it is precisely thanks to the talent that Annette Gigon and Mike Guyer showed in their open-minded, phenomenological analysis of the existing architecture and their ability to identify its spatial potential. Although the architects respect the buildings as historical monuments, they are also acutely aware of contemporary needs and see an important cultural duty in bridging the differences between them.

Accordingly, they made it a priority to create a coherent balance between the spatial structure and the functions it had to fulfill. That involved seeking appropriate uses for

Kunstmuseum Basel, window to the bar

Laurenzbau Library, reading room

the existing historical rooms while at the same time defining spaces suitable for, say, temporary exhibitions and hospitality areas. The architects recognized the potential of the cloister, which had hitherto been used to house the wardrobe and refreshment facilities. They disencumbered the existing structure and, with only a few simple adjustments—even retaining the single-glazed, bronze-framed windows—turned it into a wonderfully atmospheric space for the presentation of contemporary sculpture. They moved the museum cafe into the narrow library corridor, which they opened up to the main courtyard with elegant French windows aligned precisely with the existing pillars. The result is so entirely in keeping with the spirit of the building that it might have sprung directly from the drawing board of Bonatz and Christ themselves. The library rooms facing the rear courtyard, once a crowded mass of shelving and books, were transformed into a series of generously dimensioned exhibition spaces, while the library itself found a suitable new home on the ground floor of the Laurenzbau. The high-ceilinged entrance hall of the museum was decluttered and cleared of its shelves, booktables, and postcard-stands, and a contemporary museum shop installed in the adjacent low-ceilinged magazine room of the former library. The cloakrooms were moved from the cloister to a corridor with a now redundant stairway entrance.

As a result, the necessary alterations—from repainting to reconstruction to redesign—proved a logical consequence of this fusion of spatial and functional hierarchies. The spatial configurations of the main courtyard/entrance hall and stairway/cloister are now restored to their original state, while ancillary spaces such as the cloakrooms and shop have been provided with new built-in furnishings. One particularly ambitious aspect of the project was the transformation of the former banking hall in the Laurenzbau into the library reading room, following several of the approaches described by Mörsch. The mahogany wall paneling, the stucco cassette ceiling and the star-shaped central skylight were all left intact and merely repaired. The magnificent double swing doors with their zigzag mahogany glazing bars, on the other hand, are a modern replica of

Kunstmuseum Basel, entrance hall after renovation

Kunstmuseum Basel, entrance hall before renovation

the original. The fitted carpet was replaced by new strip parquet flooring in dark acacia wood framed by a border of stone and carefully stained to match the original woodwork of the room. Contrasting subtly with this sumptuous and exquisitely ornamental setting is a mix of mass-produced metal shelving and custom-built, uncompromisingly cuboid furnishings. The new lamps and the green library armchairs, developed in collaboration with designer Hannes Wettstein especially for this space, are in fact veritable pieces of industrial design.

Using the opposing principles of integration and contrast, Annette Gigon and Mike Guyer have defined not only the character of the new library reading room, but of all the newly refurbished rooms throughout the Kunstmuseum. What's more, they have enhanced the atmosphere through attention to seemingly minor details that convey a confidently contemporary aesthetic above and beyond their actual function. Their abstract forms—such as the coat-hooks that fold out of the brass cladding in the wardrobe area—combine aesthetic clarity with a generous pinch of playful wit. Such details bear eloquent witness to what Claude Lichtenstein has described as a manifesto of "subtlety, concealment, discovery, control of the situation, and a dexterous handling of rules."[8] Such details permeate the entire building complex, resonating like the *basso continuo* of a finely-tuned architecture. They make even the empty, seemingly untouched entrance hall appear more crystalline, colorful, and fresh than ever before. Amid the gravitas of Bonatz' and Christ's architecture, the slender rods of light between the renovated ribs of the concrete ceiling, the sharply defined, dark volume of the reception area, the minimalist black leather benches,[9] and the bright information screen create an almost subversive effect. This same effect is also translated to the old ashlar face in what is perhaps the most brilliant coup of all: the architects have opened up the museum to the street by means of six heavy, dark brass frames. The first four frames give an indirect view into the interior in the form of brightly lit posters announcing the current exhibitions. The fifth and largest frame invites visitors to step into the bistro, its shady arcades providing a view into the depths of the sculpture courtyard. The sixth frame, set at an angle, is the window of the cafe and bar. This subtle framing of the new functions is underpinned by the sculptural effect of the gray stairway/ramp that seems to emerge out of the reddish sandstone flooring, its simple metal handrail deviating subtly from the conventional in an echo of the architects' playful wit.

Traditional garden pavilion with trellis

Tony Smith, *For P.C.*, 1969, bronze, 164 × 208 × 152 cm

Capriccio

The approach taken in remodeling these two well-preserved palazzi in Basel follows a remarkably similar pattern to that adopted by the architects in the modest and anonymous context of their Davos conversion. In spite of the presence of such strongly historic architectures, they manage to introduce a remarkable wealth of architectural inventiveness. Compared to the Basel museum complex, however, the late neoclassicist Villa Annamaria in Kastanienbaum (p. 340), built in 1860 as a summer residence in a large park overlooking Lake Lucerne, offered considerably more leeway. This Italianate villa, presumably built by Franz Xaver Waller, underwent radical interior remodeling in 1927, when a rather awkward kitchen wing was also added. This raised a number of questions concerning the historical value of such modifications—questions that often give even the preservation authorities themselves a headache. Should a building that has been remodeled be returned to its original state and then gently adapted to its new function? Or does the state

Villa Kastanienbaum, extension, 2004

Villa Kastanienbaum, extension built in 1927

that has gradually developed over time bear more authentic witness to the course of history?

When Gigon/Guyer first took on this project, plans had been made in keeping with the latter approach but this proved a dead end—mainly because the kitchen extension was unsuitable for the proposed conversion to garages. Right from the start, the architects suggested replacing the unsightly addition. By contrast, they retained the heavy cassette ceiling that had been installed in 1927 when the salon was enlarged. Such a pragmatically phenomenological selection can only succeed if it is combined with extraordinary knowledge and ability, as well as great appreciation of the building itself. Gigon/Guyer's affinity for the original building is evident, for instance, in their handling of the windows, where they not only repaired the delicate original frames, but also retained the old, hand-made panes of glass wherever possible. Throughout the building, features were revealed, refurbished, and repaired with painstaking care, always with the intent of allowing the original materials and finishes to speak for themselves. In the turret room, the client and architects even decided, after stripping the wallpaper, that the original raw plaster should be left just as they found it, with its tattoo-like stencil markings, scribbles, and craftsmen's notes. In this enchanting little chamber even the old doorlock facings have been left untouched.

Anyone familiar with the finer points of architectural preservation, as applied in other restoration projects, will probably judge the originality of the work primarily on the basis of the new additions. The heavy cassette ceiling of the grand salon initially posed something of a challenge, which was overcome quite brilliantly. The richly textured plasterwork, aligned with the tectonics of the beams, probably seemed to Gigon/Guyer an all too figurative element that definitely needed to be offset by a certain degree of abstraction (echoes of the two projects in Davos). To this end, they came up with a golden *cheminée* sculpture of polished brass that hits just the right balance between abstraction and figuration, and eliminates the somewhat musty feeling of the salon. In variations on the same theme, the black metal chimney on the upper floor is shaped to

Enlarged salon, 1927

Salon with fireplace built in 2004

form a heat source and cooking area, while the demolition of the kitchen annex was compensated by a compact chromium steel unit. The exhaust hood over the freestanding kitchen island also takes the form of an abstract metal sculpture, reiterating the principle of cuboid forms as the underlying theme of the new fittings. When it comes to sophisticated solutions, function does not lag behind form: instead of the steam being extracted upwards through three stories to the roof, it is channeled just one floor down and expelled through the cellar. Even the bathroom has a freestanding cuboid chromium steel bathtub. All the other wet room fittings, including the doors, are incorporated into a dado-height wall covering of engraved mirror glass. In one corner of the room, there are two glass surfaces that can be folded out of the wall covering to create a shower cabinet.

The absolute highlight of this playful approach to the artifact is surely the new extension housing such utilitarian functions as garages and a workshop. As these specific functional requirements were not, in themselves, enough to define the architectural structure, Gigon/Guyer set about creating a whole series of smaller models to shape a complex entity with a shell of metal latticework enveloping the low-level annex and protruding above its roof height in the form of a pergola. Given that the Villa Annamaria already had a cuboid floor plan, a simple cuboid form would have been inappropriate for the extension. Instead, the irregular grid-like structure pierced by window apertures recalls a garden pavilion and is, at the same time, redolent of a crystalline Minimal Art sculpture—once again both abstract and familiar. Even the olive hues of the concrete and metal resonate in the sandstone of the main building and the various green tones of the villa's mature and flourishing gardens.

Contrapunto

Elegant responses were found to a number of different challenges: the Villa Annamaria is the Capriccio in this trio of converted buildings. "Suppleness, visual feast, insight, and serenity!" is how Annette Gigon sums up the effect that the architects sought to achieve as a refreshing respite

University of Zurich, transverse hall originally used as sculpture gallery

Socioeconomic institute in the transverse hall, c. 1996

from the usual run-of-the-mill conservational aims. These concepts could just as easily apply to the new Auditorium Maximum of Zurich University (p. 320), even though the problems they faced there were entirely different. "We'll probably always aim to create a building as a cohesive unit—in terms of material, structure, and color. But the interesting thing is that, because each project is so different, this approach actually leads to a wide variety of architectural solutions."[10] (Annette Gigon)

Together with Gottfried Semper's adjacent Polytechnic, the collegiate building of the university, built between 1911 and 1914 by architects Robert Curjel and Karl Moser, crowns the city's skyline. Today, it is mainly used as a teaching center by the institutes and seminars of the faculty of philosophy, though it also houses some departments of the central administration as well as canteen facilities. As part of an overall refurbishment plan, the cantonal building department commissioned Gigon/Guyer in 1996 to design an additional auditorium. At first, the architects sought to articulate this major undertaking in the form of an overground glass cube that would create a landmark entrance to the building.[11] This approach failed—probably quite rightly—due to conservational concerns.

Today, there are only a few subtly formulated outward clues to the auditorium, which has been developed out of the terrace and slotted in between the façade overlooking the valley, the existing canteen, and the supporting wall on

Transverse hall used as lecture hall foyer, after 2003

Künstlergasse. Once again, it was careful analysis of the existing structure that provided the solution—a solution so logical that even considering the possible alternatives seems pointless. The baseline of the design relates to the hall set transversely in front of the main atrium—formerly filled with the socioeconomic institute's books—which has now become the entrance area. Two double-flight stairways set between the cross-vault lead down into the basement, where stepped seating for an audience capacity of about 500 follows the slope of the hill. A concrete ceiling with prestressed joists, its height carefully calculated to ensure maximum structural integrity, spans the 23-meter width of the room. Hollow spaces within the joists are used to conceal the cabling. Across the entire breadth of the wall facing the valley, daylight is channeled directly towards the speaker's lectern through a long skylight ribbon.

The simple, rectangular interior is entirely clad in panels that double as sound insulation on the back wall of the auditorium. On the right-hand wall, the panels protrude slightly to counter any flutter-echo effect. In addition to these technical considerations, the interior cladding also serves an aesthetic function. As in the Vinikus restaurant, it conceals the technical infrastructure. This is undoubtedly its true raison d'être: only by concealing all the obvious functional forms does the room acquire its abstract appearance as a counterpoint to the elaborate late Jugendstil architecture of the collegiate building. The rows of box-like

Atrium, University of Zurich

lamps and the stepped sequence of long, cuboid writing desks turn the auditorium into a richly articulated sculpture. In the transverse hall of the collegiate building, the inner cladding of the auditorium is foreshadowed by the stairwells spanned between the (incidentally, hollow) pillars of the vaulting.

The architecture of this inner shell could be expressed in a number of different ways. One option would be the undisguised materiality of the paneling, as in the Vinikus restaurant; another would be embellishment with beautiful veneer, as in the library of the Kunstmuseum in Basel. In this instance, Gigon/Guyer chose to enlist the power of color. Together with the artist Adrian Schiess, who is also a personal friend, they developed a project of "art for architecture" that embraces both the exterior and the interior of the building. On the outside, the luminous pink tone of the water basin in the middle of the terrace, parallel to the long and narrow skylight, references the auditorium below.[12] The color is particularly striking because it is so unexpected—pink being on the opposite end of the color spectrum from the green that is normally used in such situations—and creates a very special effect in combination with the water feature designed by Moser. Along the narrow alleyway known as Künstlergasse, the new supporting walls consist of red-pigmented concrete, layered so that the pigmentation (8 per cent at the lowest level) becomes increasingly light towards the top (graduating from 4 to 2 and finally 0.5 per cent). In the finished building, the irregular layers of different colors used in the concreting process have an aesthetic impact.[13] These layers also link the otherwise homogeneous concrete wall with the older ashlar masonry of the supporting walls in the university complex. Finally, the increasingly vibrant hue of red towards the lower section of the wall also references the theme of gravity, which is omnipresent in the architecture of the collegiate building.

Pigmented walls

The use of color, so subtly applied on the exterior, takes on an entirely unexpected intensity inside the auditorium. All the wall and ceiling paneling is lacquered in dark pink, pale pink, blue, or grayish-green. The grass-green writing desks and chairs are mirrored in the highly polished finishes

Auditorium

and the golden reflections shining in the glazing of the interpreters' booths heighten the play of interacting colors still further, creating an overwhelming and constantly changing overall impression. Adrian Schiess related his choice of color directly to Karl Moser's palette—not only to the Great Hall with its register of reddish and ochre tones, but also to the green-hued transverse hall forming the antechamber of the new auditorium, where the intense pink of the lacquer-finished stairwells so clearly announce the subterranean world of color in which all spatial boundaries dissolve. Celebratory, intimate, transcendent—these are the descriptions that spring to mind. The riot of color turns the almost perfectly square and self-reflexive room into the modern equivalent of Moser's architectural imaginings. Here we find a counterpoint, a different voice—as in the theory of music—that thrives on the mastery of consonance and dissonance.

1 See *Die Gläserne Kette. Visionäre Architektur aus dem Kreis um Bruno Taut 1919–1920,* exh. cat. Museum Schloss Morsbroich, Leverkusen, 1963, cited in Arthur Rüegg, "Abstrakt - vertraut. Zur Architektur des Kirchner Museums" in: *Werkstoff. Annette Gigon, Mike Guyer,* exh. cat. Architekturgalerie Luzern, Lucerne, 1993, pp. 5–8.

2 Ibid., p. 5.

3 Johannes Gachnang, cited in *Werkstoff* 1993 (see note 1), p. 15.

4 Annette Gigon and Mike Guyer, interview with tox./ak., "Der Prime Tower übernimmt die Funktion eines Flaggschiffs." *Neue Zürcher Zeitung,* no. 235, 8 October 2008.

5 The building has since been repainted. All descriptions in this article refer to the original state. Where necessary, any discrepancies are pointed out in the footnotes.

6 Georg Mörsch, *Aufgeklärter Widerstand. Das Denkmal als Frage und Aufgabe,* Basel: Birkhäuser Verlag, 1989, p. 117.

7 See the publication of the competition project in *Projekte. Gigon/Guyer,* Lucerne: Quart Verlag, 2004, pp. 18–21.

8 See Claude Lichtenstein, *Klarheit und Spielwitz. Schweizer Architektur, Grafik und Design 1950–2006,* Baden: Lars Müller Publishers, 2006, p. 8. The Zurich University auditorium by Gigon/Guyer is discussed on pp. 218–221.

9 The seating designed by Jasper Morrison has since been replaced.

10 Annette Gigon in conversation with Rahel Hartmann, *Neue Zürcher Zeitung,* 1 November 2002.

11 See "'Kunst am Bau' im Hörsaal." *Neue Zürcher Zeitung,* 8 November 2002.

12 The pink has since been replaced by a less light-sensitive yellow pigment.

13 See Esther Hodel and Reto Gadola, "Rosa" in: Arthur Rüegg, Reto Gadola, Daniel Spillmann, and Michael Widrig, *Die Unschuld des Betons, Wege zu einer materialspezifischen Architektur,* Zurich: gta Verlag, 2004, pp. 82–85.

Auditorium, University of Zurich, Switzerland 011
1996/1999–2002

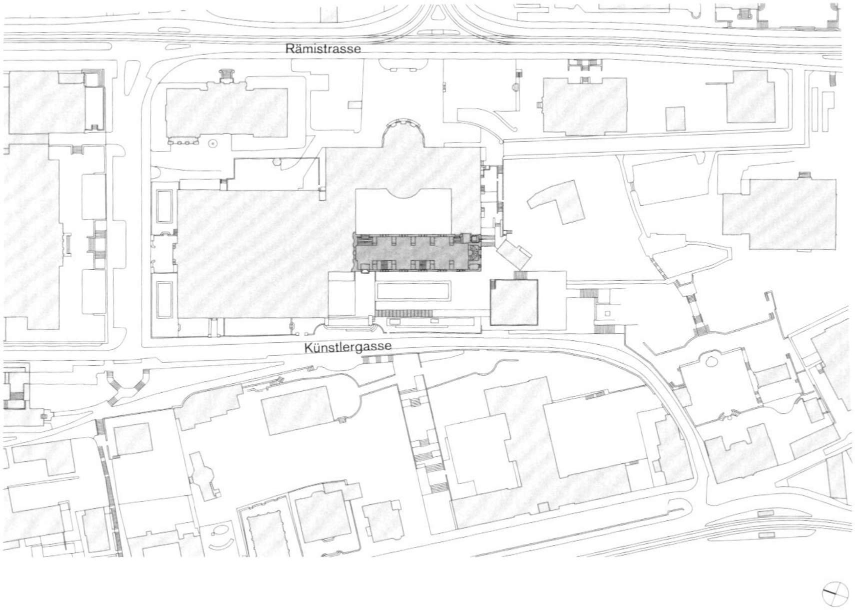

A new, large auditorium that seats 500 people was constructed under the terrace on the valley side of the university building designed by Karl Moser in 1913/1914. The space serves both as a new auditorium and a second assembly hall. On weekends and during semester breaks it can also function as a conference hall for third-party rentals.

The auditorium is accessed via the former sculpture gallery on the ground floor. This space was previously used as an institute library and can be directly approached from outside and inside the university. The open gallery now functions as a lobby, with stairs in the alcoves of the vaulting leading down to the auditorium. Another wheelchair-accessible entrance and an elevator are located on the cafeteria side of the building.

Inside the auditorium the walls and ceiling are faced with colored panels, analogous to the spirit of the original interior design of the Moser building. The panels provide acoustic absorption and cladding for ventilation and electrical services. The artist Adrian Schiess designed the color scheme for the auditorium, consisting of light and dark pink, as well as tones of light blue and gray-green. To emphasize the festive quality of the space, the glass of the interpreters' booths is printed with golden reflective patterns.

A skylight above the white projection wall provides the space underneath with daylight. Outside, both the raised skylight and a pool centered on the terrace indicate the presence of the auditorium below. The strong color of the basin contradicts conventional expectations of a natural green, which is used for the ponds in the neighboring gardens of the university. The basin with its reflective surface and artificial color resembles an independent, horizontal sculpture.

The walls facing the Künstlergasse consist of concrete poured in successive layers of various hues, from dark to light, which also references the "space-containing" nature of the base. The top layers of the wall are only faintly pigmented, and the concrete surface of the terrace and the concrete rim of the basin are left in their natural tone. These thus form a contrast with the pure, strong color of the basin.

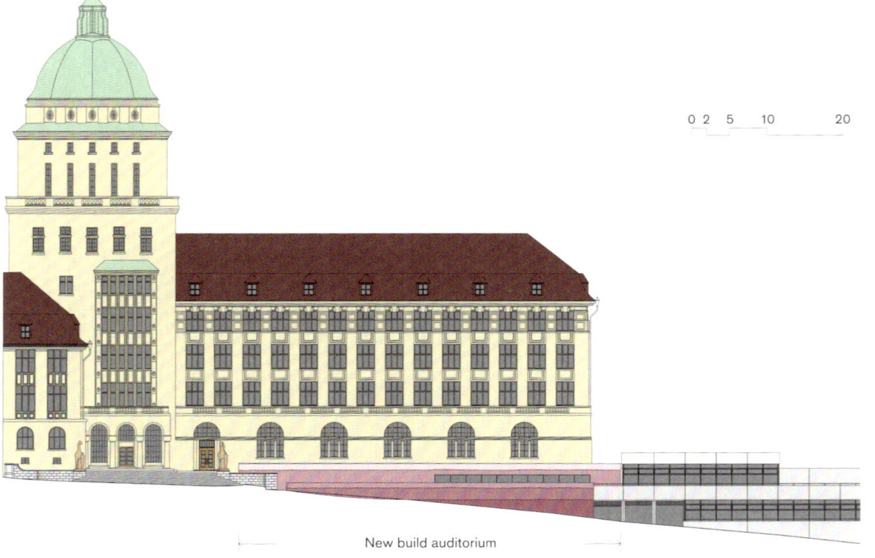

Elevation

Color studies in cast concrete

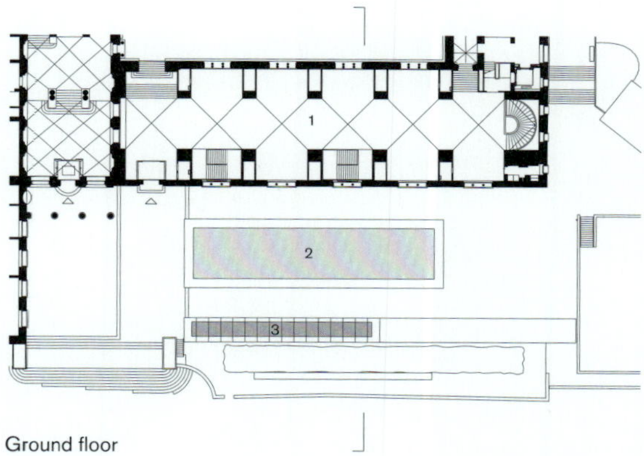

Ground floor

1 Foyer
2 Pool
3 Skylight
4 Auditorium
5 Interpreters' booths
6 Projection room

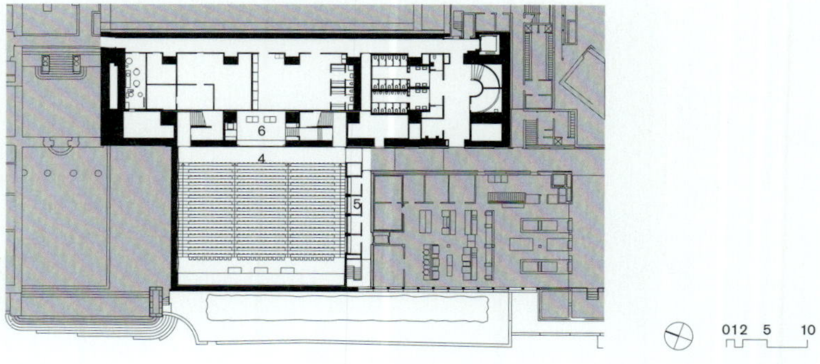

Lower floor

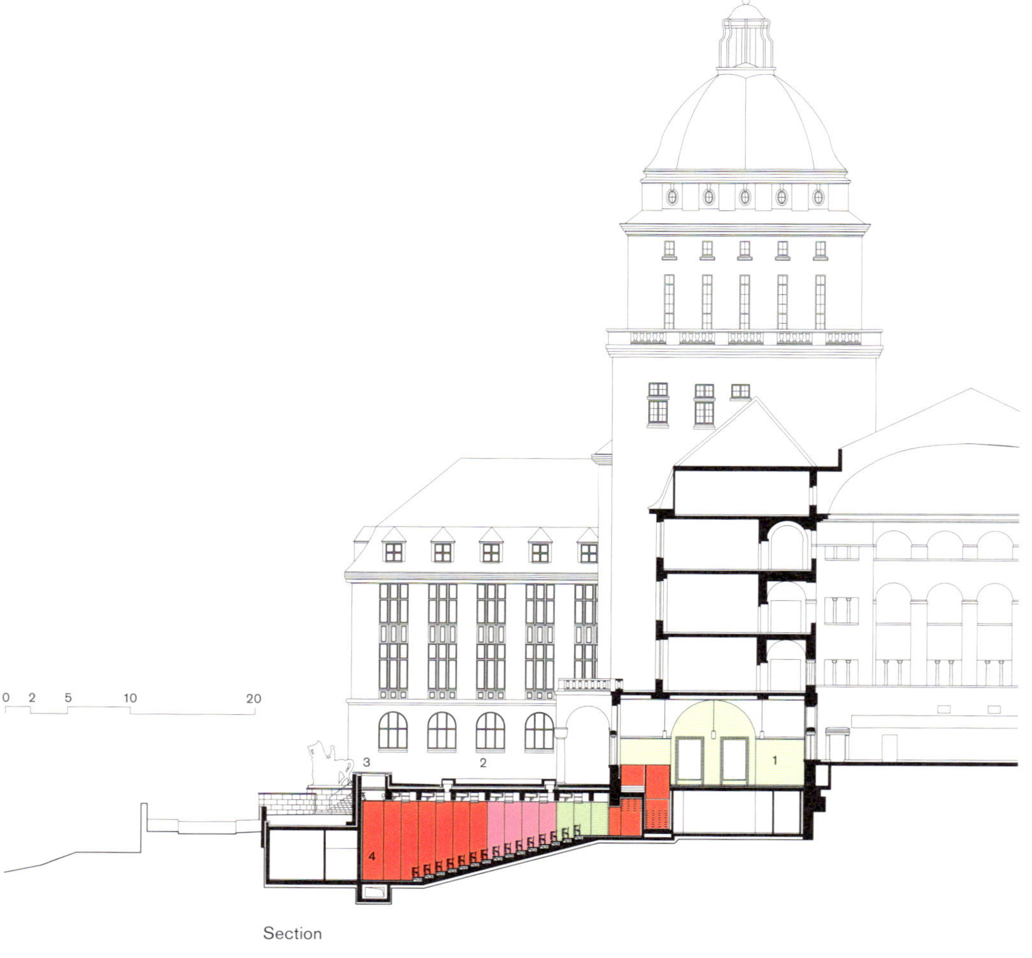

Section

Color sketch by Adrian Schiess

Remodeling of Kunstmuseum Basel and Laurenzbau Library, Switzerland 095

2001 / 2003–07

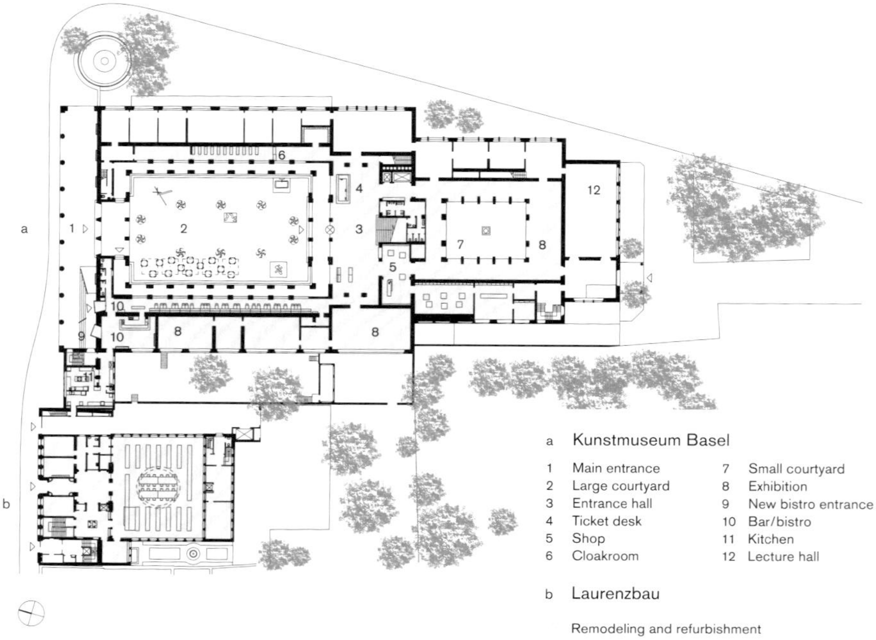

a Kunstmuseum Basel

1	Main entrance	7	Small courtyard
2	Large courtyard	8	Exhibition
3	Entrance hall	9	New bistro entrance
4	Ticket desk	10	Bar/bistro
5	Shop	11	Kitchen
6	Cloakroom	12	Lecture hall

b Laurenzbau

Remodeling and refurbishment

The expansion of the Kunstmuseum Basel into the neighboring former bank building enabled important improvements to be made to the spatial organization of the museum building and allowed additional exhibition space to be created. Both historic buildings—the Kunstmuseum, constructed in 1936 by the architects Rudolf Christ and Paul Bonatz, and the Laurenzbau, formerly home to the National-bank and built in 1926 by the architects Suter & Burckhardt—were in need of structural modifications in several areas in order to fulfill their new functions. The plan to build an extension for temporary exhibitions, as considered during the 2001 competition, was abandoned.

The character and extent of the various restructuring measures ranged from the creation of new spatial relationships to the reconstruction of original conditions, and also included light restorative retouching. The reconstruction work was carried out in various stages in order not to disrupt the functioning of the museum.

In the museum building, the former library rooms were converted into exhibition spaces and a bistro. Large new display cases, doors, and windows in the arcades open up the museum to the street and provide a welcoming countenance for museum visitors and restaurant clients. A gray sandstone staircase and ramp rises from the red-gray veined sandstone flooring of the arcades and leads to the entrance of the new bistro. The narrow former library hallway now functions as the bistro's dining area. Sitting on the elongated leather sofa, the guests look through the glazed doors at the comings and goings in the great sculpture and entrance court. In the adjoining bar, the focal point is the bar itself, which is made of highly polished brass. This treatment of the material produces a striking contrast to the matt, dark brown tones of the related material, architectural bronze, used for the windows and doors—this is true of both the historic elements and the new additions.

The gallery encircling the small courtyard and the high entrance hall were only gently renovated, with all interventions designed to restore the hall's function as the central starting point and orientation area for all visitor services. The few modifications to this space included a light wash of paint, new lighting, and the island-like placement of the ticket desk. Freeing up the gallery around the small courtyard on the ground floor represents a further important strategy in this reconstruction project. This gallery corridor was historically used as an exhibition space, but over the years it has also accommodated a cafe and cloakroom. Provided with new lighting, freshly stuccoed walls and ceilings, and a reduced number of door openings, the gallery now forms a generous exhibition space for contemporary sculpture and reliefs.

Façade opened up to the large courtyard

Bistro in former library corridor

Former library corridor

> Exhibition space, hallway around small courtyard

Hallway around small courtyard with cafeteria and cloakroom before remodeling

Exhibition space, former reading room

The library reading room was relocated to the imposing central bank hall of the neighboring Laurenzbau with its mahogany wall paneling, stuccoed ceiling, and huge central skylight. The glazed pivoting door was reconstructed and the heavily damaged stone floor was replaced with acacia parquet. The glass skylight remains the room's main source of natural light and now illuminates the reading tables positioned below it. The new furniture in the reading room consists on the one hand of standard metal bookcases and on the other of purpose-built counters, tables, and cases of dark stained acacia. New light fixtures were placed on the bookcases to illuminate the books (directly) as well as the room (indirectly). The reading room chairs were produced in collaboration with the designer Hannes Wettstein. With the green tone of their fabric upholstery they recall the feeling of traditional library reading rooms.

1 Entrance to new library
2 Library/reading room
3 Librarians' office
4 Card catalogue
5 Meeting room
6 Cloakroom
7 New entrance to museum administration
8 Garden

Library, section

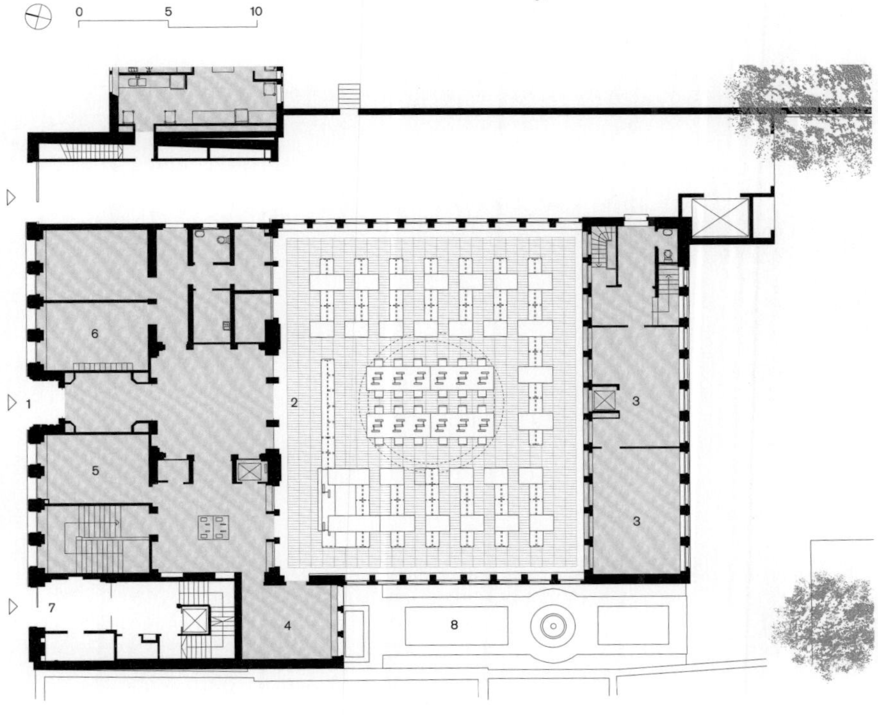

Laurenzbau with library, ground floor

Banking hall of the Nationalbank, 1936,
by architects Suter & Burckhardt

Entrance before remodeling/reconstruction

Extension/Renovation of Historical Villa, Kastanienbaum, Switzerland 111

2002–04

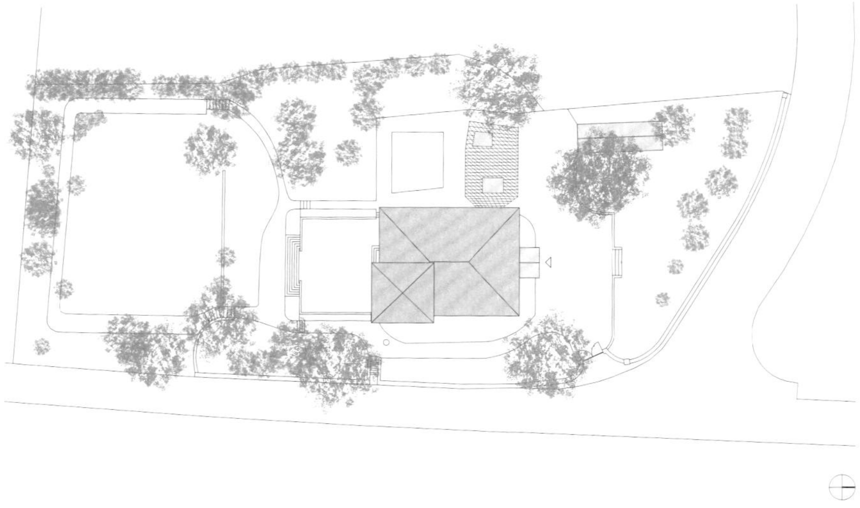

The existing, late Neoclassical villa was built in 1860 in the Italian country-house style as a summer residence within a large park overlooking Lake Lucerne. It is thought to be the work of Xaver Waller. In 1927, the villa's interior was extensively altered and an extension was built to house the kitchen.

For the villa's current owner, a remodeling project was developed involving various degrees of intervention. The modifications ranged from cleaning, the removal of wallpaper, repairs and restorations, to a series of individual, explicitly dialectical interventions, and finally the replacement of the kitchen annex with a new building. However, the decision was made not to reconstruct the spatial and structural characteristics of the original building.

Proposed restoration involved repairing the sandstone window surrounds, sanding and oiling the parquet flooring, and transforming some single-glazed windows into double-glazed ones using the existing wooden frames and glass. Of special note is the small room in the tower. Stripped of wallpaper, the walls here exhibited such a remarkable patina, along with a number of pencil drawings made by previous workers, that it was decided not to renovate them.

Selective interventions included the construction of a brass fireplace in the large salon and the installation of a chrome steel kitchen unit in the center of the former small salon. The renovation of the bathrooms (the original positions of which were retained) likewise belongs in this category. They were furnished with new fittings, oak flooring, and walls of etched mirrors. In the large bathroom a freestanding bathtub was specially commissioned.

The most radical intervention was the demolition of the kitchen annex, which was in poor repair. Replacing it is a garage with adjacent workshop. The annex building, the roof of which serves as a terrace, is accessible from both the house and the garden. Trellises cover the walls of the single-story concrete structure and continue up above the roof, forming a pavilion over the terrace. In this way, the annex acquires dimensions and proportions in keeping with those of the villa. Architectural features typical of nineteenth-century villa gardens, such as gazebos and coach houses, are in a sense interwoven in this structure and physically connected with the house. The villa, annex, and grounds are also linked in terms of color: the green of the villa's sandstone is echoed in the colored concrete, and the olive-green hues of the trellis match the greenery of the park.

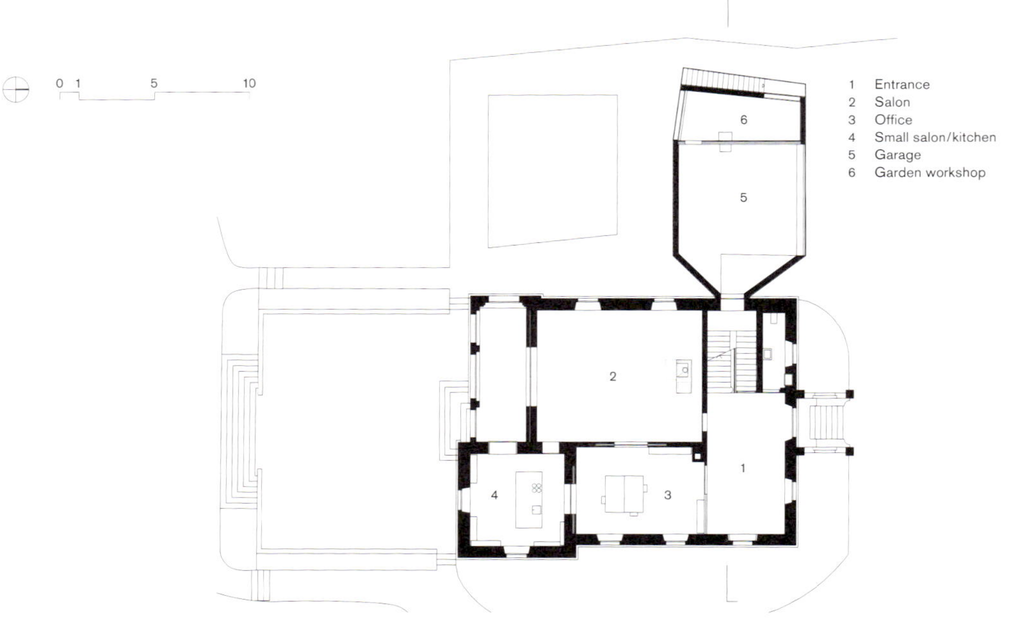

Ground floor

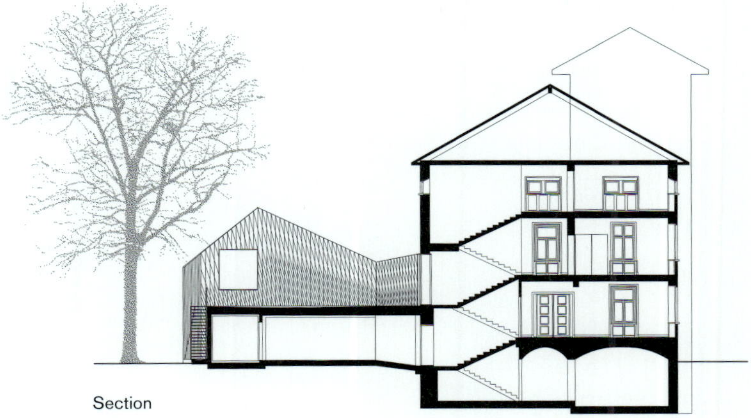

Section

Small room in the tower

Office

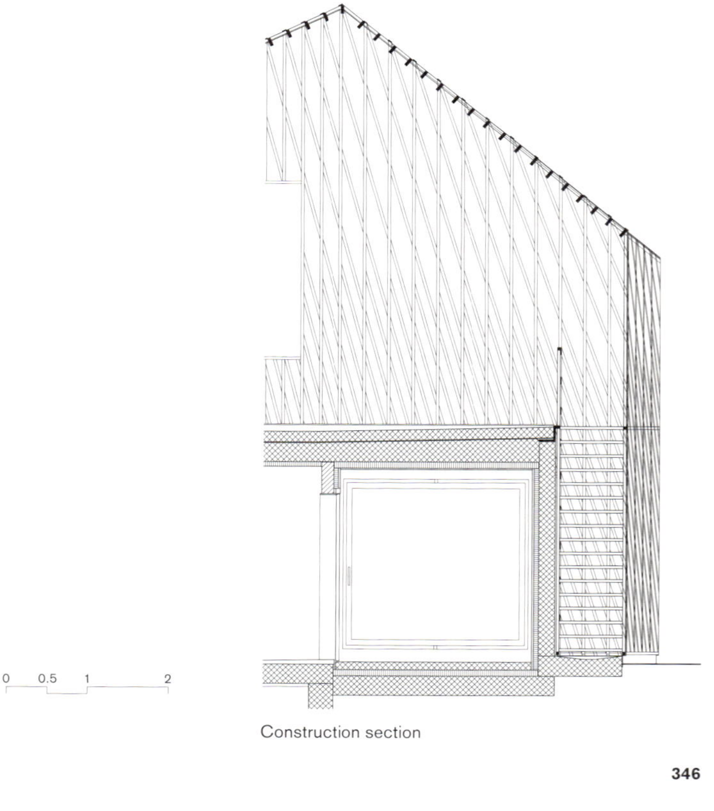

Construction section

LIVING

Detached House, Zurich, Switzerland 093

2001–03

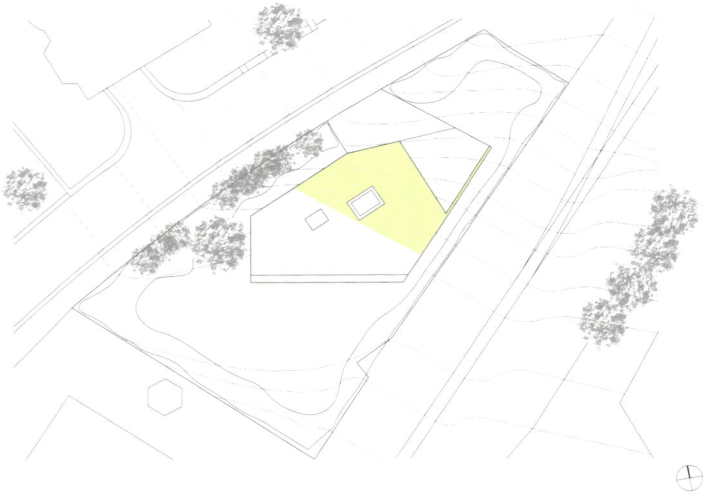

Facing south, the hexagonal volume of the detached house in Zurich is inscribed within a trapezoid-shaped plot on a steep incline. An inclined volume with a slanted roof was conceived, which resulted from going to the maximum building height possible at all six corners of the building.

The main entry to the house is located on the north side underneath a large cantilever that provides a sheltered exterior space. Inside, the entrance area is arranged into zones by "space-containing" walls with an integrated wardrobe, cabinets, and guest bathroom. This allows the adjoining bedroom and study to be separated off via sliding walls, or alternatively connected into one continuous space. The children's bedrooms are located on the lower ground floor. They are accessed via a central space that merges into the "garden room," which can also be utilized as a guest room, playroom, or study. On the upper floor, under the slanted roof, is the main living area with an exceptionally high ceiling that rises from 2.4 to 5.2 meters. This room is also organized around a "space-containing" central wall in order to allow these zones of varying height and breadth to be utilized for living, cooking, work, and play.

On the ground floor, colored surfaces of dark green and light orange accentuate the lighting effects in each room. On the upper floor, a new color concept for the main wall is to be devised periodically. The general interplay of color and space can be observed and experienced during the course of daily life, almost as if it were an ongoing experiment. The first concept was for a bright yellow-green that reacted strongly to the light, while the second was a bright raspberry, and the current incarnation is a sprayed-on high-gloss color gradient with iridescent pigments.

The exterior walls and roof consist of load-bearing concrete. The large windows are opened by sliding them into a recess between the outer concrete and inner brick wall. To the north the windows have wide frames and are mounted flush with the wall. The concrete of the roof and the outer walls is a dark gray and a mossy green-yellow. The crossover from colored to uncolored doesn't occur at the corners, but on the faces. Dense vegetation of blooming shrubs and berry bushes lines the borders of the property and forms a "clearing" in which the green/gray building is set.

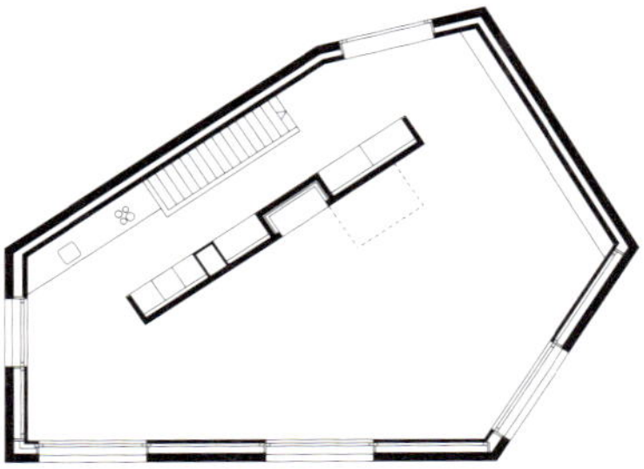

Upper floor

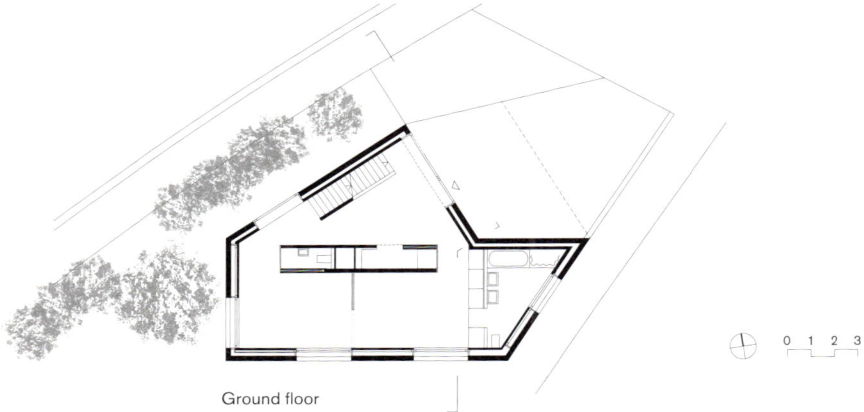

Ground floor

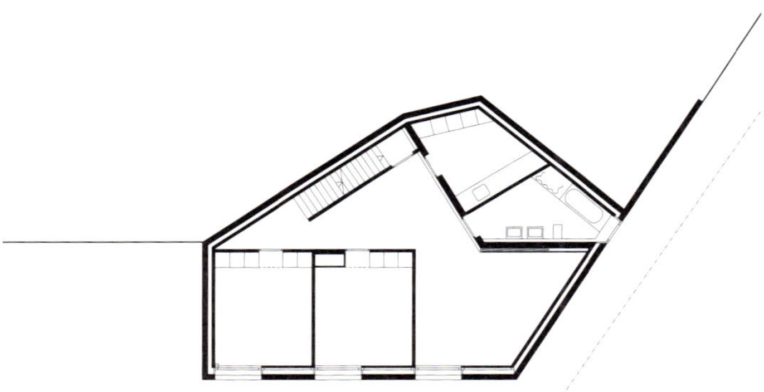

Lower floor

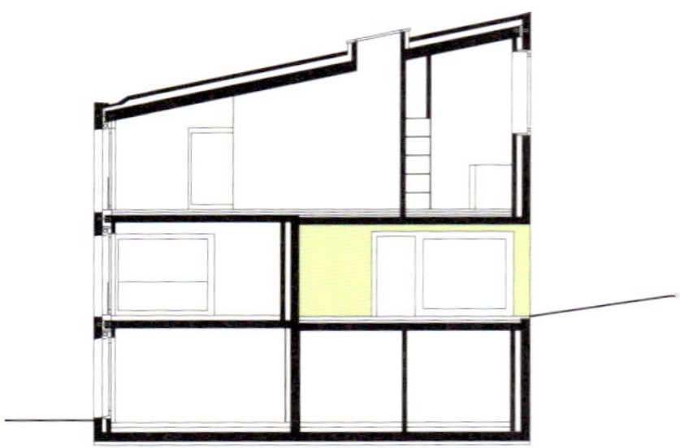

Section

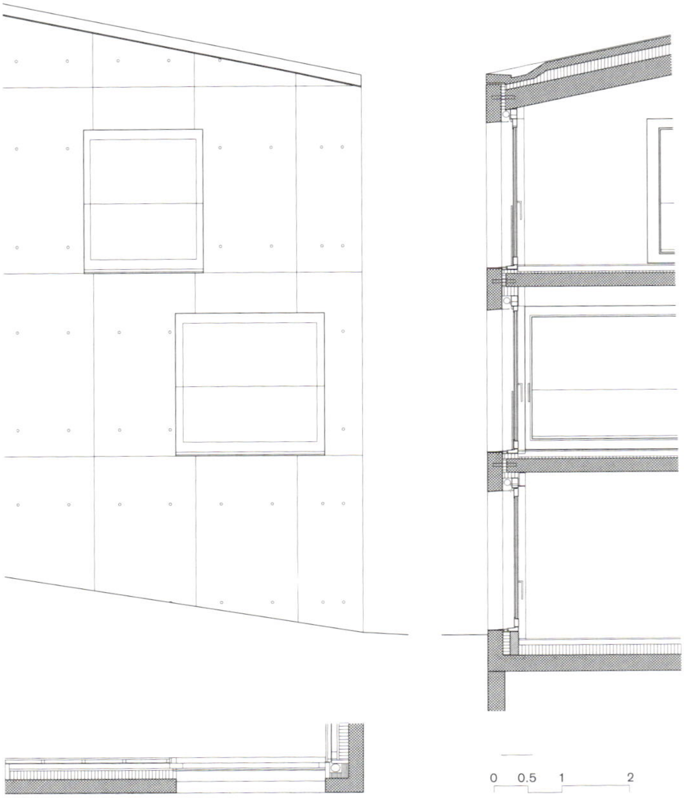

Construction detail

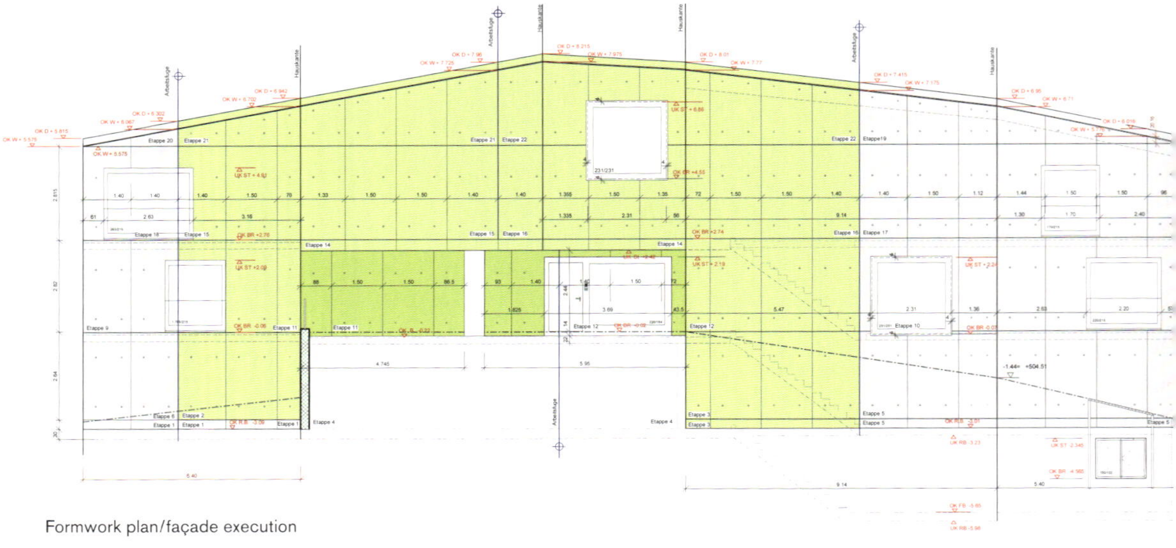

Formwork plan/façade execution

Detached House, Zurich, Switzerland

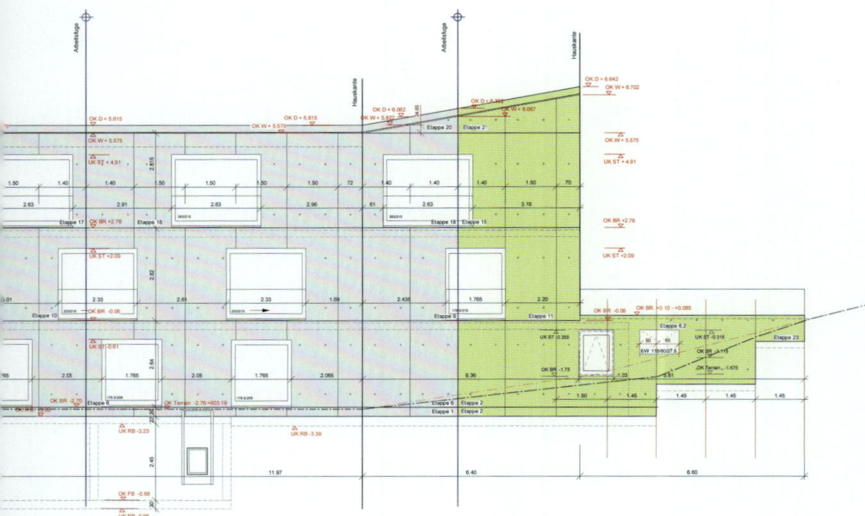

Detached House, Canton Grisons, Switzerland 172

2004–07

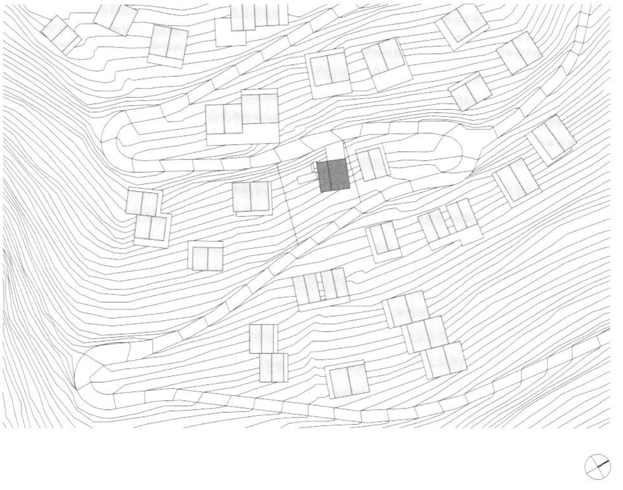

The house is located on a steep slope below the village. A wide bridge leads to it from the street above, forming a level courtyard and a parking area.

The building form is defined by the mountain community's strict building code, which stipulates the height and a pitched roof oriented toward the village church. The ridge of the roof runs parallel to the incline and the house is cantilevered toward the valley, seemingly suspended over the slope. With the façades and the roof uniformly clad in brownish-red copper shingles, the structure blends in with the timber buildings of the village. As a complete rain screen, the cladding allows for a reduced, contemporary formal vocabulary.

The topography is also reflected in the interior. Under the slanted roof, the living/dining room reaches a height of seven meters, and staggered mezzanine levels follow the sloping hillside. The central staircase links all four mezzanine levels with a single flight of stairs each. Wide floor-to-ceiling sliding doors allow generous connections between the spaces as well as closing them off at night.

The load-bearing structure consists of pre-fabricated timber elements filled with thermal insulation and protected from the weather by the rear-ventilated copper shingling. The inner surfaces of the timber panels are whitewashed. Pivot windows of uniform size appear to be scattered across the façade at random, but they actually reflect the spatial layout of the interior. The tall viewing window offers a spectacular vertical panorama down into the valley, across to the hills, and up the mountains on the other side.

The site remains nearly untouched by the house, with wild grasses now growing again all around, seamlessly joining the neighboring pastures. The only intervention is a level deck cut into the hillside to the west.

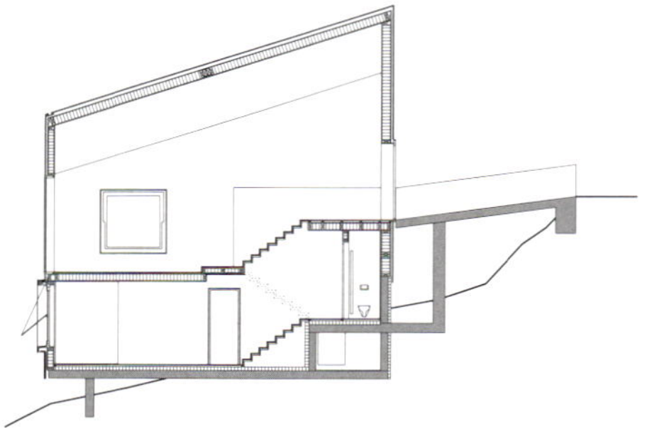

Section

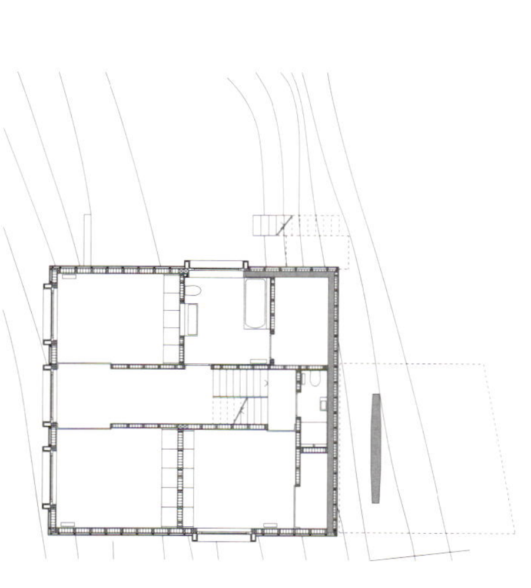

Lower floor

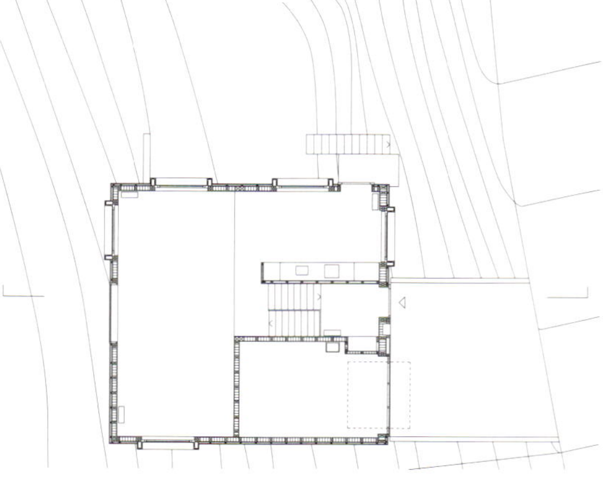

Ground floor

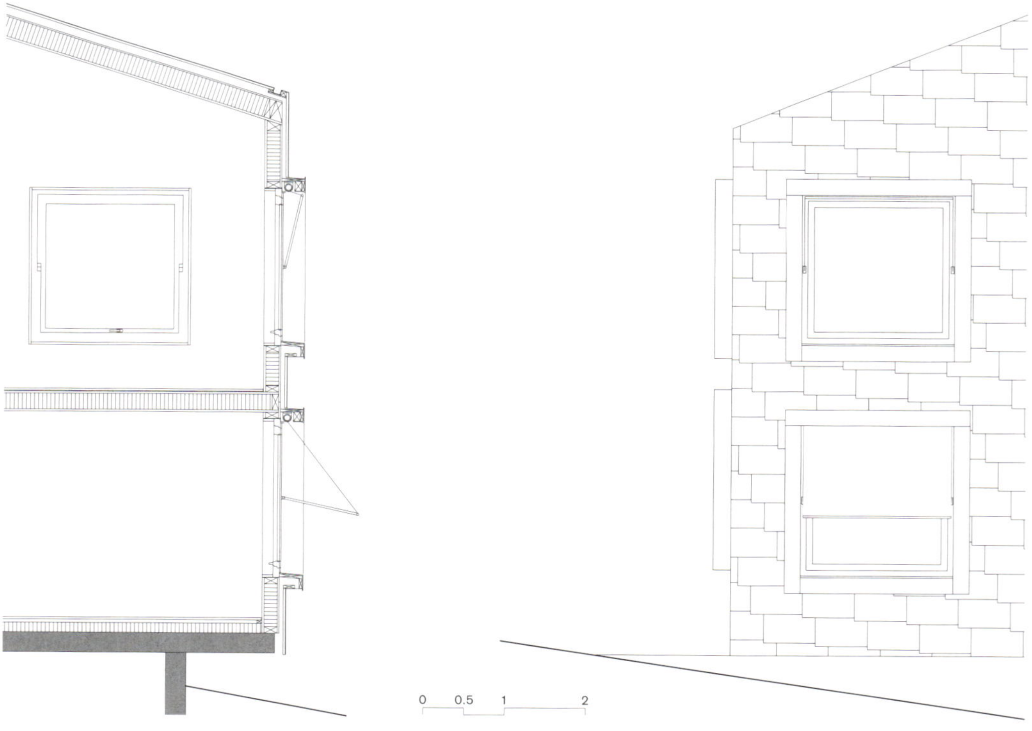

Construction detail

Detached House, Küsnacht, Switzerland 173
2005–07

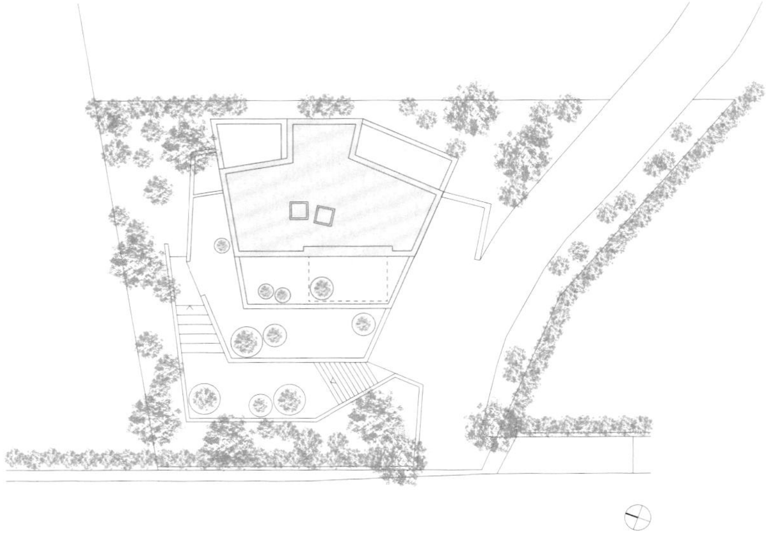

The tree-framed garden of an old villa forms the building site of the new family home. The geometry of the garden plot, the existing trees including a magnificent cedar, and the steep terrain dictate a polygonal structure which rises in tiers up the slope. The entrance and garage form the basement level with terrace, topped by two stories and an attic level.

A generously proportioned multi-angular staircase with a wide wellhole links all four levels not only physically, but also optically and acoustically: from the entrance hall to the children's rooms, the living area, and the parents' bedroom. The living/dining room is on the second floor and benefits from its elevated position, while the children's rooms on the first floor have direct access to the garden, and the parents' bedroom on the top level has its own large rooftop terrace.

In collaboration with the artist Harald F. Müller and the family, certain internal surfaces have been painted in strong colors. The ceilings in the children's rooms are bright orange and gold, one wall of the parents' bedroom is light blue, the wall beneath the skylight in the living room is black, and the ceiling above the large stairwell is an orangey-red.

The dark terrazzo floors throughout the house give the various rooms an overall muted coloration and establish a correlation with the concrete used for the support structure, whose load-bearing external concrete shell forms the façade. Internal masonry walls are not load-bearing and conceal the insulation.

Due to the texture of the vertical rough planking used as formwork and the deep reveals of the window openings, the exposed concrete façade gains a striking physical presence. This underlines the structure's sturdiness against the slope. The white scumble on the surface of the concrete emphasizes with delicate tonal nuances the play of shadows across the surfaces and perforations. The glazed parapet has a slightly reflective finish to afford privacy while also mirroring the trees in the garden.

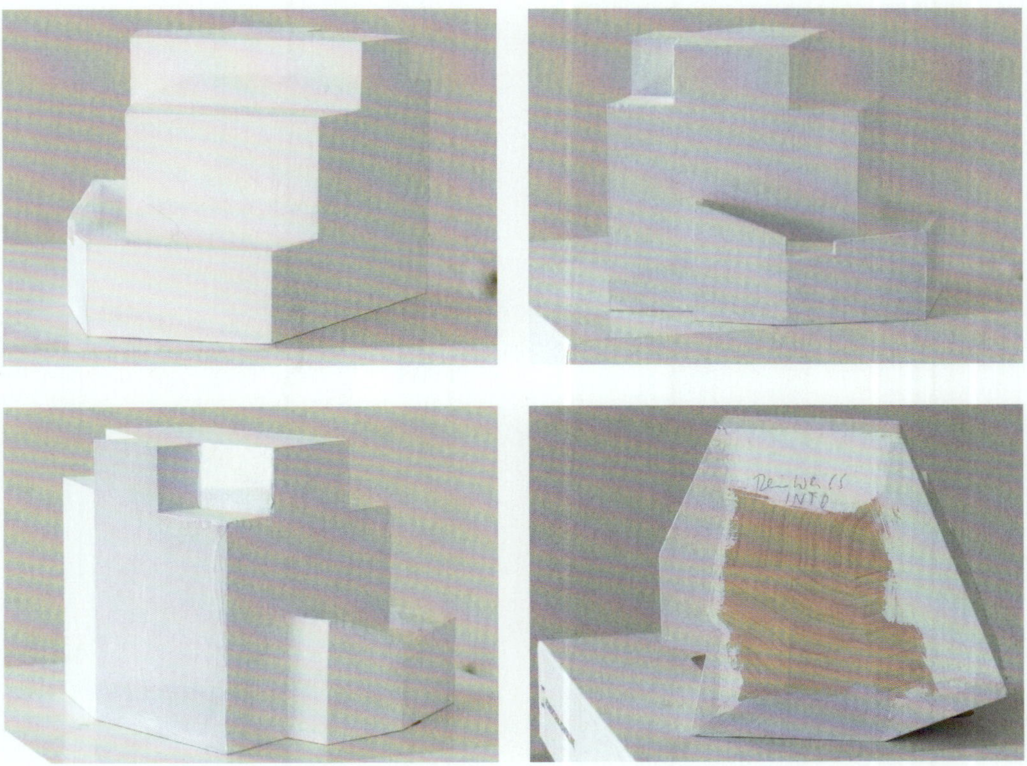

Study model, shades of white

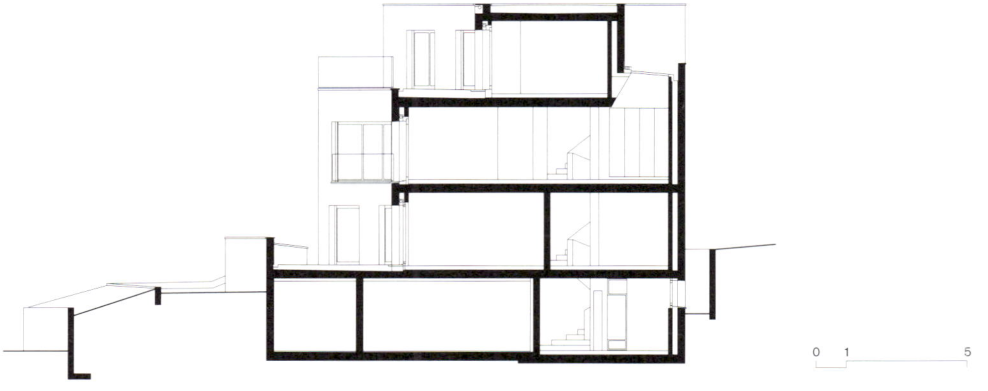

Section

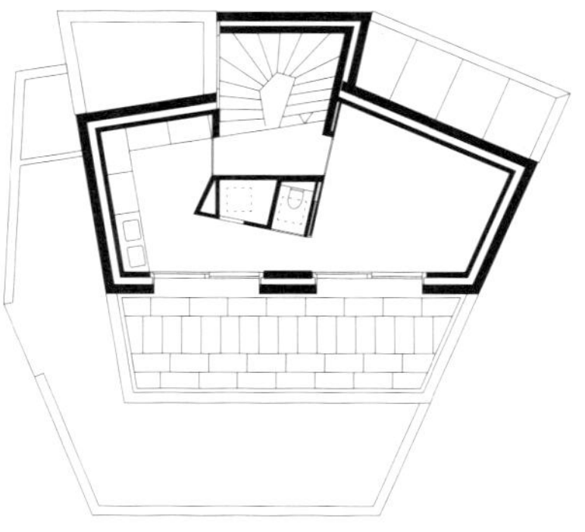

Top floor

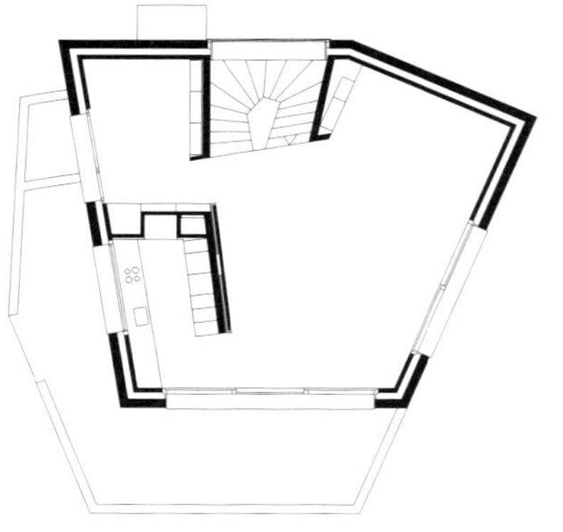

Upper floor

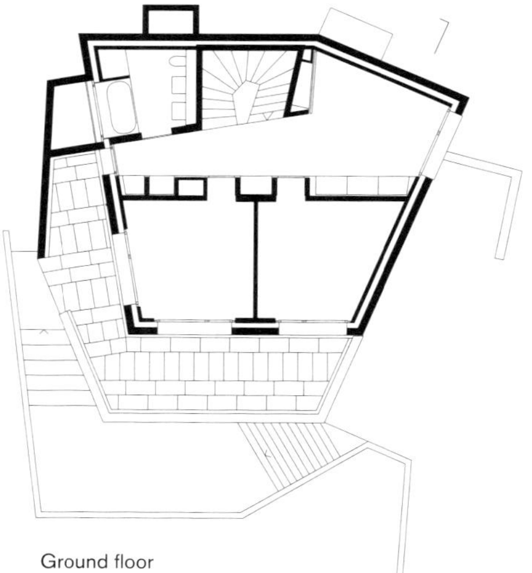

Ground floor

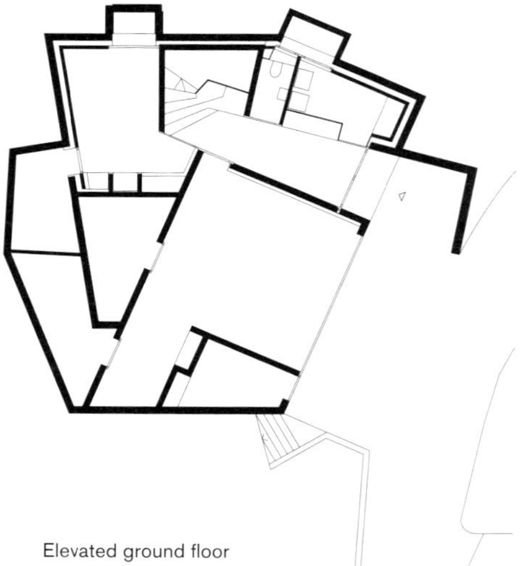

Elevated ground floor

Detached House on Zürichberg, Zurich, Switzerland 222

2008–11

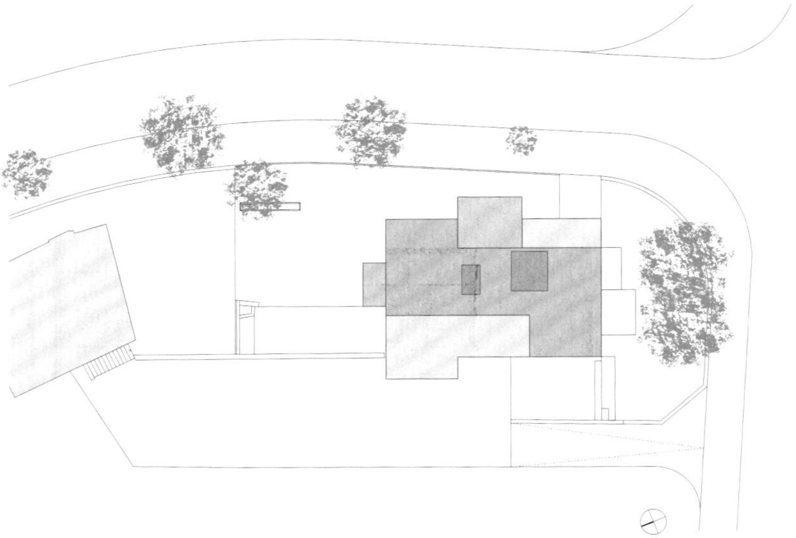

The current residential building replaces a pair of 1940s semi-detached houses. The building volume is widened with three projecting sections and forms terraces through setbacks on the top level.

Two residential units have been created on four floors: a small apartment, which opens onto a front garden on the lowest floor, and a large apartment that extends over the remaining floors.

A cut-out volume on the ground floor forms the entrance area. Here a circuit connects the entry hall with the living room, the two-story dining room, and the kitchen. The double-height dining area extends up to the first floor, which is divided into two sleeping areas, each with separate bathrooms—one private area and one for guests, with scope to separate off the latter space with sliding doors. Above this, on the top floor, two similar rooms are used as study and library, each featuring its own terrace.

A central stairway structures the space; an angled stair winds between the walls to the lowest floor, and a straight stair with a deeper first step emerges from the fireplace and kitchen block and leads upwards. The upper staircase leading up to the rooftop terrace is lent transparency by offset cut-outs in the risers.

Dark oak windows, with separate ventilation sashes behind curtain-like latticework, frame and structure the range of differently proportioned openings in the various rooms. In the interior, the doors, built-in furniture, and bookshelves, in dark oak veneer or glossy white paint, complement the spatial ambience created by the chalk-colored cast concrete floors and the cream tone of the walls with their white lazure. The outer layer of the double concrete shell is also executed in beige limestone concrete. Some of the surfaces were heavily sandblasted, while others were left with a smooth formed finish.

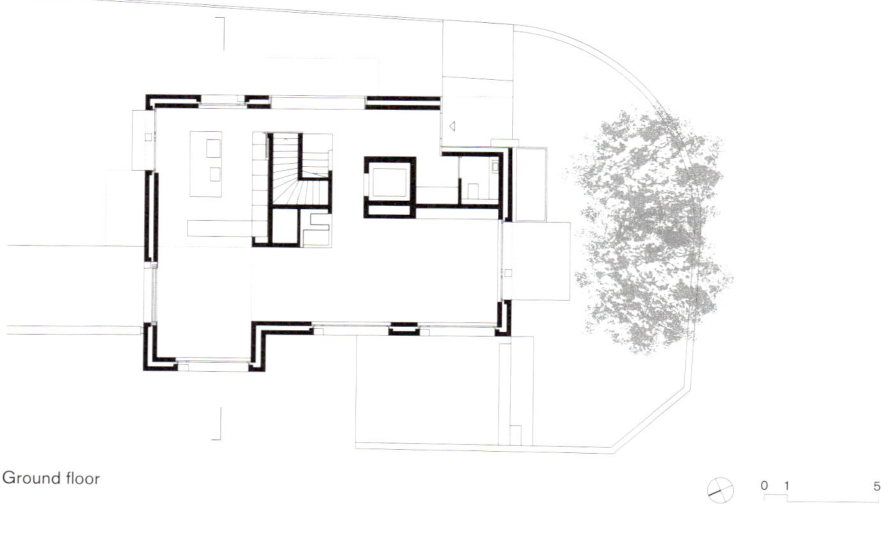

Ground floor

Detached House on Zürichberg, Zurich, Switzerland

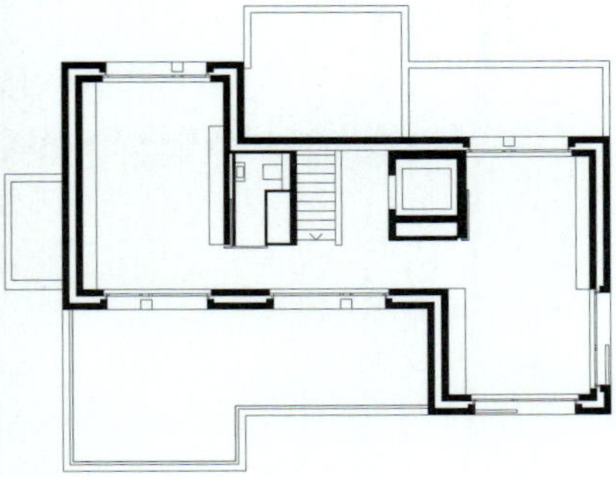

Top floor

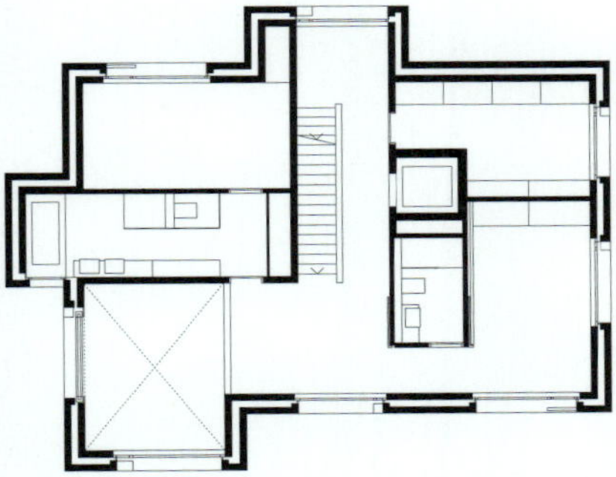

1st floor

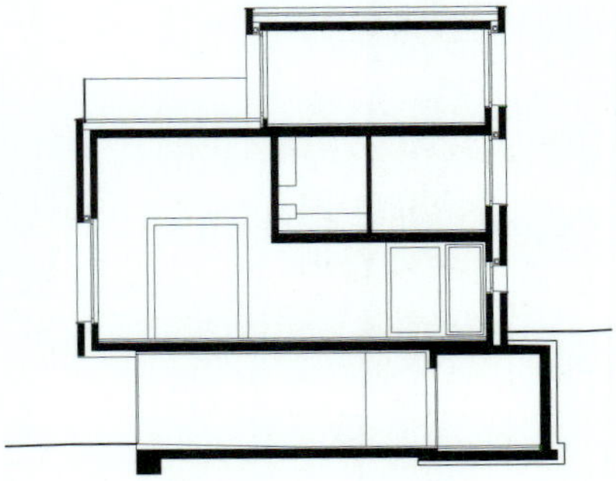

Section

Housing Construction

A Conversation with Martin Steinmann, Patrick Gmür, Annette Gigon, and Mike Guyer

Martin Steinmann: In the past ten years, there has been a boom in the construction of housing in Zurich. I'm not just talking about quantity because there has been a lot of building going on in other cities, too. You've been involved in various aspects of housing construction for over a decade. To what extent have the circumstances changed in that time?

Annette Gigon: Even though most of our housing projects have been built in and around Zurich, much depends on the time, the place, and the specifications. The first housing development we built was Broëlberg I 002 in Kilchberg above Lake Zurich. At the time, 15 years ago, it was one of the few examples of high quality rental apartments. There weren't many spacious apartments in Zurich and the middle classes were moving out to the suburbs, usually into detached houses. The projects that followed were in the city and comprised large apartments in good locations. Architectural design competitions have given us the opportunity to build a wide variety of housing at both ends of the spectrum—expensive and affordable, rental and owner-occupied, large and small. The tide has turned a little now, and city life is regaining its appeal.

MS: Zurich has undoubtedly made a significant contribution to "research" in the field of housing projects. The floorplans have become increasingly distinctive. At first I was delighted by what I saw as a real change in the development of housing. But now I can't help wondering just how far this distinctiveness can go without restricting the freedom of individuals to appropriate their living space. To what extent does a floorplan have to be neutral so that people can put their own stamp on where they live? I think that is especially important in the case of rental accommodation. Adolf Behne, for instance, distinguished between the social aspect of rationalism, which emphasizes society, and functionalism, which foregrounds the significance of the individual.

Patrick Gmür: Today's individualistic lifestyle is mirrored in architecture and in the way it is used. There are about 207,500 apartments in the city of Zurich, with a vacancy rate of 0.05 percent—in other words, practically nil. And yet some 80,000 people move house every year—that's 20 percent of the city's total population. It's an interesting phenomenon: people move due to changing circumstances—first-time tenants, apartment sharing, growing families, retirement—there is a lot of flexibility. The Brunnenhof development for large families (p. 490) shows that housing can be designed for very specific needs. It illustrates how social change has affected the design of the floorplan. In 1995, when you designed your first projects, the emphasis was on versatility of layout. The floorplan had to meet as many different requirements as possible.

Mike Guyer: How did this typological innovation come about in Zurich? Here sometimes larger sites are given a special status that allows a certain degree of architectural freedom, which offsets the city's otherwise strict building regulations and provides an opportunity for a number of design competitions in Zurich. Such sites are big enough to be divided into various lots which, together, form a mixed-use neighborhood. Each lot offers a certain freedom to develop specific housing types. The developing areas of Zurich are especially interesting in that such a diversity of housing is required to meet the needs of many different sectors of the population—families, singles, students, the elderly, temporary accommodation, shared apartments—along with relevant facilities such as nurseries, kindergartens, shops, restaurants, and community centers.

PG: There's also a political dimension to this diversity. We want Zurich to be a city for everyone. A city can only function if people from all income groups are able to afford suitable housing. Cooperative housing associations currently account for one quarter of the housing stock. We want to increase that share. To save money, floorplans in cooperative housing are shrinking. Three-room apartments are being reduced from 100 to 90 square meters, reflecting the average wage, which is currently 5500 Francs in the city of Zurich. That curtails the freedom of developing new housing.

MS: What is the difference between rental accommodation and condos? Is it merely a question of quantity, of room sizes and budgets, or are there more fundamental issues involved?

AG: Financial considerations are a factor right across the housing spectrum. Condos and high-end rental accommodation are also subject to certain pressures that can be just as restrictive as the budgetary constraints of low-income housing. On the other hand, it was possible to build the Brunnenhof development for large families to a relatively high standard because the city authorities subsidized the costs so that current real estate prices for land didn't have to be offset by higher rents. Cooperative housing construction in Zurich is an important regulatory factor in terms of construction quality and counteracts an overheated market.

MG: The ideal situation for us is when we can take an all-inclusive approach from urban design through to the interior finishings. Large housing estates with specific residential typologies and outdoor spaces become special places that actually enhance the neighborhood. They have a more open, public feel—this is clearly evident in the Pflegi (p. 436), Thalwil (p. 516), Geneva (p. 528), and Brunnenhof developments.

The units in condos are individually finished. The design of both the structural and the technical installations determine how flexible they are. The shell of the building and the outdoor areas have to be designed robustly enough to absorb the individuality of these living spaces without forfeiting the impact of the project as a whole within the urban setting. Basically, it is the owner of the land who decides whether to build rental apartments or condos. If the plot is already owned and is not going to be sold, the owner has more leeway in setting the value of the land and can build more interesting rental apartments (Broëlberg, Zellweger-Areal [p. 566], Pflegi, Brunnenhof). But if the owner sells the land, the subsequent sale or rent of the housing units is necessarily based on current property values (Grünenberg [p. 474], Erlenhof [p. 538], Goldschlägi [p. 546], Zollikerstrasse [p. 556]).

MS: In other words, the basically arbitrary ownership factor sometimes favors high quality planning, and sometimes it doesn't.

MG: A remarkable example of this is our project in the city of Geneva, which has suffered from a housing shortage for many years. For this major housing development, an increase in housing density was permitted on condition that half the apartments be condos at regulated purchase prices, and one quarter subsidized rental units. The result is a broad spectrum of housing types of varying standards.

MS: Handover and resale of projects has become commonplace. How does this affect the type of housing? Does it make the architects' task more difficult?

MG: Different circumstances influence the type and quality of housing in different ways. As mentioned, the Brunnenhof housing development was funded by the local authorities. The client is a municipal foundation and the value of the land played a secondary role in the construction of new housing. The Goldschlägi project was developed by SBB with the express intention of selling the developed site at the best possible market price. The size and rental rates had to be tailored to the needs of housing in Schlieren and the construction budget was tight due to the value of the land itself. In the case of the Löwenbräu site (p. 288), the standard of the condos was determined largely by the price of the land. On the one hand, the investor, PSP, was aiming for maximum returns, but on the other, the overall plan and the high-rise demanded exacting standards of urban planning and architectural design. As a result, the volume, façade, and structure of the building had to be adapted to suit the sophisticated, individual needs of these high-end condos.

PG: The Löwenbräu high-rise brings us back to the initial question about the generic and the specific: in this vertically stacked building, you offer a number of different floorplans to cater to a maximum of different functions and layouts.

MS: You are inscribing different worlds—different apartments—within a given framework. That means making strategic overall decisions on things such as the placement of cores, load-bearing walls, conduits, and ducts. I wonder whether that's possible without a uniform room layout, without one basic type that can be individually modified as required.

MG: Yes, basic types and their variations determine the layout of the fixed elements. In general, the type of apartment reflects the qualities of the location with all its pros and cons and it is developed in accordance with the permitted density. We have explored a wide range of apartment types in different buildings: ones that are layered like an onion, open-plan living, others that stretch right through the building from façade to façade, apartments built around a courtyard, and two and three-story maisonettes. In principle, free-standing apartment blocks can be adapted best to their surroundings thanks to their all-round views and the floorplans can be varied enormously.

PG: Given the current housing shortage, there is little option but to examine the possibilities of different

Apartment type with "onion-style" layout

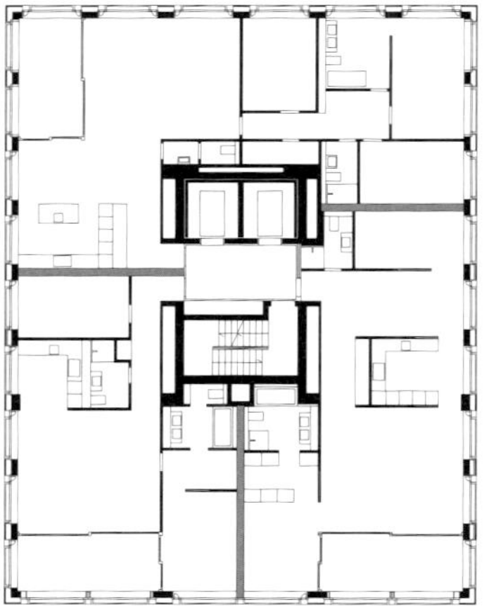

Löwenbräu

Pflegi

Apartment type with open-plan areas

Susenbergstrasse

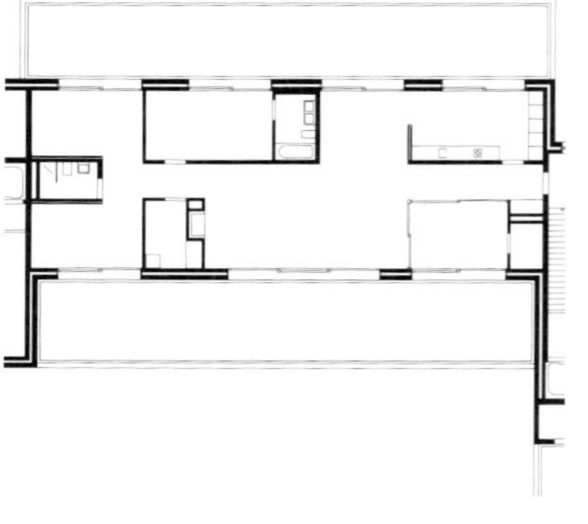

Broëlberg II

Apartment type with living room extending from front to back

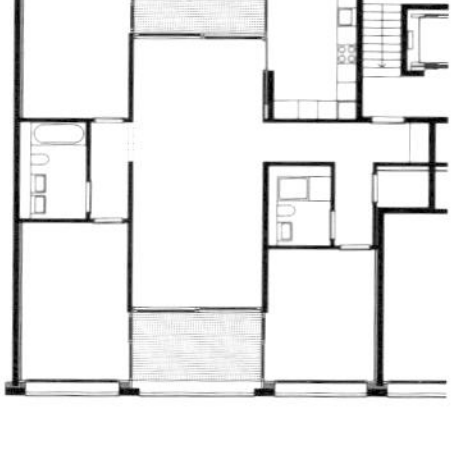

Thalwil

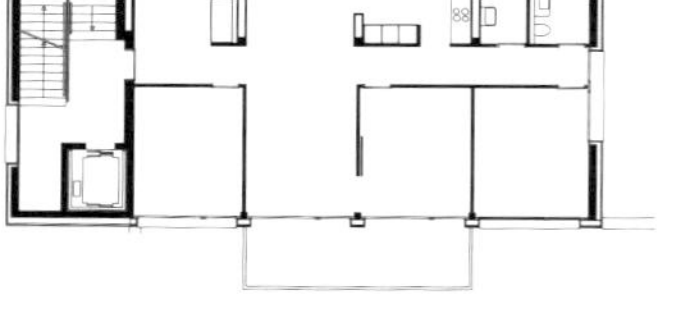

Goldschlägi

Apartment type with courtyard

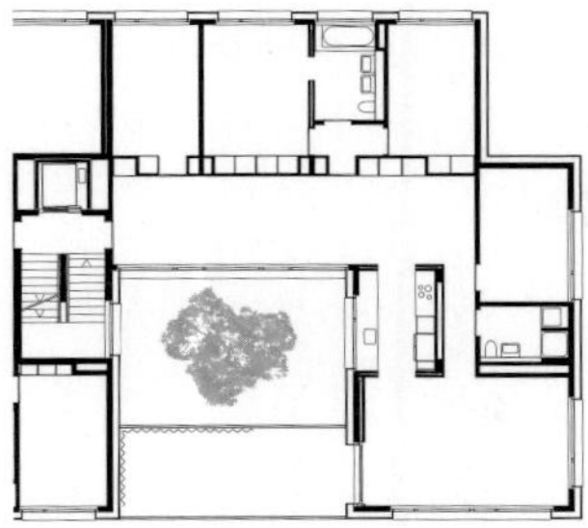

Neumünsterallee

Duplex type

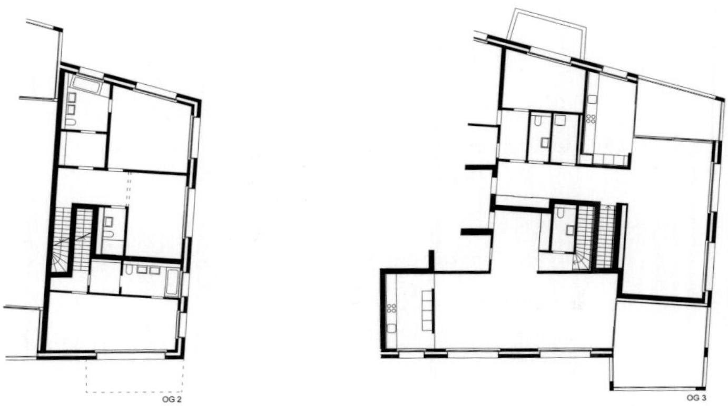

Grünenberg

Freestanding building with several apartments per floor

Geneva I

types of high-density housing. Northeast or northwest facing apartments are now being built again, which may not provide the most ideal lighting conditions. Compromises are being made that would not have been deemed acceptable ten years ago, but which do help to provide affordable housing.

AG: The trend towards more compact, in other words deeper, apartment buildings is also fostered by the increasing emphasis on ecological factors. This brings new challenges, because good lighting conditions and views are very important aspects of our work. AG: But at the same time there is a trend against these deeper floorplans. New building regulations are quite rightly stricter about sound insulation. That has repercussions for building volume and for urban planning. It meant, for example, that the Brunnenhof and Goldschlägi projects were designed with very narrow floorplans.

MS: But I think we would more or less agree that light, air, and movement—the key tenets of 1920s housing design—are no longer as important, given today's living conditions. Those tenets were a response to the appalling housing conditions in those days. Today, we can have rooms with low levels of natural light. Patrick has built deep apartment blocks in which some rooms are intended mainly for evening use. In the French-speaking part of Switzerland such apartments have been around for quite a while. Some have a very large entrance hall, often with a fireplace.

PG: In my experience, such layouts work better in condominiums. When you build deep apartments, the handling of space becomes an interesting challenge. But, of course, that increases the floor area.

MG: A twenty-meter deep apartment with a two-room axis easily oversteps the 90-square-meter mark for four rooms. The alternative is a split-level or two-story maisonette layout, which is not really feasible

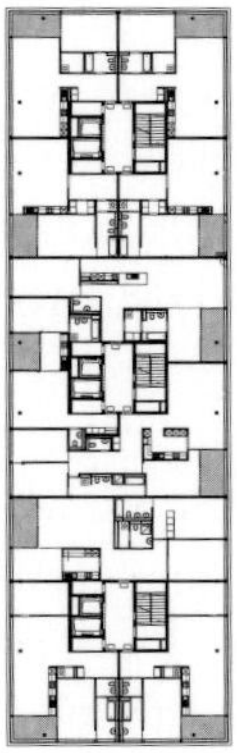

Standard floor, James Residential and Commercial Complex, Albisrieden, Zurich, by architects Gmür & Geschwentner

for low-income housing. There have been competitions in which we worked with deep apartment layouts, as in Neumünsterallee (p. 482), although that was an exception because, on the whole, more conventional designs end up being built. For the Goldschlägi project, the two-story accommodation envisaged in the competition design proved too expensive—that's sobering.

MS: Another consideration is the effect that production processes have on the floorplan. Take housing construction in the Netherlands, for example. The tunnel formwork that is widely used there creates a structure of parallel walls. It is possible to create exciting layouts on this basis—simple floorplans developed out of the structure itself, as in the past. This brings the housing back to the reality of the building site. I think that also applies to your layouts in Almere (p. 448). That's another example of a very deep building.

MG: In contrast to the apartments in our housing projects abroad, in Almere, Amsterdam 146, and Paris 233, where rigid cross-wall construction methods determine the typology, the structure of our housing in Switzerland is developed on the basis of the apartment layout: this means that there are either load-bearing walls in the façade and core areas or every second room axis is conceived as a load-bearing wall with concrete internal reinforcement walls forming the access areas—or there are load-bearing core areas with supports in the façade zone.

MS: So far, we have spoken mainly about external factors, the legal, technical, and economic factors that determine the outcome of a building. But there are also the living conditions themselves. So floorplans are influenced from two directions. In the past, an architect would design a nice layout, and that would form the basis for a building. This is often no longer the case: external factors determine the area on which the floorplan has to be inscribed, sometimes resulting in layouts that don't correspond to conventional typologies. It's a whole different approach to design: the floorplan is not based on ideal conditions. Not that this is a new problem—but we'll come back to that later.

AG: Maybe even more interesting than the basic housing types is the actual transformation they undergo in each specific case. That brings us back to the original topic: just how specific can a building or apartment type be if it is to serve as many people for as long as possible? Just how well does this lend itself to multiplication as part of town planning and general use? And what are the exceptions that may function beautifully as highlights, but don't necessarily lend themselves to repetition and adaptation? Which apartment types can be multiplied to shape the urban fabric, to form street plans and districts, and which are more suited to expansion in green areas—for instance, the development and restructuring of former private gardens and their parks—like a new "garden city," an idea that has always been of interest to us?

MS: What answers do you have to those questions?

AG: Actually very site-specific and task-specific ones, which makes them so different. We aren't necessarily looking for the ultimate housing type although there are certain patterns which can be discerned in our work—arranging rooms, creating views, providing freedom of movement—that have been proven in several instances. There are also some exceptions, such as the Zollikerstrasse project, where we had a relatively small site with protected trees, which meant that we had to depart from the right-angled approach in order to leave enough room for the roots. It was an unusual solution, among those mature trees, and not one that could be applied to an urban situation. But while working on that housing project we also worked on others with entirely different dimensions—very generalized, low key, and urban, as in the Thalwil project.

PG: Those are indeed two extremes.

AG: The oscillation between the typical and the specific is something that can only be grasped by considering the different projects within their respective contexts and functions.

The competition brief of the Susenbergstrasse project (p. 416), for instance, called for spacious apartments for singles! We came up with a "spatial continuum" but it has large sliding partitions so that the rooms can be divided up in a way that would also suit a small family. The overall building volume was split into three individual buildings, with just one apartment on each floor, ensuring maximum light and views. For the Pflegi urban housing development, the layout offers room for movement around the core. Structurally, the building would have permitted more spacious layouts without subdivisions, but in the end, because of the rental market, the apartments had to be divided into as many rooms as possible. One project that is especially defined by the site itself is the development of the Grünenberg Park in Wädenswil. We tried to give each apartment a fair share of sunshine and views of the lake. Given the odd shape of the gardens, the end result was a trio of buildings with spacious stairways and apartments that interlock in various ways.

In the Neumünsterallee development, the dimensions of the former business site required a deep building, so we added an inner courtyard to ensure that each apartment receives adequate light.

PG: Context is the most important factor in the process of design, which actually contradicts the idea of type because every site is, after all, unique. That could be seen as a challenge to generate diversity and create not just one type of apartment, but many, very

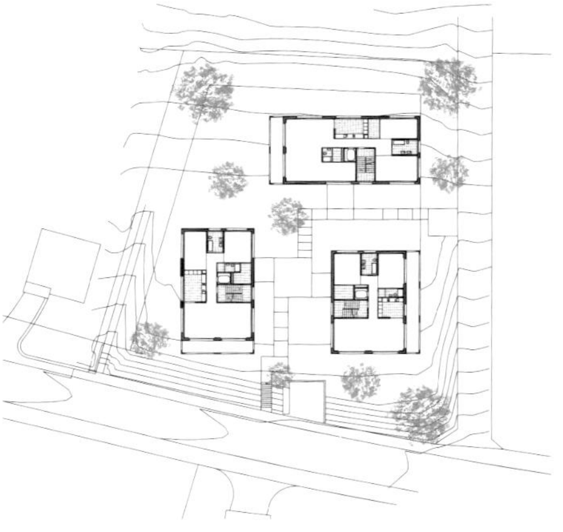

Susenbergstrasse

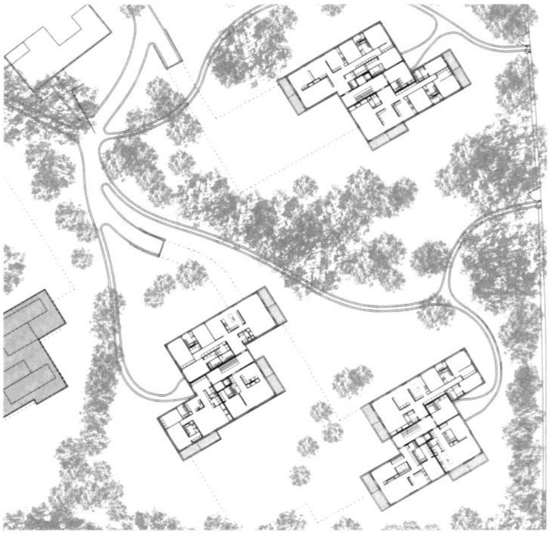

Geneva I

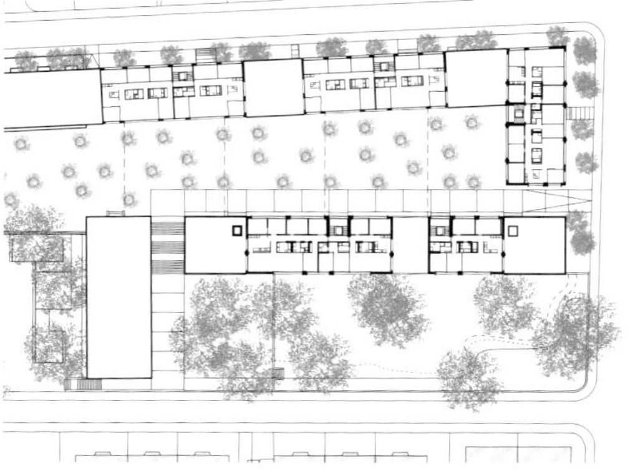

Pflegi

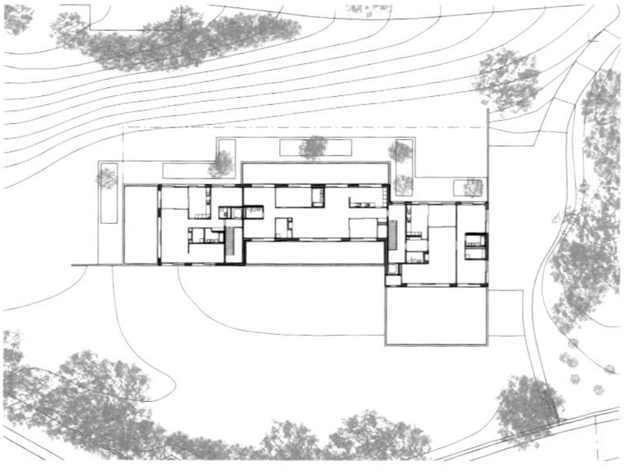

Broëlberg II

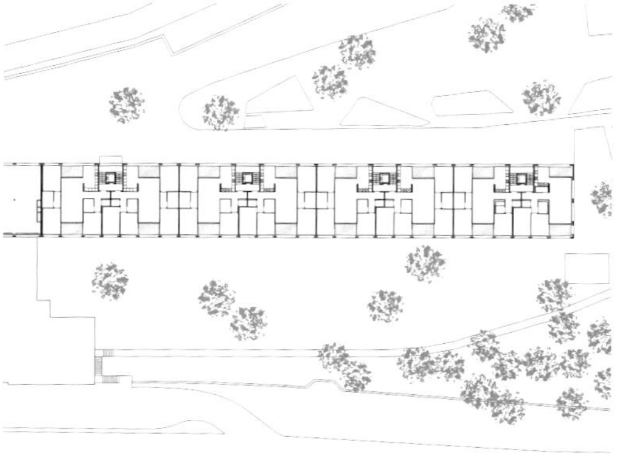

Thalwil

Grünenberg

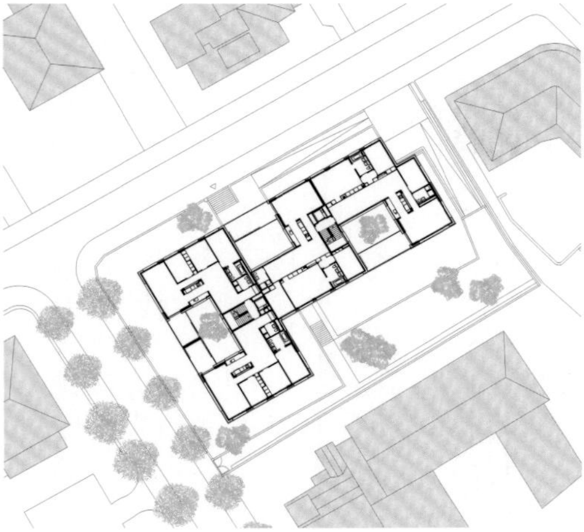

Neumünsterallee

Brunnenhof

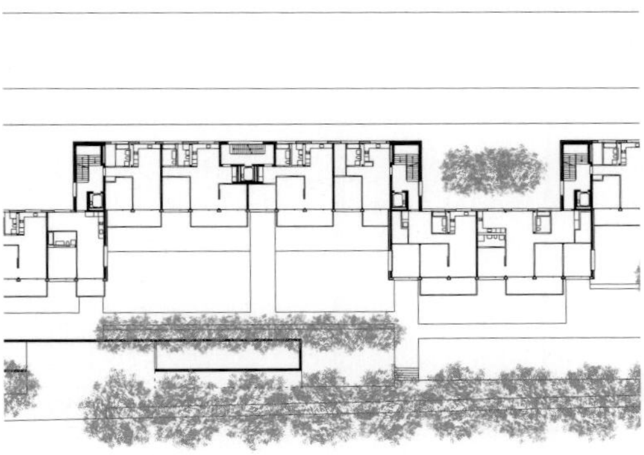

Goldschlägi

Zellweger-Areal

Zollikerstrasse

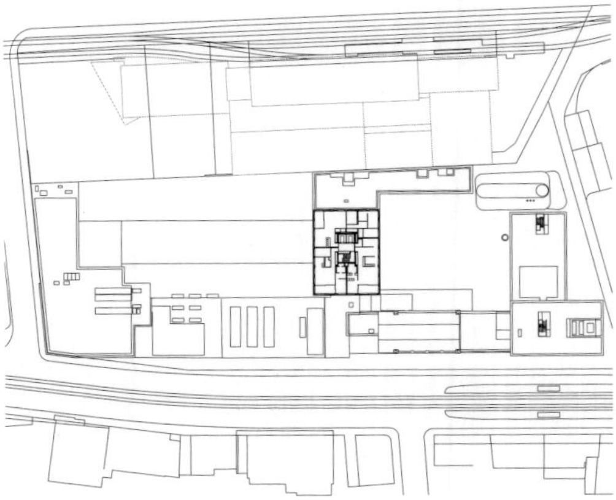

Löwenbräu-Areal

different types of apartments that appeal to as many different users as possible.

MG: Yes, function and context influence the design in equal measure. The wish for diversity also reflects the wishes of an increasingly heterogeneous population. And yet all these variations and different layouts, shaped by the respective context, can still be traced back to a few fundamental types. Attics are the most unusual types because the specifications conflict with the building regulations and the layout has to be reinvented.

MS: A very good illustration of this struggle between type and context can be found in housing construction in Paris after 1850. The network of streets built according to Haussmann's urban planning criteria often produced plots with ridiculously challenging outlines. The three-volume publication by César Daly about this project shows just how inventively these plots were developed. Of course, the apartment types were prescribed by the requirements of the bourgeois lifestyle of the time: a sequence of public rooms facing the street, and the servants' quarters and functional areas facing the courtyard.

AG: Smaller projects, especially, tend to be defined by the context and inscribed into urban or park-like surroundings. Sometimes it is even possible to make a virtue of necessity. And sometimes the phenotype of an architecture developed under difficult circumstances proves more interesting than the genotype produced under normal conditions.

PG: What makes your layouts stand out is their functionality in spite of all context-specific deformations. They are precisely tailored to fit the brief and the budget. Housing construction means keeping an eye on the task in hand, and on the floorplan, which has to be constantly adjusted, so you're not talking so much about radical innovation but about patient research.

AG: Yes, it certainly is. Housing construction is not a freestyle exercise It's always a question of building economically because housing costs make a direct impact on people's everyday living expenses. The modernists tackled this too by asking how you could give as much as possible to as many people as possible at the lowest possible cost. Space, light, air, openings: these are still the issues that define housing construction, just as they did in the past. In addition to the work on the layout and the quest for site-specific architecture, there have also been endeavors and innovations in the past decades in terms of materials—for instance, when aiming for more sustainability.

MS: Another issue is the idea of apartments based on the typology of a certain period. There's a lot of talk about how that has changed fundamentally in lockstep with changing social circumstances. I'm not so sure about that. Old habits die hard …

AG: It is symptomatic that we have, for the most part, pushed our innovations through with a lot of persuasion and have been criticized for not meeting conventional expectations—such as seasonal rooms instead of the usual balcony, or the robust gastro-kitchen and the cast concrete flooring that we have, incidentally, used in high-end apartments …

And, of course, changing technical and social parameters have also impacted housing design in recent years: sound insulation, wheelchair access, thermal insulation, larger balconies that can take dining tables instead of just pot plants, as well as more wet rooms and better storage. The most important interior changes, however, have been the location and size of the kitchen—often a dining kitchen—which goes hand in hand with a wider range of available foodstuffs and, more importantly, the changing role of the woman in the family and in society as a whole. I also think that the apartments are going to change even more, given the increasing number of people working from home, thanks to communication technology. This brings up new questions: does this require larger apartments, or will the bedroom double as an office? We're touching on a very sensitive aspect of living here. Home is meant to be a place of regeneration, of family life, of warmth and comfort.

MS: In addition to working from home, there is the other extreme: homes used simply as a place to sleep. What do you need for that? Not much, really. In those cases, 90 square meters is far too much.

AG: The apartment as an oversized hotel room and a logistics center with a bed, shower, desk, and wardrobe, a television and a handful of books. People who travel a lot, young people, or people who are more inclined to spend their time out and about rather than in their own four walls, need something more suited to their lifestyle than the conventional three-to-four-room apartment.

MS: This trend is already quite far advanced in Japan. A lot of "domestic" activities now take place outside the home. People tend to invite friends to a restaurant rather than to their own home. They eat out, take their clothes to the cleaners, or have their laundry washed and ironed. The neighborhood has become an extension of the home. People don't just live in their apartments, but in the surrounding area, where they make use of services that used to be part of a traditional household.

PG: I like that idea of urban life—the neighborhood as living room. It's all about networking and making new friends, for instance at the laundromat.

AG: That depends on the individual. Family, age, and employment situation can all be factors that shift the line between the desire for privacy and the need for neighborly, social interaction.

It also touches on the theme of physical boundaries and the transition between home and the outside world. Here, too, there has been a change, for instance, bigger window apertures or the way outdoor spaces are designed. You might have balconies, loggias, winter gardens, or a combination of those things: seasonal rooms that can alternate between being outdoor and indoor spaces. All this has changed the way houses relate to the outside and to one another. I actually think that the modernist mantra of light, air, and openness is only now really coming into its own.

PG: But the trend towards bigger windows is disrupting the cityscape. We've talked a lot about how to conserve neighborhoods and in Zurich's District 4, for example, we've noted that when new buildings replace old ones, large windows and balconies are proposed in keeping with current trends. And before you know it, you feel you're in suburbia, rather than in the city center.

As far as the floorplan goes, we don't have much room for innovation. In competition design projects, the floorplans are mostly of a high standard, pretty well planned and optimized. Façades, on the other hand, involve lots of variables and that's where the real difference comes into play; the skills may not be there yet, but the potential certainly is. And besides, there's all this new technology leading to more variables, like windows that can't be opened anymore because of low-energy standards, known as "Minergie" in Switzerland.

Apartment floor plan, Hard Turm Park high-rise, Zurich-West, by architects Gmür & Geschwentner

MS: In contrast to the House on Zürichberg (p. 376), which we looked at together, the buildings don't just face trees, they face other buildings. So it's about protection from the gaze of others, but also about using windows as a framework for the rooms, about giving the rooms a clear shape. That's the problem with big windows: the room loses its shape. For me, finding the right size of a window has a lot to do with a sense of space. It's something a lot of architects don't have —if I may be so bold—and they often don't build spaces any more.

PG: The problem is even more pronounced in the case of a freestanding high-rise, which creates an entirely different situation. There's no shade on the 24th floor, so the light becomes a problem. Large windows can be unpleasant at that height. What would be ideal is a layered, onion-like floorplan. We tried that in our Hard Turm Park apartment block. We placed the bathrooms and kitchens on the side of the façade. Living and sleeping areas were placed in the second row. I believe there are still more options.

AG: It's not just a question of how big the windows are. It's also about how they sit in the façade. A building with big windows can still be urban. It's only when the building has all glass walls, like the Farnsworth house, that it needs to be set in an extensive green area. On the other hand, it is actually more difficult to articulate a balcony in an urban context when it has a certain depth. The open balcony, seen from outside, is the most visible and public space, whereas from inside it is a very private area that can be used for anything from a deckchair or a dining table to a laundry rack. That makes it hard to create an urban environment with balconies. Solid walls with apertures is a proven means of defining urban space—though there are also examples of skimpy windows, which are just as non-urban as big balconies.

MS: As Patrick pointed out, a lot of today's architects have a hard time designing façades. The easiest way out is to create a framework and then fill it with windows. That way you think you don't have any problems with the façade, and in the process you forget the proportions… I don't have to spell out the name Mies van der Rohe to remind you how important proportions are.

MG: In housing construction, there is always a repetitive, serial element to the alignment of similar modules—usually in the form of grid structures, horizontal window ribbons, parapets, or rhythmic lines of vertical glazing and floor-to-ceiling windows. Walls with smaller, more precisely positioned windows are seldom found, because the deep rooms in high-density apartment blocks don't have much façade surface and require a lot of light and views. There's been an inversion of closed and open areas in the design of façades. Older buildings with a ratio of about 30 percent window area to 70 percent wall area are being replaced by ones with reverse proportions. The whole look of the urban setting is changing; the difference between private and public is becoming blurred. I see this as a challenge. In new developments, it presents an opportunity of shaping the public space differently. In existing neighborhoods, on the other hand, where only specific sites are redeveloped, the overall appearance of urban spaces suffers.

AG: This kind of openness, with big windows and fewer curtains, is also a reflection of a society that has become more open.

MG: The whole thing about big windows reaches a critical point when it comes to living on the ground floor, where private space and public space clash. This is where innovative solutions are required both outside and within the buildings themselves, because a lot of people are still going to be living in ground floor apartments in the future.

MS: Or in raised ground floor apartments.

MG: That's the usual solution in existing urban districts where the street and the pavement are directly adjacent to the apartment. In newer developments, the outdoor areas tend to be mixed zones, without any through traffic, so they can be exploited for ground floor use. The private merges with the public; the outdoor area appears more indistinct and less urban. Buildings appear as objects and are no longer anchored by any hierarchical outdoor space.

PG: I think about that a lot. We have to encourage more debate about the city—about the role of public spaces. It's a thorny issue even here in our department, and in terms of traffic planning too.

AG: The old-fashioned solution of the raised ground floor has proved its worth—especially in urban areas. But usually the prescribed maximum building height and the topography don't allow for that in Zurich. Clients are not willing to waste an entire story just so that the ground floor can be raised. Urban planning would benefit enormously if Zurich could be a little more flexible about its building heights and ground floor usage—then apartments wouldn't have to be buried, but could be raised and there would be more leeway to install shops and offices in higher ground floor spaces.

Urban planning, Sulzerareal Werk 1, Winterthur

MG: For the urban masterplan to redevelop the Sulzerareal 238 in Winterthur, the client and the municipal authorities agreed on a raised ground floor once we had presented various layouts and suggested usages, and showed the potential that was there: upper ground floor apartments, high-level work spaces and studios, vertically organized apartments and office spaces as well as local services such as nurseries, kindergartens, stores, and communal rooms and laundry facilities. Overall building potential was optimized by shifting floor areas. This allowed for interesting hybrid solutions.

PG: But you always have to have an idea of what urban means. Now, since I no longer build, I would argue for a return to the exploration of certain themes, like the three-part division of a building into a base, a wall, and a roof.

MS: That's an interesting point: what is housing construction? It's something inherently urban. Does an architect really have to do something special? Is it not enough for you to do something simple and urban in the spirit of, say, Heinrich Tessenow?

MG: Thanks to competitions, the discussion and debate on housing construction in Zurich over the past ten years, with the active involvement of politicians and local authorities, has attracted a lot of talented and also young architects. As a result, some remarkable buildings have been realized which are outstanding in themselves, but which also challenge and change the existing urban fabric. This is something that has not been closely analyzed and in this respect I agree with your call for a return to thinking about the urban environment and sustainable simplicity. However, as impassioned architects, we try to explore the substantive, architectural, and design potential of each and every project—and that includes housing. We do this with the conviction that architecturally successful buildings can have a positive influence on the development of a city.

AG: Let's round off the discussion by taking a look at the question of color, which is also a component in the relationship between the individual and the collective, between architecture and the city. We have repeatedly worked with color in our architectural designs—occasionally in cooperation with artists. For the most part, we have incorporated color wherever we felt that the means at our disposal were not enough to imbue a place with a sense of identity—in such cases, we have deployed color as a cost-effective "fourth dimension."

Signal Box, Zurich

MS: For the Signal Box 018 and Römerholz 006 projects, you experimented with unusual material colors such as iron oxide and copper powder. I like both of those projects. In your housing designs, there is a very varied use of color. Let's just say that not all of them appeal to me in equal measure.

Extension of Oskar Reinhart Collection, Winterthur

AG: When it comes to housing, the starting point and the end results are also very project-specific and site-specific—but the use of color is applied more freely, in the sense that it is not necessarily linked to the

Susenbergstrasse

Pflegi

Broëlberg I

Broëlberg II

Grünenberg

Neumünsterallee

Brunnenhof

Diggelmannstrasse

Geneva I

Erlenhof

Goldschlägi

Zollikerstrasse

material used. There are indeed very different approaches, and it is not so easy to categorize these in groups or "families." An analysis of solutions would start, for instance, with the urban planning aspect of individualizing houses by means of color.

This was done in the case of the three apartment buildings on Susenbergstrasse in the sensitive Zürichberg area: we did this to make them fit in with the surrounding villas and make them look less like a housing development. We took a similar approach in Grünenberg Park, where we worked with various shades of green, echoing the former English-style garden there. That was done in collaboration with the artist Pierre André Ferrand, with whom we had an invigorating and at times critical dialogue. Green can often be a difficult color for houses—perhaps because the eye is so accustomed to seeing endless variations of green in the trees, meadows, and surrounding scenery. When it is applied evenly to a flat surface, it can seem out of place. In both instances, we used mineral pigments on concrete structures. It was the same in the Pflegi project.

In the urban situation of the Pflegi project, we and Adrian Schiess were not simply looking to color the building; we also wanted to use color to define the mood of the semi-public outdoor spaces, the large courtyard and the garden area. In the Brunnenhof project, Adrian Schiess developed a similar theme, but with a completely different material—glass. The park becomes a landscape space in which the building forms a powerful, multi-colored "horizon." By contrast, the dark blue and violet hues of the building façades on the street side are relatively subdued.

Alienation and familiarity were a key theme in our first housing development, Broëlberg I. We wanted to indicate the organic wall structure of the rendered outer insulation. Together with Harald F. Müller, we chose brown rendering for the outside and orange for the courtyard. In the second phase of the Broëlberg

Extension of Villa Kastanienbaum

project (p. 426)—situated within a green hollow—we reiterated the orange theme and also used the concept of dyed concrete, along the lines of the Stellwerk project in Zurich. We tinted the concrete with reddish-orange pigment as a complementary color to offset the predominance of green among the surrounding trees.

In another example of a garden context, the Zollikerstrasse project, we explored the potential of dark tones. Somewhat paradoxically, the buildings appear quite subtle because of their dark brown sheen, but also eye-catching because the reflection of the gardens in the façades creates a live, organic ornament. The extension to the villa (p. 340) in Kastanienbaum has a similarly strong yet subtle use of color with its dark olive green fitting in with the hues of the mature trees.

MG: But we do have a keen awareness of the urban context when it comes to color. If at all, our use of color for apartment buildings in urban situations is more subtle as opposed to suburban areas where it is bolder. You can see that in the Diggelmannstrasse project (p. 508), as well as in the apartment developments at Goldschlägi and Erlenhof. The latter two bring a colorful presence as the first buildings to be erected on former agricultural and industrial sites. These places are changing rapidly and their focus will soon be tempered by the scale of development.

AG: To complete the spectrum, we have to touch on some examples of housing that don't involve such vibrant colors. Examples in densely populated areas include the Rüschlikon project (p. 502) and Neumünsterallee, where we worked with Adrian Schiess to come up with tones of gray and silver. Neumünsterallee is like an oyster: a little rough on the outside, but richer, more vibrant and varied on the inside, with iridescent walls and fittings. And then there's also the detached home in Küsnacht with its subtle gradations of white on the façade by Harald F. Müller,

Two Houses in Zurich

but with an interior that harbors bright and radiant colors.

In some cases, the colors were determined primarily by the materials, as in the Zellweger project with its wood and concrete, or the two earlier houses in Zurich 013 with their lime cement rendering, as well as the latest lime concrete house on Zürichberg, where the variations in sandblasting alone defined the subtle differences in color.

MG: In comparison to our office and museum buildings, we have used color more often in our housing designs because these are often projects with relatively limited potential. Color is a fairly economical way of generating atmosphere and identity; a building can respond more to outdoor spaces and assert itself in its surroundings. Color as the topmost layer is simple to apply and has a broad spectrum of use—sometimes color is part of the material itself. Together with carefully exploited daylight, this expands the possibilities for any design project. We work with artists because they are freer and more experienced in addressing visual concerns and they tend to question the project itself in an independent, sharp-minded and sometimes even subversive way. We choose to subject ourselves to this outside influence because we believe that these challenging forms of cooperation enrich our designs.

MS: I found the grayish brown color for Broëlberg I very appealing, but I found Broëlberg II more problematic because orange is a color that pushes itself to the forefront, at the cost of other surrounding colors such as the green of the trees. I don't like that kind of predominance of one element, whether it is a color or a form. And I would also differentiate between the colors of the rendering and the colors of the glass. Which brings me to the Brunnenhof development: I wouldn't want an artist to place a yellow or blue panel in front of the window that would determine the light in my apartment. Front doors used to be painted yellow or gray or green—so I could tell which one was mine. That might even apply to the whole building if the color is fairly subtle—but not when it affects the light and colors everything in my apartment.

AG: The colored glass panes in the Brunnenhof project can be pushed aside by the residents if they don't want to see that color. In the Goldschlägi project the glass parapets are fixed and the colors and their shadows actually infiltrate the apartment. But when you are inside, the bluish tinge seems quite normal, presumably because it's associated with natural elements like the sky or water.

MG: Color can actually trigger emotions. That may explain why it has never really been accepted as a fundamental tool of architecture since the days of modernism. Color is a very individual and subjective thing, sometimes even irrational, and it often breaks with convention. Every city has found its own canon of color over the years, and has continued to develop that. New colors, when they are introduced, can quickly override that established urban image and draw attention in ways that may be inappropriate. And yet those experiments are important.

PG: As an architect, I also enjoyed working with colors. But now in my new position, I ask an additional question: how do they relate to the city? What happens when the buildings in a city are painted in bright colors? There have been follow-up projects that I vetoed because the reasoning was not compelling enough. The colors had too little to do with the city and the urban context. Aldo Rossi once said that the city should be a gray mass and that only the church and the town hall should be a little more colorful.

MS: But even Rossi took that back when it came to his own housing designs in Berlin.

PG: We made a catalogue of the color canon in Zurich in our atlas *Farbraum Stadt* (Haus der Farbe in collaboration with the Urban Planning Office of the City of Zurich)—a huge project that is also useful as a handbook for architects.

MG: That atlas is a valuable tool as an inventory and also heightens the awareness of color in the urban environment. But if it is to serve as a point of reference for new color applications, it is important to find new and contemporary solutions through analysis and interpretation.

AG: Strong, beautiful, and even inappropriate colors—these all existed before we started coloring our buildings and working with artists. To some extent, our use of color is a response to the colors of the environment, including the traffic and the advertising, because we want to get to grips with the awkwardness and clumsiness, with the less satisfactory aspects of our surroundings; we want to redefine and reinvent them, to transform them into something tolerable and even pleasurable.

Color can substantially enhance buildings and spaces. The Pflegi courtyard springs to mind; before it was colored, it was gloomy and oppressive. And then along came the layer of yellowish-green and the whole exterior took on an almost magical impact and scope.

PG: If you can achieve the kind of variation in the city center that the Pflegi project achieved, then that is what I would call the right use of color. Color and architecture can be combined to good effect.

MS: At this point, I could quote from Tessenow's essay on the external colors of buildings—*Die äussere Farbe unserer Häuser*. He really nails it when he says that "subtle and simple forms, like subtle and simple colors, are always essentially urban, or, to put it another way, inherently social," and so on. But for

Tessenow, gray is the color of the city. And if color serves to distinguish the public nature of streets and courtyards, then that's okay. I wouldn't want to prohibit color as a vehicle of atmosphere, as you put it. It is simply a question of how bright those colors should be so that they can play that role without being overwhelming.

AG: We have tried experimenting with that in various ways, for instance by using the colors of the materials themselves, camouflage colors, bright colors, subtle colors, and working with and without the advice of artists. In the case of the Pflegi project, Adrian Schiess refused to color the street façade, against the client's wishes; in the Diggelmannstrasse project, he pulled out all the stops; and in the Neumünsterallee project, he took a more subtle approach. In Wädenswil, Pierre André Ferrand worked with subdued colors: we almost had to put in a plea for a stronger yellowish green for the third building. So it can't be said that artists are always hell bent on a maximum of color—and neither are we.

I think it's fair to say that many of our apartment buildings make the world a little better for the people who live in them than if they were simply gray or white. I would definitely say that is the case in the Brunnenhof project, in particular, because it was designed for low-income families with many children and gives them a diversity and elegance that creates a positive sense of identity. The brightly colored sliding sunscreens in this large housing development are today's equivalent of the colored front doors of yesteryear.

Three Houses on Susenbergstrasse, Zurich, Switzerland 039

1998–2000

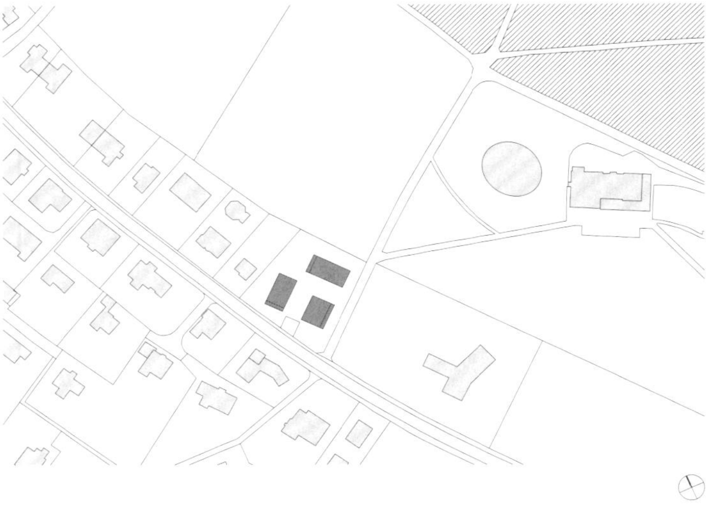

The articulation of the building mass into three volumes takes place within the context of the small-scale, "fine-grained" housing structure in the immediate and extended upscale neighborhood on the Zürichberg. In contrast to the solitary houses and villas, the building volumes react to each other by means of their proportions and with respect to their openings.

The division into three buildings allows the apartments to be oriented in all four directions, which also provides natural light and ventilation for the bathrooms and kitchens. The apartments are laid out in such a way that the service spaces—wet rooms, kitchens, bathrooms, and ancillary spaces—act as closed cores that generate a spatial articulation of the open "living space area." The area thus defined can be easily subdivided into more conventional rooms or living spaces using large sliding doors. Nevertheless, this living area can still be understood as a continuous space aligned with the four points of the compass and correspondingly proportioned and formed.

The four-sided orientation of the apartments is differently accentuated depending on the varying location of the loggias to the east, south, and west. The loggias themselves are conceived as projections from the concrete façades that form narrow open-air rooms along the entire length and width of the building volumes.

The building structure is determined by the space-forming, load-bearing cores of the service blocks. A double-layered concrete façade completes the support framework. The exterior layer, made of in-situ concrete, forms the cantilevered loggias and the perforated parapets of the penthouses. The floor surfaces are made of concrete in various forms and finishes: poured concrete flooring for the living space areas, prefabricated polished cast stone tiles for the secondary rooms, and unpolished tiles for the terraces.

Mineral-based pigments, applied to the concrete with silicate, enable a highly matt, pollen-like "powdered" building surface. An additional intention was to attain the individualization of the three buildings by varying the colors used, while simultaneously emphasizing their compositional coherence. The final coloring was achieved in collaboration with the artist Adrian Schiess. The smallest building is painted a bright yellow, the largest, north-facing one is in grayish green with pink-painted loggias, and the medium-sized building is yellowish apricot with the west-facing façade painted light blue.

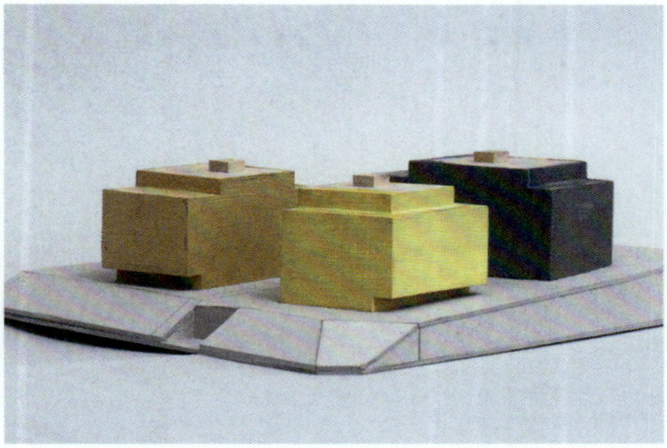

Color studies

Ground floor with studios and ancillary rooms

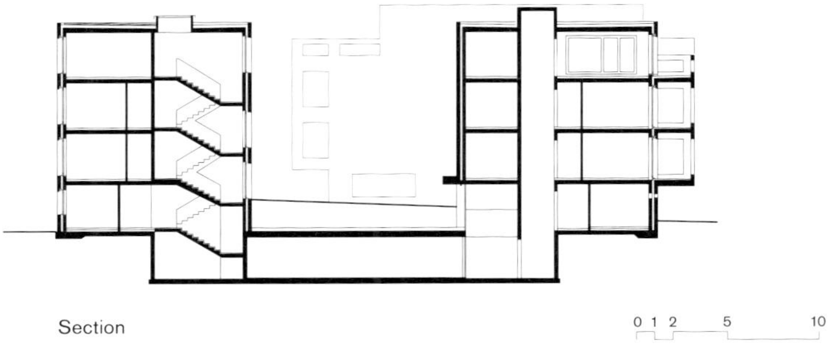

Section

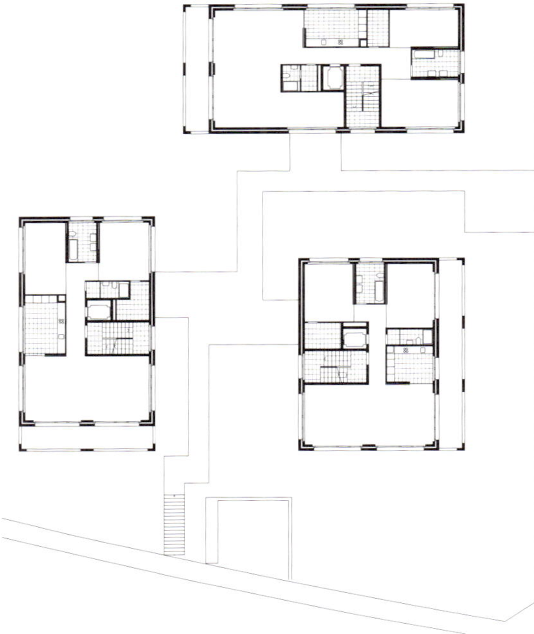

1st and 2nd floors

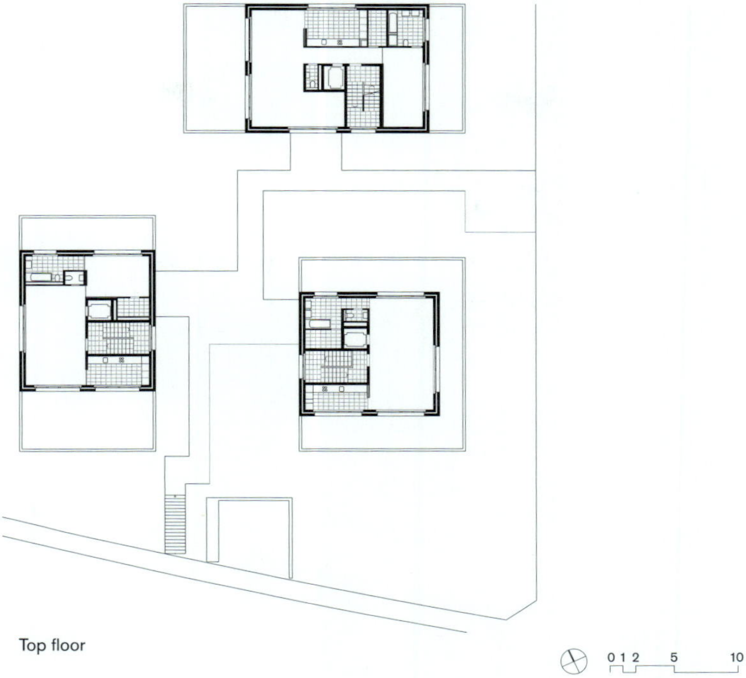

Top floor

Housing Development Broëlberg II, Kilchberg, Switzerland 040

1999–2001

1 Broëlberg I
2 Broëlberg II

The complex is located in the eastern part of Broëlberg Park in a hollow between the old manor house and a villa built in the 1950s. Through variations in shape, height, and depth, the angled complex responds to the features of the site: the topography, the surrounding groups of trees, and the view to the lake.

The qualities and aspects of the site are reflected in a multitude of different apartment types. The structural cores for stairs, elevators, kitchens, bathrooms, and service installations define the living areas. These areas can be further subdivided with non-load-bearing walls, allowing individual arrangements ranging from traditional rooms to an open space.

Closely linked to kitchen and living room, the glazed loggias become focal points in the apartments. On the ground floor they access an outdoor patio and on the top floor large terraces. Shifts in the ground plan allow each apartment to face in several directions. The height of the rooms (2.70 m), the large horizontal openings with sliding windows, and the dark, solid oak floors throughout lend the apartments a sense of spaciousness.

Outside, the smooth, seamless, fairfaced concrete enhances the volumetric presence of the building. Its orange-red tone, pigmented with iron oxide, complements the saturated green of the surroundings in summer and harmonizes with the dark brown of the bare trees in winter. The color scheme was developed in close collaboration with Harald F. Müller. The windows with their dark brown anodized aluminum frames reinforce the twofold reading of the façade as a grid or perforated wall.

An elongated lobby provides access to the building and leads to two sets of stairs with an elevator serving each. Along one side of the hallway the color of the façade continues on the inside and is additionally accentuated through the windows, which are mounted flush with the exterior and have an orange-red painted frame on the interior. The green of the park and the orange of the façades are reflected in the lacquered, natural concrete wall opposite. The worked surfaces of the lobby and staircases mediate between the colorful exterior façades and the white plaster walls in the apartments. Lamps placed alternately in the ceilings and walls complement the effects of space, material, color, and light.

Floor plan staked out

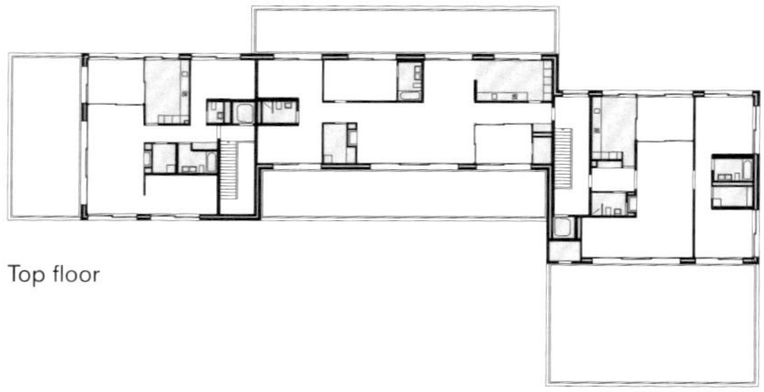

Top floor

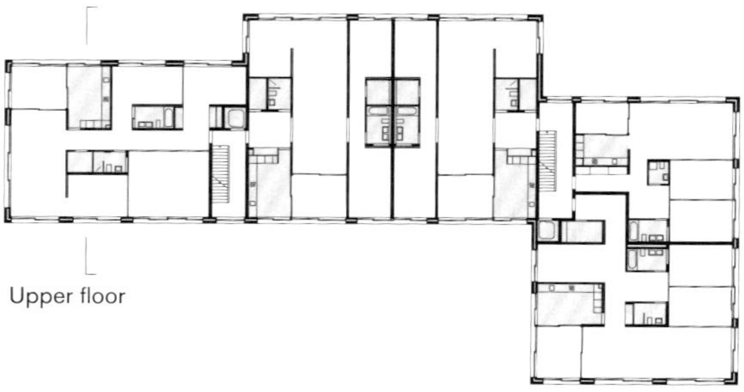

Upper floor

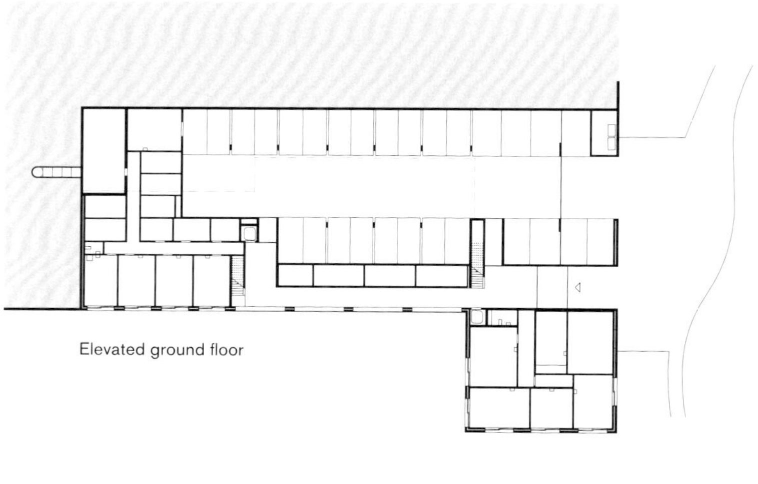

Elevated ground floor

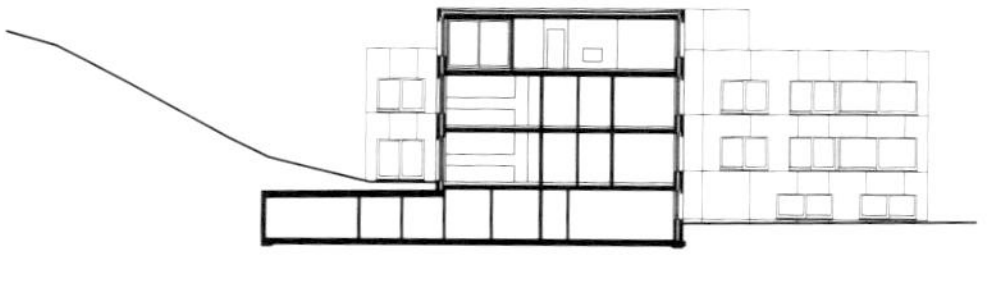

Section

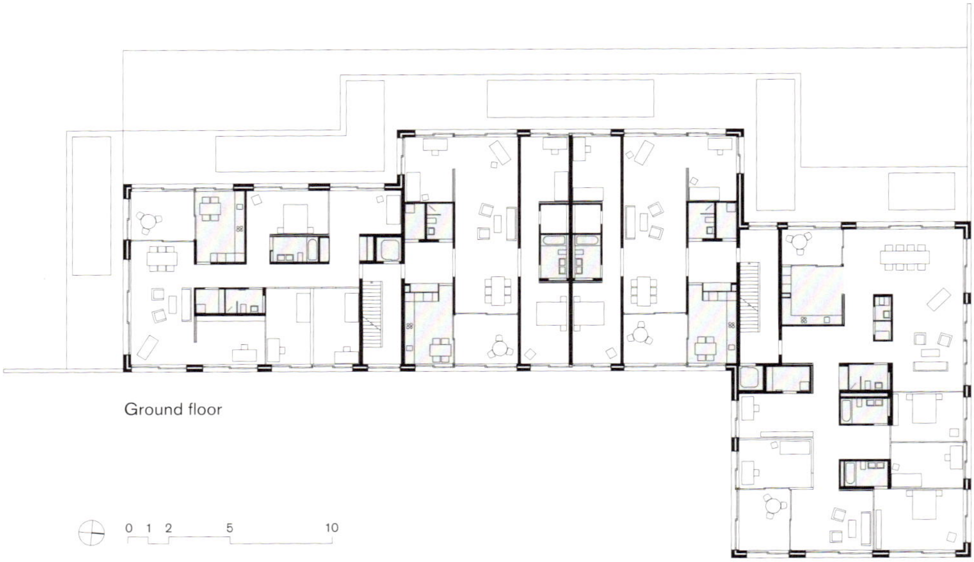

Ground floor

Housing Development and Remodeling, Pflegi-Areal, Zurich, Switzerland 071
1998–2002

The quality of the building stock of the former hospital "Pflegerinnenschule Zürich" indicated a clear allocation of the new functions—offices and housing—within the existing and newly constructed buildings. It was possible to retain the buildings to the southwest by Pfister Architects from 1933/34 and convert the former hospital wards into offices, while the heterogeneous hospital buildings to the northeast were replaced by housing.

Despite substantial interventions, the goal was to retain the spatial character of the large-scale facility. Akin to the former hospital building complex and the neighboring freestanding houses, the new buildings form a hybrid ensemble between a closed block development and individual building volumes.

Together with the existing buildings, the new housing complex demarcates and defines three large exterior spaces: the garden, the Samaritan Court, and the Carmen Court. The former patients' garden, with its beautiful trees, was left almost untouched. The Samaritan Court serves as new access area for the underground parking garage and offers drop-off and parking space. The Carmen Court, in place of the former nurses' garden and lying atop the new parking garage, now stretches across the entire length of the site. The ground here consists of fine gravel as well as large poured concrete slabs, which form a wide access path to the apartment entrances. Willows are planted in large baskets made of steel reinforcement bars and filled with stones and earth. Set atop the garage roof, these baskets form a nutrient-rich habitat as well as providing root space and acting as a counterweight for the trees.

Housing in the newly constructed buildings consists primarily of single-level apartments with generous floor plans. A total of forty-eight apartments with twenty-two different floor plan types offer 2.5 to 6.5 rooms. In addition, nine work studios were built at courtyard level. To cater to contemporary living/working constellations, some ground-level apartments are connected with the courtside studio spaces via internal stairs. Placing the ancillary and service spaces at the center of the apartments permits free circulation, while the load-bearing use of the service core allows for minimal, as well as conventional room divisions. Several apartments have exterior spaces in the form of terraces. Most of them, however, possess a kind of "fresh-air space," also called a "seasonal room." It transforms into an open loggia in good weather and can be used as a normal, heated interior space during the rest of the year.

Concrete is used for the basic construction as well as for the interior flooring. Gravel and sand, two ingredients of concrete, form the floor surfaces outside and on the roofs. The load-bearing cores and double-layered exterior walls form the support structure. Generous window openings provide the apartments with ample daylight and a sense of space. The highly perforated wall surfaces become skeleton-like structures and give the apartments—analogous to the existing buildings—a pragmatic, urban air.

Colors applied in the form of mineral-based, highly matt pigments contrast with the unpretentious, commonplace expression of the architectural language. The use of color was developed in collaboration with the artist Adrian Schiess as a means of defining the atmosphere of the outdoor spaces (Carmen Court, garden). Thus, only three of the long façades are painted, while the street front, the short façades, and the reveals were left unpainted. The colors chosen are yellow-green and white in the Carmen Court, and blue toward the garden. The yellow-green tone on the southwest façade of the Carmen Court colors the light and reflects its hue when the sun shines onto the opposite, white-painted façade, thereby "bathing" the entire courtyard space. The blue coat of paint on the garden side mingles with the green of the trees to transform the old garden into a blue-green "landscape space"—right in the middle of the city.

Former hospital "Pflegerinnenschule"

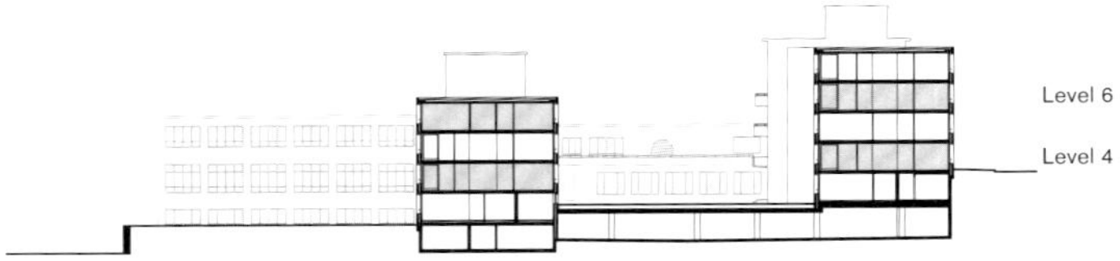

Cross section through new builds

Level 6 / 2nd floor Carmenstrasse / 3rd floor Samariterstrasse

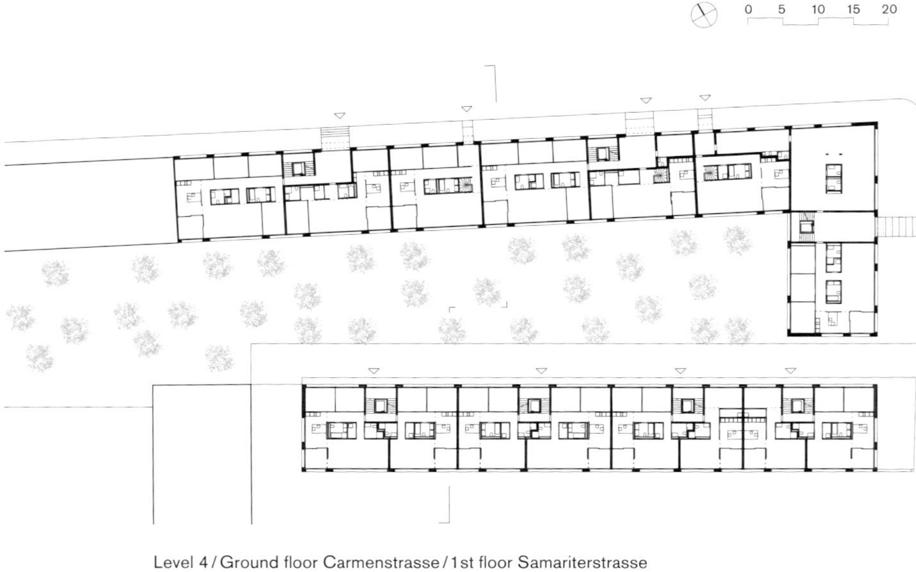

Level 4 / Ground floor Carmenstrasse / 1st floor Samariterstrasse

Color studies

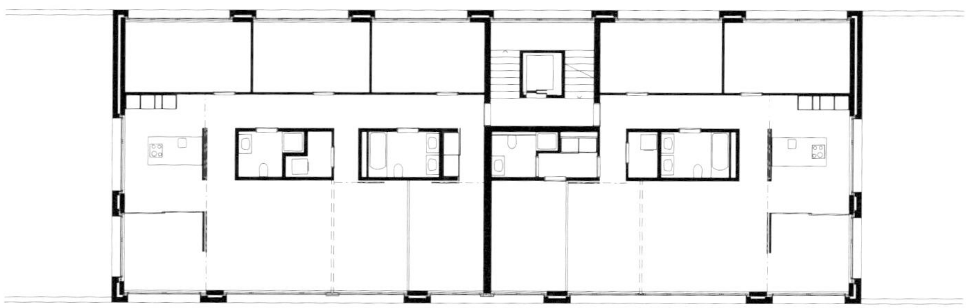

Apartments with seasonal rooms, Level 6 / 2nd floor Carmenstrasse

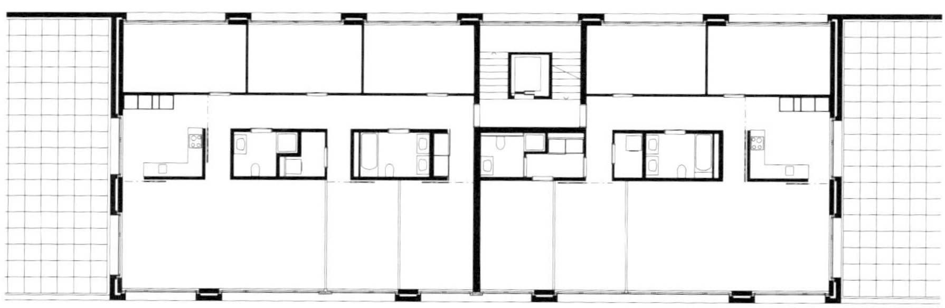

6.5/5.5-room-apartments with terraces, Level 5 / 1st floor Carmenstrasse

Seasonal room

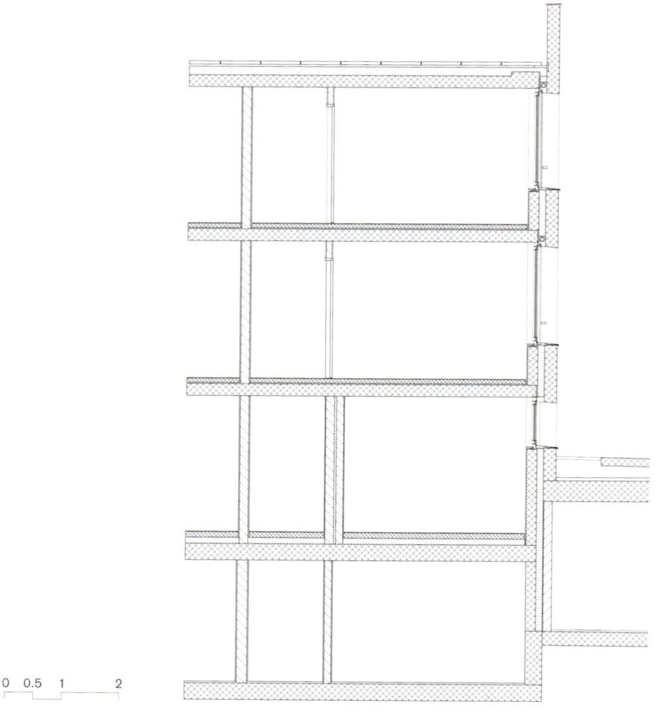

Construction detail

HEMA
HEMA
pure beauty
RITUALS

NEW

Residential and Retail Building, Almere, The Netherlands 108
2002–07

The Dutch town of Almere is not a place that has grown successively, but was planned on a drawing board, originating after the war as polder land reclaimed from the Ijsselmeer Lake. The masterplan for the new, enlarged town center was developed by the OMA architecture studio. A striking characteristic of this city center area is an artificially raised, curved slab ("Gebogen Maaiveld"), which connects the existing retail center with the Weerwater Lake as a new pedestrian level. Underneath this floor slab is an area for local east-west vehicular traffic, as well as for deliveries, parking, and buses. The new residential and retail building is situated at the highest point of the curved slab, where access roads lead to the "underworld" of services and infrastructure.

The masterplan envisioned the combined residential and retail structure to be a high and very deep building volume with a footprint measuring 27 × 55 meters. With a trapezoidal floor plan that bends inward on both sides, it was possible to achieve the maximum possible amount of natural light for the residential spaces within the given perimeter. The volume does not rise up in a straight vertical line, but inclines toward the south and east while broadening as it ascends.

On the ground and first floors the retail areas are occupied by the Hema department store chain, with the second floor used as storage space. Both basement levels serve as a parking garage. Originally conceived as condominiums, a total of 72 apartments are now offered for rental over eight floors. As a result of the expansion of the building volume toward the top, larger, south-facing apartments can be offered on the higher, more desirable floors. The floor plans are largely derived from the tunnel formwork technique commonly used in the Netherlands.

On the residential floors the building form is defined by the bands of glazed balcony parapets. In plan the glazed façade of each apartment describes an obtuse angle, thereby forming triangular balcony spaces as well as providing privacy from the neighboring balconies. The jagged shape of the floor plan repeats to a lesser extent the principle followed by the greater building volume of maximizing surface area and natural light.

The façade is wrapped entirely in glass: color-enameled glazing is employed for the cladding of the ground floor, while the parapets of the apartment balconies consist of safety glass laminated with colored film. The residential areas have floor-to-ceiling windows to maximize natural light. The color concept for the building's façades was developed in collaboration with the artist Adrian Schiess: orange for the corners facing the south and east, light green toward the pedestrian area, light blue facing north, and finally, highly reflective silver for half of the two longest, angled façades toward the north and south. The inward- and outward-slanting glazed surfaces reflect the sky and surroundings, while the obtuse-angled surfaces additionally reflect the building itself as well as the nearby exterior spaces. The immediate surroundings thus play an integral part in how the building is perceived.

HEMA
Hospitaalgarage
Esplanade
Bioscoop
Schouwburg
Kunstencentrum

Residential and Retail Building, Almere, The Netherlands

Façade model

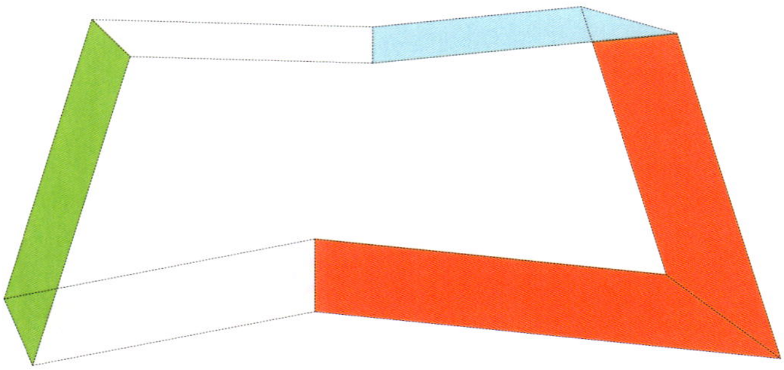

Color concept for façade

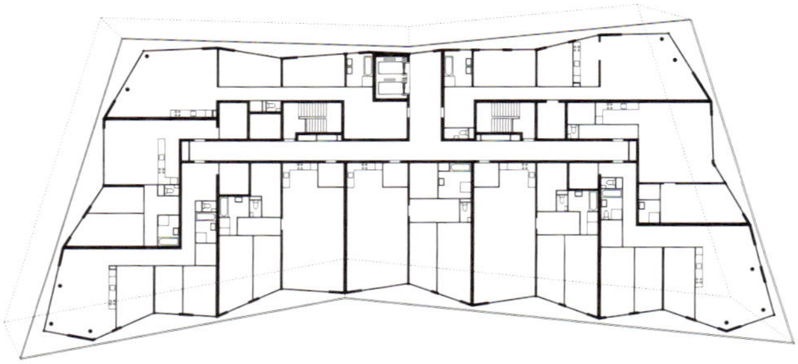

10th floor

3rd floor

Ground floor with retail use

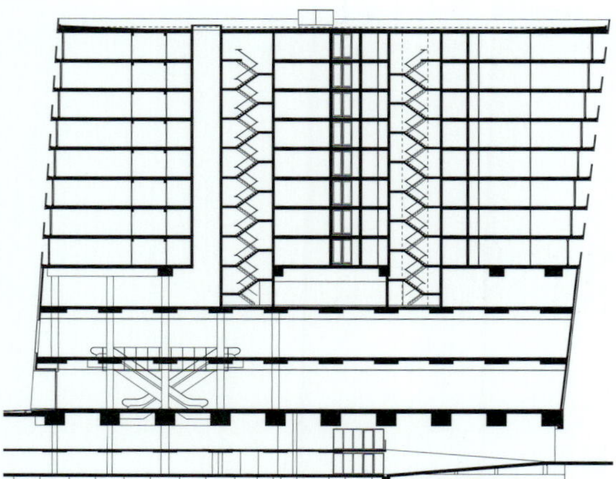

Section A–A

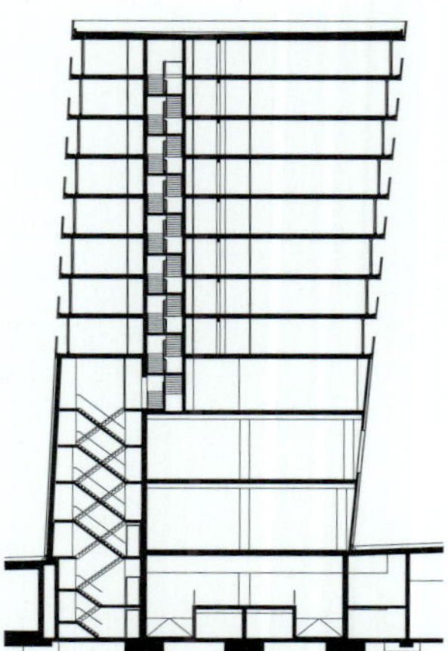

Section B–B

Dear Annette, Dear Mike,

When we met in 1994 and began to work together for the first time on the Davos Sports Center, our cooperation gave me an opportunity to experiment with my painting in public space and to put my ideas into practice. In the eighties these notions of painting outside the traditional exhibition setting in a museum or a gallery had a very pronounced influence on my work. Nowadays my position is somewhat different. Back then I was working mainly on the panels series, although all the other groups of works, such as photos, videos, paintings, watercolors, and murals were also taking shape at the same time. In all of our projects during that period it was important for me to show each particular place by means of the colors I used—to paint a place, not to describe it! The focus for me was not on painting the architecture, making it more visible or even concealing it. In each of our projects the emphasis for me was explicitly on showing the particular place, the sky, the surroundings, the light, the seasons, through the dispersing, scattering effect of the colors I used. I enjoyed rendering these things visible in a way that could generate fleeting images for someone looking at these places. In each of our projects—I'm thinking here of "Susenbergstrasse," the "Pflegerinnenschule" complex, and particularly "Almere," "Diggelmannstrasse," and "Brunnenhof"—I tried to use your buildings in a sense as reflectors, in order to present these places as they are and to offer a way of experiencing them on those terms. For the "Diggelmannstrasse" project I aimed to direct the gaze toward this district at the foot of the Üetliberg, set below the forest, with the forsythias and shrubs in the small gardens and with the colored shadows on the sidewalks. I read the southern façades of the "Brunnenhof" as a kind of backdrop to the park in front with its large beeches, birches, and fir trees, and of course the people there. On the reflecting surface of the pool in front of the university, the world appears as a transient illusion, inviting us to plunge in and lose ourselves within it. Two stairs below this, entering the underground lecture hall, the colors seem to open up psychedelic parallel worlds, a kind of alternative universe existing alongside the humanities and sciences taught there.

It seems to me that we share a tacit consensus about the intermeshing of art/painting and architecture in order to reveal the particular features of the places and spaces in question, an approach that has been the basis informing our cooperation over the years. This entails the painting dovetailing with the architecture, conjoining with it, so that the combined impact of the distinct media can grow out of this interaction. In the process, I always found it important to introduce a note of "discontinuity" into these sites, inviting the gaze to wander, to lose its way.

As I mentioned earlier, I see all this somewhat differently nowadays, and some of the emphases have shifted. I am much more interested now in classic wall painting, classic murals in interiors, and I find myself fascinated once again by the possibilities they present. Perhaps this has something to do with the rampant plagiarism of our colorful projects, manifested in forlorn copies bereft of any real link to their settings. Probably a greater insistence on my artistic concerns has something to do with it too. However, these imitations are what have led me to realize how readily our aims, outlined above, can be turned into the opposite of what we were seeking, producing banal, unintelligent, and irksome results. In projects over the last few years, I have responded to this by seeking to be more selective in incorporating my painting into the architecture and demarcating it from everything else. In 2005 Hans-Jörg Ruch invited me to participate in a project in S-chanf, where I was fortunate to be able to develop a painting for a private interior. This picked up on my experience with the Davos Sports Center hallway, yet went beyond it, opening up new possibilities for me with regard to wall paintings. Shortly afterward, I painted a work for Mike on one of the walls in his home, designed as a classic mural. It has a strong presence as an autonomous image that relates to the light, place, and time, while striking a balance with the asymmetrical architecture and mediating between indoors and outdoors. Similar considerations also informed the large mural for the lobby of the Prime Tower in Zurich. With its iridescent transitions from yellow-green, golden yellow, orange, and crimson to violet, light blue, ultramarine, and dark green, it oscillates between wall, frieze, ornamentation, and image. As the light shifts throughout the day, this transit area and the space above the reception desk are reflected as phosphorescent illusions in the velvety-looking, yet glossy surface of the painting. Like the hallway in the Davos Sport Center, the pool and lecture hall at Zurich University, and the glass façades in Almere and in the Brunnenhof residential complex, this giant mural perpetually seeks to banish time, to create a sense of the immediacy of the present moment almost as if it were doing so casually, in passing, while simultaneously highlighting the indeterminacy of painterly objectives. Yet, to paraphrase Paul Valéry: What would painting be without architecture, the mother of the arts?

Adrian Schiess

Water basin, University of Zurich, 2002
Exhibition, Domaine de Kerguéhennec, 1993

Exhibition, Indianapolis Museum of Art, 2007
Wall painting, entrance hall, Prime Tower, 2011

Freshly Prepared en Route

Adopting an open attitude toward cooperation and not having everything cast in stone at the outset makes it possible to break down rigid preconceptions and allows scope for new visions—for serenity and lightness in the spirit of Matisse. The things I share with Annette and Mike are an interest in the whole and a delight in attentive discovery and in developing ideas further, right down to the smallest detail, right down to the composition of the pigments. Intensive exchanges produce fresh impulses, inviting interventions with their own individual stamp. Our cooperation is most fruitful when it is rooted in movement, in the process of consciously being en route.

The source for the colors and materials I bring to the architecture are my color archive and my pigments, along with visual material discovered during my rambles, such as color combinations I observe along the way. In this process of finding the right mix, almost all the combinations I see fail to pass muster; only a few linger, those that are able to challenge the individual building and its setting. Just as in my "Cuts," which are increasingly developing out into space, the principle underlying my work involves cutting out a particular detail and shifting it from its original context into a new setting. This same modus operandi applies to transpositions in architectural projects.

In this context, the question of the autonomy of art versus architecture is subsumed in a process of research—the focus is not on the one or the other; it is about the entire ensemble. The artistic process always begins anew, looking with an impartial gaze and an openness to discovering the powerful potential within the relationship between architect and artist, between an architectural situation and an artistic intervention. Empathetically engaging with existing or planned structures with heightened attention is a crucial ingredient for success—and as a result the interventions are not submerged in the whole, but rather unfurl within it. In my vision of how my contributions meld with the architecture, color systems and established formulas do not count—what counts is courage.

"Broëlberg I," our first joint project, was based on my studies on the color brown—the umber of Italy, the dark brown of an exhibition design in Cairo's Museum of Art, and a very attentively observed color combination of neutral brown and light red in the felt uniforms worn by Malév Airlines' flight attendants. It was the architects' idea to use brown to add a touch of "alienating" unfamiliarity to the coloring of the plastered façades, at the same time creating a grounding link to the existing park landscape—I found the right brown tone in a pure clay earth pigment. Early on in the process I had thought of including red in the project, but this idea only took on tangible form when I bought a notebook with a light-red hardboard cover during a stopover at Nice airport—and realized I had found the right color for the courtyard.

The most recent project, "First Cuts" in the Prime Tower, emerged from Mike's notion of using image-covered screens made of perforated aluminum sheeting to provide noise absorption. I was glad to be invited to tease out the idea of intermeshing images with architecture a little further. At this stage in Zurich's urban development the Prime Tower marks an incisive turning point. In keeping with this spirit, I selected "First Cuts" from cultural and scientific history (both generic and specific to Switzerland and Zurich), along with motifs from classical Modernism that are emblematic of a new era in art and have had an enduring impact—just like the urban planning decision to construct the Prime Tower as a pioneering intervention. Even if some day new skyscrapers in Switzerland may soar even higher than the Prime Tower, the outstanding aspect of the architecture is inscribed in the building in its "First Cuts."

Harald F. Müller

Housing Complex Broëlberg II, Kilchberg, 1999–2001
Housing Complex Goldschlägi, Schlieren, 2005–2009
Extension of Workshop School Buildings Appisberg, Männedorf, 1998–2002
Detached House, Küsnacht, 2005–2007

First Cuts: Silberpfeil, Prime Tower, Zurich, 2011
First Cuts: Röntgen, Prime Tower, Zurich, 2011
Color samples for interior courtyard, Housing Complex Broëlberg I, Kilchberg, 1990/1994–1996

EDELSTAHL
KOHLER
EDELSTAHL

Ft A 4 210 x 297
RÉF. 7928

NICE AIRPORT

Brölhorg I

LA COURONNE

35F

bloc buro

100 Feuilles Détachables

Format 70 x 100	REF. 7921
Format 85 x 120	REF. 7922
Format 100 x 145	REF. 7923
Format 110 x 170	REF. 7924
Format 148 x 210	REF. 7926
Format 210 x 297	REF. 7928

3 240180 079282

Une baie rouge
a roulé
sur la gelée blanche du jardin

Masaoka Shiki (1867–1902)

Il faut partir de l'idée que la couleur est présente dans le projet architectural dès sa conception bien que, dans sa phase initiale de réalisation, elle demeure invisible aux yeux de chacun. Rendre cette couleur visible, voilà ce qui est demandé. Dans cette situation qu'il sait unique, le peintre doit en quelque sorte agir sans agir … c'est-à-dire que sa tâche est accomplie avec précision si à la fin on ne perçoit ni son intervention, ni son travail.

Pierre André Ferrand, juillet 2011

The point of departure should be the notion that color is present in an architectural project right from the moment when it is conceived, even if it is still invisible for everyone in the initial phase of realization. The challenge lies in rendering this color visible. In this situation, aware that it is unique, the painter must in a sense act without acting … in other words, the painter has brought the requisite precision to the task if ultimately neither his intervention nor his labor are perceptible.

Pierre André Ferrand, July 2011

3560

Housing Complex Park Grünenberg, Wädenswil, Switzerland 114

2002/2004–07

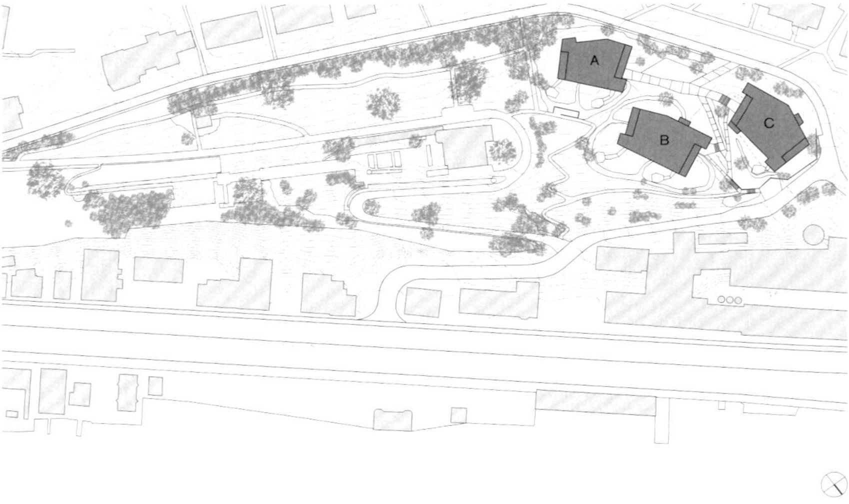

One of the goals of this project was to make the existing Park Grünenberg the key theme of the new housing development. Three residential buildings were set in the western area of the park, formerly a landscape garden, while the architectural section of the garden to the east, along with the listed villa (Robert Bischoff and Hermann Weideli, 1910) were preserved as is. The new volumes are arranged and formed in a manner that guarantees vistas and perspectives onto the park or the lake. In conjunction with the vegetation, these polygonal volumes give the impression of a colorful "rock garden."

The material used for the façades and construction is concrete—or "cast stone." The exterior concrete shells extend into cantilevered structures, forming and bearing balconies. The concrete surfaces are finely sandblasted and coated with a glaze of mineral pigments. The artist collaborating on the color scheme, Pierre André Ferrand, envisioned a different tone for each building—dark gray, ochre, and yellow—each containing the color green. The appearance of the pigments themselves is completely matt, similar to a colored powder coating. From the outside, large windows reflect the surrounding trees, the sky, and the lake, while affording sweeping views from inside the apartments.

The careful arrangement of the apartments with their varying layouts enables each to benefit from the buildings' orientation and location. In the smallest building (A), situated to the south, two apartments share each floor, enjoying either the virtues of slightly more lake views and evening sun in summertime, or more southern light. For the larger buildings located to the east and north (B and C), a variety of apartment types ensures that each is provided with both optimal natural light and vistas to the lake. The eight different types range from single-story units oriented toward three sides, to others with a living room that extends all the way through the building, to duplexes.

In analogy to the former landscape gardens, the green areas between the buildings are dotted with scattered trees and copses. Blooming bushes and evergreen shrubs adorn and organize the green spaces and distinguish the public areas from private gardens. The pathways are laid out as light-colored concrete surfaces that broaden and narrow, their effect comparable to large, level slabs of rock within the landscape.

Color studies

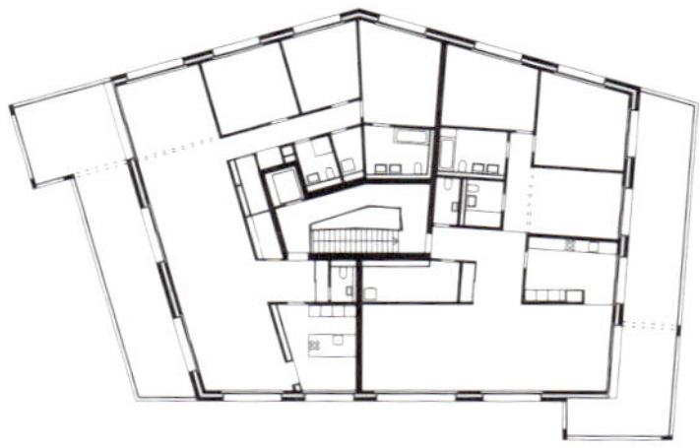

4th floor

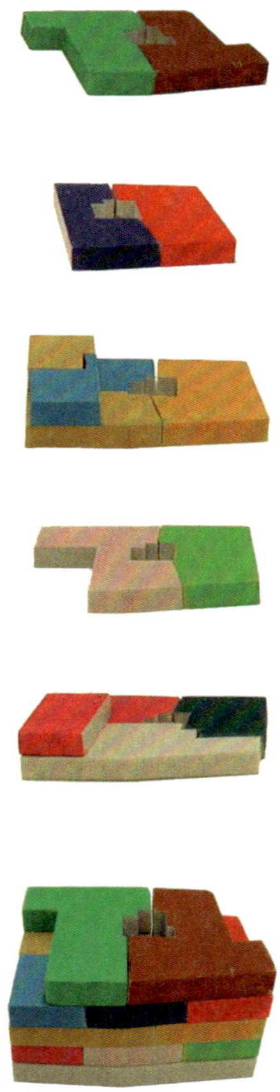

Arrangement of apartments within the volume

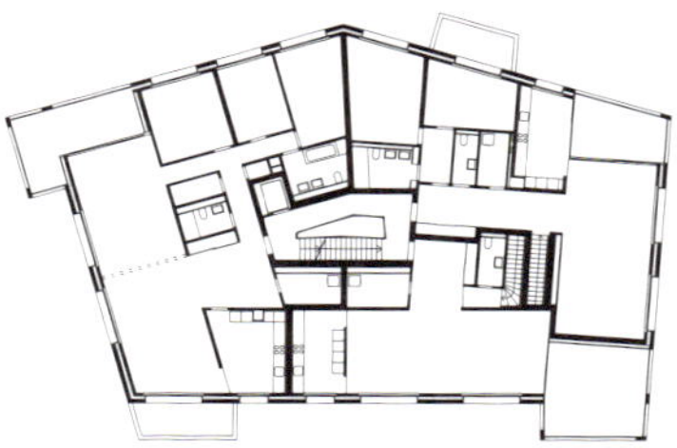

3rd floor

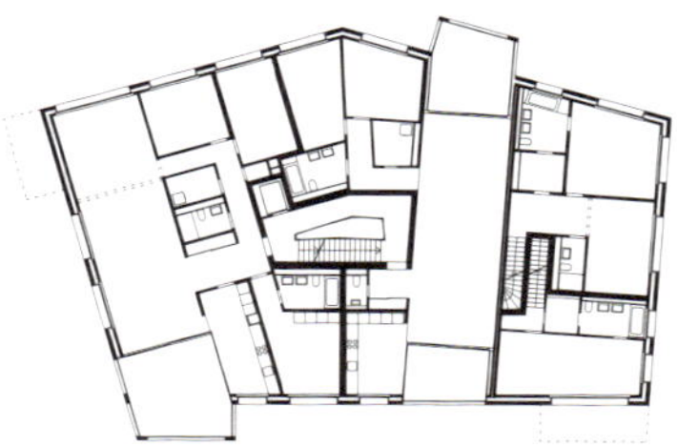

2nd floor

1st floor

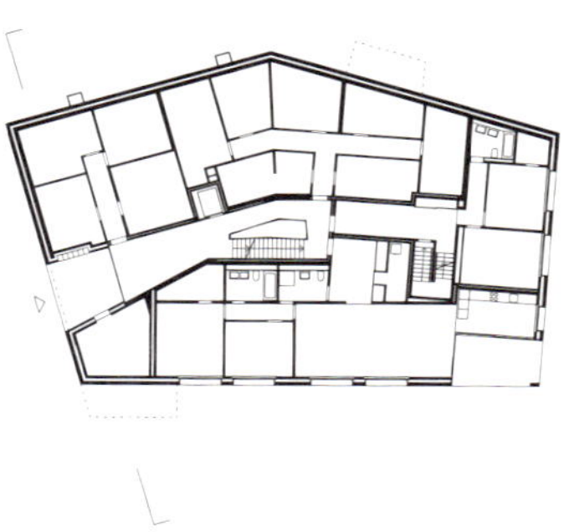

Ground floor

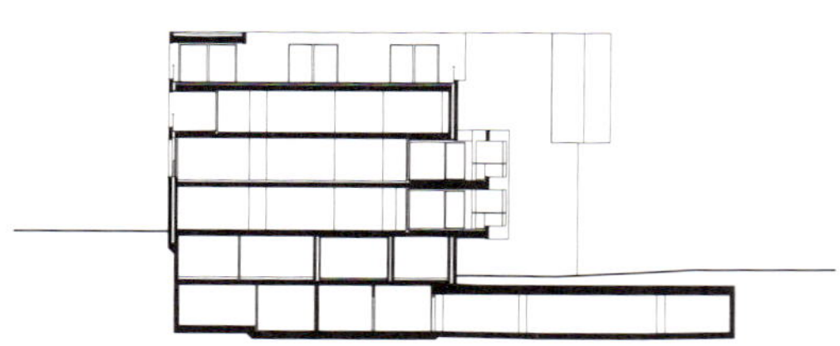

Section

House A

3rd floor

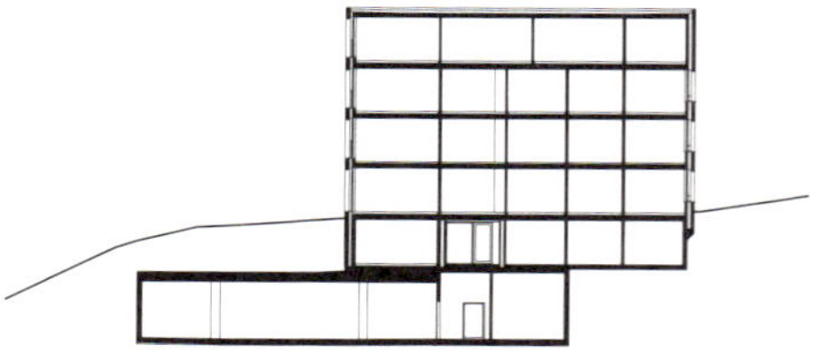

Section

House A

House B

3rd floor

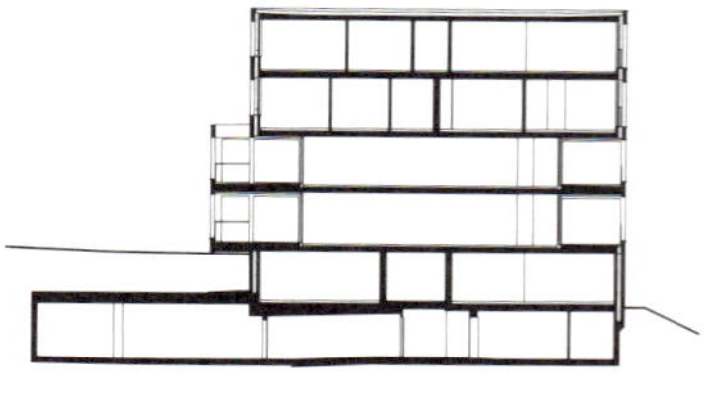

Section

House B

Housing Development Goldschlägi, Schlieren, Switzerland 169
2005–09

The Goldschlägi site is located adjacent to the railway station in the center of Schlieren. The site borders a wide stretch of railway track to the north and a green space to the south that serves as a vista and access area for the apartments. The elongated, narrow residential buildings emphasize the orientation of the plot parallel to the tracks, but rigidity is alleviated by their offset alignment. The height of the complex varies between three and six floors, resulting in a division of the overall volume that creates differentiated outdoor spaces.

The urban concept is reflected in the individual apartment types. Those rooms in which noise level is of less relevance, such as the access cores, kitchens, and bathrooms, are located on the north, facing the tracks. All living rooms and bedrooms, as well as the generously proportioned, projecting balconies, face south over the garden area. Their staggered positioning provides residents with an outdoor space one or two stories high. The parapets and the side elements are composed of colored glass panels that ensure privacy and cast bright blue shadows when the sun shines.

The complex is divided into 105 apartments with different floor plans and of varying sizes (with 1, 2, or 3 bedrooms). All have one open-plan living/dining/kitchen area that is naturally lit from both sides. The kitchen and bathroom form one module in each unit, and a large number of different floor plans have been generated through its alternate siting.

The projecting and recessed façades facing the tracks have been finished in a bright red. The black-framed windows of various sizes and division—belonging to the kitchens, bathrooms, dining areas, and staircases—create a rhythmic pattern. The south-facing façades and the end walls are of white plaster, with the window frames and sunblinds executed here in anodized aluminum.

Concrete floor slabs cast in-situ and prefabricated concrete supports give the complex a regular structure. Bracing is achieved by means of the stairwells and the external end walls. The concrete structure is encased in large, prefabricated and insulated timber elements, clad with a rear-ventilated and plastered façade. Using frame construction throughout and avoiding load-bearing internal walls wherever possible has ensured a high degree of flexibility with regard to the floor plans.

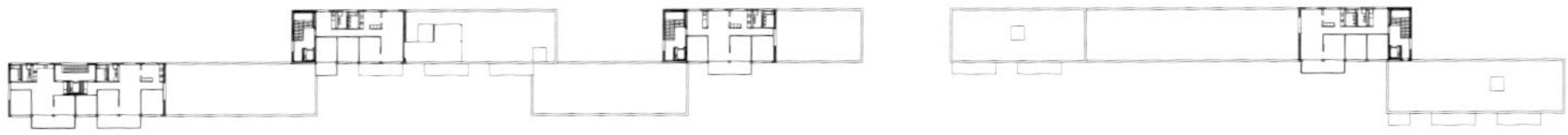

5th floor

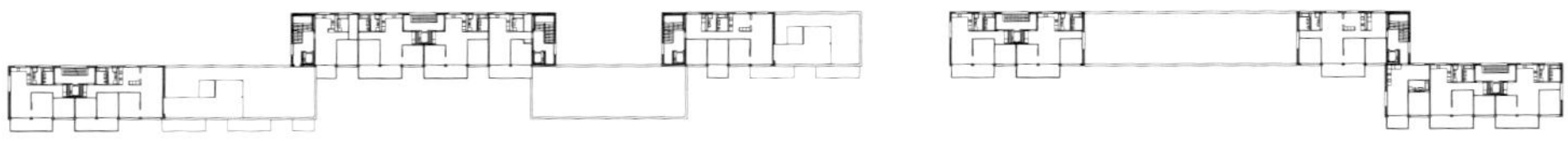

4th floor

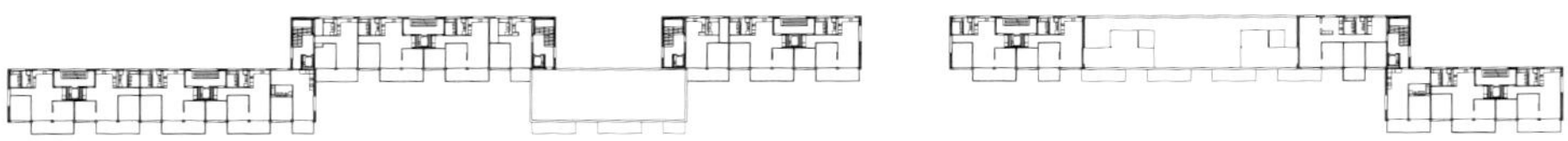

3rd floor

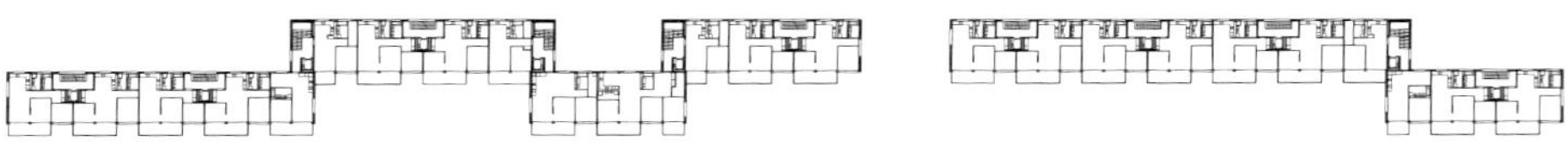

2nd floor

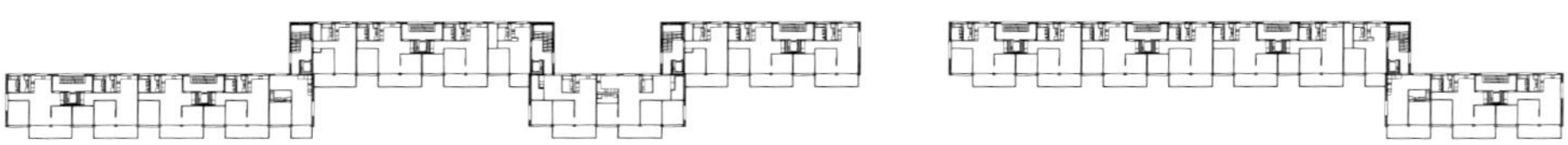

1st floor

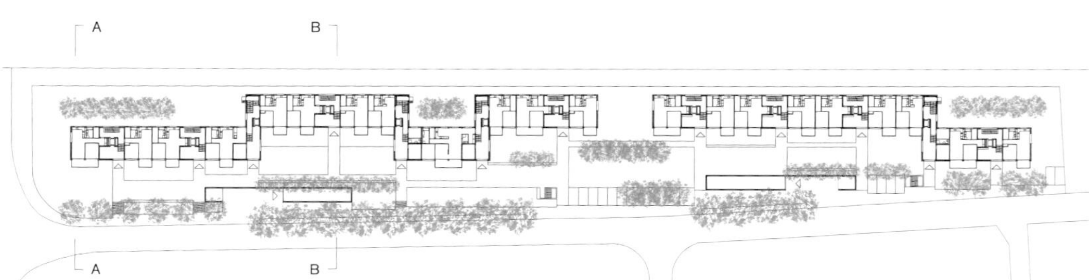

Ground floor

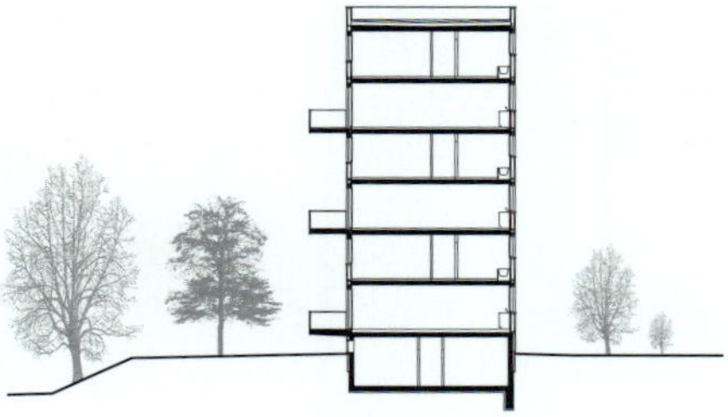

Section A–A

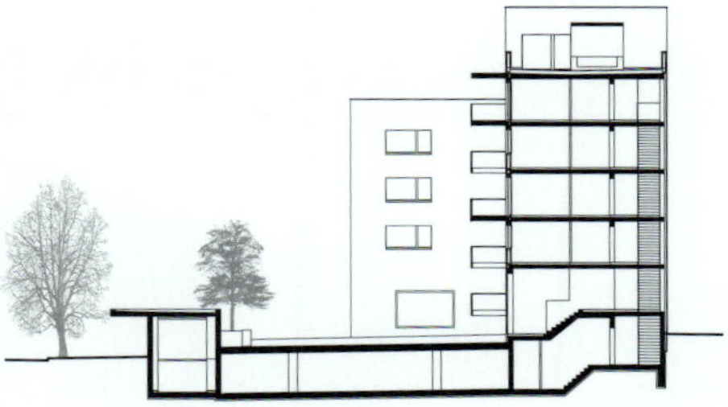

Section B–B

0 2 5 10 20

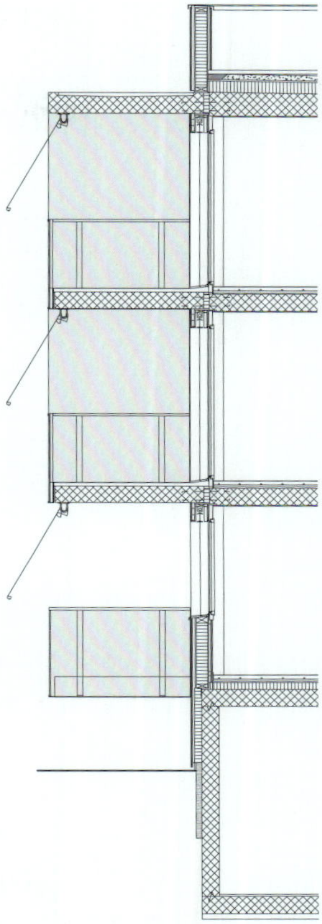

Construction section, south façade

0 0.5 1 2

5th floor

4th floor

4.5-room apartments

1st and 3rd floors

3.5-room apartments

2nd floor

1st and 3rd floors

2.5-room apartments

Ground floor and 2nd floor

Housing Complex Zollikerstrasse, Zurich, Switzerland 178
2005–11

The impressive existing trees on the site of the former villa—a copper beech, a redwood, and a pine tree—influenced the architecture of the replacement buildings in several ways. The trees had an impact on the position, shape, materials, and also the colors of the new structures, calling for a specific architectural reaction to the immediate surroundings.

The new built volume is much larger than the previous building and is divided into two units. An unusually narrow space establishes a visual connection between the shady garden beneath the trees on the street side and the private garden to the west. The narrow interspace is widened and opened up by reflections in the façades' glazed surfaces, which visually "duplicate" the garden.

The fulfillment of various specifications regarding noise protection, the spacing required by the building code, and also the protection of the trees' roots calls for footprints that are not rectangular. However, an orthogonal structure is inscribed within the irregular polygons.

In total, the complex houses eight owner-occupied apartments and one studio, which differ widely in size and character. This is expressed in the number of levels, the ceiling heights, and the respective outdoor spaces. For example, the penthouses have terraces while the apartments on the first and second floors have covered loggias. The three apartments on the ground floor are duplexes, two of which feature living rooms with high ceilings and direct access to a private garden.

Large slabs of in-situ concrete define the private outdoor spaces of the ground-floor apartments. Low yew hedges, interspersed with blooming plants, form loose green divisions between the various garden spaces. The hedges also constitute green boundaries toward the street. Ferns and low shrubs cover the "forest soil" underneath the trees.

The polygonal buildings are covered with dark brown enameled glass panels that reflect the garden space like a kaleidoscope and therefore enhance the presence of the small garden. The mirrored vegetation casts a lively ornamental pattern across the façades, paying homage to the exterior painted decoration on nearby Villa Patumbah.

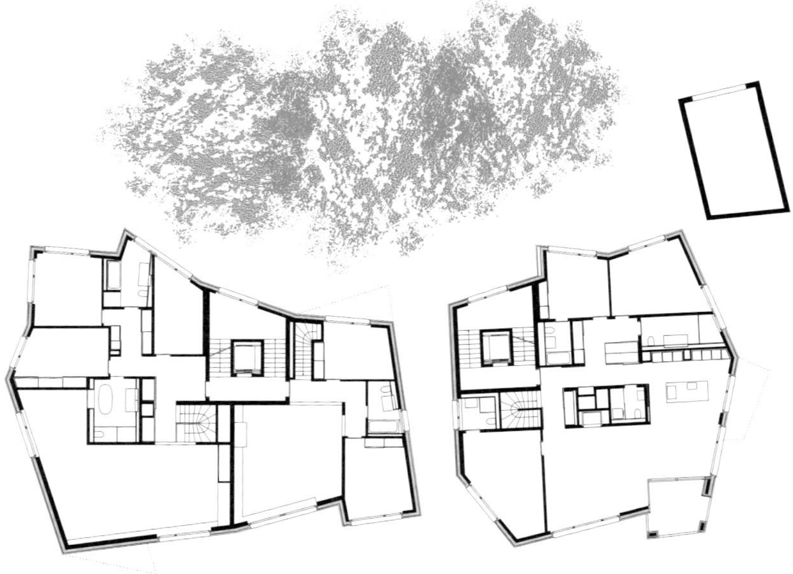

1st floor

Ground floor

Top floor

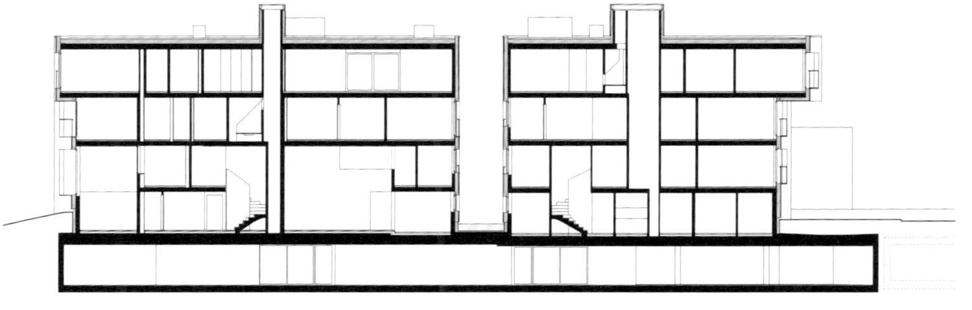

Section

Housing Development Zellweger-Areal, Uster, Switzerland 224

2008–13

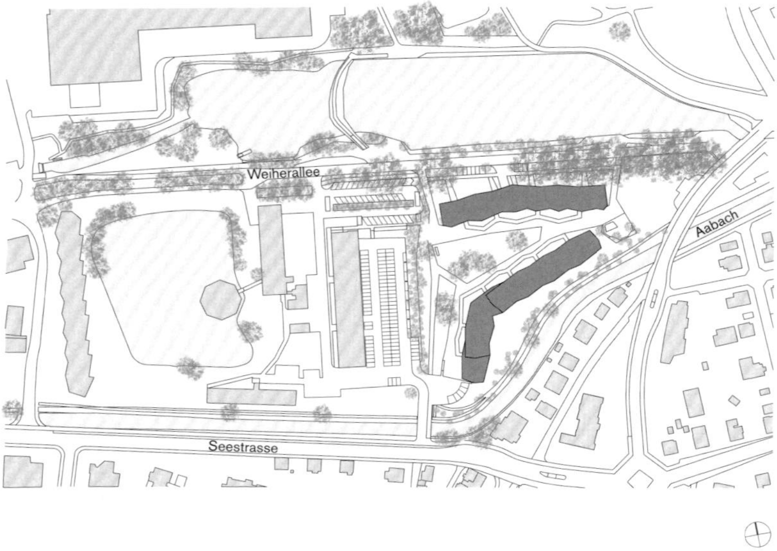

The Zellweger complex, set on a former industrial site, boasts outstanding landscape features. Two large ponds, originally created to generate energy from hydropower, a stretch of river, and a park-like area with mature trees define the site. Site B is demarcated by the Gehretswiesen pond and the Aabach stream. Two residential buildings of differing heights are positioned here in alignment with the promenade of plane trees by the pond in the north and the tree-lined course of the stream in the southeast. The two buildings create an L-shaped green area between them, opening up to the west onto a group of trees and an existing high-rise office building, which will be preserved.

Broad paths lead to the buildings through the open garden area, beneath which the garage is located. Pines will grow on the gently contoured lawn like green sculptures. The private front gardens at ground level are set off from the public green areas with slatted larchwood fences. These are framed by open, elegant concrete structures that also provide parking spaces for bicycles and contain mailboxes and shafts providing natural ventilation for the underground garage.

The northern eight-story building along Weiherallee contains 74 rental apartments, a bistro, and a daycare center. The building on the new Zellwegerweg, set along the Aabach, ranges from three to five stories in height and houses 61 rental apartments along with a multi-purpose common room. Most of the apartments in both buildings have living/dining/kitchen areas that extend through the building, opening onto both the green inner courtyard and the pond or stream. The principle of the living/dining room extending from front to back was articulated differently in the two buildings. In the building on Zellwegerweg the space narrows in the middle to form an entrance area and then widens again to either side to form distinct zones for the living room and eat-in kitchen at opposite ends of the apartment. The rooms are arranged around the periphery of this central space. In the building on Weiherallee the entrance area provides access to the rooms and leads to the living/dining room that runs across the apartment. The subtle angling of the balconies offers outdoor areas of varying depths and provides a formal echo to the large-scale angled sections of the two buildings, adding a lively and sculptural touch to the volumes of these two housing ensembles.

The façades are articulated by layers of rhythmically offset flamed larchwood planks and openwork prefabricated concrete parapets, which protrude somewhat beyond the wooden cladding to protect it from the weather. On the balconies, the concrete band projects further forward to form the parapet.

Ground floor with surroundings

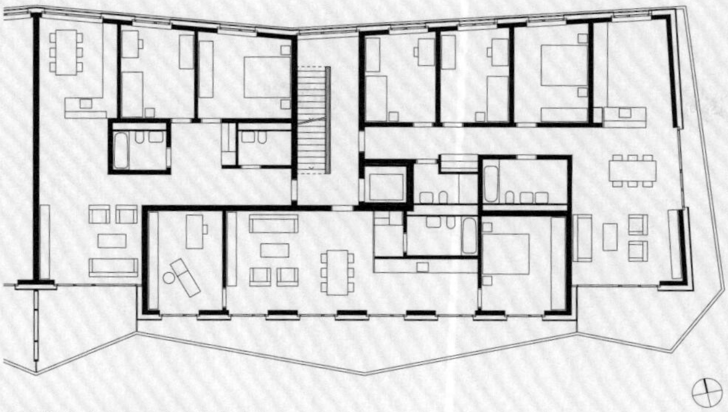

3.5-/3-/4.5-room apartments
Building on Weiherallee

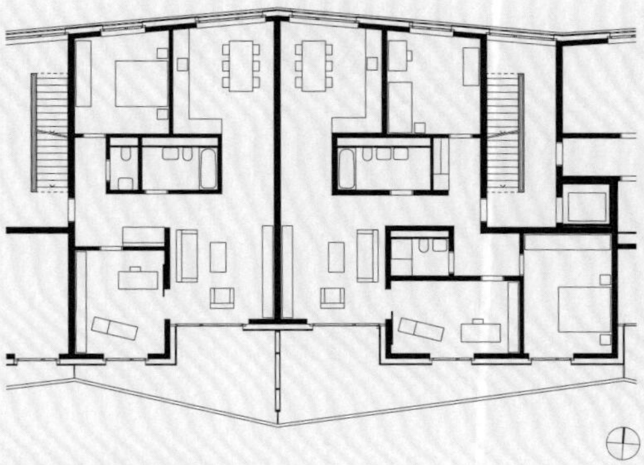

3.5-/4.5-room apartments
Building on Weiherallee

3.5-/4.5-room apartments
Building on Zellwegerweg

Typical floor plans

1st floor

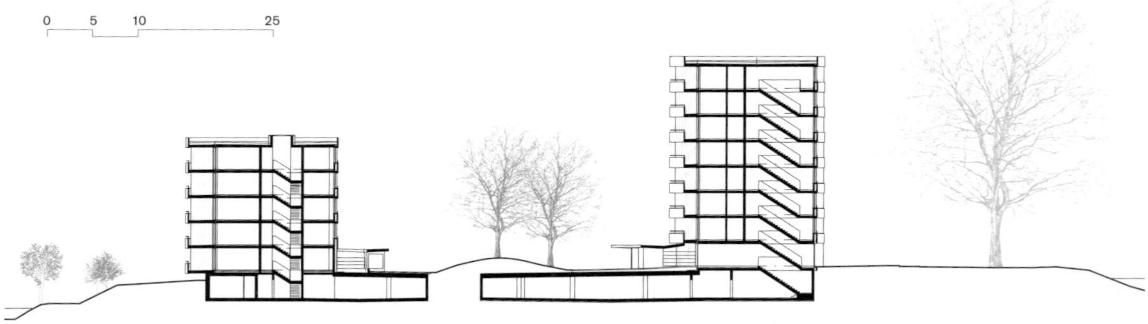

Building on Zellwegerweg

Building on Weiherallee

Section

Housing Development Zellweger-Areal, Uster, Switzerland

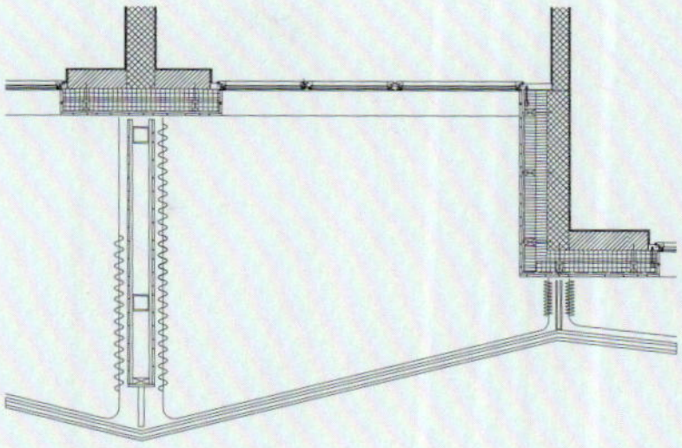

Construction detail

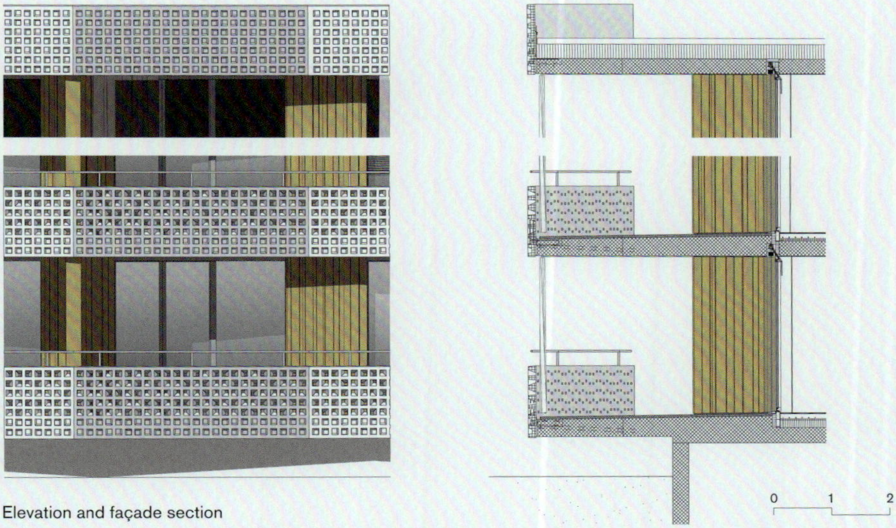

Elevation and façade section

Façade studies

APPENDIX

Index of Works & Projects

000
Training Center and Museum on the Schia Brook, Davos, Switzerland
Planning Study: 1989

00A
Kirchner Museum Davos, Switzerland
Competition: 1989, First Prize
Planning/Construction: 1990–92
Collaborators G/G: Judith Brändle, Urs Schneider (Construction Manager), Raphael Frei
Client: Kirchner Stiftung Davos
Structural Engineer: Preliminary Project: Aerni + Aerni AG, Zurich; Execution: Davoser Ingenieure AG, Davos
Lighting Consultant: Institut für Tageslichttechnik, Stuttgart, Germany
Building Services Engineer: 3-Plan AG, Winterthur
Graphic Design: Lars Müller, Baden

00B
Vinikus Restaurant, Reconstruction and New Building, Davos, Switzerland
Commission: 1990
Planning/Construction: 1990–92
Collaborators G/G: Dieter Bachmann (Project and Construction Manager), Gabriella Güntert
Client: Christoph Künzli, Scala Vini Davos
Structural Engineer: Davoser Ingenieure AG, Davos
Graphic Designer: Lars Müller, Baden

00C
School for Stone Sculptors, St. Gallen, Switzerland
Competition: 1990, Second Prize
Collaborators G/G: Dieter Bachmann, Judith Brändle
Competition: City of St. Gallen
Structural Engineer: Aerni + Aerni AG, Zurich
Consultant: Ruth Gossweiler, sculptor

00D
Hotel Park Hyatt, Zurich, Switzerland
Competition: 1993, First Prize
Collaborators G/G: Michael Widrig, Rina Plangger, Raphael Frei, Dieter Bachmann
Competition Organizer: City of Zurich, Suter + Suter, Hyatt
Landscape Architecture: Raderschall AG, Meilen
Structural Engineer: Aerni + Aerni AG, Zurich

00E
***Werkstoff,* Exhibition at the Architekturgalerie Lucerne, Switzerland**
1993

001
Davos Sports Center, Switzerland Converted into: Davos Tourism and Sports Center
Competition: 1992, First Prize
Planning/Construction: 1993–96
Collaborators G/G: Competition: Raphael Frei, Judith Brändle, Rina Plangger, Planning/Construction: Raphael Frei, David Leuthold
Client: Kur- und Verkehrsverein, Davos
Construction Manager: Othmar Brügger, Davos
Structural Engineer: Competition: Aerni + Aerni AG, Zurich; Construction: DIAG Davoser Ingenieure AG, Davos
Stands: Branger + Conzett AG, Chur
Colors: Adrian Schiess, Mouans-Sartoux, France
Graphic Designer: Trix Wetter, Zurich

002
Housing Development Broëlberg I, Kilchberg, Switzerland
Layout Plan: 1989–1992
Planning/Construction: 1994–96
Partnership with R.+E.Guyer Architekten, Zurich
Collaborators G/G: Matthias Stocker (Project Manager), Ivana Vallarsa, Andrea Roth
Client: Dr. Otto P. Haab, Küsnacht
Construction Manager: R.+E. Guyer Architekten, Zurich
Structural Engineer: Aerni + Aerni AG, Zurich
Building Services Engineer: 3-Plan AG, Winterthur
Electrical Engineer: Bühler + Scherler AG, Chur
Colors: Harald F. Müller, Öhningen, Germany
Graphic Designer: Trix Wetter, Zurich

003
Extension of Kunstmuseum Winterthur, Switzerland
Competition: 1993, First Prize
Planning/Construction: 1994–95
Collaborators G/G: Competition: Michael Widrig; Planning/Construction: Michael Widrig (Project Manager), Stefan Gasser, Dieter Bachmann (Construction Manager)
Client: Kunstverein Winterthur
Structural Engineer: Branger & Conzett AG, Chur
Building Services Engineer: Waldhauser AG, Münchenstein
Lighting Consultant: Institut für Tageslichttechnik, Stuttgart, and Lichtdesign Ingenieurgesellschaft mbH, Cologne, Germany

004
Remodeling House for Two Families Flawil, Switzerland
Commission: 1992
Planning/Construction: 1993–94
Collaborator G/G: Dieter Bachmann (Project and Construction Manager)
Client: Private

005
Detached House for a Doctor's Family, Canton Zurich, Switzerland
Commission: 1992
Planning/Construction: 1992–94
Collaborators G/G: Dieter Bachmann (Project and Construction Manager), Michael Widrig, Roberto Azzola
Client: Private
Structural Engineer: Aerni + Aerni AG, Zurich

006
Renovation and Extension Oskar Reinhart Collection "Am Römerholz," Winterthur, Switzerland
Competition: 1993, First Prize
Planning/Construction: 1995–98
Collaborators G/G: Competition: Raphael Frei, Michael Widrig, Judith Brändle; Planning/Construction: Andreas Sonderegger (Project Manager), Markus Jandl, René Kümmerli, Peter Steiner (Construction Manager)
Client: Federal Office for Construction and Logistics, Bern
Landscape Architecture: Kienast Vogt Partner, Zurich
Electrical Engineer: Elkom Partner AG, Chur
Building Services Engineer: Waldhauser AG, St. Gallen
Lighting Consultant: Institut für Tageslichttechnik, Stuttgart, and Lichtdesign Ingenieurgesellschaft mbH, Cologne, Germany
Graphic Designer: Trix Wetter, Zurich

007
Single-family House, Hergiswil, Switzerland
Planning Study: 1993

008
Extension "Stadthauskeller" Aarau, Switzerland
Competition: 1993
Collaborators G/G: Raphael Frei, Judith Brändle, Dieter Bachmann

009
Library Extension, Winterthur, Switzerland
Competition: 1995, First Prize
First Project: 1995–96
Second Project: 1996–97
Collaborators G/G: Competition: Michael Widrig, Urs Birchmeier
First Project: Urs Birchmeier; Second Project: Philippe Vaucher (Project Manager), Markus Jandl
Competition Organizer: Building Office of City of Winterthur
Structural Engineer: Dr. Deuring + Oehninger AG, Winterthur
Building Services Engineer: IBG AG Ingenieure, Winterthur

010
Reinsurance Company Training Center, Rüschlikon, Switzerland
Competition: 1995, purchase
Collaborators G/G: Urs Birchmeier, David Leuthold
Competition: Schweizerische Rückversicherung Zurich
Structural Engineer: Aerni + Aerni AG, Zurich

011 → p. 320
Auditorium, University of Zurich, Switzerland
Commission: 1996
Preliminary Project: 1996–98
Planning/Construction: 1999–2002
Collaborators G/G: Christian Brunner (Project Manager), Thomas Hochstrasser (Construction Manager), Stefan Gasser, Michael Bucher
Client: Building Office of Canton Zurich
Cost Planning: Othmar Brügger, Davos
Landscape Architecture: Hager AG, Zurich
Structural Engineer: SKS Ingenieure AG, Zurich
Colors: Adrian Schiess, Mouans-Sartoux, France

013
Two Houses in Zurich, Switzerland
Competition: 1995
Planning/Construction: 1997–98
Collaborators G/G: Michael Widrig (Project and Construction Manager), Michael Bucher
Client: Private
Landscape Architecture: Dieter Kienast, Thomas Steinmann, Zurich
Structural Engineer: Aerni + Aerni AG, Zurich
Colors: Harald F. Müller, Öhningen, Germany

014
Shop and Office Building at Winterthur Railway Station, Switzerland
Competition: 1996, Second Prize
Collaborators G/G: Urs Birchmeier, Raphael Frei
Client: Schweizerische Bundesbahnen SBB, Zurich
Structural Engineer: Branger + Conzett, Chur

016
Cultural Center and Workshop, Schauspielhaus, Zurich, Switzerland
Competition: 1996
Collaborators G/G: Urs Birchmeier, Raphael Frei, Lorenz Baumann
Competition Organizer: Neue Schauspielhaus AG, Zurich
Graphic Designer: Trix Wetter, Zurich

017
Museum Liner Appenzell, Switzerland
Commission: 1996
Planning/Construction: 1996–98
Collaborators G/G: Urs Birchmeier (Project Manager), Daniel Kaufmann (Construction Manager)
Client: Stiftung Museum Carl Liner Vater und Sohn
Landscape Architecture: Kienast Vogt Partner, Zurich
Structural Engineer: Aerni + Aerni AG, Zurich
Electrical Engineer: Elkom Partner AG, Chur
Building Services Engineer: Waldhauser AG, St. Gallen
Lighting Consultant: Institut für Tageslichttechnik, Stuttgart, and Lichtdesign Ingenieurgesellschaft mbH, Cologne, Germany
Graphic Designer: Trix Wetter, Zurich

018
Signal Box, Zurich, Switzerland
Competition: 1996, First Prize
Planning/Construction: 1997–99
Collaborators G/G: Competition: David Leuthold; Planning/Construction: Philippe Vaucher (Project and Construction Manager), Markus Lüscher
Client: Schweizerische Bundesbahnen SBB
Structural Engineer: Conzett, Bronzini, Gartmann AG, Chur
Colors: Harald F. Müller, Öhningen, Germany

019
Detached House, Tscherlach, Switzerland
Project Study: 1998
Collaborator G/G: Matthias Stocker
Client: Private

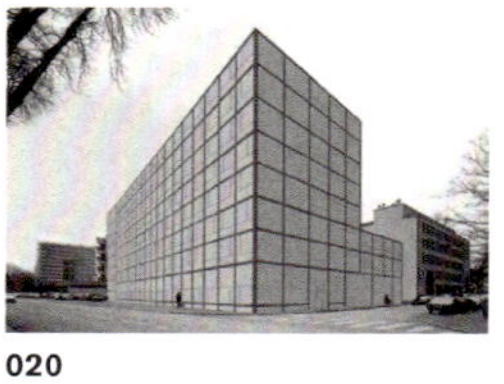

020
Technical Vocational School Salzmagazin, Zurich, Switzerland
Competition: 1997, Fifth Prize
Collaborators G/G: Markus Lüscher, Katrin Jaggi
Competition Organizer: Building Office of Canton Zurich

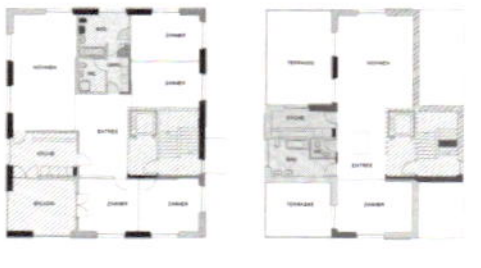

022
Housing Development Wallisellen, Switzerland
Planning Study: 1997
Competition Organizer: Streich AG, Brüttisellen, and Wüest & Partner, Zurich
Development Concept with: Burkhalter + Sumi, Haerle + Hubacher, Bearth + Deplazes, Grego + Smolenicky, J. Steib, Morger + Degelo

023
Extension of Kunsthaus Aarau, Switzerland
Competition: 1997, Third Prize
Collaborator G/G: Katrin Jaggi
Competition Organizer: Building Office of Canton Aargau
Structural Engineer: Aerni + Aerni AG, Zurich

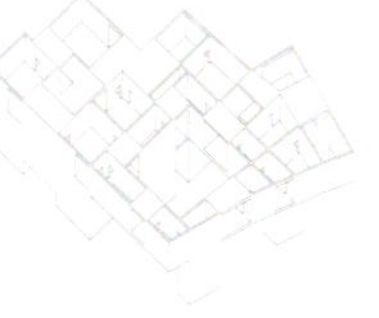

024
Kolumba Art Museum of the Archdiocese of Cologne, Germany
Competition: 1997, Second Prize
Collaborators G/G: Markus Lüscher, Katrin Jaggi
Competition Organizer: Archdiocese of Cologne, Germany
Structural Engineer: Branger + Conzett, Chur

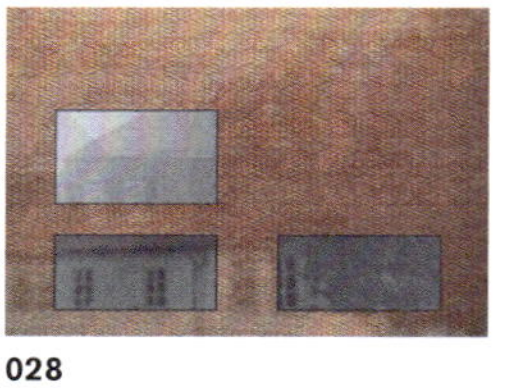

028
Kunsthalle Adolf Würth, Schwäbisch Hall, Germany
Competition: 1997, Second Prize
Collaborator G/G: Markus Lüscher
Competition Organizer: Adolf Würth GmbH + Co. KG, Künzelsau, Germany
Structural Engineer: Aerni + Aerni AG, Zurich

029
Housing Development Hohenbühl, Zurich, Switzerland
Competition: 1997
Collaborator G/G: Markus Lüscher
Competition Organizer: Hardturm Immobilien, Zurich

030
Kunstmuseum Vaduz, Liechtenstein
Competition: 1997
Collaborators G/G: Roberto Azzola, Markus Lüscher
Competition Organizer: Stiftung zur Errichtung eines Kunstmuseums, Vaduz, Liechtenstein
Structural Engineer: Branger + Conzett, Chur

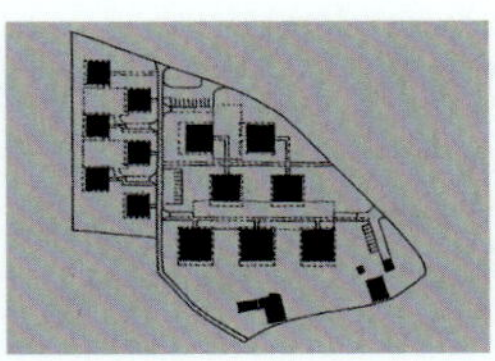

032
Layout Plan Hohenrain Complex, Kilchberg, Switzerland
Development Study: 1997
Layout Plan: 1998–99
Partnership R.+ E. Guyer Architekten, Zurich
Client: Hohenrain Family Heirs

033
District Office Building, Dietikon, Switzerland
Competition: 1998
Collaborator G/G: Markus Lüscher
Competition Organizer: Building Office of Canton Zurich

035
Municipal Works Yard, Davos, Switzerland
Competition: 1998, First Prize
Planning/Construction: 1998–99
Partnership Gigon/Guyer with Othmar Brügger, Davos
Collaborators G/G: Competition: Markus Lüscher; Planning/Construction: Christian Brunner (Project Manager)
Client: Davos Tourismus
General Contractor: Zschokke, Chur
Structural Engineer: Conzett, Bronzini, Gartmann AG, Chur, and Peter Flütsch, Chur
Graphic Designer: Trix Wetter, Zurich

036
Kunstmuseum Linz, Austria
Collaborator G/G: Michael Widrig
Competition Organizer: City of Linz, Austria

037 → p. 258
Extension of Workshop School Buildings Appisberg, Männedorf, Switzerland
Competition: 1998, First Prize
Planning/Construction: 1999–2002
Collaborators G/G: Competition: Markus Lüscher; Planning/Construction: Markus Lüscher (Project Manager), Mathias Brühlmann
Client: Gemeinnütziger Verein Appisberg, Abklärungs- und Ausbildungsstätte, Männedorf
Construction Manager: Caretta Weidmann Baumanagement AG, Zurich
Landscape Architecture: Zulauf Seippel Schweingruber, Baden
Colors: Harald F. Müller, Öhningen, Germany

038 → p. 34
Archeological Museum and Park Kalkriese, Osnabrück, Germany
Competition: 1998, First Prize
Gigon/Guyer in collaboration with Zulauf Seippel Schweingruber, Landschaftsarchitekten, Baden
Planning/Construction: 1999–2002
Collaborators G/G: Competition: Markus Lüscher; Planning/Construction: Volker Mencke (Project Manager), Caspar Bresch, Christian Brunner, Massimo Wüthrich
Client: Varusschlacht im Osnabrücker Land GmbH, Museum and Park Kalkriese, Germany
Construction Manager/Cost Planning: pbr Planungsbüro Rohling AG, Osnabrück, Germany
Landscape Architecture: Planning/Execution: Zulauf Seippel Schweingruber, Baden
Construction Manager: Heimer + Herbstreit, Hildesheim, Germany
Exhibition Concept Museum and Pavilions: Integral Concept, Ruedi Baur, Lars Müller, Paris/Baden
Structural Engineer: Gantert + Wiemeler, Münster, Germany

039 → p. 416

Three Houses on Susenbergstrasse, Zurich, Switzerland

Competition: 1998, First Prize
Planning/Construction: 1998–2000
Collaborators G/G: Competition: Michael Widrig; Planning/Construction: Peter Steiner (Project Manager), Samuel Thoma
Client: Zürcher Frauenverein (ZFV)
Construction Manager: Generalunternehmung Göhner Merkur AG, Zurich
Landscape Architecture: Zulauf Seippel Schweingruber, Baden
Structural Engineer: Dr. Lüchinger + Meyer AG, Zurich
Colors: Adrian Schiess, Mouans-Sartoux, France

040 → p. 426

Housing Development Broëlberg II, Kilchberg, Switzerland

Commission: 1999
Planning/Construction: 1999–2001
Collaborators G/G: Pascal Müller, Esther Righetti, Carmelo Hochstrasser (Construction Manager)
Client: Dr. Otto P. Haab, Küsnacht, Baukonsortium im Broëlberg c/o HALIMA, Kilchberg
Landscape Architecture: Zulauf Seippel Schweingruber, Baden
Structural Engineer: Dr. Lüchinger + Meyer AG, Zurich
Electrical Engineer: Elkom Partner AG, Chur
Building Services Engineer: 3-Plan AG, Winterthur
Colors: Harald F. Müller, Öhningen, Germany

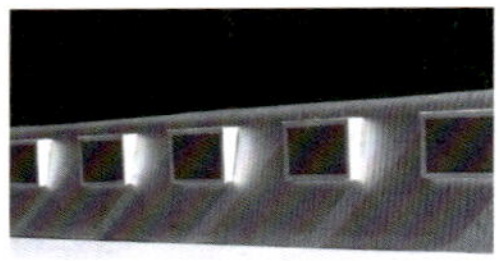

041

Municipal Works Yard and Fire Station, Olten, Switzerland

Competition: 1998
Collaborator G/G: Thomas Kurz
Competition Organizer: City of Olten

043 → p. 516

Residential and Office Building, Färberei-Areal, House 1, Thalwil, Switzerland

Competition: 1998, First Prize
Planning/Construction: 2005–08
Collaborators G/G: Michael Winklmann (Team Manager), Esther Righetti, Marius Baumann, Stine Henckel Schultz, Hiroaki Tanaka
Client: Weidmann Management AG, Thalwil
General Contractor: Karl Steiner AG, Zurich
Landscape Architecture: Schweingruber Zulauf, Zurich
Structural Engineer: Dr. Lüchinger + Meyer AG, Zurich
Electrical Engineer: Elkom Partner AG, Chur
Building Services Engineer: HL-Technik AG, Schaffhausen
Colors: Harald F. Müller, Öhningen, Germany

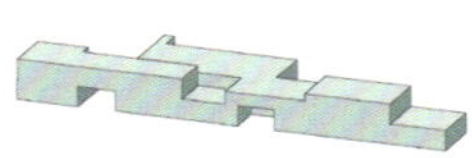

045

Museum of World Culture, Gothenburg, Sweden

Competition: 1998
Collaborator G/G: Markus Lüscher
Competition Organizer: City of Gothenburg, Sweden

046

Office and Service Center Coesfeld, Germany

Competition: 1998
Collaborator G/G: Pascal Müller
Competition Organizer: Ernsting's Family

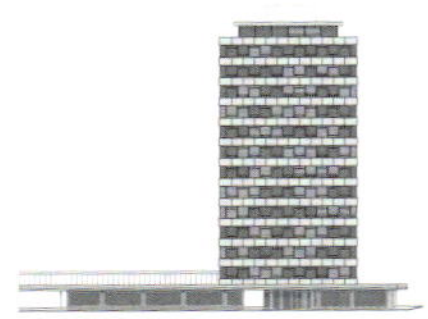

047

"Zur Schanze" High-rise, Renovation of Building Envelope, Additional Floors, Zurich

Competition: 1998
Collaborator G/G: Pascal Müller
Competition Organizer: "Zur Schanze" Owners' Consortium, Zurich

048

Alfried Krupp House, Greifswald, Germany

Competition: 1999
Collaborator G/G: Pascal Müller
Competition Organizer: Alfried Krupp von Bohlen und Halbach-Stiftung, Germany

049
Swiss Museum of Transport, Lucerne, Switzerland, Road Transport Hall, Urban Development Concept
Competition: 1999, First Prize (cf. 166)
Collaborators G/G: Markus Lüscher, Dalila Chebbi
Competition Organizer: Swiss Museum of Transport, Lucerne
Exhibition Concept: Lars Müller, Baden
Structural Engineer: Dr. Lüchinger + Meyer AG, Zurich

050
Extension of The Nelson-Atkins Museum of Art, Kansas City, Missouri, USA
Competition: 1999
Collaborators G/G: Urs Birchmeier, Arnault Biou, Caspar Bresch, Stefan Thommen
Competition Organizer: The Nelson-Atkins Museum of Art, Kansas City, Missouri, USA
Landscape Architecture: Zulauf Seippel Schweingruber, Baden
Structural Engineer: Aerni + Aerni AG, Zurich
Graphic Designer: Trix Wetter, Zurich

051
Cidade da Cultura, Santiago de Compostela, Spain
Competition: 1999
Collaborators G/G: Dalila Chebbi, Markus Lüscher, Arnault Biou
Competition Organizer: City of Santiago de Compostela, Spain
Landscape Architecture: Zulauf Seippel Schweingruber, Baden

053
Training Center Roche Forum, Buonas, Switzerland
Competition: 1999
Collaborators G/G: Pascal Müller, Caspar Bresch
Competition Organizer: F. Hoffmann-La Roche AG, Basel
Landscape Architecture: Zulauf Seippel Schweingruber, Baden
Structural Engineer: Conzett, Bronzini, Gartmann AG, Chur

054 → p. 62
Albers-Honegger Donation, Espace de l'Art Concret, Mouans-Sartoux, France
Competition: 1999, First Prize
Planning/Construction: 2001–03
Collaborators G/G: Competition: Eva Geering, Dalila Chebbi; Planning/Construction: Gilles Dafflon (Project Manager)
Client: Ville de Mouans-Sartoux, France; Etat, Ville, Conseil Régional PACA, France; Conseil Général des Alpes-Maritimes, France
Costs, Construction Manager, Structural/Electrical/Building Services Engineer: BET G.L. Ingénierie, Nice, France
Structural Engineer: Preliminary Project: Dr. Lüchinger + Meyer AG, Zurich
Electrical Engineer: Preliminary Project: Elkom Partner AG, Chur
Building Services: Preliminary Project: 3-Plan AG, Winterthur

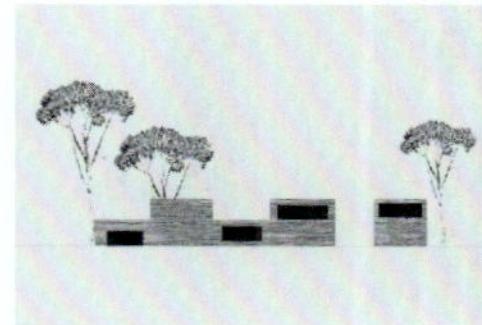

055
House in Greenwich, Connecticut, USA
Planning: 1999
Collaborators G/G: Dalila Chebbi, Eva Geering
Client: Private

059
Museum für Kunst und Design, Ingolstadt, Germany
Competition: 2000
Collaborators G/G: Caspar Bresch, Christof Bhend
Competition Organizer: City of Ingolstadt, Germany

061
Restaurant Pavilion, Swiss Museum of Transport, Lucerne, Switzerland
Commission: 1999
Planning/Construction: 1999–2000
Demolition: 2008
Collaborators G/G: Markus Seiler (Project Manager), Markus Lüscher, Caspar Bresch
Client: Swiss Museum of Transport, Lucerne
Construction Manager: Sepp Zurfluh, Rothenburg
Landscape Architecture: Christoph Fahrni, Lucerne
Structural Engineer: Dr. Lüchinger + Meyer AG, Zurich, Ingenieurbüro B. Trachsel, Lucerne
Building Services/Electrical Engineer: Integral, Lucerne
Colors: Harald F. Müller, Öhningen, Germany
Graphic Designer: Trix Wetter, Zurich

062
Extension of Air and Space Travel Hall, Remodeling Restaurant and Planetarium, Swiss Museum of Transport, Lucerne, Switzerland
Commission: 1999
Planning: 1999–2001
Collaborators G/G: Markus Lüscher (Project Manager), Markus Seiler, Caspar Bresch
Client: Swiss Museum of Transport, Lucerne
Exhibition: Fabritastika, Brüttisellen
Structural Engineer: Dr. Lüchinger + Meyer AG, Zurich

064
Expo Pavilion 2002, SAirGroup, Yverdon, Switzerland
Extension of Air and Space Travel Hall, Swiss Museum of Transport, Lucerne, Switzerland
Commission: 2000
Planning: 2000–01
Collaborators G/G: Markus Seiler, Eva Geering, Pieter Rabijns
Client: SAirGroup, Zurich
Exhibition: Fabritastika, Brüttisellen
Structural Engineer: Dr. Lüchinger + Meyer AG, Zurich

071 → p. 436
Housing Development and Remodeling, Pflegi-Areal, Zurich, Switzerland
Competition: 1998–99, First Prize
Planning/Construction: 1999–2002
Collaborators G/G: Competition: Gaby Kägi, Pascal Müller; Planning/ Construction New Buildings: Christian Maggioni (Project Manager), Gaby Kägi, Philippe Vaucher, Ivo Lenherr, Arnault Biou; Existing Buildings: Christian Maggioni (Project Manager), Peter Steiner (Construction Manager), Andrea Fiechter, Eva Geering
Client: Stiftung Diakoniewerk Neumünster, Schweizerische Pflegerinnenschule, Zurich
Construction Manager New Buildings: Witzig Architekten, Zurich
Landscape Architecture: Zulauf Seippel Schweingruber, Baden
Structural/Building Services Engineer: Basler & Hofmann AG, Zurich
Colors: Adrian Schiess, Mouans-Sartoux, France

081
Rotkreuz-Areal, Zurich Fluntern, Switzerland
Competition: 2000
Collaborators G/G: Christof Bhend, Caspar Bresch, Markus Seiler
Competition Organizer: Stiftung Schwesternschule and Krankenhaus vom Roten Kreuz, Zurich
Landscape Architecture: Zulauf Seippel Schweingruber, Baden

082
Cafe Kunsthalle, Zurich, Switzerland
Project Study: 2000
Collaborators G/G: Markus Seiler, Pieter Rabijns
Client: Kunsthalle Zurich

083
Landesmuseum Zürich, Switzerland
Competition: 2002
Collaborators G/G: Esther Righetti, Sarah Righetti
Competition Organizer: Federal Office for Construction and Logistics, Bern

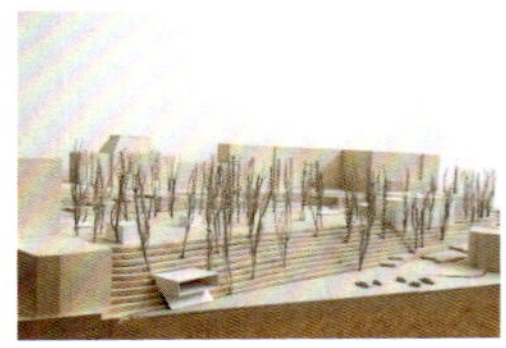

084
Underground Garage, Kirchner Platz, Davos, Switzerland
Planning as Alternative Proposal: 2002
Collaborator G/G: Christoph Bhend
Cost Planning: Othmar Brügger, Davos

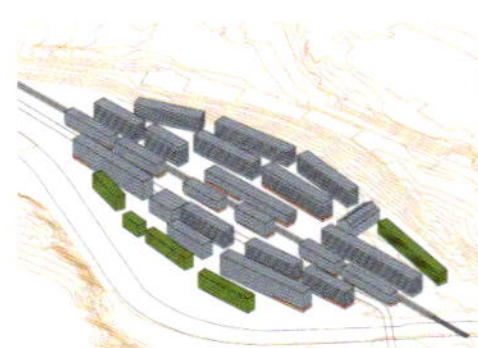

085
Urban Development Study Manegg, Zurich, Switzerland
Competition: 2000
Collaborator G/G: Christoph Bhend
Competition Organizer: Manegg Owners' Association and City of Zurich
Landscape Architecture: Zulauf Seippel Schweingruber, Baden

086
Housing Development Broëlberg III, Kilchberg, Switzerland
Competition: 2000–01
Collaborators G/G: Barbara Schlauri, Gilles Dafflon
Competition Organizer: Bodmer Family
Landscape Architecture: Zulauf Seippel Schweingruber, Baden

088
Parliament Building, Vaduz, Liechtenstein
Competition: 2000
Collaborators G/G: Christof Bhend, Pieter Rabijns
Competition Organizer: Government of the Principality of Liechtenstein
Structural Engineer: Aerni + Aerni AG, Zurich

091
Visitors Center and Park Kalkriese, Osnabrück, Germany
Competition: 2002–03, First Prize
Collaborator G/G: Volker Mencke
Competition Organizer: Varusschlacht im Osnabrücker Land GmbH, Museum and Park Kalkriese, Germany

093 → p. 352
Detached House, Zurich
Commission: 2001
Planning/Construction: 2001–03
Collaborators G/G: Markus Seiler (Project and Construction Manager), Pieter Rabijns
Client: Private
Landscape Architecture: Zulauf Seippel Schweingruber, Baden
Structural Engineer: Dr. Lüchinger + Meyer AG, Zurich
Building Services Engineer: 3-Plan AG, Winterthur
Colors: Adrian Schiess, Mouans-Sartoux, France

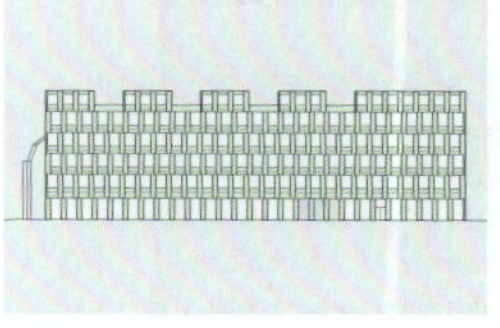

094
AZ-Media AG Office Building, Aarau, Switzerland
Competition: 2001
Collaborators G/G: Sergej Klammer, Samuel Thoma
Competition Organizer: ABB Immobilien AG, Baden

095 → p. 330
Remodeling of Kunstmuseum Basel and Laurenzbau Library, Switzerland
Competition: 2001, First Prize (Reconstruction and Extension)
Planning/Construction: 2003–07 in four stages (Reconstruction without Extension)
Collaborators G/G: Competition: Barbara Schlauri, Sergej Klammer, Christof Bhend; Planning/Construction: Christian Maggioni (Project Manager), Florian Isler, Thomas Hochstrasser (Construction Manager)
Client: Building and Planning Office, Main Building Division, Construction Department of Canton Basel City
Furnishings: Gigon/Guyer and Hannes Wettstein, Zurich
Structural Engineer: Rapp Infra AG, Basel
Electrical Engineering: Elektrizitäts AG, Basel
Building Services: Aicher, De Martin, Zweng AG, Lucerne

097
Installation in Courtyard of Museum and Library Building, Winterthur, Switzerland
Competition: 2001, Second Prize
Collaborators G/G: Competition 2001: Markus Seiler; Revision 2002: Barbara Schlauri, Christof Bhend, Esther Righetti, Sarah Righetti
Competition Organizer: City of Winterthur
Structural Engineer: Conzett, Bronzini, Gartmann AG, Chur
Building Services Engineer: 3-Plan AG, Winterthur

098
BMW Experience and Delivery Center, Munich, Germany
Competition: 2001
Collaborators G/G: Markus Seiler, Raul Mera
Competition Organizer: BMW AG, Munich
Structural Engineer: Dr. Lüchinger + Meyer AG, Zurich

099
Office Building, No. 2–7 Leipziger Platz, Berlin, Germany
Competition: 2001, Third Prize
Collaborators G/G: Christof Bhend, Esther Righetti, Markus Seiler
Competition Organizer: Berlin Leipziger Platz 2–7 Grundbesitz GmbH represented by Sony Berlin GmbH and Württembergische Lebensversicherung AG

100
Kiosk in Riesbach Harbor, Zurich, Switzerland
Competition: 2001
Collaborators G/G: Markus Seiler, Barbara Schlauri
Competition Organizer: City of Zurich

102
Media City Port, Hamburg, Germany
Competition: 2001, Third Prize
Collaborators G/G: Esther Righetti, Christof Bhend, Sergej Klammer, Pascal Müller, Veronika Steiger
Competition Organizer: Grundstücksgesellschaft MCP, Media City Port GmbH + Co. KG
Structural Engineer: Dr. Lüchinger + Meyer AG, Zurich

103
Research, Teaching, and Services Building, e-Science Lab, HIT, ETH Hönggerberg, Zurich, Switzerland
Competition: 2001
Collaborators G/G: Barbara Schlauri, Markus Seiler, Veronika Steiger, Sergej Klammer, Christof Bhend, Esther Righetti, Raul Mera
Competition Organizer: ETH Zurich
Landscape Architecture: Zulauf Seippel Schweingruber, Baden
Structural Engineer: Aerni + Aerni AG, Zurich
Building Services: 3-Plan AG, Winterthur

104
Office Building Thurgauerstrasse, Opfikon, Switzerland
Project Study: 2001
Collaborators G/G: Barbara Schlauri, Christof Bhend, Markus Seiler
Competition Organizer: Private, represented by Kuoni, Müller + Partner, Zurich
Structural Engineer: Dr. Lüchinger + Meyer AG, Zurich

105
Training Hall HCD, Davos, Switzerland
Competition: 2001, Second Prize
Gigon/Guyer in collaboration with Othmar Brügger, Davos
Collaborators G/G: Pascal Müller, Raul Mera
Competition Organizer: Landschaft Davos Gemeinde
Structural Engineer: Walter Bieler AG, Chur (timber construction), DIAG Davoser Ingenieure AG, Davos (foundations, piles)
Building Services Engineer: Waldhauser AG, Münchenstein

106
Contribution to Exhibition *Arne Jacobsen – Absolutely Modern* at the Louisiana Museum of Modern Art, Humlebæk, Denmark
Exhibition Contribution: 2002
Louisiana Museum of Modern Art, Humlebæk, Denmark
Publication: *Gigon/Guyer: Seen by Kjeld Vindum*

107 → p. 108
Extension of Rietberg Museum, Zurich
Competition: 2002, Third Prize
Collaborators G/G: Esther Righetti, Sarah Righetti, Barbara Schlauri, Raul Mera
Competition Organizer: Building Office of City of Zurich
Landscape Architecture: Hager AG, Zurich
Structural Engineer: Dr. Lüchinger + Meyer AG, Zurich

108 → p. 448
Residential and Retail Building, Almere, The Netherlands
Workshop Process with Interview: 2002
Planning/Construction: 2002–07
Collaborators G/G: Preliminary/Building Project Phase: Christof Bhend; Tender Documentation Phase: Volker Mencke; Construction Phase: Pieter Rabijns
Local Contact Architect: B+M, Den Haag, The Netherlands
Client: Blauwhoed Eurowoningen, Rotterdam, The Netherlands
General Contractor: J.P. van Eesteren bv, Barendrecht, The Netherlands
Structural Engineer: ABT bv, Arnhem, The Netherlands
Building Services Engineer: Huygen Elwako bv, Rotterdam, The Netherlands
Colors: Adrian Schiess, Mouans-Sartoux, France

109
Islisberg Süd Bridge, Switzerland
Competition: 2002
Gigon/Guyer in collaboration with Dr. Lüchinger+Meyer AG, Zurich
Collaborator G/G: Barbara Schlauri
Competition Organizer: Buildings Management of Canton Zurich
Structural Engineer: Dr. Lüchinger+ Meyer AG, Zurich
Colors: Adrian Schiess, Mouans-Sartoux, France

110 → p. 74
Kunst-Depot, Henze & Ketterer Gallery, Wichtrach, Switzerland
Commission: 2002
Planning/Construction: 2002–04
Collaborators G/G: Esther Righetti (Project Manager), Thomas Hochstrasser (Construction Manager)
Client: Henze & Ketterer Gallery, Ingeborg Henze-Ketterer, Dr. Wolfgang Henze, Günther Ketterer
Structural Engineer: Aerni+Aerni AG, Zurich
Electrical Engineer: Elkom Partner AG, Chur
Building Services Engineer: 3-Plan AG, Winterthur

111 → p. 340
Extension/Renovation of Historical Villa, Kastanienbaum, Switzerland
Commission: 2002
Planning/Construction: 2002–04
Collaborator G/G: Barbara Schlauri (Project Manager)
Client: Private
Construction Manager: Witzig Architekten, Zurich
Structural Engineer: Dr. Lüchinger+ Meyer AG, Zurich
Electrical Engineer: Bühlmann Engineering AG, Lucerne
Building Services Engineer: 3-Plan AG, Winterthur

112 → p. 100
National Park Center, Zernez, Switzerland
Competition: 2002
Gigon/Guyer in collaboration with Othmar Brügger, Davos
Collaborators G/G: Volker Mencke, Barbara Schlauri
Competition Organizer: Stiftung Schweizerischer Nationalpark
Structural Engineer: Walter Bieler, Bonaduz

113
Residential Towers Kattendijkdok, Antwerp, Belgium
Commission: 2002
Planning: 2002–04
Urban planning in collaboration with Diener & Diener Architekten, Basel/Berlin, and David Chipperfield Architects, Berlin
Collaborator G/G: Volker Mencke
Competition Organizer: Project² NV/SA, Antwerp, Belgium
Partner Office: ELD, Antwerp, Belgium

114 → p. 474
Housing Complex Park Grünenberg, Wädenswil, Switzerland
Competition: 2002, First Prize
Planning/Construction: 2004–07
Collaborators G/G: Competition: Volker Mencke; Planning/Construction: Barbara Schlauri (Project Manager), Caspar Bresch, Marjana Sigrist, Juan Gonzalez
Client: Grünenberg Baugesellschaft c/o Beat Odinga AG, Uster
Construction Manager: Karl Steiner AG, Zurich
Structural Engineer: Basler & Hofmann AG, Zurich
Electrical Engineer: Innovative Elektrotechnik, Gossau
Building Services Engineer: Schoch Reibenschuh AG, Nänikon
Colors Consultant: Pierre André Ferrand, Geneva/Krakow

115 → p. 502
Three Single-Family Row Houses, Rüschlikon, Switzerland
Competition: 2002, First Prize
Planning/Construction: 2002–05
Collaborators G/G: Gaby Kägi (Project Manager)
Client: Weidstrasse 8 Clients' Association, Rüschlikon
Construction Manager: Karl Steiner AG, Zurich
Landscape Architecture: Vogt Landschaftsarchitekten, Zurich
Structural Engineer: Henauer Gugler AG, Zurich
Electrical Engineer: Elkom Partner AG, Chur
Building Services Engineer: 3-Plan AG, Winterthur
Colors: Adrian Schiess, Mouans-Sartoux, France

116
Lake and Congress Hotel Beau-Rivage, Biel, Switzerland
Competition: 2002
Collaborator G/G: Ulrike Horn
Competition Organizer: Hotel Beau-Rivage, Biel

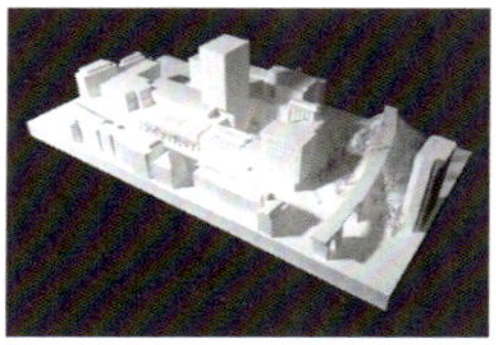

118 → p. 288

Löwenbräu-Areal – Arts Center, Residential Tower, and Office Building, Zurich, Switzerland

Competition: 2003, two ex aequo First Prizes: Gigon/Guyer and Atelier WW Architekten SIA AG, Founding of the ARGE Löwenbräuareal
Collaborators G/G: Competition: Volker Mencke; Collaborators Atelier WW: Martin Danz
Layout Plan: 2004
Planning/Construction: 2006–12
Collaborators G/G: Mike Guyer (General Manager), Volker Mencke (Planning and Team Manager), Bettina Gerhold, Daniel Friedmann, Reto Killer, Kathrin Sindelar, Damien Andenmatten, Yvonne Grunwald, Alex Zeller, Pieter Rabijns; Collaborators Atelier WW: Walter Wäschle (General Manager), Peter Epprecht (Project Manager), Tatjana Abenseth, Özgül Kale, Eric Hoffmann, Claudia Keichel, Martin Pellkofer, Thomas Huber; General Contractor Submission: Roman Züst, Daniel Bünzli, Christian Verasani, Mario Ercolani, Boris Deister
Client: PSP Property AG, Zug
General Contractor: Steiner AG, Zurich
Landscape Architecture: Schweingruber Zulauf, Zurich
Structural Engineer: Dr. Lüchinger + Meyer AG, Zurich, in conjunction with Henauer Gugler AG, Zurich
Electrical Engineer: Planning/Submission: Schneider Engineering + Partner Zurich AG, Zurich; Execution: Mosimann & Partner, Zurich, Schmidiger + Rosasco, Zurich
Building Services Engineer: Gruenberg + Partner AG, Zurich
Façade: Planning/Submission: gkp fassadentechnik ag, Aadorf; Construction: Josef Gartner GmbH, Gundelfingen
Apartment Sales: Rhombus Partner Immobilien AG, Zurich
Signage: Integral Ruedi Baur, Zurich
Colors: Harald F. Müller, Öhningen, Germany

119

Housing and Office Complex Areal Hauptwerkstätte SBB Chur, Switzerland

Competition: 2003
Collaborators G/G: Ulrike Horn, Raul Mera
Competition Organizer: Schweizerische Bundesbahnen SBB
Landscape Architecture: Zulauf Seippel Schweingruber, Baden

120

Letzigrund Stadium, Zurich, Switzerland

Competition: 2003
Collaborators G/G: Volker Mencke, Christof Bhend, Ulrike Horn, Raul Mera
Competition Organizer: City of Zurich, Building Department, School, and Sports Department
Landscape Architecture: Zulauf Seippel Schweingruber, Baden
Structural Engineer: Dr. Lüchinger + Meyer AG, Zurich

121 → p. 482

Housing Development Neumünsterallee, Zurich, Switzerland

Competition: 2003, First Prize
Planning/Construction: 2004–07
Collaborators G/G: Competition: Markus Lüscher; Planning/Construction: Kim Sneyders (Project Manager from 2005), Markus Lüscher (Project Manager until end 2004), Lorenzo Igual, Markus Seiler
Client: Personalvorsorgestiftung der SV Group, Dübendorf
Client's Representative: Daniel Nyfeler
General Contractor: Karl Steiner AG, Zurich
Landscape Architecture: Schweingruber Zulauf, Zurich
Structural Engineer: Dr. Lüchinger + Meyer AG, Zurich
Electrical Engineer: Elkom Partner AG, Chur
Building Services Engineer: 3-Plan AG, Winterthur
Colors: Adrian Schiess, Mouans-Sartoux, France
Graphic Design: Trix Wetter, Zurich

122 → p. 116

New Museum of Contemporary Art, New York, NY, USA

Competition: 2003
Collaborators G/G: Stefan Thommen, Raul Mera
Competition Organizer: New Museum of Contemporary Art, New York, NY, USA
Consultant: Jan Kinsbergen
Structural Engineer: Dr. Lüchinger + Meyer AG, Zurich

123

New Ritter Sport Museum, Waldenbuch, Germany

Competition: 2003, First Prize
Collaborators G/G: Ulrike Horn, Raul Mera
Competition Organizer: Ritter Sport, Alfred Ritter GmbH & Co. KG, Waldenbuch, and Marli Hoppe-Ritter-Stiftung zur Förderung der Kunst, Germany

124

Extension of Tel Aviv Museum of Art, Israel

Competition: 2003
Collaborators G/G: Stefan Thommen, Ulrike Horn, Raul Mera
Competition Organizer: Tel Aviv Museum of Art
Structural Engineer: Aerni + Aerni AG, Zurich

125
Retail and Residential Building on Oberanger, Munich, Germany
Competition: 2003, Third Prize
Collaborators G/G: Markus Seiler, Christof Bhend, Raul Mera
Competition Organizer: Wöhr+Bauer GmbH
Structural Engineer: Dr. Lüchinger+Meyer AG, Zurich

126
"Alte Chemie" Hotel, Retail, and Residential Buildings, Munich, Germany
Competition: 2003
Collaborators G/G: Stefan Thommen, Raul Mera
Competition Organizer: Frankonia Eurobau Max Viertel GmbH, Nettetal, Germany
Landscape Architecture: Zulauf Seippel Schweingruber, Baden

129
Elementary School Burg, Näfels, Switzerland
Competition: 2003
Collaborators G/G: Stefan Thommen, Raul Mera
Competition Organizer: Näfels School Association

130
Development Archareal, Winterthur, Switzerland
Competition: 2003
Collaborators G/G: Ulrike Horn, Volker Mencke, Raul Mera
Competition Organizer: Halter Generalunternehmung AG, Zurich
Landscape Architecture: Vetsch Nipkow Partner AG, Zurich

131
Railway Station with Shops, Offices, and Apartments, Baar, Switzerland
Competition: 2004, First Prize
Planning/Construction: 2004–09
Collaborators G/G: Competition: Mathias Brühlmann, Ulrike Horn; Planning/Construction: Pit Brunner (Team/Project Manager), Mathias Brühlmann, Alex Zeller, Ingo Brinkmann, Reto Killer
Client for Entire Complex: Migros-Pensionskasse, Zurich
Client for Design of Public Space: Einwohnergemeinde Baar
Client for Railway Facilities: Schweizerische Bundesbahnen SBB, Lucerne
General Contractor: Halter Generalunternehmung AG, Zurich
Landscape Architecture: Vetsch Nipkow Partner AG, Zurich
Structural Engineer: ARP André Rotzetter+Partner AG, Baar
Electrical Engineer: Mosimann & Partner AG, Affoltern am Albis
Building Services Engineer: Hans Abicht AG, Zug
Colors: Adrian Schiess, Mouans-Sartoux, France

132
Casa de la Historia, Archeological Museum, La Coruña, Spain
Competition: 2003
Collaborators G/G: Stefan Thommen, Raul Mera
Competition Organizer: Ayuntamiento de La Coruña
Landscape Architecture: Zulauf Seippel Schweingruber, Baden

133 → p. 62
Préau des Enfants, Espace de l'Art Concret, Mouans-Sartoux, France
Commission: 2003
Planning/Construction: 2003
Collaborators G/G: Gilles Dafflon (Project Manager), Leander Morf
Client: City of Mouans-Sartoux
Financing: Michael Hilti and Gottfried Honegger
Planning Office: BET G.L. Ingénierie, Nice
Structural Engineer: Dr. Lüchinger+Meyer AG, Zurich

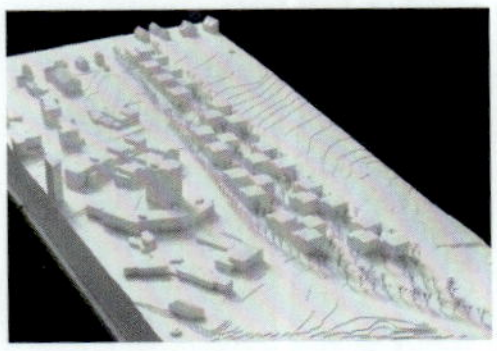

134
Housing Development Wolfswinkel, Zurich, Switzerland
Competition: 2003
Collaborators G/G: Mathias Brühlmann, Raul Mera
Competition Organizer: ABZ – Allgemeine Baugenossenschaft Zurich
Landscape Architecture: Zulauf Seippel Schweingruber, Baden

135 → p. 490

Housing Development Brunnenhof, Zurich, Switzerland

Competition: 2003, First Prize
Planning/Construction: 2004–07
Collaborators G/G: Markus Seiler (Project Manager), Lorenzo Igual, Rolf-Werner Wirtz, Ulrike Horn
Client: Stiftung Wohnungen für kinderreiche Familien, Zurich
Construction Manager/Cost Planning: b+p baurealisation ag, Zurich
Landscape Architecture: Hager Landscape Architecture AG, Zurich
Structural Engineer: Dr. Lüchinger + Meyer AG, Zurich
Electrical Engineer: Elkom Partner AG, Chur
Building Services Engineer: 3-Plan AG, Winterthur
Colors: Adrian Schiess, Mouans-Sartoux, France

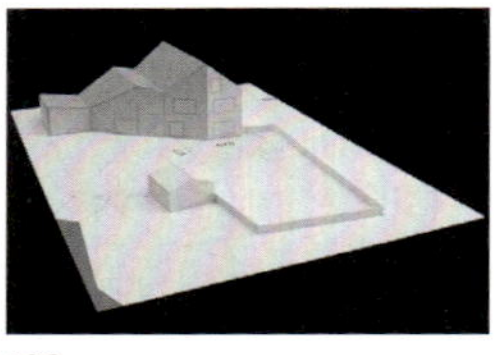

136

House former "Schäfli" Inn, Busskirch, Switzerland

Project Study: 2003
Collaborator G/G: Stefan Thommen
Client: Marc & Valérie Dentand

137

Novartis Laboratory and Knowledge Center, Basel, Switzerland

Competition: 2003
Collaborators G/G: Stine Henckel Schultz, Stefan Thommen, Raul Mera
Competition Organizer: Novartis Pharma AG, Basel
Cost Planning: PBK AG, Rüti
Structural Engineer: Dr. Lüchinger + Meyer AG, Zurich
Building Services Engineer: HL-Technik AG, Zurich
Laboratory Technology: Volker Krieger, Freiburg-Opfingen, Germany

139 → p. 508

Housing Complex Diggelmannstrasse, Zurich, Switzerland

Competition: 2003, First Prize
Planning/Construction: 2004–07
Collaborators G/G: Competition: Katja Schubert; Planning/Construction: Pit Brunner (Team Manager), Katja Schubert (Project Manager until 04/2007), Matthias Clivio (Project Manager from 04/2007), Gaby Kägi
Client: Gemeinschaftsstiftung der Zellweger Luwa AG, Uster, represented by Hesta Immobilien AG, Zurich
General Contractor: HRS, Hauser Rutishauser Suter AG, Zurich
Landscape Architecture: Schweingruber Zulauf, Zurich
Structural Engineer: Henauer Gugler AG, Zurich
Building Services Engineer: HL-Technik AG, Zurich
Colors: Adrian Schiess, Mouans-Sartoux, France

140

Test Planning for Urban Space, Main Railway Station, Zurich, Switzerland

Development Concept: 2003–04
Architecture ARGE HB Zurich: Theo Hotz AG, Burkhalter Sumi Architekten, Gigon/Guyer, Zurich
Collaborators G/G: Pieter Rabijns, Stefan Thommen

141 → p. 528

Résidence du Pré-Babel, Geneva, Switzerland

Competition: 2003–04, First Prize
Planning/Construction: 2004–08
Collaborators G/G: Competition: Gilles Dafflon, Katja Schubert; Planning/Construction: Gilles Dafflon (Project Manager), Matthias Clivio, Christine Jahn, Andréanne Pochon, Pieter Rabijns, Katja Schubert, Michael Wagner
Client: Frontimmo SA, Chêne-Bougeries, Geneva
Construction Manager/Cost Planning: Roberto Carella Architectes, Geneva
Landscape Architecture: Schweingruber Zulauf, Zurich
Structural Engineer: Fiechter Ingénierie SA, Chêne-Bourg
Electrical Engineer: ECE SA, Bernex
Building Services Engineer: Ryser Eco Sàrl, Geneva, and Mike Humbert, Geneva

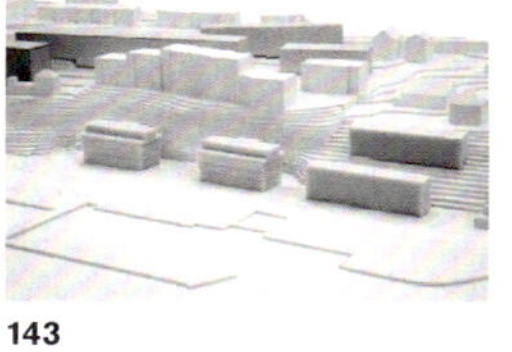

143

Commercial, Office, and Residential Building, Seestrasse, Thalwil, Switzerland

Project Study: 2003–04
Collaborators G/G: Stine Henckel Schultz
Competition Organizer: Weidmann Management AG, Thalwil
Landscape Architecture: Zulauf Seippel Schweingruber, Baden

144
New City Casino, Basel, Switzerland
Competition: 2004
Collaborators G/G: Stefan Thommen, Raul Mera
Competition Organizer: Stadtcasino AG, Basel, Building Office of City of Basel
Structural Engineer: Aerni + Aerni AG, Zurich

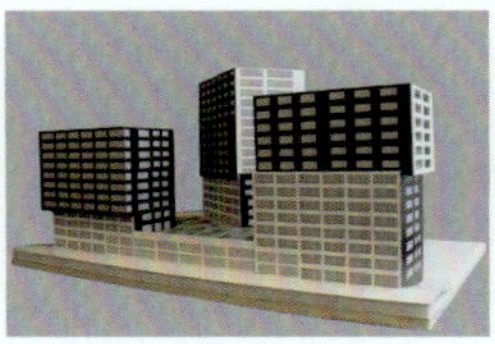

146
Housing Development De Driehoek, Science Park, Amsterdam, The Netherlands
Commission: 2004
Planning/Submission: 2004–06
Collaborators G/G: Pieter Rabijns (Project Manager), Brigitte Rüdel, Daniel Friedmann, Kim Sneyders, Daniela Schadegg, Peter Graf
Client: Blauwhoed bv, Rotterdam, The Netherlands
Construction Economics: BBN, Amsterdam, The Netherlands
Landscape Architecture: Schweingruber Zulauf, Zurich
Structural Engineer: Van Rossum bv, Amsterdam, The Netherlands
Building Services Engineer/Electrical Engineer: Huygen installatie adviseurs, Rotterdam, The Netherlands, and Cauberg-Huygen Raadgevende ingenieurs bv, Amsterdam, The Netherlands
Colors: Harald F. Müller, Öhningen, Germany

148
Façade envelope for l'île Seguin, Paris, France
Competition: 2004
Collaborator G/G: Stefan Thommen
Competition Organizer: Val de Seine Aménagement, Boulogne-Billancourt, France
Art: Adrian Schiess, Mouans-Sartoux, France

149
Solo Exhibition *Gebaut/Nicht gebaut*, Architekturforum, Zurich, Switzerland
December 9, 2004 – February 12, 2005
Planning/Execution: 2004–05
Collaborator G/G: Alexia Zydel
Graphic Designer: Trix Wetter

151 → p. 528
Résidence du Parc de Grange-Canal, Geneva, Switzerland
Competition: 2003–04, First Prize
Planning/Construction: 2007–12
Collaborators G/G: Competition: Gilles Dafflon, Katja Schubert; Planning Application Buildings 38, 40, 42: Gilles Dafflon, Andréanne Pochon, Karin Schultze, Pieter Rabijns, Sebastian Beck; Planning/Construction Buildings 40, 42: Gilles Dafflon (Team Manager until 2008), Markus Seiler (Team Manager from 2008), Vanessa Tardy-Klikar (Project Manager 2008–2011), Martin Schwarz (Project Manager from 2011), Eric Sommerlatte, Christine Jahn, Karla Pilz
Client: Frontimmo SA, Chêne-Bougeries
Interior Designer Condominiums: Yvan Prokesch, Gigon/Guyer
Detail Planning, Construction Building 38: Cerutti architectes, Vésenaz
Construction Manager Buildings 40, 42: Cerci SARL and AML Immo Conseils SA, Plan les Ouates, Geneva
Landscape Architecture: Preliminary Project: Schweingruber Zulauf, Zurich; Execution: Jacquet SA, Geneva
Structural Engineer: ESM & Fiechter Ingenieries SA, Geneva
Electrical Engineer: DSSA Dumont Schneider SA, Plan-les-Ouates
Ventilation/Heating: Enerlink, Geneva
Plumbing: Ryser ECO SARL, Geneva

152 → p. 208
Prime Tower Office High-rise with Annex Buildings Cubus and Diagonal, Maag-Areal, Zurich, Switzerland
Competition: 2004, First Prize (cf. 155, 247, 258, 261, 272)
Planning/Construction: 2005–11
Collaborators G/G: Competition: Stefan Thommen
Prime Tower: Stefan Thommen (Team Manager), Christian Maggioni (Deputy Team Manager), Christoph Rothenhöfer (Project Manager until 2007), Pieter Rabijns (Project Manager from 2007), Alex Zeller, Urs Meyer, Franziska Bächer, Raffaella Bisceglia, Armin Baumann, Karin Schultze, Roberto Outumuro, Rafael Schmid, Martin Bischofberger, Leander Morf
Client: Swiss Prime Site AG, Olten
Client's Representative: Perolini Baumanagement AG, Zurich
General Contractor ARGE Prime Tower: Losinger Construction AG und Karl Steiner, Zurich
Landscape Architecture: Schweingruber Zulauf, Zurich
Cost Planning: Building Project/General Contractor Submission: b+p baurea-lisation ag, Zurich
Structural Engineer Competition: Dr. Schwartz Consulting AG, Zug; Submission: Dr. Schwartz Consulting AG, Zug, Dr. Lüchinger + Meyer AG, Zurich, and Freihofer & Partner AG, Zurich
Construction: Walt + Galmarini AG, Zurich, with Dr. Schwartz Consulting AG, Zug, Dr. Lüchinger + Meyer AG, Zurich, Bänzinger Partner AG, Richterswil, and Freihofer & Partner AG, Zurich

Electrical Engineer: Submission: IBG Graf AG, St. Gallen; Execution: Hefti Hess Martignoni AG, Zurich
Heating/Cooling: Submission/Execution: PB P. Berchtold, Sarnen
Ventilation: Competition/Submission: Waldhauser AG, Münchenstein; Execution: Hans Abicht AG, Zurich
Plumbing/Sprinklers: Submission: PB P. Berchtold, Sarnen; Execution: GRP Ingenieure, Rotkreuz
Façade: Competition/Submission: gkp fassadentechnik ag, Aadorf; Execution: Reba Fassadentechnik AG, Chur
Collaborator for Interior Design: Competition/Submission: Studio Hannes Wettstein, Zurich
Art: Adrian Schiess, Zurich and Mouans-Sartoux, France, and Harald F. Müller, Öhningen, Germany
Cubus and Diagonal: Construction: Stefan Thommen (Team Manager), Urs Meyer, Alex Zeller, Karin Schultze
General Contractor ARGE Prime Tower: Losinger Construction AG and Karl Steiner, Zurich
Landscape Architecture: Schweingruber Zulauf, Zurich
Cost Planning: Building Project/General Contractor Submission: b+p baurealisation ag, Zurich
Structural Engineer Competition: Dr. Schwartz Consulting AG, Zug; Submission: Dr. Schwartz Consulting AG, Zug, Dr. Lüchinger + Meyer AG, Zurich, and Freihofer & Partner AG, Zurich
Construction: Walt + Galmarini AG, Zurich, with Dr. Schwartz Consulting AG, Zug, Dr. Lüchinger + Meyer AG, Zurich, Bänzinger Partner AG, Richterswil, and Freihofer & Partner AG, Zurich
Electrical Engineer: Submission: IBG Graf AG, St. Gallen; Execution: Hefti Hess Martignoni AG, Zurich
Heating/Cooling: Submission/Execution: PB P. Berchtold, Sarnen
Ventilation: Competition/Submission: Waldhauser AG, Münchenstein; Execution: Hans Abicht AG, Zurich
Plumbing/Sprinklers: Submission: PB P. Berchtold, Sarnen; Execution: GRP Ingenieure, Rotkreuz
Façade: Competition/Submission: gkp fassadentechnik ag, Aadorf; Construction: Reba Fassadentechnik AG, Chur

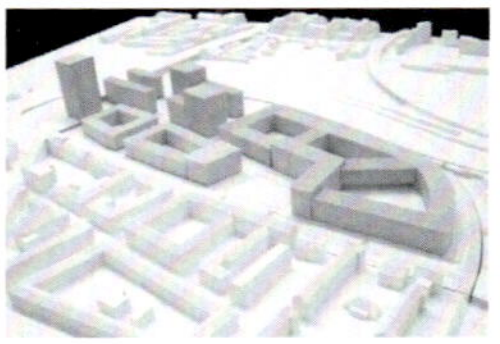

153
Urban Planning Police and Justice Center Site, Zurich, Switzerland
Competition: 2004, First Prize (cf. 234)
Development Study/Layout Plan: 2005–06
Collaborators G/G: Competition: Gilbert Isermann, Stefan Thommen; Layout Plan: Gilbert Isermann
Client: Buildings Management of Canton Zurich, Building Office of Stab
Planning Report/Layout Plan: Metron AG, Brugg
Landscape Architecture: Schweingruber Zulauf, Zurich
Traffic Consultant: Ernst Basler + Partner AG, Zurich

154
Housing Development CU West, Uetikon, Switzerland
Competition: 2004
Collaborators G/G: Volker Mencke, Pieter Rabijns, Raul Mera
Competition Organizer: CPH Chemie + Papier Holding AG, Perlen
Landscape Architecture: Hager AG, Zurich
Real Estate Consultant: Colliers CSL AG, Zurich

155 → p. 224
Tenant Fit-out for Homburger, Prime Tower, Zurich, Switzerland
Commission: 2007 (cf. 152)
Planning/Construction: 2010–2011
Collaborators G/G: Stefan Thommen (Team Manager), Raffaella Bisceglia, Karla Pilz, Alex Zeller
Client: Swiss Prime Site AG, Olten
Client's Representative: Perolini Baumanagement AG, Zurich
Contractor ARGE Prime Tower: Losinger Construction AG und Karl Steiner, Zurich
Structural Engineer: Walt + Galmarini AG, Zurich
Electrical Engineer: Hefti Hess Martignoni AG, Zurich
Heating/Cooling/Building Automation: PB P. Berchtold, Sarnen
Ventilation: Hans Abicht AG, Zurich
Plumbing/Sprinklers: GRP Ingenieure, Rotkreuz

156 → p. 272
Rosau Office Building, Zurich, Switzerland
Commission: 2008
Planning Residential/Office Building: 2008–09
Collaborators G/G: Michael Winklmann (Team Manager), Christoph Justies (Project Manager), Mark Zjörjen, Christoph Dober, Cornelia Schmidt, Karin Schultze
Planning/Construction Office Building: 2010–15
Collaborators G/G: Michael Winklmann (Team Manager), Mathias Rösner (Project Manager from 2011), Martin Bischofberger (Project Manager until end of 2010), Christoph Dober, Brigitte Rüdel, Griet Aesaert
Client for Basic Fit-out: Villa Rosau AG, Zurich
Client's Representative: Conarenco AG, Zurich
Client for Tenant Fit-out: Bank Sarasin & Cie AG, Basel
Tender Documentation/Construction Manager: ARGE Rosau: Gigon/Guyer and b+p baurealisation ag, Zurich
Landscape Architecture: Vogt Landschaftsarchitekten, Zurich
Structural Engineer: Ingenieurgemeinschaft Residenz Rosau: Dr. Lüchinger + Meyer AG mit Grünenfelder + Lorenz AG, St. Gallen
Building Services Engineer: Gruenberg + Partner AG, Zurich
Electrical Engineer: IBG B. Graf AG, St. Gallen
Coordination: Portmann Planning GmbH
Façade Planning: gkp fassadentechnik ag, Aadorf

158
Row Houses Bosrijk, Eindhoven, The Netherlands
Commission: 2007
Planning: 2007–08
Collaborators G/G: Kim Sneyders (Project Manager), Daniela Bergmann, Peter Graf
Client/Project Developer: AM Wonen, Eindhoven, The Netherlands
Urban Planning, Landscape Architecture: Karres en Brands landschapsarchitecten bv, Hilversum, The Netherlands

159
Maison du Livre et Parking du Château, Mouans-Sartoux, France
Competition: 2005, First Prize
Planning Preliminary Project: 2006
Gigon/Guyer in collaboration with Actom Architecture, Valbonne, France
Collaborators G/G: Competition: Gilles Dafflon; Preliminary Project: Gilles Dafflon (Project Manager), Andri Gartmann, Christine Jahn
Competition Organizer: Ville de Mouans-Sartoux
Structural/Building Services Engineer: GLI, Nice, and SETEF, Nice, France

162 → p. 538
Housing Development Erlenhof, Dietikon, Switzerland
Competition: 2005, First Prize
Planning/Construction: 2006–09
Collaborators G/G: Competition: Matthias Clivio; Planning/Construction: Marjana Sigrist (Team Manager until planning application), Michael Winklmann (Team Manager from planning application), Matthias Clivio (Project Manager), Martin Bischofberger, Karin Schultze, Cornelia Schmidt, Daniel Trepte, Daniela Bergmann
Client House 2 (Rental Apartments): PV-Promea, Schlieren
Client Houses 1 and 3 (Condominiums): Wohnbaugenossenschaft Blumenrain, Zurich
Development Houses 1, 2, 3: Halter Entwicklungen, Zurich
General Contractor: Halter Generalunternehmung, Zurich
Landscape Architecture: Schweingruber Zulauf, Zurich
Structural Engineer: Basler & Hofmann AG, Zurich
Electrical Engineer: R+B engineering AG, Zurich
Building Services Engineer: 3-Plan AG, Winterthur
Colors: Harald F. Müller, Öhningen, Germany

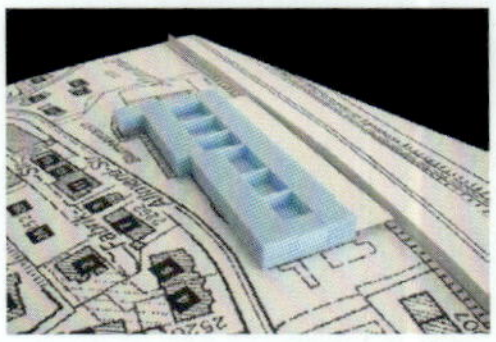

163
Conversion Flower Market, Oberengstringen, Switzerland
Project Study: 2004
Collaborators G/G: Gilbert Isermann, Stefan Thommen
Competition Organizer: Colliers CSL AG, Zurich
Cost Planning: Bosshard + Partner Baurealisation AG, Zurich
Landscape Architecture: Schweingruber Zulauf, Zurich

164
Landesmuseum für Kunst und Kulturgeschichte, Münster, Germany
Competition: 2005
Collaborators G/G: Gilbert Isermann, Pieter Rabijns, Caspar Bresch, Leander Morf, Raul Mera
Competition Organizer: Landschaftsverband Westfalen-Lippe, Münster, Germany

166 → p. 84
Swiss Museum of Transport, Lucerne, Switzerland
Entrance Building and Road Transport Hall
Competition: 1999, First Prize (cf. 049)
Planning/Construction: 2005–09
Collaborators G/G: Caspar Bresch (Team/Project Manager), Mark Zjörien, Damien Andenmatten, Gaby Kägi, Gilbert Isermann, Elise Camus, Andreas Rothen
Client: Swiss Museum of Transport, Lucerne
General Contractor: Karl Steiner AG, Lucerne
Landscape Architecture: Schweingruber Zulauf, Zurich
Structural Engineer: Henauer Gugler AG, Lucerne
Electrical Engineer: Scherler AG, Lucerne
Building Services Engineer: Wirthensohn AG, Lucerne
Consultants: Lars Müller, Baden, and Peter Regli, Zurich

167
Fuglsang Kunstmuseum, Toreby Lolland, Denmark
Competition: 2005
Partner in Denmark: Jensen + Jørgensen + Wohlfeldt, Copenhagen
Collaborators G/G: Stefan Thommen, Stine Henckel Schultz, Raul Mera
Competition Organizer: Building Foundation, represented by: Akademisk Arkitektforening, Arkitekternes Hus, Copenhagen, Denmark
Landscape Architecture: Schweingruber Zulauf, Zurich
Lighting Consultant: Institut für Tageslichttechnik, Stuttgart, Germany

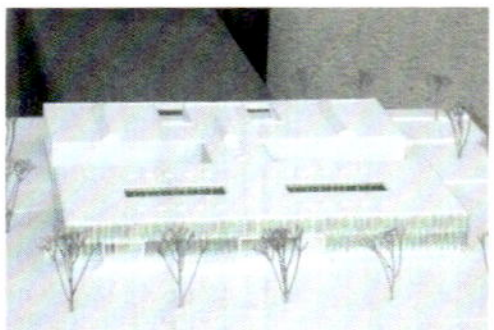

168
Extension of Office Building UICN, Gland VD, Switzerland
Competition: 2005
Collaborators G/G: Caspar Bresch, Karin Schultze, Leander Morf, Raul Mera
Competition Organizer: UICN, Union Internationale pour la Conservation de la Nature
Landscape Architecture: Schweingruber Zulauf, Zurich

169 → p. 546
Housing Development Goldschlägi, Schlieren, Switzerland
Competition: 2005, First Prize
Gigon/Guyer in collaboration with Halter Generalunternehmung AG
Planning/Construction: 2005–09
Collaborators G/G: Competition: Gilbert Isermann; Planning/Construction: Markus Seiler (Team Manager), Martin Bischofberger (Project Manager), Rolf-Werner Wirtz, Florian Isler, Daniel Trepte, Kristin Sasama, Sebastian Beck, Daniela Bergmann
Competition Organizer: Schweizerische Bundesbahnen SBB, Zurich
Client: Migros Pensionskasse Immobilien, Zurich
General Contractor: Halter Generalunternehmung AG, Zurich
Landscape Architecture: Rotzler Krebs Partner AG, Winterthur
Structural Engineer: ARP André Rotzetter + Partner AG, Baar
Electrical Engineer: R+B engineering AG, Zurich
Building Services Engineer: Project: HL-Technik AG, Schaffhausen; Execution: Turrin Engineering, Hegnau
Colors: Harald F. Müller, Öhningen, Germany

170
ZürichForum – New Congress Center, Zurich, Switzerland
Competition: 2005
Collaborators G/G: Caspar Bresch, Volker Mencke, Leander Morf, Raul Mera
Competition Organizer: Zürich Forum AG
Structural Engineer: Henauer Gugler AG, Zurich

171
Residential and Retail Building Terrains Renault, Rives de Seine, Paris, France
Competition: 2005
Collaborators G/G: Karin Schultze, Gaby Kägi, Leander Morf
Competition Organizer: Ville de Boulogne-Billancourt, ZAC Seguin Rives de Seine
Landscape Architecture: Hager AG, Zurich

172 → p. 360
Detached House, Canton Grisons, Switzerland
Commission: 2004
Planning/Construction: 2005–07
Collaborator G/G: Christian Maggioni (Planning, Construction, Construction Manager)
Client: Private
Structural Engineer: Bruno Patt, Zurich
Electrical Engineer: Elkom Partner AG, Chur
Plumbing: Marco Felix, Chur
Heating: Remo Collenberg, Chur

173 → p. 368
Detached House, Küsnacht, Switzerland
Commission: 2005
Planning/Construction: 2005–07
Collaborators G/G: Marjana Sigrist (Project Manager), Caspar Bresch, Florian Isler
Client: Private
Construction Manager: Ruoss Witzig Architekten, Zurich
Landscape Architecture: Robin Winogrond, Zurich
Structural Engineer: Dr. Lüchinger + Meyer AG, Zurich
Electrical Engineer: Elkom Partner AG, Chur
Building Services Engineer: 3-Plan AG, Winterthur
Colors: Harald F. Müller, Öhningen, Germany

174
Contribution to Exhibition *Utopie réalisée* at Haus Konstruktiv, Zurich, Switzerland
Contribution to exhibition marking Gottfried Honegger's 90th birthday, 2007
Projection: Museum "Albers-Honegger Donation"; Pictures: Harald F. Müller, Öhningen, Germany, and Gigon/Guyer

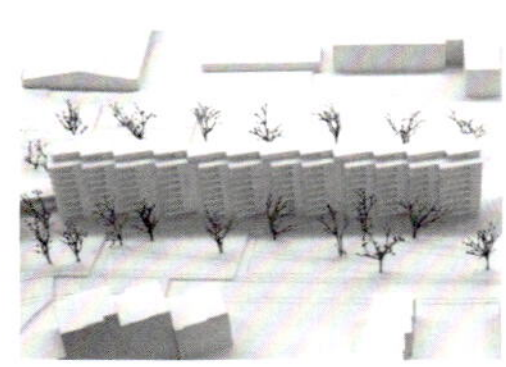

175
Housing Development Schaffhauserstrasse, Zurich, Switzerland
Competition: 2005
Collaborators G/G: Mathias Brühlmann, Andréanne Pochon
Competition Organizer: Baugenossenschaft ASIG, Zurich
Landscape Architecture: Schweingruber Zulauf, Zurich

176 → p. 516

Housing Development, Färberei-Areal, House 5, Thalwil, Switzerland

Competition: 1998, First Prize
Planning/Construction: 2005–08
Collaborators G/G: Michael Winklmann (Team Manager), Ilka Tegeler (Project Manager), Ingo Brinkmann, Reto Killer
Developer: Lerch Immobilien AG, Winterthur, with Colliers CSL AG, Zurich
General Contractor: Bauengineering.com AG, Zurich
Colors: Harald F. Müller, Öhningen, Germany

177 → p. 56

Visitors Center, Museum Kalkriese, Osnabrück, Germany

Competition: 2005, First Prize
Planning/Construction: 2006–09
Collaborators G/G: Competition: Volker Mencke, Leander Morf; Planning/Construction: Michael Winklmann (Team Manager), Christoph Justies (Project Manager)
Client: Varusschlacht im Osnabrücker Land GmbH, Museum und Park Kalkriese, Germany
Construction Manager/Cost Planning: pbr Rohling AG, Osnabrück, Germany
Structural Engineer: Competition: Dr. Lüchinger + Meyer AG, Zurich; Planning/Construction: pbr Planungsbüro Rohling AG, Osnabrück, Germany
Electrical Engineer: Jacobi + Richter, Osnabrück, Germany
Building Services Engineer: pbr Planungsbüro Rohling AG, Osnabrück, Germany

178 → p. 556

Housing Complex Zollikerstrasse, Zurich, Switzerland

Competition: 2005, First Prize
Planning/Construction: 2006–11
Collaborators G/G: Competition: Monica Knechtle; Planning/Construction: Markus Seiler (Team Manager from 2009), Barbara Schlauri (Team Manager until 2009), Damien Andenmatten (Project Manager), Ilka Tegeler, Monica Knechtle
Client: Floor Owners' Association Zollikerstrasse, Zurich
Construction Manager: Agora Baumanagement, Zurich
General Contractor: Gross AG, Brugg
Landscape Architecture: Hager Partner AG, Zurich
Structural Engineer: Basler & Hofmann AG, Zurich
Electrical/Building Services Engineer: Ernst Basler + Partner AG, Zurich

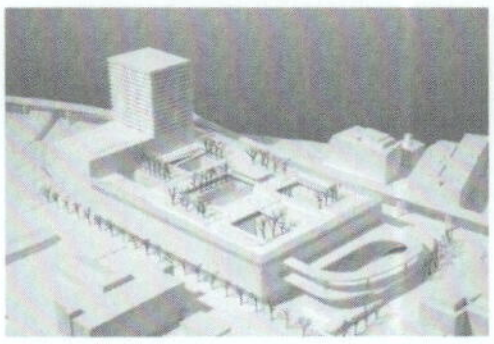

179

Zurich University of the Arts, Toni-Areal, Zurich, Switzerland

Competition: 2005–06
Collaborators G/G: Competition: Volker Mencke, Andréanne Pochon, Mathias Brühlmann, Michael Wagner, Christoph Ramser, Ivana Vukoja, Raul Mera
Client: Zürcher Kantonalbank
Landscape Architecture: Vetsch Nipkow Partner AG, Zurich
Structural Engineer: Dr. Lüchinger + Meyer AG, Zurich
Building Services Engineer: PB P. Berchtold, Sarnen
Signage: Integral Ruedi Baur, Zurich

181

Detached House, Oetwil an der Limmat, Switzerland

Commission: Project 2006
Collaborator G/G: Gilbert Isermann
Client: Private

182

Zurich University of Teacher Education and Sihlpost Office Complex, Zurich, Switzerland

Competition: 2006, Second Prize (cf. 206)
Architecture: Gigon/Guyer in collaboration with David Chipperfield Architects, Berlin, Germany
Collaborators G/G: Mathias Brühlmann, Raphaela Schacher, Christoph Ramser, Andri Gartmann, Ivana Vukoja, Raul Mera
Competition Organizer: Die Schweizerische Post, Bern, and Schweizerische Bundesbahnen SBB, Bern
Landscape Architecture: Schweingruber Zulauf, Zurich
Structural Engineer: Dr. Lüchinger + Meyer AG, Zurich
HVAC and Plumbing: PGMM Schweiz AG, Winterthur

183

Kunst(Zeug)Haus, Rapperswil-Jona, Switzerland

Competition: 2006
Collaborators: Raphaela Schacher, Raul Mera
Competition Organizer: Dr. Peter Bosshard, Rapperswil
Consultant: Mirjam Varadinis
Cost Planning: Ruoss Witzig Architekten, Zurich

184
Office Building, Färberei-Areal, Kesselhaus, Thalwil, Switzerland
Commission: 2006
Planning/Construction: 2006–08
Collaborators G/G: Michael Winklmann (Team Manager), Ivana Vukoja
Client: Weidmann Management AG, Thalwil
Client's Representative: MS Bautreuhand AG, Zurich
General Contractor: Bauengineering.com AG, Zurich
Structural Engineer: Henauer Gugler AG, Zurich
Building Services Engineer: HL Technik AG, Schaffhausen
Electrical Engineer: Elkom Partner AG, Chur
Colors: Harald F. Müller, Öhningen, Germany

186
Railway Station, Swiss Museum of Transport, Lucerne, Switzerland
Commission: 2006
Planning/Construction: 2006–07
Collaborators G/G: Caspar Bresch (Team Manger), Mark Ziörjen (Project Manager)
Client: Canton Lucerne, Department of Building, Environment, and Economy
Project Manager: Schweizerische Bundesbahnen SBB, Lucerne
Landscape Architecture: Schweingruber Zulauf, Zurich
Structural Engineer Safety Barriers: Conzett, Bronzini, Gartmann AG, Chur
Structural Engineer Commuter Railway Station: Emch + Berger WSB AG, Emmenbrücke

187
Housing Development Denzlerstrasse, Zurich, Switzerland
Competition: 2006
Collaborators G/G: Christoph Justies, Roberto Outumuro, Martin Bischofberger
Competition Organizer: BDZ Baugenossenschaft Denzlerstrasse Zurich
Landscape Architecture: Hager AG, Zurich

188
Orange County Museum of Art OCMA, Newport Beach, Los Angeles, USA
Competition: 2006
Collaborators G/G: Monica Knechtle, Andrei Koshelev, Raul Mera
Competition Organizer: Orange County Museum of Art
Cost Planning: Davis Langdon
Structural/Building Services Engineer: Arup, Los Angeles, USA, and London, UK, Ernst Basler + Partner, Zollikon
Lighting Design: Arup, Los Angeles, USA, and London, UK

189
Development of Central Area, Bleiche-Areal, Schaffhausen, Switzerland
Competition: 2007, Second Prize
Gigon/Guyer in collaboration with SPS Immobilien AG as investor
Collaborators G/G: Stefan Thommen, Rolf-Werner Wirtz, Karin Schultze, Monica Knechtle, Christoph Justies, Karsten Buchholz
Competition Organizer: City of Schaffhausen, Building Office
Landscape Architecture: Vetsch Nipkow Partner, Zurich
Structural Engineer: Dr. Lüchinger + Meyer AG, Zurich
Building Services Engineer: Waldhauser AG, Münchenstein

190
Day School with Sports Facilities Sydhaven, Copenhagen, Denmark
Competition: 2006
Architecture in collaboration with Erik Møller Arkitekter, Copenhagen
Collaborators G/G: Raphaela Schacher, Andri Gartmann, Ivana Vukoja, Karsten Buchholz, Raul Mera
Competition Organizer: City of Copenhagen
Landscape Architecture: Schweingruber Zulauf, Zurich
Structural Engineer: Dr. Lüchinger + Meyer AG, Zurich
Building Services Engineer: Birch & Krogboe A/S, Virum, Denmark

192
Housing Project Areal Schleife, Zug, Switzerland
Competition: 2006
Collaborators G/G: Franziska Bächer, Martin Bischofberger, Karsten Buchholz, Christoph Justies, Andrei Kosholev, Raul Mera, Stefan Thommen, Ivana Vukoja
Competition Organizer: Schweizerische Bundesbahnen SBB
Landscape Architecture: planetage GmbH, Zurich
Structural Engineer: Dr. Schwartz Consulting AG, Zug
Building Services Engineer: PB P. Berchtold, Sarnen

193
Museum Folkwang, Essen, Germany
Competition: 2007, Third Prize
Collaborators G/G: Raphaela Schacher, Karsten Buchholz, Andri Gartmann, Brigitte Rüdel, Pieter Rabijns, Ivana Vukoja, Raul Mera
Competition Organizer: City of Essen
Landscape Architecture: Schweingruber Zulauf, Zurich
Structural Engineer: Dr. Lüchinger + Meyer AG, Zurich
Building Services Engineer: Waldhauser AG, Münchenstein
Lighting Consultants: Institut für Tageslichttechnik, Stuttgart, Germany, and Lichtdesign Ing. gesellschaft mbH, Cologne, Germany

194
Refurbishment of Residential Building, Färberei-Areal, Farbstrasse, Thalwil, Switzerland
Commission: 2006
Planning/Construction: 2006–08
Collaborators G/G: Michael Winklmann (Team Manager), Martin Bischofberger, Franziska Bächer, Ivana Vukoja
Client: Weidmann Management AG, Thalwil
Client's Representative: MS Bautreuhand AG, Zurich
General Contractor: Unirenova AG, Zurich
Colors: Harald F. Müller, Öhningen, Germany

196
Urban Planning Study Cloche d'Or, Luxembourg
Competition: 2006–07
Collaborators G/G: Stefan Thommen, Gilbert Isermann
Competition Organizer: Grossfeld PAP SA, Luxembourg

197 → p. 240
Platform Office Building, Zurich, Switzerland
Tenant Fit-out for Ernst & Young Ltd, Platform, Zurich
Commission: 2007
Planning/Construction: 2007–11
Collaborators G/G: Christian Maggioni (Team Manager), Franziska Bächer (Project Manager from 11/2007), Stefan Thommen (Project Manager until 06/2007), Christoph Rothenhöfer (Project Manager until 05/2007); Planning/Construction: Markus von Dellingshausen, Philippe Volpe, Karla Pilz, Armin Baumann, Pieter Rabijns
Client: Swiss Prime Site AG, Olten
Main Tenant: Ernst & Young Ltd, Zurich
General Contractor: HRS Real Estate AG, Zurich
Structural Engineer: Planning: ARGE Dr. Schwartz Consulting AG, Zug, Dr. Lüchinger + Meyer AG, Zurich, and Freihofer & Partner AG, Zurich; Construction: Ribi + Blum AG, Romanshorn
Façade: Planning: gkp fassadentechnik ag, Aadorf; Construction: Fahrni Fassadensysteme AG, Lyss
Electrical Engineer: Planning: IBG B. Graf AG, St. Gallen; Execution: Herzog Kull Group Zurich, Schlieren
Ventilation: Planning: Waldhauser AG, Münchenstein; Construction: Lippuner Energie- und Metallbautechnik AG, Grabs
Heating/Cooling/Building Automation: Planning: PB P. Berchtold, Sarnen; Execution: Lippuner Energie- und Metallbautechnik AG, Grabs
Lighting Consultant: Planning: Ernst Basler + Partner AG, Zurich; Execution: Regent, Zurich
Atmospheric Lighting: Planning: Gigon/Guyer, Studio Hannes Wettstein, Zurich; Execution: Fluora, Herisau
Plumbing: Planning: PB P. Berchtold, Sarnen; Execution: Huustechnik Rechberger AG, Zurich
Fire Safety Engineer: Planning: Makiol + Wiederkehr, Beinwil a.S.; Execution: AFC Air Flow Consulting AG, Zurich
Sprinklers: Planning: PB P. Berchtold, Sarnen; Execution: GRP Ingenieure, Rotkreuz
Building Physics Engineer: BAKUS GmbH, Zurich
Landscape Architecture: Schweingruber Zulauf, Zurich
Furnishings: Gigon/Guyer
Work Places, Internal: Off Consult, Zurich
Art: Nic Hess, Zurich; Herbert Lachmayer and Margit Nobis, Vienna; Ernesto Neto, Brazil

198
Training Center Academy of Art and Design, Dreispitz-Areal, Basel, Switzerland
Competition: 2007
Collaborators G/G: Gilbert Isermann, Raphaela Schacher, Brigitte Rüdel, Ivana Vukoja, Karsten Buchholz
Competition Organizer: Christoph Merian Stiftung, Basel, Building Department of the Canton Basel City
Landscape Architecture: Schweingruber Zulauf, Zurich

200
University of Applied Sciences Northwestern Switzerland, Brugg-Windisch
Competition: 2007
Collaborators G/G: Stefan Thommen, Gilbert Isermann, Raphaela Schacher, Pieter Rabijns, Karsten Buchholz
Competition Organizer: Publica (Pensionskasse des Bundes), Bern, and HRS Campus AG, Madetswil
Landscape Architecture: Planetage GmbH, Zurich

201
Fondazione Arp, Locarno, Switzerland
Commission: 2008
Planning/Construction: 2008–13
Collaborators G/G: Barbara Schlauri (Project Manager), Damien Andenmatten
Client: Fondazione Marguerite Arp, Solduno
Costs/Construction Manager: Architetti associati, Verscio
Structural Engineer: De Giorgi & Partner, Muralto
Electrical Engineer: Scherler Ingegneri Elettrici, Lugano
Building Services Engineer: Studio AGS, Locarno

202
Housing Development Langhagweg, Zurich, Switzerland
Competition: 2007, Third Prize
Collaborators G/G: Karin Schultze, Kim Sneyders, Raphaela Schacher, Karsten Buchholz
Competition Organizer: Gemeinnützige Baugenossenschaft Limmattal, Zurich
Landscape Architecture: Schweingruber Zulauf, Zurich
Structural Engineer: Basler & Hofmann AG, Zurich
Building Services Engineer: 3-Plan AG, Winterthur

203
"Der Spiegel" Headquarters Building, Ericusspitze, Hamburg, Germany
Competition: 2007
Collaborators G/G: Stefan Thommen, Nicolai Rünzi, Karin Schultze, Monica Knechtle, Karsten Buchholz
Competition Organizer: ROBERT VOGEL GmbH & Co. KG, Hamburg, Germany
Construction Economics: pbr Planungsbüro Rohling AG, Magdeburg, Germany
Landscape Architecture: Planetage GmbH, Zurich
Structural Engineer: Dr. Lüchinger + Meyer AG, Zurich
Building Services Engineer: PBP. Berchtold, Sarnen, IPB GmbH Ingenieurgesellschaft, Frankfurt am Main, Germany

204
Tourism and Sports Center, Davos (formerly Sports Center Davos), Switzerland
Commission: 2007
Planning/Construction: 2007–09
Collaborators G/G: Markus Seiler (Project Manager), Kristin Sasama, Marjana Sigrist, Sebastian Beck
Client: Davos Destinations-Organisation, Davos
Construction Manager: Othmar Brügger, Davos
Structural Engineer: DIAG AG, Davos
Electrical Engineer: Elkom Partner AG, Davos
Building Services Engineer: Waldhauser AG, Münchenstein
Colors: Adrian Schiess, Zurich
Art: Joël Tettamanti, Lausanne
Graphic Design: Trix Wetter, Zurich

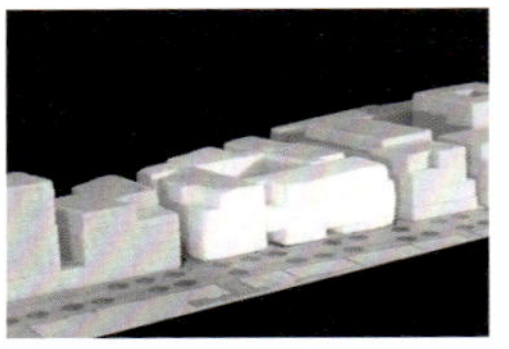

206 → p. 280
C10 Office Building, Europaallee 21, Zurich, Switzerland
Competition: 2006, Second Prize (cf. 182)
Planning/Construction: 2007–12
Gigon/Guyer (Building C10); Max Dudler, Zurich (Buildings C20, C30); David Chipperfield Architects, Berlin, Germany (Building C40)
Collaborators G/G: Barbara Schlauri (Team Manager), Brigitte Rüdel (Project Manager until 08/2010), Urs Meyer (Project Manager from 08/2010), Luisa Wittgen, Katharina Löble, Bettina Gerhold, Ingo Brinkmann
Development: Schweizerische Bundesbahnen SBB, Bern, and Schweizerische Post, Bern
Client: UBS AG, Zurich
General Contractor: Implenia Generalunternehmung AG, Dietlikon
Landscape Architecture: Schweingruber Zulauf, Zurich
Structural Engineer: Leonhardt, Andrä und Partner, Berlin, Germany, and Dr. J. Grob & Partner AG, Winterthur
Electrical Engineer: Bürgin & Keller Management & Engineering AG, Adliswil, and Thomas Lüem Partner AG, Baar
Building Services Engineer: Polke, Ziege, von Moos AG, Zurich
Façade: Planning: gkp fassadentechnik ag, Aadorf; Construction: Gig Fassaden GmbH, Attnang-Puchheim, Austria

207
Redesign of Visitors Zone, Feller AG, Horgen, Switzerland
Competition: 2007
Collaborators G/G: Pieter Rabijns, Franziska Bächer, Raphaela Schacher, Karsten Buchholz
Competition Organizer: Feller AG, Horgen
Consultant: Hannes Wettstein, Zurich
Structural/Building Services Engineer: Ernst Basler + Partner AG, Zurich

209
Housing/Office Complex Altes Warteck-Areal, Basel, Switzerland
Competition: 2007
Collaborators G/G: Nicolai Rünzi, Raphaela Schacher, Ivana Vukoja, Karsten Buchholz
Competition Organizer: Warteck Invest AG, Basel
Landscape Architecture: Schweingruber Zulauf, Zurich
Colors: Harald F. Müller, Öhningen, Germany

213
Housing Complex Villa Pax, Baden, Switzerland
Competition: 2007–08, First Prize
Planning/Construction: 2008–11
Collaborators G/G: Competition: Nicolai Rünzi, Ivana Vukoja, Karsten Buchholz; Planning/Construction: Pit Brunner (Team/Project Manager), Daniela Schadegg, Christoph Dober, Brigitte Rüdel
Client: Dr. Peter + Pia Conrad, Baden
Client's Representative: AK Bautreuhand, Zurich
Costs/Construction Manager: Witzig Architekten, Zurich
Landscape Architecture: Balliana Schubert AG, Zurich
Structural Engineer: MWV Bauingenieure AG, Baden
Building Services Engineer: Nanotech AG, Baden
Electrical Engineer: P. Keller + Partner AG, Baden

214
Extension of Städel Museum, Frankfurt am Main, Germany
Competition: 2008, Second Prize ex aequo
Collaborators G/G: Ivana Vukoja, Nicolai Rünzi, Karsten Buchholz
Competition Organizer: Städelsches Kunstinstitut, Frankfurt am Main, Germany
Landscape Architecture: Vogt Landschaftsarchitekten, Zurich
Lighting Consultant: Lichtdesign Ingenieurgesellschaft mbH, Cologne, Germany

215 → p. 516
Housing Development, Färberei-Areal, Houses 2 and 3, Thalwil, Switzerland
Commission: 2008
Planning/Construction: 2008–12
Collaborators G/G: Michael Winklmann (Team Manager), Cornelia Schmidt (Project Manager from 2010), Lucía Gratz, Anna Dreykluft, Ingo Brinkmann, Daniela Bergmann, Martin Schiess, Meret Morgenthaler, Martin Bischofberger, Christoph Dober, Alex Zeller, Griet Aesaert, Daniel Trepte
Client: Ornak AG, Thalwil
Client's Representative: MS Bautreuhand AG, Zurich
General Contractor: HRS Real Estate AG, Zurich
Landscape Architecture: Schweingruber Zulauf, Zurich
Structural Engineer: Synaxis AG, Zurich
Electrical Engineer: R+B engineering AG, Zurich
Building Services Engineer: HL Technik, Schaffhausen
Colors: Harald F. Müller, Öhningen, Germany

216
Window Factory, Goldach, Switzerland
Project Study: 2007–08
Collaborators G/G: Mark Ziörjen, Katharina Löble
Client: Vogel Fensterbauer AG, Rorschach

218
Hawa Administration and Production Building, Mettmenstetten, Switzerland
Competition: 2008, Third Prize
Gigon/Guyer in collaboration with Studio Hannes Wettstein, Zurich
Collaborators G/G: Karla Pilz, Markus von Dellingshausen, Karsten Buchholz
Competition Organizer: HAWA AG, Mettmenstetten
Landscape Architecture: Schweingruber Zulauf, Zurich
Structural Engineer: Dr. Lüchinger + Meyer AG, Zurich

219
Living Architecture, A House on the Sea, Thorpeness, UK
Project Study: 2008
Collaborators G/G: Andréanne Pochon, Karsten Buchholz
Client: Living Architecture

220
Curling and Training Hall HCD, Davos, Switzerland
Project Study: 2007–08
Collaborators G/G: Markus Seiler, Daniel Trepte, Katharina Löble, Karsten Buchholz
Client for Curling Hall: Curlingclub Davos
Client for Training Hall HCD: Hockeyclub Davos
Timber Construction: Walter Bieler AG, Bonaduz
Planning for Ice Rinks: Benjamin W. Bührer, Meggen

221
Extension of Congress House Davos, Switzerland
Competition: 2008, Second Prize
Collaborators G/G: Nicolai Rünzi, Ivana Vukoja, Karsten Buchholz, Markus Seiler
Competition Organizer: Landschaft Davos Gemeinde, represented by Kleiner Landrat Davos
Landscape Architecture: Schweingruber Zulauf, Zurich
Structural Engineer: DIAG Davoser Ingenieure AG, Davos and Aerni + Aerni AG, Zurich

222 → p. 376
Detached House on Zürichberg, Zurich, Switzerland
Commission: 2008
Planning/Construction: 2008–11
Collaborators G/G: Markus Seiler (Team/Project Manager), Kristin Sasama, Adréanne Pochon
Client: Private
Construction Manager: Witzig Architekten, Zurich, and Gigon/Guyer
Structural Engineer: Aerni + Aerni AG, Zurich
Building Services Engineer/Electrical Engineer: Ernst Basler + Partner AG, Zurich

223
Residential District Blaricummermeent, Area B, The Netherlands
Competition: 2008, Second Prize
Collaborators G/G: Kim Sneyders, Daniela Schadegg, Daniela Bergmann, Andréanne Pochon
Competition Organizer: Town of Blaricum
Gigon/Guyer in collaboration with three architecture studios under the direction of two project developers and the landscape architect
Project Developer: Blauwhoed Euro-woningen, Amsterdam, Vorm Ontwikkeling B.V., Papendrecht, The Netherlands
Landscape Architecture: Karres en Brands landschapsarchitecten bv, Hilversum, The Netherlands
Architecture Studios: Onix bv, Groningen, The Netherlands, ANA architecten, Amsterdam, The Netherlands, DAAD architecten bv, Beilen, The Netherlands

224 → p. 566
Housing Development Zellweger-Areal, Uster, Switzerland
Competition: 2008, First Prize
Planning/Construction: 2009–13
Collaborators G/G: Competition: Daniel Friedmann, Reto Killer, Eric Sommerlatte, Karsten Buchholz; Planning/Construction: Caspar Bresch (Team Manager until 02/2011), Markus Seiler (Team Manager from 02/2011), Daniela Schadegg (Project Manager), Karin Winklmann, Kristin Sasama, Philippe Volpe, Martin Feichtner, Lena Ehringhaus
Client: Zellweger Park AG, Uster
Client's Representative: Immopoly, Zurich
Construction Manager/Cost Planning: b+p baurealisation ag, Zurich
Landscape Architecture: Hager Partner AG, Zurich
Structural Engineer: Schnetzer Puskas Ingenieure AG, Zurich
Building Services Engineer: Ernst Basler + Partner AG, Zurich
Art: Lutz/Guggisberg

225 → p. 124
Extension of Kunsthaus Zürich, Switzerland
Competition: 2008, Second Prize
Collaborators G/G: Ivana Vukoja, Nicolai Rünzi, Christian Maggioni, Damien Andenmatten, Karsten Buchholz
Competition Organizer: Zürcher Kunstgesellschaft, Stiftung Zürcher Kunsthaus, City of Zurich
Construction Economics: Ghisleni Planen Bauen GmbH, Rapperswil
Landscape Architecture: Schweingruber Zulauf, Zurich
Structural Engineer: Dr. Schwartz Consulting AG, Zug
Building Services Engineer: Waldhauser AG, Münchenstein
Lighting Consultants: Arup Lighting, London, UK, Lichtdesign Ingenieurgesell-schaft mbH, Cologne, Germany

227
Housing Development Areal Letzibach, Area C, Zurich, Switzerland
Competition: 2008
Collaborators G/G: Nicolai Rünzi, Kim Sneyders, Karsten Buchholz, Martin Schiess, Luisa Wittgen
Competition Organizer: Schweizerische Bundesbahnen SBB, Real Estate, Development Zurich
Landscape Architecture: Balliana Schubert, Zurich
Colors: Adrian Schiess, Mouans-Sartoux, France

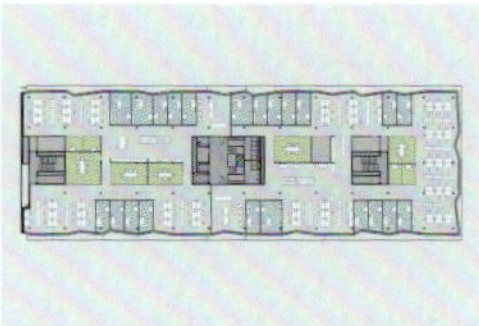

229
Retail and Office Building Sévelin, Lausanne, Switzerland
Competition: 2008, First Prize ex aequo
Collaborators G/G: Vanessa Tardy, Martin Schwarz, Eric Sommerlatte, Thomas Möckel
Competition Organizer: PSP Swiss Property AG, Zug
Cost Planning: b+p baurealisation ag, Zurich
Façade: Reba Fassadentechnik, Chur

231
Housing Development Hunziker-Areal, Zurich, Switzerland
Competition: 2008–09
Collaborators G/G: Damien Andenmatten, Martin Schiess, Karsten Buchholz
Competition Organizer: City of Zurich, Building Office
Landscape Architecture: Hager Landscape Architecture AG, Zurich

232 → p. 130
Munch Museum and Stenersen Museum Collections, Oslo, Norway
Competition: 2008–09
Collaborators G/G: Nicolai Rünzi, Luisa Wittgen, Damien Andenmatten, Karsten Buchholz, Martin Schiess, Thomas Möckel
Competition Organizer: HAV Eiendom AS, Oslo, Norway
Landscape Architecture: Schweingruber Zulauf, Zurich
Consultants: Lars Müller, Baden, Erik Møller Arkitekter, Copenhagen, Denmark, A.L. Høyer Skien AS, Skien, Norway

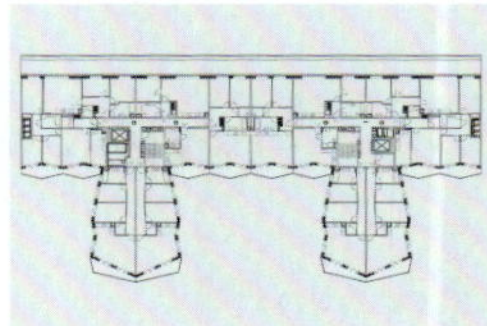

233
Housing Development Entrepot MacDonald, Paris, France
Commission: 2008
Planning/Construction: 2008–12
Collaborators G/G: Caspar Bresch (Team Manager until 2010), Pieter Rabijns (Team Manager from 2011), Eric Sommerlatte
Client: SHC Parci MacDonald Promotion, Paris, France
Construction: in collaboration with DVVD, Architectes, Paris, France
Technical Planning Office: ARCOBA, Saint Denis, France

234
Urban Master Plan Police & Justice Center PJZ, Switzerland
Feasibility Study: 2009 (cf. 153)
Collaborators G/G: Pit Brunner, Eric Sommerlatte
Client: Building Office Canton Zurich, Urban Planning Office, City of Zurich

235
Hotel, Housing, Office, and Commercial Complex, Lindberghallee, Glattpark, Opfikon, Switzerland
Competition: 2009, Fourth Prize
Collaborators G/G: Reto Killer, Daniel Friedmann, Daniela Schadegg, Karsten Buchholz, Thomas Möckel, Pit Brunner
Competition Organizer: Karl Steiner AG, Zurich
Landscape Architecture: Rotzler Krebs Partner GmbH, Winterthur
Structural Engineer: Walt + Galmarini AG, Zurich

236
Housing Development Tramstrasse/ Funkwiesenstrasse, Zurich, Switzerland
Competition: 2009
Collaborators G/G: Martin Schiess, Bettina Gerhold, Karsten Buchholz, Damien Andenmatten, Thomas Möckel
Competition Organizer: BAHOGE Wohnbaugenossenschaft, Wohnsiedlung Tram-/Funkwiesenstrasse
Structural Engineer: Dr. Lüchinger + Meyer AG, Zurich

237 → p. 264
Würth Administration Building with Educational and Training Center, Rorschach, Switzerland
Competition: 2009, First Prize
Planning/Construction: 2009–13
Collaborators G/G: Competition: Nicolai Rünzi, Luisa Wittgen, Bettina Gerhold, Thomas Möckel, Matthias Clivio; Planning/ Construction: Christian Maggioni (Team Manager), Matthias Clivio (Project Manager), Nicolai Rünzi, Christoph Lay, Katja Fröhlich, Rus Carnicero, Martin Schneider, Michael Kloiber
Client: Würth International AG, Chur
Construction Manager/Cost Planning: Walter Dietsche Baumanagement AG, Chur
Structural Engineer: Dr. Lüchinger + Meyer AG, Zurich
Building Services Engineer: Waldhauser Building Services Engineer AG, Basel
Electrical Engineer: Bühler + Scherler AG, St. Gallen
Kitchen Planning: HoGaKa Profi GmbH, Ludwigsburg, Germany
Fire Safety: Makiol + Wiederkehr, Beinwil am See

238
Urban Planning Concept, Sulzerareal Werk 1, Winterthur, Switzerland
Competition: 2009, First Prize
Layout Plan: 2009–10
Collaborators G/G: Competition: Bettina Gerhold, Eric Sommerlatte, Ingo Brinkmann, Kristin Sasama, Daniel Friedmann, Hauke Jungjohann
Guideline Project/Concept: Christoph Justies (Project Manager), Andréanne Pochon, Daniel Friedmann, Ingo Brinkmann
Client: Sulzer Immobilien, Winterthur, taken over by Implenia Immobilien AG, 10/2010
Landscape Architecture: Vogt Landschaftsarchitekten, Zurich
Layout Plan: Suter von Känel Wild AG, Zurich
Construction Economics: Rhombus Partner Immobilien AG, Zurich

239 → p. 272
Refurbishment of Villa Rosau, Zurich, Switzerland
Commission: 2009
Planning/Construction: 2009–15
Collaborators G/G: Michael Winklmann (Team Manager), Mathias Rösner (Project Manager), Martin Bischofberger, Christoph Dober, Karla Pilz, Griet Aesaert, Daniel Friedmann
Client for Basic Fit-out: Villa Rosau AG, Zurich
Client's Representative: Conarenco AG, Zurich
Interior Design, Club Baur-au-Lac: Pierre Yves Rochon, Paris, France
Tender Documentation/Construction Manager: ARGE Gigon/Guyer, b+p baurealisation ag, Zurich
Landscape Architecture: Vogt Landschaftsarchitekten, Zurich
Structural Engineer: Ingenieurgemeinschaft Residenz Rosau: Dr. Lüchinger+Meyer AG, Zurich, with Grünenfelder+Lorenz AG, St. Gallen
Building Services Engineer: Gruenberg+Partner AG, Zurich
Electrical Engineer: IBG B. Graf AG, St. Gallen
Kitchen Planning: Simeta AG, Niederwil

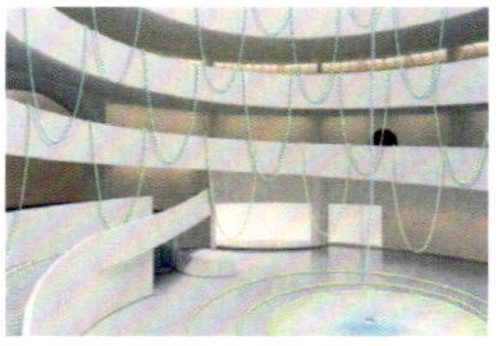

240
Contribution to 50th Anniversary of the Guggenheim Museum, New York, USA
Sketch of Idea for Installation: 2009
Collaborators G/G: Ilka Tegeler, Thomas Möckel

242
The Circle, Airport Extension, Zurich, Switzerland
Competition: 2009
Collaborators G/G: Nicolai Rünzi, Daniel Friedmann, Thomas Möckel, Hauke Jungjohann
Competition Organizer: Unique (Flughafen Zürich AG), Corporate Development, Zurich Airport
Landscape Architecture: Rotzler Krebs Partner GmbH, Winterthur

243
High-rise Office Buildings, Baden Nord, Switzerland
Competition: 2009
Collaborator G/G: Martin Schiess
Competition Organizer: ABB Immobilien AG, Baden
Landscape Architecture: Schweingruber Zulauf, Zurich
Structural/Building Services Engineer: Ernst Basler+Partner AG, Zurich

244
Town Hall, Volketswil, Switzerland
Competition: 2009
Gigon/Guyer Architekten in collaboration with HRS Real Estate AG, Zurich
Collaborators G/G: Reto Killer, Luisa Wittgen, Hauke Jungjohann, Thomas Möckel
Competition Organizer: Municipal administration of Volketswil
Landscape Architecture: Schweingruber Zulauf, Zurich
Structural Engineer: Synaxis AG, Zurich
Building Services Engineer: Meierhans+Partner AG, Schwerzenbach

245 → p. 136
Extension of Kunstmuseum Basel, Switzerland
Competition: 2009
Collaborators G/G: Bettina Gerhold, Katharina Löble, Thomas Möckel, Hauke Jungjohann
Competition Organizer: Canton Basel City
Structural Engineer: Conzett, Bronzini, Gartmann AG, Chur
Lighting Consultant: Institut für Tageslichttechnik, Stuttgart, Germany

246
Housing Development Bombach, Zurich Höngg, Switzerland
Competition: 2009–10
Collaborators G/G: Martin Schiess, Katharina Löble, Thomas Möckel, Roger Sidler
Competition Organizer: Construction and Housing Cooperative Höngg
Landscape Architecture: Westpol, Basel
Structural Engineer: Aerni+Aerni AG, Zurich

247 → p. 228

Tenant Fit-out for Clouds Restaurant, Bistro, Cocktail Bar, Lounge, and Conference Center, 34th and 35th Floor of Prime Tower, Zurich, Switzerland
Competition: 2010, First Prize (cf. 152)
Planning/Execution: 2011
Collaborators G/G: Competition: Stefan Thommen, Karla Pilz, Griet Aesaert; Planning/Execution: Stefan Thommen (Team Manager), Karla Pilz (Project Manager), Yvonne Grunwald, Julia Löscher, Markus von Dellingshausen
Client: Swiss Prime Site AG, Olten
Operator: Jürg Landert, Peter Herzog
Costs/Construction Manager: Steiner AG, Zurich
Ventilation: Hans Abicht AG, Zurich
Heating/Air Conditioning: PB P. Berchtold AG, Sarnen
Electrical Engineer: Hefti, Hess Martignoni AG, Zurich
Kitchen Planning: Promafox, Bad Zurzach
Lighting Consultant: Ernst Basler + Partner AG, Zurich
Furnishings: Gigon/Guyer, Teo Jakob AG, Zurich
Art: Adrian Schiess, Zurich

248

House for Two Families, Zumikon, Switzerland
Commission: 2009
Planning up to planning application: 2010
Collaborators G/G: Markus Seiler (Team Manager), Armin Baumann, Martin Bischofberger, Daniel Friedmann
Client: Private

249

Apartment Building, Rüschlikon, Switzerland
Project Study: 2010
Collaborators G/G: Markus Seiler (Team Manager), Ingo Brinkmann
Client: Rhombus Partner Immobilien AG, Zurich

250 → p. 144

Cultural Center Les Arts, Gstaad, Switzerland
Competition: 2010, Third Prize
Collaborators G/G: Bettina Gerhold, Katharina Löble, Thomas Möckel, Roger Sidler
Competition Organizer: Verein Les Arts, Gstaad
Structural Engineer: Dr. Lüchinger + Meyer AG, Zurich
Landscape Architecture: Schweingruber Zulauf, Zurich

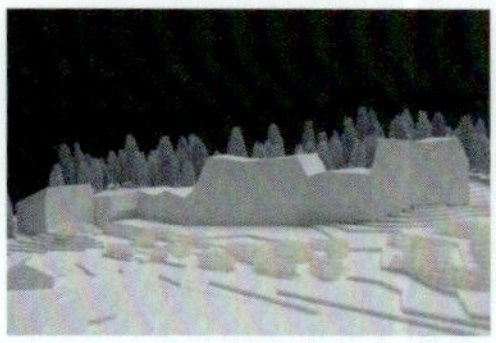

251

Hotel, Schwägalp, Switzerland
Competition: 2009
Collaborators G/G: Reto Killer, Roger Sidler, Thomas Möckel
Competition Organizer: Säntis-Schwebebahnen AG, Schwägalp
Landscape Architecture: Schweingruber Zulauf, Zurich

252

Musée National des Beaux-Arts du Québec, Québec, Canada
Competition: 2009
Collaborators G/G: Daniel Friedmann, Luisa Wittgen, Thomas Möckel, Vanessa Tardy
Competition Organizer: Musée National des Beaux-Arts du Québec

253

Indoor Swimming Pool/Sports Center, St. Moritz, Switzerland
Competition: 2010
Collaborators G/G: Luisa Wittgen, Rico Oberholzer, Christoph Justies
Competition Organizer: Municipal administration of St. Moritz
Landscape Architecture: Westpol GmbH, Basel
Swimming Pool Technology: Schneider Aquatec AG, Staad

254

Apartment Building Brunner, Kilchberg, Switzerland
Project Study: 2010
Collaborators G/G: Barbara Schlauri
Client: Brunner Family Heirs
Cost Planning: b+p baurealisation ag, Zurich

255

Exhibition in ETH Main Building, Zurich, Switzerland
December 9, 2011–January 26, 2012
Invited by gta, ETH Zurich Architecture Department
Planning/Execution: 2010–12
Collaborators G/G: Arend Kölsch, Jennifer Hauger, Veronika Weisner, Ilka Tegeler
Films: Severin Kuhn, Zurich
Projection Technology: videocompany.ch, Zofingen

256
Detached House, Herrliberg, Switzerland
Project Study: 2010
Collaborators G/G: Markus Seiler, Armin Baumann
Client: Hans Sachs, Küsnacht

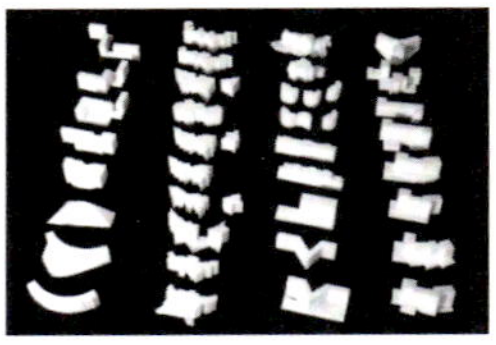

257
Hotel Dolder Waldhaus, Zurich, Switzerland
Urban Planning Feasibility Studies: 2010
Collaborators G/G: Luisa Wittgen, Rico Oberholzer, Armin Baumann
Client: Dolder Waldhaus, Zurich
Client's Representative: Fazun AG, Zurich

258
Tenant Fit-out Bar "Hotel Rivington & Sons", Ground Floor of Prime Tower, Zurich, Switzerland
Concept: raumzuerich 05 AG, Zurich
Commission: 2010 (cf. 152)
Planning/Construction: 2010–11 in close collaboration with raumzuerich 05 AG, Zurich
Collaborators G/G: Stefan Thommen, Karla Pilz, Raffaella Bisceglia, Griet Aesaert
Client: raumzuerich 05 AG, Zurich, Daniel Ferrari, Jonas Herde, Emil Looser, Livio Sergio Notaro
Costs/Construction Manager: Eidos AG, Ralf Gubler and raumzuerich 05 AG, Zurich
Construction of Bar: Almo, Bergamo

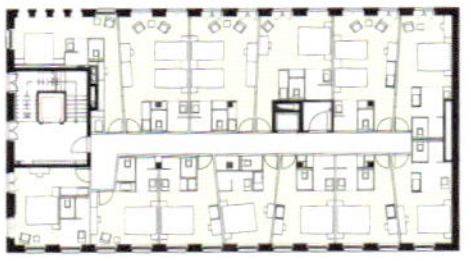

259
Hotel Weberhaus, Zurich, Switzerland
Project Study: 2010
Collaborators G/G: Markus Seiler, Karla Pilz, Luisa Wittgen
Client: Hans Sachs, Küsnacht
Furnishings: Studio Hannes Wettstein, Zurich

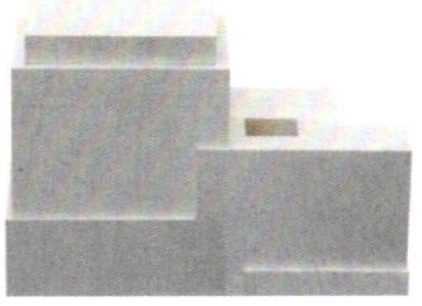

260
High-rise Office Building Taunusanlage 8, Frankfurt am Main, Germany
Competition: 2010, Fourth Prize
Collaborators G/G: Luisa Wittgen, Thomas Möckel, Armin Baumann, Reto Killer
Competition Organizer: Credit Suisse Asset Management, Frankfurt am Main, Germany
Cost Planning: Wenzel + Wenzel, Freie Architekten, Frankfurt am Main, Germany
Structural/Building Services Engineer: Ernst Basler + Partner AG, Zurich

261
Tenant Fit-out Transammonia AG, 16th and 17th Floor of Prime Tower, Zurich, Switzerland
Commission: 2011 (cf. 152)
Planning/Construction: 2011
Collaborators G/G: Stefan Thommen (Team Manager), Alex Zeller
Client: Transammonia AG
Cost Planning/Construction Manager: Ghisleni Planen Bauen GmbH, Rapperswil
Ventilation: Waldhauser AG, Münchenstein
Heating/Cooling/Building Automation: PB P. Berchtold AG, Sarnen
Electrical Engineer: Herzog Kull Group, Schlieren
Light Planning: Ernst Basler + Partner AG, Zurich
Furnishings: Gigon/Guyer, Wohnbedarf Zurich

262
Extension of Museum der Weltkulturen, Frankfurt am Main, Germany
Competition: 2010
Collaborators G/G: Luisa Wittgen, Arend Kölsch
Competition Organizer: Magistrate of the City of Frankfurt am Main, Department VII Culture and Science, Museum der Weltkulturen
Landscape Architecture: Schweingruber Zulauf, Zurich

263
Blumenfeld School, Zurich, Switzerland
Competition: 2010
Collaborators G/G: Mathias Rösner, Christoph Justies, Arend Kölsch, Markus von Dellingshausen
Competition Organizer: Building Office of City of Zurich
Landscape Architecture: Hüsler & Associés Sàrl, Lausanne

264
Housing Development Mattenhof, Zurich, Switzerland
Competition: 2010
Collaborators G/G: Armin Baumann, Thomas Möckel, Markus von Dellings-hausen

Competition Organizer: Siedlungsgenossenschaft Sunnige Hof, Zurich
Landscape Architecture: Vogt Landschaftsarchitekten, Zurich
Construction Economics: planungsboom, Zurich

266
Extension of Kirchner Museum Davos, Switzerland
Project Study: 2010–11
Collaborators G/G: Markus Seiler, Damien Andenmatten

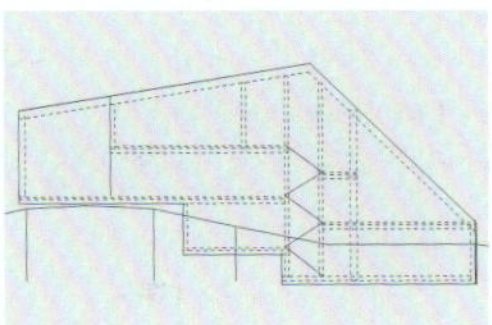

268
Holiday House, Saint-Blaise, Switzerland
Project Study: 2010
Collaborator G/G: Damien Andenmatten
Client: Private

269
Research Building GLC with Laboratories and Offices, ETH Zurich, Switzerland
Competition: 2010
Collaborators G/G: Luisa Wittgen, Thomas Möckel, Armin Baumann, Arend Kölsch
Competition Organizer: ETH Zurich Immobilien, Buildings Management, Zurich
Laboratory Consultant: Morgan Sindall, Basel
Landscape Architecture: Schweingruber Zulauf, Zurich
Structural Engineer: Dr. Schwartz Consulting AG, Zug
Building Services Engineer: Waldhauser AG, Münchenstein

270 → p. 252
Extension of Hardbrücke Railway Station, Zurich, Switzerland
Competition: 2010, First Prize
Gigon/Guyer in collaboration with Walt + Gamarini AG, Zurich, and Ernst Basler + Partner AG, Zurich
Collaborators G/G: Armin Baumann, Moritz Pürckhauer, Christoph Justies
Competition Organizer: Civil Engineering Office of City of Zurich
Structural Engineer: Walt + Galmarini AG, Zurich
Pedestrian Traffic Management: Ernst Basler + Partner AG, Zurich
Cost Planning: b + p baurealisation ag, Zurich
Signage: Weber Harbecke Werbeagentur AG, Zurich

271 → p. 150
Nouveau Musée cantonal des Beaux-Arts MCBA, Lausanne, Switzerland
Competition: 2010–11, Fifth Prize
Collaborators G/G: Arend Kölsch, Kathrin Sindelar, Thomas Möckel, Damien Andenmatten
Competition Organizer: Canton Waadt, Service Immeubles, Patrimoine et Logistique, Département des infrastructures, Lausanne
Structural Engineer: dsp Ingenieure and Planer AG, Zurich
Building Services Engineer: Ernst Basler + Partner AG, Zurich
Museography Consultant: Dieter Schwarz, Kunstmuseum Winterthur

272
Tenant Fit-out Deutsche Bank, 13th to 16th and 33rd Floor of Prime Tower, Zurich, Switzerland
Commission: 2011 (cf. 152)
Planning/Construction: 2011
Collaborators G/G: Stefan Thommen (Team Manager), Pieter Rabijns (Project Manager), Raffaella Bisceglia
Client: Deutsche Bank, Switzerland
Cost Planning/Construction Manager: Ghisleni Planen Bauen GmbH, Rapperswil
Building Services Engineer: PB P. Berchtold AG, Sarnen
Electrical Engineer: Hefti Hess Martignoni AG, Zurich
Lighting Consultant: Ernst Basler + Partner AG, Zurich
Furnishings: Vitra, Gigon/Guyer

273
Würth Office Tower, Künzelsau, Germany
Competition: 2011
Collaborators G/G: Thomas Möckel, Arend Kölsch, Moritz Pürckhauer
Competition Organizer: Adolf Würth GmbH & Co. KG, Künzelsau, Germany
Structural Engineer: Dr. Lüchinger + Meyer AG, Zurich
Construction Economics: Wenzel + Wenzel, Frankfurt am Main, Germany

276
Hotel Dolder Waldhaus, Zurich, Switzerland
Competition: 2011 Phases 1 + 2
Collaborators G/G: Thomas Möckel, Arend Kölsch, Moritz Pürckhauer, Meret Morgenthaler, Sarah Haubner, Rodrigo Jorge
Competition Organizer: Dolder Waldhaus, Zurich
Client's Representative: Fazun AG, Zurich
Landscape Architecture: Schweingruber Zulauf, Zurich
Structural Engineer: Walt + Galmarini AG, Zurich
Building Services Engineer: Polke, Ziege, von Moos AG, Zurich

Biographies

Artists

Pierre André Ferrand
Born 1952 in Geneva, painter. Studied at the Ecole Supérieure d'Art Visuel in Geneva and at the Academy of Fine Arts in Krakow. Lives and works in Geneva and La Chaux-de-Fonds, Switzerland.

Harald F. Müller
Born 1950 in Karlsruhe. Studied art at the Kunstakademie Stuttgart and art history at the University of Stuttgart. Freelance artist, creates sculptural wall installations combining painting and photography. Has realized numerous color and interior concepts for private and public buildings in collaboration with architects in Switzerland and Germany. Lives and works in Öhningen/Lake Constance, Germany

Adrian Schiess
Born 1959 in Zurich, freelance artist. Preparatory course at the Kunstgewerbeschule Zurich in 1975/1976. Graphic design apprenticeship in Zurich from 1976 to 1980. Represented Switzerland at the Venice Biennale in 1990. Invited by Jan Hoet to participate in Documenta IX in Kassel in 1992. Lives and works in Zurich.

Authors

Patrick Gmür
Born 1961 in Lucerne, Dipl. Arch. ETH/BSA/SIA. Studied at ETH Zurich. Appointed Professor of Design and Construction at the Fachhochschule beider Basel, Architecture Department, Muttenz, in 2000. From 1989 to 2009 he had his own architecture studio in Zurich. From 2000 he cooperated with Jakob Steib, architect in Zurich, founding a second firm, Gmür & Steib Architekten AG. Director of the Architectural Institute at the Fachhochschule Nordwestschweiz from 2004 to 2009. Appointed Director of Zurich's Urban Planning Office in September 2009.

Gerhard Mack
Born 1956 in Speyer am Rhein, Germany. Art and architecture editor, *NZZ am Sonntag*, Zurich. Numerous publications on architecture, art, literature, and theater, including: *Kunstmuseen: Auf dem Weg ins 21. Jahrhundert (Art Museums into the 21st Century)* (2000); a monograph on the oeuvre of architects Herzog & de Meuron, 4 volumes to date (1996–2009); and monographs on Hans Josephsohn and Rémy Zaugg (both 2005).

Arthur Rüegg
Born 1942 in Bülach. Studied architecture at ETH Zurich, worked as an architect in Paris and Boston. Has been a freelance architect in Zurich since 1971. Professor of Architecture and Construction at ETH Zurich from 1991 to 2007. Numerous essays and books on construction, interior design, and polychromy in the twentieth century, along with a number of articles on the history of photography. Editor of books including: *Le Corbusier. Polychromie architecturale* (1997/2006) and *Schweizer Möbel und Interieurs im 20. Jahrhundert (Swiss Furniture and Interiors in the 20th Century)* (2002).

Martin Steinmann
Born 1942 in Zurich, Dipl. Arch. ETH and Dr. sc. ETH. From 1987 to 2006 Professor of Architecture and Architectural Theory at ETH Lausanne, Director of Laboratoire de l'habitation urbaine. Exhibition curator and author of numerous publications on twentieth-century and contemporary architecture, including *Forme forte: Écrits/Schriften 1972–2002*. Lives and works in Aarau.

Philip Ursprung
Born 1963 in Baltimore, USA. Studied art history, history, and German language and literature in Geneva, Vienna, and Berlin. Professor of Modern and Contemporary Art at Zurich University's Institute of Art History from 2005 to 2011 and visiting professor at the Graduate School of Architecture, Planning, and Preservation, Columbia University, New York, in 2007. In 2011 he was appointed Professor of Art History and Architectural History at ETH Zurich. Editor of *Herzog & de Meuron: Naturgeschichte (Herzog & de Meuron: Natural History)* (2002); author of *Grenzen der Kunst: Allan Kaprow und das Happening, Robert Smithson und die Land Art* (2003), and *Die Kunst der Gegenwart: 1960 bis heute* (2010).

Annette Gigon
Born 1959 in Herisau, Switzerland. Graduated from ETH Zurich in 1984. Ran her own architecture studio from 1987 to 1989. Since 1989 joint practice with Mike Guyer under the name Gigon/Guyer Architects. From 1997 to 2000 member of Salzburg's Advisory Urban Design Committee. In 2001/2002 guest lecturer at EPF Lausanne, in 2008 guest lecturer at ETH Zurich. 2011 Professeur invitée at the UCL, Tournai. From 2012 Professor for Architecture and Technology at the ETH Zurich. Annette Gigon has been married to Stefan Zwicker since 2008 and lives in Zurich.

Mike Guyer
Born 1958 in Columbus, Ohio, USA. Graduated from ETH Zurich in 1984. Ran his own architecture studio from 1987 to 1989. Since 1989 joint practice with Annette Gigon under the name Gigon/Guyer Architects. From 1996 to 2003 member of Baden Urban Planning Commission, and from 1998 to 2003 member of Quality Team Kop van Zuid in Rotterdam. From 2002 to 2006 member of Zurich's Advisory Urban Planning Commission. Guest lecturer at EPF Lausanne in 2002 and guest lecturer at ETH Zurich in 2009. From 2012 Professor for Architecture and Technology at the ETH Zurich. Mike Guyer has been married to Loe van Scherpenberg since 1989, has two children, and lives in Zurich.

Christian Maggioni
Born 1969 in Leuggern, Switzerland. Graduated from ETH Zurich in 1996. From 1996 to 1999 worked at Bearth & Deplazes, Chur. He has been with Gigon/Guyer Architects since 1999, from 2006 as a team manager and a member of Gigon/Guyer Architects' company management.

Pit Brunner
Born 1957 in Tanga, Tanzania. Studied interior design/industrial design at ZHdK Zurich from 1981 to 1984. Worked in various architecture studios from 1984 to 1991. From 1992 to 1996 studied architecture at TWI/ZHAW Winterthur. Graduated from ETH Zurich in 2000. From 2002 to 2004 worked with Hopf & Wirth, Winterthur. Has been with Gigon/Guyer Architects since 2004, team manager since 2006.

Volker Mencke
Born 1969 in Hofheim am Taunus, Germany. Graduated as Dipl. Ing. (Architecture) from FH Karlsruhe in 1995. From 1995 to 1999 post-graduate course (M. Arch.) at Berlage Institute, Rotterdam. In 1997/1998 worked with Daniel Libeskind, Berlin. Has been with Gigon/Guyer Architects since 1998, team manager since 2006.

Pieter Rabijns
Born 1974 in Mechelen, Belgium. Graduated as Dipl. Arch. from Sint-Lukas Institute of Architecture, Brussels, in 1997. Completed postgraduate degree in architecture at Leuven Catholic University in 1998. From 2001 to 2003 worked with West 8, Rotterdam. Has been with Gigon/Guyer Architects since 2003, team manager since 2006.

Barbara Schlauri
Born 1973 in Münsterlingen, Switzerland. Graduated from ETH Zurich in 2001. Has been with Gigon/Guyer Architects since 2001, team manager since 2006. In 2008/2009 design assistant to visiting lecturers Miller & Maranta, ETH Zurich.

Markus Seiler
Born 1969 in Sarnen, Switzerland. Graduated from FH Luzern in 1996, worked from 1997 to 1999 with Rolf Mühlethaler, Bern. Has been with Gigon/Guyer Architects since 1999, team manager since 2006.

Stefan Thommen
Born 1975 in St. Gallen, Switzerland. Graduated from ETH Zurich in 2002, worked with Meili+Peter, Zurich, in 2002/2003. Has been with Gigon/Guyer Architects since 2003, team manager since 2006.

Michael Winklmann
Born 1971 in Roding, Germany. Graduated from TU München in 1999. From 1999 to 2005 worked in various architecture studios. Has been with Gigon/Guyer Architects since 2005, team manager since 2006.

Past and Present Team at Gigon/Guyer Architects

Griet Aesaert
Sandro Agosti
Yasemin Akdag
Luis Bruno Jose Alves
Julian Amann
Matthias Amsler
Damien Andenmatten
Marène Augsburger
Tuba Ay
Roberto Azzola
Franziska Bächer
Dieter Bachmann
Ivo Barao
Alexander Barina
Armin Baumann
Lorenz Baumann
Marius Baumann
Peter Baumberger
Sebastian Beck
Theo Bellmann
Katrin Belz
Verena Berchtold
Daniela Bergmann
Christof Bhend
Marco Bill
Arnault Biou
Urs Birchmeier
Raffaella Bisceglia
Martin Bischofberger
Christine Blaas
Ute Bleile
Mark Block
Andreas Böhler
Michael Bösch
Anuschka Bossi
Judith Brändle
Claude Brauchli
Caspar Bresch
Ingo Brinkmann
Mathias Brühlmann
Christian Brunner
Pit Brunner
Michael Bucher
Karsten Buchholz
Oscar Buson
Corina Cadisch
Didier Callot
Elise Camus
Rus Carnicero Moreno
Alicia Casals San Miguel
Romana Castiglioni
Yun Hee Choi
Matthias Clivio
Gilles Dafflon
Markus von Dellingshausen
Elisabeth Deutschmann
Björn Dittrich
Christoph Dober
Anna Dreykluft
Sonja Eberle
Lena Ehringhaus
Roy Engel
Carolin Engelhardt
Andreas Ernst
Marc Faber
Deborah Fehlmann
Martin Feichtner
Andrea Fiechter
Patrick Fischer
Corina Flury
Raphael Frei
Daniel Friedmann
Christina Friedrich
Katja Fröhlich
Sonja Furrer Stitz
Michal Gabas
Andri Gartmann
Stefan Gasser
Eva Geering
Annika Geiger
Adrien Genre
Bettina Gerhold
Adinda van Geystelen
Daniel Giezendanner
Jeannette Göldi
Gregor Goldinger
Ireen Gommlich
Juan Gonzalez
Peter Graf
Lucia Gratz
Matthias Greschner
Yvonne Grunwald
Gabriella Güntert
Simone Gutknecht
Roland Harnist
Simon Harrison
Angela Hasler
Sarah Haubner
Jennifer Hauger
Alis Haxhi
Armenak Haydeyan
Felix Heisel
Stine Henckel Schultz
David Hermann
Carmelo Hochstrasser
Thomas Hochstrasser
Esther Hodel
Beatrice Hollenstein
Ulrike Horn
Anna Hotz
Aja Huber
Marius Hug
Florian Husemeyer
Lorenzo Igual
Chantal Imoberdorf
Nicole Ineichen
Gilbert Isermann
Florian Isler
Katrin Jaggi
Christine Jahn
Markus Jandl
Rodrigo Jorge
Hauke Jungjohann
Christoph Justies
Gaby Kägi
Yuta Kanezuka
Miyun Kang
Daniel Kaschub
Daniel Kaufmann
Reto Killer
Serge Klammer
Michael Kloiber
Monica Knechtle
Arend Kölsch
Andrei Koshelev
Stephanie Kühnle
René Kümmerli
Dario Lanfranconi
Christoph Lay
Ivo Lenherr
David Leuthold
Yifang Liu
Katharina Löble
Mario Locci
Jakob Loock
Julia Löscher
Christoph Lötscher
Huihui Lü
Giulia Luraschi
Markus Lüscher
Chantal Lutz
Faye Maerki
Christian Maggioni
Marc Major
Andrin Martig
Mirella Mascolo
Michelle Meier
Katja Mencke
Volker Mencke
Lisa Menje
Raul Mera
Harry Metzler
Christian Meyer
Lucius Meyer
Urs Meyer
Andreas Michel
Thomas Möckel
Leander Morf
Meret Morgenthaler
Basil Morscher
Sandra Mosbacher
Maxim Moskalenko
Claudia Motalli
Adrian Müller
Pascal Müller
Roger Naegeli
Ayaka Nakamura
Rico Oberholzer
Caspar Oswald
Roberto Outumuro
Martino Pedroli
Iris Perl
Jan Pfenning
Christian Pflug
Karla Pilz
Andréanne Pochon
Dirk Podbielski
Tomasz Podniesinski
Moritz Pürckhauer
Pieter Rabijns
Christoph Ramser
Annina Reber
Simone Reiter
Nina Renner
Nina Richner
Lea Rickenbacher
Esther Righetti
Sarah Righetti
Dirk Rinker
Daniela Risoli
Christopher Rofe
Patrizia Roos
Mathias Rösner
Andrea Roth
Andreas Rothen
Christoph Rothenhöfer
Brigitte Rüdel
Nicolai Rünzi Heraeus
Esther Rusnak
Hannes Rutenfranz
Anna Ryf
Julia Sagorodny
Kristin Sasama
Raphaela Schacher
Daniela Schadegg
Marcel Schaufelberger
Loe van Scherpenberg
Daniel Scheuner
Martin Schiess
Barbara Schlauri
Rafael Schmid
Cornelia Schmidt
Frank Schneider
Martin Schneider
Martin Schwarz
Andrea Seiler
Markus Seiler
Konstantin Seufert
Roger Sidler
Marjana Sigrist
Kathrin Sindelar
Jakub Smagacz
Kim Sneyders
Hyung-Sup Soh
Eric Sommerlatte
Andreas Sonderegger
Samuele Squassabia
Karin Stegmeier
Veronika Steiger
Peter Steiner
Matthias Stocker
Annabarbara Suter
Tomas Szczebiot
Hiroaki Tanaka
Philipp Tännler
Vanessa Tardy-Klikar
Ilka Tegeler
Sebastian Thaut
Samuel Thoma
Mireille Thomann
Stefan Thommen
Tobias Tonch
Daniel Trepte
Ivana Vallarsa
Philippe Vaucher
Lucie Vencelidesova
Johannes Vogt
Philippe Volpe
Ivana Vukoja
Michael Wagner
Marcel Weiler
Veronika Weisner
Clara Welbergen
Daniel Weller
Anja Widmer
Michael Widrig
Regula Wiesner
Karin Winklmann
Michael Winklmann
Rolf-Werner Wirtz
Luisa Wittgen
Koni Witzig
Niko Wolfromm
Claudia Wunderlich
Massimo Wüthrich
Liang Xu
Nicolas Yerly
Florian Zahn
Mimouna Zaidi
Francesco Zanchi
Alex Zeller
Libei Zhao
Mark Ziörjen
Stefan Zopp
Alexia Zydel

The names printed in bold type are those members of staff working at Gigon/Guyer Architects at the time of the publication of this book.

Image Credits

Unless stated otherwise, the copyright for illustrations, plans, and photographs is held by Gigon/Guyer Architects.

The numbers in square brackets refer to the images in the Index of Works & Projects and indicate the project number.

t = top, m = middle, b = bottom, l = left, r = right

Georg Aerni: 407 tl, 488f, 494, 496, 498f, [135]
Architron GmbH (Visualization): 270f, 274 b, [156]
Architron GmbH, Gigon/Guyer (Visualization): 274 b, [247]
ARGE Löwenbräuareal: 289, 300
© Astock/A Stock/Corbis: 203 m
Baugeschichtliches Archiv der Stadt Zürich: 277 l
Ferenc Berko (photo: 1952/53), © berkophoto.com: 198
Pit Brunner: 212
René Burri: 184–187
Katalin Deér: 164–167
Serge Demailly: 22, 23, 67–71, [133]
René C. Dürr : 241
Hans Ege: [197]
Ralph Feiner: 358f, 362–365
Pierre André Ferrand: 406 bl, 467, 469–471, [114]
© Gemeinnütziger Verein Appisberg: 259
Gigon/Guyer, David Chipperfield Architects (Visualization): [182]
Gmür & Geschwentner Architekten (Plans): 392, 401
Google Earth: 272
© Gosteli-Stiftung, SPZ, F2: 437
Maurice Haas: 201 b, 350f
© Amanda Hall/Robert Harding World Imagery/Corbis: 202 b
Andrea Helbling: 18, 407 tr, 506f, 511, 513, [139]
Heinrich Helfenstein: 13 t, 14, 16 t, 19, 21 tl b, 29 , 40 t bl, 42 bl, 43f, 51 b, 53, 55 t, 72f, 75f, 78–83, 85, 87 t, 89 t, 90f, 94–97, 180–183, 201 m, 203 t, 305 t, 306, 307 m, 309, 310 t, 315–317, 318f, 322, 324f, 326, 327 b, 328f, 331, 332 t, 333f, 336 b, 337, 406 t, 410, 414f, 419–421, 423, 429 b, 432, 433 b, 434f, 439 b, 442–445, 500f, 503, [00A, 00B, 00E, 001–003, 009, 011, 013, 014, 016, 018, 023, 035, 039, 053, 061, 071, 093, 095, 115, 149, 152]
Hannes Henz: 493, 495 b
Valentin Jeck: 158–161
Kantonale Denkmalpflege Zürich: 277 r, 314 t
Christian Kerez: [005]
Severin Kuhn (Filmstill): 197, 201, 341, 354f, 409, 514f, [111]
Walter Mair: 192–195, 214 l, 217 b, 225 t, 234–236
André Morin: 60f, 64f, [054]
Harald F. Müller: 256f, 260, 261 b, 405, 406 m, 424f, 429 t, 430f, 433 t, 462f, 465, 547, [006, 037, 040]
Jeroen Musch: 446f, 449, 453 l, [108]
Claude Opprecht, Galerie Henze & Ketterer: 21 tr
Klemens Ortmeyer: 31, 32f, 40 br, 41 br, 45, 47 t, 51 t, 52, 57–59, [177]
Lucas Peters: 312 t, 313 b, 338f, 342–347, 353, 357, 366f, 371, 373, 406 br, 407 mr bl, 477–479, 483 t, 484, 487, 504, 517–520, 536f, 541, 543, 544f, 549 l, 550f, 553, [043, 131, 162, 169, 186]
Projekt 172, Bauherr: 361, [172]
© 2011, ProLitteris, Zurich: 311 b
raumgleiter gmbh (Visualization): 250f, 252 b, 253f, 286f, 294 t, 295f, 297 t, 298 t, 299, 300 m b, 301
Adrian Schiess: 327 t, 454–455, 458–459
Hanspeter Schiess: 288, 291, [118]
© Steffi Schmedes: 311 t
Christian Scholz: 172–175
Filippo Simonetti: 370, [173]
Erik Steinbrecher: 168–171
Annelies Štrba: 162f
Albert Teichmann, Basel: 336 tl
Joël Tettamanti: 176–179, 407 ml, 526f, 529, 531–533, [141, 204]
Tiefbauamt Zürich/hochparterre. wettbewerbe: 252 t, [270]
© VARUSSCHLACHT im Osnabrücker Land: 28 b
Thies Wachter: 188–191, 199, 202 m, 203 b, 204 t, 206f, 211, 214 r, 215, 217 t, 220, 222f, 225 m b, 226f, 229–233, 237, 238f, 243–249, 374f, 377–383, 407 br, 464, 525 tl b, 554f, 557, 559, 561–563, [155, 178, 222, 255, 258, 261, 272]
Gaston Wicky: 17 t, [017]
© Helga Zoppke, Foto Oleg Woinoff: 28 t (From: *Varusschlacht im Osnabrücker Land, Museum und Park Kalkriese,* hg. von VARUSSCHLACHT im Osnabrücker Land GmbH – Museum, Verlag Philipp von Zabern, Mainz, 2009)
Thomas Zwyssig: 205, 297 m b

The editors have endeavored to identify all copyright holders and photographers. If despite our intensive research any person entitled to rights should have been overlooked, legitimate claims shall be compensated within the usual provision.

Monographs

El Croquis, "Annette Gigon Mike Guyer 2001–2008, The Everyday and Its Reinvention," no. 143, Madrid, 2009

WA. World Architecture, "The Complexity of Colour, Gigon/Guyer Architects," no. 12, 2006, Peking, 2006

a+u. Architecture and Urbanism, "Gigon/Guyer – Matter, Colour, Light and Space," special edition, Tokyo, November 2006

Projekte. Gigon/Guyer (De aedibus, no. 7), Quart Verlag, Lucerne, 2004

Gigon/Guyer. Seen by Kjeld Vindum, Louisiana Museum of Modern Art, Humlebæk, 2002

Gigon/Guyer. The 2000 Charles & Ray Eames Lecture (Michigan Architecture Papers, no. 8), edited by Annette W. LeCuyer, University of Michigan, Ann Arbor, 2000

Gigon & Guyer. Museum Liner Appenzell (Archiv kunst architektur. Werkdokumente, no. 18) edited by Edelbert Köb, Kunsthaus Bregenz, Hatje Cantz Verlag, Ostfildern-Ruit, 2000

El Croquis, "Annette Gigon Mike Guyer 1989–2000, The Variegated Minimal," no. 102, Madrid, 2000

Gigon/Guyer Architekten. Arbeiten 1989–2000, edited by Christoph J. Bürkle, Niggli Verlag, Sulgen, 2000

Gigon/Guyer Architects. Works & Projects 1989–2000, edited by Christoph J. Bürkle, Barcelona, Editorial Gustavo Gili, Barcelona, 2000

Fenster-Fassade. Annette Gigon/Mike Guyer, edited by Arthur Rüegg, ETH, Zurich, 1998

Werkstoff. Annette Gigon/Mike Guyer, Architekturgalerie, Lucerne, 1993

Awards (selection)

2012
Daylight-Award Velux Stiftung (Kirchner Museum Davos)

2009
International Fellowship of the RIBA Royal Institute of British Architects

Schweizer Denkmalpreis awarded by the Konferenz der Schweizer Denkmalpflegerinnen und Denkmalpfleger (for the Extension/Renovation of the Historical Villa, Kastanienbaum)

2008
"Auszeichnung Gute Bauten" awarded by the Municipality of Wädenswil (for the Housing Complex Park Grünenberg, Wädenswil)

2007
Bautenprämierung awarded by Heimatschutz Basel (for the Remodeling of Kunstmuseum Basel)

2005
"Auszeichnung für gute Bauten" awarded by the City of Zurich (for the Housing Development Pflegi-Areal in Zurich)

2003
BDA Prize awarded by the Lower Saxony branch of the Bund Deutscher Architekten (for the Archeological Museum and Park Kalkriese, Osnabrück, Germany)

2002
Fritz Schumacher Prize awarded by the Alfred Toepfer Foundation, Hanover, for outstanding contributions to architecture

Deutscher Stahlbaupreis (for the Archeological Museum and Park Kalkriese, Osnabrück, Germany, awarded)

2001
"Auszeichnung für gute Bauten" awarded by the City of Zurich (for Two Buildings in Zurich)

Weser-Ems Prize for Architecture and Civil Engineering (for the Archeological Museum and Park Kalkriese, Osnabrück, Germany)

"Auszeichnung guter Bauten" awarded by the Canton of Grisons (for Davos Sports Center, Switzerland)

"Auszeichnung für gute Bauten" awarded by the Canton of Zurich (for Three Houses on Susenbergstrasse, Zurich, Switzerland)

1999
Mies van der Rohe Award for European Architecture (for Museum Liner Appenzell; finalist)

1997
Mies van der Rohe Award for European Architecture (for the Extension of Kunstmuseum Winterthur; finalist)

1995
Bauen in den Bergen Prize awarded by Sexten Kultur (for the Kirchner Museum Davos; first prize)

"Auszeichnung guter Bauten" awarded by the Canton of Grisons (for the Kirchner Museum Davos)

Exhibitions

Solo Exhibitions

2012
Zeit Räume
Annette Gigon/Mike Guyer
Architektur Galerie Berlin, May–June 2012

2011
Annette Gigon/Mike Guyer
Main Hall, Center, ETH Zurich, December 2011–January 2012

2004
gebaut nicht gebaut
Architekturforum Zurich, December 2004–February 2005

1993
Werkstoff
Architekturgalerie Lucerne

Group Exhibitions (selection)

2012
Common Ground
13th Venice Architecture Biennale, Italy

2011
Hochhaus – Wunsch und Wirklichkeit
Museum für Gestaltung Zurich (Prime Tower, Zurich)

2010
Building for Brussels – Architecture and Urban Transformations in Europe
Centre for Fine Arts, Brussels, Belgium (Prime Tower, Zurich)

2009
Wohnhochhäuser für die Stadt Zürich
Architekturforum Zurich (student projects produced during the visiting professorship of Gigon/Guyer at ETHZ)

Lern- und Begegnungszentrum für Science City
ETH Halle Hönggerberg, Zurich (student projects produced during the visiting professorship of Gigon/Guyer at ETHZ)

2005
Utopie réalisée
Haus Konstruktiv, Zurich (contribution to the exhibition on Gottfried Honegger and his connections with Haus Konstruktiv, Zurich, and with Espace de l'Art Concret, Mouans-Sartoux)

2004
1st Beijing Architecture Biennale
National Art Museum, Beijing, China (Museum Liner Appenzell)

9th Venice Architecture Biennale, Italy (Kunst-Depot, Henze & Ketterer Gallery, Wichtrach; Auditorium, University of Zurich)

2003
Work in Progress – Contemporary Architecture in Switzerland. CH in SHA
Bund Center, Shanghai, China (Museum Liner Appenzell)

2002
Nouvelle Simplicité
Espace de l'Art Concret, Mouans-Sartoux, France (Archeological Museum and Park, Kalkriese, Osnabrück, Germany; Signal Box, Zurich; Design for the Museum of Mouans-Sartoux)

Arne Jacobsen – Absolutely Modern
Louisiana Museum of Modern Art, Humlebæk, Denmark (contribution by Gigon/Guyer to the exhibition marking the centenary of the birth of Arne Jacobsen)

2001
Matière d'art – Architecture contemporaine en Suisse
touring exhibition by the Centre Culturel Suisse, with stops in Glasgow, Lausanne, Bordeaux, Copenhagen (Museum Liner Appenzell)

2000
Construire des logements
EPFL, Lausanne (Housing Development Broëlberg II, Kilchberg)

1999
Die neue Sammlung: Schenkungen und Akquisitionen 1995–1999
Architekturmuseum Frankfurt (Museum Liner Appenzell)

1997
Espaces pour l'art – Espace de l'art
Fondation Louis Moret, Martigny (Extension of Kunstmuseum Winterthur; Kirchner Museum Davos)

1995
Light Constructions
MoMA Museum of Modern Art, New York (Kirchner Museum Davos)

1994
Schweizer Museen
Centre Pasquart, Biel (Kirchner Museum Davos; Extension of Kunstmuseum Winterthur)

This book is published on the occasion of the exhibition *Annette Gigon/Mike Guyer* at the ETH Zurich (December 2011–January 2012). The exhibition and publication have been made possible by the kind support of the following companies and institutions:

Amt für Hochbauten der Stadt Zürich; Ruedi und Thomas Bechtler, Zellweger Park AG, Uster; Dr. Lüchinger+Meyer Bauingenieure AG, Zurich; Eberhard Bau AG, Kloten; Eduard Truninger AG, Zurich; Ernst Schweizer AG, Metallbau Hedingen; Ernst & Young AG, Zurich; Fahrni Fassadensysteme AG, Lyss; Fluora Leuchten AG, Herisau; Gruenberg+Partner AG, Zurich; IBG B. Graf AG Engineering, St. Gallen/Winterthur; Jansen AG, Oberriet; Lippuner Energie- und Metallbautechnik AG, Grabs; NÜSSLI Gruppe, Switzerland; OLMeRO AG, Glattbrugg; Perolini Baumanagement AG, Zurich; Rhombus Partner Immobilien AG, Zurich; Schär AG Wil, Fensterbau; Schindler Aufzüge AG, Zurich; Villa Rosau AG, Zurich; Walt+Galmarini AG, Zurich; Wartmann Immobilien AG, Brugg

b+p baurealisation ag, Zurich

Implenia AG, Dietlikon

Losinger Marazzi AG, Berne

Luc Prokesch Investissements Immobiliers, Geneva

Georg und Bertha Schwyzer-Winiker Stiftung, Zurich

Steiner AG, Zurich

WÜRTH GROUP

Gigon/Guyer Architects. Works & Projects 2001–2011

Editors: Annette Gigon, Mike Guyer
Concept: Gigon/Guyer Architects with Lars Müller
Editorial office: Jennifer Hauger, Veronika Weisner, Ilka Tegeler
Editorial assistance: Arend Kölsch, Sonja Furrer Stitz, Claudia Motalli, Alis Haxhi, Tom Szczebiot
Design: Gigon/Guyer Architects with Integral Lars Müller/Martina Mullis and Lars Müller
Copyediting: Catherine Schelbert (Essays, Conversation, Foreword, Acknowledgments), Jennifer Taylor (Project texts & Appendix)
Proofreading: Roderick O'Donovan
Translations: Fiona Elliott (Essay Ursprung), Ishbel Flett (Essays Mack, Rüegg, Conversation, Foreword, Acknowledgments), Helen Ferguson (Project texts, Artist statements, Appendix)
Prepress: Photolitho AG, Gossau ZH
Paper: 135 g/m², Gardapat Kiara, 1.3
Printing and binding: Kösel, Altusried-Krugzell, Germany

Lars Müller Publishers
CH-8005 Zürich
www.lars-mueller-publishers.com

ISBN 978-3-03778-276-7

Deutsche Ausgabe: *Gigon/Guyer Architekten. Arbeiten 2001–2011*, ISBN 978-3-03778-257-6

Printed in Germany